A Play of Passion

Other books by Stephen Coote

BYRON: THE MAKING OF A MYTH
WILLIAM MORRIS: HIS LIFE AND WORK
A SHORT HISTORY OF ENGLISH LITERATURE

A Play of Passion

THE LIFE OF
SIR
WALTER
RALEGH

STEPHEN COOTE

MACMILLAN
LONDON

First published 1993 by Macmillan London Limited

a division of Pan Macmillan Publishers Limited
Cavaye Place London SW10 9PG
and Basingstoke

Associated companies throughout the world

ISBN 0 333 55741 7

1 3 5 7 9 8 6 4 2

A CIP catalogue record for this book is available from
the British Library

Phototypeset by Intype, London
Printed and bound in Great Britain by
Mackays of Chatham Plc

What is our life? It is a play of passion.
What is our mirth? The music of division.
Our mothers, they the tiring houses be,
Where we are dressed for time's short tragedy.
Earth is the stage, heaven the spectator is
Who doth behold whoe'er doth act amiss.
The graves that hide us from the parching sun
Are but drawn curtains till the play be done.

Sir Walter Ralegh

Contents

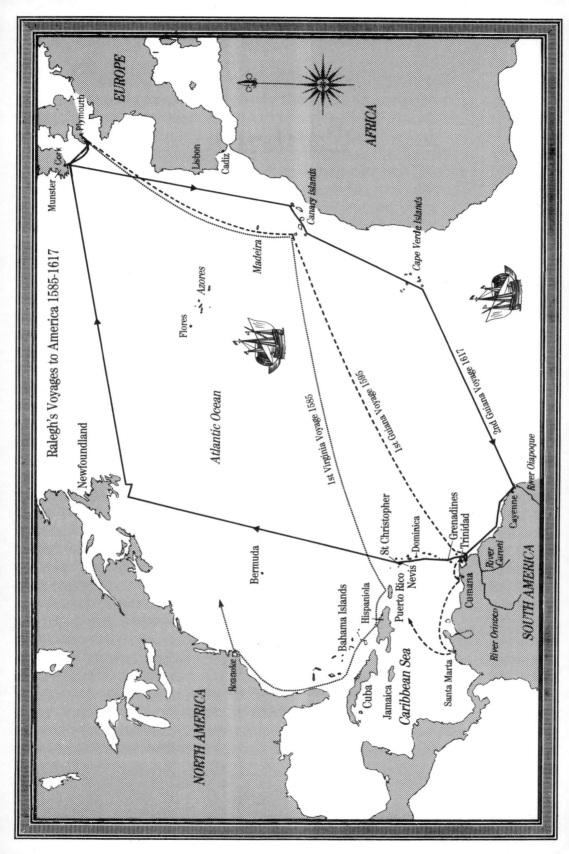

List of Illustrations

Between pages 116 and 117

Preface

The figure of Sir Walter Ralegh stands against his age high-lighted by the brilliance of his career but masked by shadows that are deep, troubling and obscure. In the court of Elizabeth I, Ralegh was among the most polished of courtiers, while in the range of his activities he appeared the universal renaissance man. He was a poet, scholar, soldier and explorer, a business man and an administrator of brilliance. In the reign of Elizabeth's successor, and isolated as the last great figure of that great age, Ralegh was forced into opposition and became the hero of a Jacobean tragedy.

Images of the drama inevitably crowd about him and, with them, ideas of role playing. These are fundamental to any appreciation of his achievements. The personal Ralegh – the subjective and private man – is all but impossible to reconstruct. The record is too fragmentary and, besides, the revelation of such things ran counter to the true direction of his genius. Ralegh was, in the fullest sense of that phrase, a self-made man. In his rise from being the youngest son of a small tenant farmer, he exploited all the forces of a remarkable imagination and intellect to shape for himself a variety of roles to act on 'this stage-play world'.[1]

This is the Ralegh with which this book is principally concerned, the Ralegh who interests me. He was a man whose powers of mind and ambition caused him to seize on some of the leading ideas of his day and to transform them in the light of his own needs, only to discover that they had in their turn entrapped him and threatened his destruction. If drama is one image by which Ralegh may be understood, the other is the prison.

The thirteen years Ralegh spent in the Tower – the years in which so much of his power was lavished on his monumental *History of the World* – are at one with the altogether more insidious entrapment he knew throughout his life – the various prisons of early poverty, of the fantastic and factitious love he elaborated for his queen, and of the lethal fantasy of El Dorado and an empire in South America which led directly to his death. It is between these poles – the theatre and the prison – that I have attempted to interpret this man and to present his life as what he himself called 'a play of passion'.

In writing this book I have incurred many debts which, I hope, are adequately recorded in the bibliography. I would however like to single out here the work of some scholars which has been of particular importance to me. The works of A. L. Rowse – *The Expansion of Elizabethan England* and *Ralegh and the Throckmortons* especially – are established classics of luminous scholarship. Professors Quinn and Andrews have notably advanced understanding of Ralegh's privateering and his imperialist ambitions. The canon of Ralegh's poetry presents one of the most formidable problems of renaissance textual scholarship, and here I have drawn gratefully on the work of Michael Rudick, as I have on Steven May for the prose works. Stephen J. Greenblatt has influenced all concerned with the period with his concept of renaissance self-fashioning. Charles Nicholl's work on Ralegh's relation to Marlowe has brought thrilling detective work to the solution of a most complex problem.

A Note on Names

I have adopted the now standard spelling 'Ralegh' for the hero of this book. To avoid confusion, various others of its characters are referred to by a single name or title although these often changed as their careers progressed. Lord Burghley is called thus throughout while his son remains Cecil although eventually elevated to the Earldom of Salisbury. The Indian chief Wingina is always referred to thus although changing his name to Permisapan in the last years of his life. I have called James's spouse Queen Anna (rather than the more common Anne) in deference to her own usage.

CHAPTER ONE

The Gentlemen of the West

He was the most famous prisoner in England, and every day a crowd gathered in the hope of seeing him as he walked for his exercise along the high, broad wall by his lodgings in the Bloody Tower. He was an old man according to the standards of the time – a little over sixty – and he leant on a stick because of the wound he had received in the attack on Cadiz. But prison, age and ill-health had failed to break him. His eyes, although sunk in his face, were still bright. His mind was still keen. Despite disgrace and the hatred of his king, despite the long years of ignominy in which a lesser man would have been forgotten, he had succeeded in making himself one of the sights of London and he rejoiced in the fact, playing his role with the skill of a great actor.

The presence of the crowd below him, these people alert and excited, whispering to each other and pointing up at him, proved he was still alive, that his cause was still worth fighting for. He accepted their adulation, knowing that when the bell rang and he was summoned back to his cell, they would return to their families and say that even to catch a glimpse of the great Sir Walter Ralegh was a token of better times, a more heroic age.

He had made his own way to this eminence and his path had been arduous, for by the time of his birth in about 1554 the ancient Ralegh family of Devon had fallen in the world. Earlier generations had produced a bishop and a distinguished judge, another ancestor had fought at Agincourt. In 1526, however, when Ralegh's father attained his majority, he found himself heir to a diminished estate. The ancestral lands at Smallridge had been made over, while others remained in the care of his uncle, a man who had exercised his right to pass on his interest in the older Ralegh's marriage to the merchant adventurer John Drake of Exmouth. In time, Ralegh's father duly wedded Joan Drake and, towards 1528, moved south with her from the fringes of Dartmoor to lands he leased at Hayes Barton, near East Budleigh. Here he set up as a gentleman farmer.

East Budleigh was an attractive location, its single street of thatched and whitewashed houses winding up a hill to the church of All Saints whose tower looked out over woods and pasturelands. These Devon fields were not uniformly fertile, but even in Tudor times local farmers were praised for their abundant harvests. Generations had worked to clear the granite-strewn wastes and then build and repair the miles of stone walling that helped make up a landscape of irregular meadows, muddy lanes and isolated farmsteads. As prosperity increased, so these farmhouses were reconstructed or extended, and it is possible that the older Ralegh was responsible for building his own home. Its cob walls still stand, little altered, set foursquare against wind and time. Before them lay the slope of Hayes Wood, to the west a broad common, while to the south red and jagged cliffs rose out of the sea, the salt spray mingling with the sweeter smells of harvest.

In addition to being a family home, the house at Hayes Barton was also the centre of a business, for it was from here, along with George and John, his sons by his first marriage, that the older Ralegh supervised the considerable grazing rights he enjoyed on Woodbury and Lympstone Commons. Sheep rearing was the county's major industry, and an experienced farmer like the older Ralegh had a practised eye 'for an ewe that is well quartered, and of a good stable, with a handsome straight lamb at her heels'.[1] Such knowledge was also part of a boy's growing up and, as a man, Walter Ralegh was to speak knowledgeably and with feeling as he defended the livelihoods of England's farmers in the House of Commons.

On the surface, such a life at Hayes Barton was typical of that lived by many of the gentry families of the West, a life varied with frequent and intricate disputes over land and supported by a modest prosperity. In 1540, the older Ralegh was assessed on property to the value of £60, a figure which put him on a level with neighbours such as the Fords and the St Cleres. It was with these people he also did business, witnessing deeds or taking his part in arranging marriages such as that between his brother-in-law John Drake and Amy, sister of Sir Richard Grenville.

There were also griefs and changes. Sometime around 1530,

Ralegh's first wife died and was buried at the east end of All Saints under a stone whose inscription, incised in reverse by an illiterate mason, has been partly worn away. The details of the older Ralegh's second marriage (it may have been to the daughter of a Genoese merchant) are disputed and obscure. By the 1540s however he was considered an influential man. Certainly, at the close of the decade, he was in a position to make a third and favourable marriage, for around 1548 he wedded Katherine Champernowne, the mother of his famous son.

It seems that Katherine Champernowne brought no property with her, but she may well have brought money and she certainly introduced her new husband to an influential web of relatives and kinsmen. Her brother, Sir Arthur Champernowne, became vice-admiral of Devon, while her aunt, Katherine Ashley, had held the robe of Princess Elizabeth at her christening and then taught the future queen her letters. Nearer home, the Carews were among her cousins, while by her earlier marriage to Otto Gilbert of Compton, Katherine Champernowne had not only secured her place in Devon society but become the mother of three famous sons: John, Humphrey and Adrian Gilbert, seafaring men and eminent Elizabethans all. To her new husband, Katherine was in time to bear a daughter and two more sons: Carew and her youngest, Walter.

It was thus through his mother that Walter Ralegh grew up associated with the leaders of that most dynamic and thrusting group of Elizabethans, the gentlemen of the West. These were a body of men asserting themselves amid a profoundly traditional society, and their new initiatives were nowhere clearer than in the all important matters of religion and local custom.

Among Ralegh's labourers, and to relieve a life at once arduous and controlled, a rich tradition of customs had grown up that was often geared to the cycle of the seasons. In the dark days around Christmas, for example, the people of Devon went out to wassail in the orchards, sprinkling cider on the roots of the apple trees, drinking the remainder, and then dancing round the blackened boughs. The primitive thus lay very close to the ordered surface of life, and in a world at once hard and uncertain there had grown up between the rites of the Church and the superstitions of the cottage a web of practices in which magic and faith combined. Worried villagers would pay their priest 'to come and say masses when our cattle were plagued',[2] while many resorted to the wise woman and the cunning man for charms, horoscopes, and the detection of stolen goods. In such a world, the ritual prayers provided by the Catholic Church blended easily with the spells offered by the conjuror, and helped make up a pattern of beliefs which the forces of the Reformation were soon to try roughly to shake off.

The older Ralegh early declared himself a local leader in these. In 1546, he gained entry to All Saints church, tore down its crucifix, broke off its precious metals, and refused to return these to the parish. To the reformers, such religious objects smacked of papist superstition, and Ralegh's display of deep if raw conviction suggests the forces at work in Tudor society and the energies that motivated the gentry of the West especially. To men who were throwing off the yoke of Rome, the reformed Anglican Church – a national Church based less on ritual than on prayer, preaching and the Bible – became the outward sign of the society in which they wished to play their part. Sunday church attendance was compulsory, and as the older Ralegh and his sons walked up the aisle to their front pew with its elaborately emblazoned coat of arms, so their role as the dominant Protestant gentlemen of the parish was made visible to all.

Such changes, at once violent and profound, were not achieved without opposition. The local people were unwilling to discard generations of slowly accreted and comforting practices. Nor, though few if any of them could understand its Latin, did they welcome the replacement of the old forms of the mass with the new, metropolitan English of the Prayer Book. This last was imposed by laws which the local authorities were not always able easily to enforce.

By the Whitsun of 1549, for example – the date on which the new Prayer Book was to be introduced – feelings in Devon were running high. The older Ralegh, riding out towards Exeter, came across a woman mumbling over her rosary. He rebuked her for her superstition and threatened her with the rigour of the law. The woman, fired by the resentment felt by the greater number of the ordinary people, at once rushed to her local church at Clyst St Mary. Here she interrupted the new service and enthused the congregation with a spirit of revolt. Parishioners at nearby Sampford Courtenay had already forced their priest to wear his vestments and say mass in the old form. They then killed one of the gentry who urged them to obedience and set out to join the bands of local villagers who had assembled at Crediton in alliance with an army of rebellious Cornishmen.

The villagers at Clyst St Mary, convinced the older Ralegh's Protestant zeal was part of a gentry plan to steal their property, started erecting barricades. Some hewed down great trees and began to fortify the bridge over the river Clyst. Others began to set in place the guns they had managed to get from Topsham. Yet a third party pursued Ralegh himself, eventually catching up with him when he hid in a chapel. By chance, Ralegh was saved by the intervention of some sailors from Exmouth, but he was almost immediately recaptured and taken to Exeter. Here he was locked in the tower of St Sidwell's church, just outside the city walls, and was obliged to watch as a rebel force of some two thousand, marching under the banner of the Five Wounds of Christ, the pyx carried before them and the air sweetened with incense, advanced to besiege the city.

But Exeter did not fall. Although the mayor and the greater part of the citizens were 'of the old stamp and of the Romish religion',[3] they put duty to their king before religious conviction. Men were mustered and armed, watches were assigned to every ward of the city, and guns placed along its walls. For a month there was stalemate. The rebels took pot shots at those citizens rash enough to show themselves at their windows. They broke down bridges, stopped supplies, burned the gates which were then barricaded, and tried unsuccessfully to mine the walls. Letters were also smuggled between the rebels and their friends within the city, while a hundred of the loyalists entered into an agreement to keep a permanent watch. Their action just managed to foil a Catholic plan to let the enemy in by a postern gate.

Two of Ralegh's relatives – Sir Gawen Carew and his nephew Sir Peter – were sent by the Lords of the Council to try to exert their local influence. When they failed, Lord Russell was despatched with inadequate troops to enforce more violent means. The rebels themselves, determined to attack before greater government forces arrived, marched out to Fenny Bridges. There, on 28 July, and after two fierce engagements, Russell's forces eventually routed them. It was only on 3 August, however, when Lord Grey finally arrived with a band of Italian mercenaries, that the government felt able to press its advantage home. The rebels who had advanced around Clyst St Mary were forced to retreat, and every house in the main street of the village was put to the torch. Russell then attacked the remaining rebels from the rear. The few despondent people left around the city itself decamped, and on 6 August Russell set up the royal standard outside the walls while the mayor and gentry advanced in procession to greet him.

By the end of the rebellion, it was said that the bodies of some four thousand West Countrymen lay in the summer fields. The Protestant gentry had secured a bloody if temporary victory, a triumph nowhere more brutally symbolized than in Exeter itself. Here, the vicar of St Thomas's was hanged from his church tower in his vestments and with 'a holy-water bucket, a sprinkle, a sacring bell, a pair of beads and such other like popish trash hanged about him'.[4] What had once been the instruments of divine intercession were now an awful warning of new political power. Ralegh and the gentlemen of the West, it seemed, had established the dominance of their class and faith by the edges of their swords.

While 1549 saw the older Ralegh caught up in public affairs, it also saw him active in other areas that were later to be of the greatest importance to his son. It is from this year that the records of the High Court of Admiralty provide the first evidence of his involvement in privateering.

At the outbreak of the wars with France five years earlier, the government had issued letters of marque authorizing English ships to seize the cargoes of the French and their Scots allies. The government were so convinced by the strategic value of privateering that they were by and large content to turn a blind eye to the fine line between privateering itself – the authorized seizure of enemy merchant shipping in time of war – and outright piracy. It followed that the government was also prepared to accept that, once permission had been given, such activities were extremely hard to stop. Indeed, in the years between 1543 and 1549, the wars with France and Scotland ensured that the Channel, the Irish Sea and the Atlantic were riven with violence. More than three hundred French ships were taken in this period, and as early as 1546 the Lord Admiral was obliged to admit that no Spanish, French or Portuguese vessel sailing round Biscay was safe from what were euphemistically referred to as 'the merchant adventurers of England'.

The records of the High Court of Admiralty give a vivid account of one such attack and the Raleghs' part in it. By 1549, the older Ralegh had gone into partnership with Gilbert Drake to victual a privateer under the command of John Ralegh, then aged about twenty-one. The ship herself was moored at Exmouth, and it was probably a look-out on the beacon above the harbour who gave warning as a boat from Dartmouth hove into view. She was a Spanish vessel carrying wine and salt under the command of a Flemish merchant, George de Fever.

The Ralegh vessel came sharking out of her harbour and, catching up with her prey, her men ordered the captain to strike his topsail. This was immediately done, but John Ralegh and his crew at once commanded de Fever to lower the rest of his canvas 'or else they said they would sink the same ship'.[5] de Fever, aware of the hands into which he had fallen, immediately obeyed, even sending out a 'follower' or small boat from which the English privateers could board. Thirty men at once leapt on to their prize, and while some carried off casks of wine, others, with bloody-minded savagery, smashed a number of the remaining barrels so that their contents ran into the salt.

With his cargo wrecked or stolen, de Fever determined to preserve at least the money and papers he kept in his private chest. When he tried to protect these from the English, however, 'they threw him down and trod him under their feet', wounding him with a dagger before taking their prize into Exmouth. Here a riot of plundering ensued, the mariners' wives especially hurrying on board to drink what they could and then carrying the rest of the wine away in earthenware pots.

It was now, perhaps when his more experienced father apprised him of the situation, that John Ralegh realized the mistake he had made. de Fever was not French but a subject of Spain, not an enemy but nominally at least an ally. John Ralegh at once promised to make amends. 'He would not be known so to misuse the king's friends'. A hot-blooded disingenuousness is audible in this, the tone of a scoundrel who suddenly finds he is a patriot. If only de Fever would say the wine and salt were French, Ralegh continued, he would see to it that ample recompense was paid. Would de Fever swear so? He would not. John Ralegh immediately vowed he would throw the foreign captain overboard. For a day or two he kept the man a prisoner, but in the end he was obliged to let him go. de Fever took his case to the Admiralty court, but its verdict is unknown. It probably inclined little to the justice of the case, however, for the partiality of the judges was notorious, and in such ways as these the Ralegh family could set about repairing their fortune.

In this atmosphere, life in Devon was becoming ever more unsettled, and during the early 1550s, while Ralegh and his older sons were privateering, his friends among the gentry were plotting rebellion. The defeat of the religious revolts in Exeter and elsewhere had shown that religious change was now in the hands of the government who greatly accelerated its pace. During the brief reign of Edward VI, Catholic bishops were deprived of their livings, the communion table was ordered to replace the altar, while the Second Prayer Book instituted a wholly reformed service. Those religious treasures that had been neither hidden nor looted were taken by commissioners to the royal Jewel House, while a government desperate for money released church lands to the gentry in what was one of the most far-reaching redistributions of wealth the country had ever seen.

But, with the king's early death and the accession of the Catholic Mary, the process of reform was thrown into reverse. Mary's first parliament repealed the Edwardian religious legislation and returned the country to the position it had known in the last years of her father. The religious victory of the gentlemen of the West was under threat, and Protestant Members of Parliament, the Raleghs' kinsmen the Carews among them, feared especially the queen's betrothal to Philip II of Spain. It seemed the nation might now be absorbed into the mighty Spanish empire and be forced to pay tribute to finance her wars. The Protestant religion appeared to be at risk, while men who had done well for themselves out of the new wealth the Reformation had devolved on them were concerned lest this might pass to Spanish grandees. They therefore sought to depose the queen through armed rebellion. Carew himself was to lead the forces from the West, but his plans were revealed. Assuring the authorities he was making for London, he rode secretly to Weymouth where he 'persuaded with Walter Ralegh esquire to convey him away in his bark'.[6]

Exile gave Carew time for study. Settled in Rouen, he began an intensive reading of the newsletters sent by Peter Martyr to the princes of the church, the first three of which had recently been translated by Richard Eden as *The Decades of the New World*. The margins of Sir Peter's copy of this work are full of notes scribbled in his excitement, for here was a revelation of Spanish power, Spanish achievement and, above all, of the fabulous empires the Spaniards had discovered on the farther shores of the Atlantic. To an embittered exile, all this was the stuff of Utopia – an image of the Golden Age – while Eden's additional material on the barbarity with which the Spaniards had subdued the native peoples so as to rifle their natural resources deepened his loathing of Spain – the conviction that the Spanish Atlantic empire must be crushed – which was again to be central to Walter Ralegh's ambitions.

In England, such beliefs were being hardened in the fires of the Marian persecutions. Soon after the defeat of Carew's rebellion the burnings began, and the time came for Ralegh's mother to show the strength of her Protestant faith. In 1558, she visited Agnes Prest in the bishop of Exeter's prison. Prest had made a nuisance of herself by repeated and aggressive avowals of extreme Protestantism, and while in her cell she continued to berate her visitors. Katherine Ralegh listened with patient interest and, in the end, found herself impressed. The two women said the creed together, and Agnes Prest then made a more general declaration of her beliefs.

She told her visitor that God did not dwell in temples made with human hands and that the sacrament was no more than a remembrance of the Passion, adding, in the words of the Protestant hagiographer Foxe, that 'as they now use it, it is but an idol, and far wide from any remembrance of Christ's body – which will not long continue, and so take it, good Mistress'.[7] This was not a prophecy Agnes Prest herself would live to see fulfilled. Aged about fifty, cheerful, sober and resolute, she was burned to death outside Exeter, convinced she was 'going to a city where money beareth no mastery'.

The older Ralegh meanwhile was greatly enriching himself. Between

1555 and 1558 he was acting deputy to John Yonge, the vice-admiral of Devon. His duties included valuing ships and their cargoes which had been restrained at the Lord Admiral's order and arresting pirates whose goods automatically fell forfeit to the Admiral himself.

The employment of such a man as the older Ralegh in this post was an open invitation to dishonesty. In 1557, his eldest sons captured the Portuguese *Conception* off the Scillies and successfully evaded trouble until they were arrested by an admiralty officer at Looe. The older Ralegh, hearing of this, at once despatched £120 to Yonge so that he would satisfactorily arrange the trial. Matters did not proceed as planned however, and Ralegh was obliged to stand five hundred marks for George's bail which the young man promptly jumped. He and his brother were then 'by means of their father Walter Ralegh so conveyed from place to place and from time to time kept so secretly'[8] that they evaded rearrest. When the matter finally came to trial, Ralegh appears to have tried to bargain his way out of the difficulty.

He could also exercise his right of immunity from arrest as a Member of Parliament, for in 1558 he was returned as a non-resident member for the borough of Wareham in Dorset. No doubt, in the light of continued trouble with France and the imminent loss of Calais, Ralegh voted for the measure requiring all substantial persons to maintain armour and equipment for a horseman and a footman, just as he was soon to be involved as a petty-captain in local measures for the defence of the realm. He was nominated one of those who were 'upon the sight of the first beacon fired, [to] make their speedy repair to the sea coasts, where their charge lieth'.[9] Such instructions recall the far greater part played by his son during the Armada terror of 1588.

While the brief reign of Queen Mary saw the older Ralegh at the height of his prestige, the first decade of the reign of Elizabeth, the period of his youngest son's boyhood, saw initiative passing to other hands. The energies and ambitions released in the gentlemen of the West were no longer satisfied by farming and privateering. Local perspectives gave way to international horizons. Protestantism, expansion and the desire for wealth and power drove men to wider seas.

The leading of such initiatives required figures of great imaginative daring and physical courage, and among these was Ralegh's half-brother Humphrey Gilbert. In 1563, when Ralegh himself was about twelve, Gilbert returned wounded from the wars in France, his mind busy with the excitement of the new discoveries. As Gilbert recuperated, working on a document he was preparing for the queen, he exercised an incalculable influence on the dark-eyed, watchful boy. Ralegh's volatile half-brother was an image of what the younger generation were now trying to achieve.

After the death of his father in 1547, Gilbert had been made the ward of a wealthy guardian who, along with his mother, decided to send him first to Eton and then to Oxford. Gilbert was to be given that education in the classics which was becoming the distinguishing mark of a gentleman. Hooker, the historian of Devon and a man who knew Gilbert personally, declared him to have been a precociously intelligent boy, and it was such qualities, along with the desire to help a promising young kinsman, that also brought Gilbert to the attention of Katherine Ashley, the adored if somewhat irresponsible governess of Princess Elizabeth.

Just turned twenty, and a woman already made wise by the political peril that surrounded her, Elizabeth took a liking to the fiery young man 'and very oftentimes would familiarly discourse with him'.[10] To Gilbert, such friendship opened golden vistas. None the less, with her instinctive judgement of the men who circled in ruthless competition about her, Elizabeth was well aware of the true nature of his qualities. Humphrey Gilbert, she saw, was a man to be used in minor extremes – courageous, fanatically loyal and intelligent, yet rendered all but unstable by the very ferocity of the merits that recommended him. He was the sort of man whose promise is constantly dogged by bad luck.

In 1562, and indulging her first essay in foreign affairs, Elizabeth dispatched Gilbert to France as part of an army allied to the Protestant Huguenots and ordered to hold Le Havre until Calais was restored to the English. This was a catastrophic exercise. The English army was ill-equipped, Le Havre was blockaded, Calais was not restored and, as plague set in, so the Huguenots turned against their English allies and entered a pact with the Catholic queen of France. The whole business had been wasteful and pointless, and early in August Gilbert himself was invalided home.

If his military hopes had been sorely disappointed, conversations with the Huguenots and, just possibly, meetings with the French geographer Thevet and Richard Eden, the English translator of Peter Martyr, had stimulated other concerns. As a younger son with all the world to win, Gilbert began contemplating plans for English expansion overseas. The Spaniards and Portuguese had carved out mighty empires in the Americas, and the French were slowly following suit. England, meanwhile, had achieved very little, the initiatives that sent the Cabots to North America in the early decades of the century having faded away. Now however, in 1563, there was talk of an Anglo-French expedition to America. Thevet's *The Whole and True Discovery of Terra Florida* had been published in May, while the Hawkinses were sailing to the West Indies, there illicitly to trade with Spanish settlers. Amid such enterprises, Gilbert's mind revolved schemes yet more ambitious. Before him glittered the fabled wealth of the East.

He was in part reviving an old ambition. Some ten years earlier, in 1554, three ships funded by the great men of the court and City had set out on 'the intended voyage for Cathay'.[11] Chiefly under the aegis of Richard Chancellor, detailed technical preparations were made for a north-easterly voyage, past the cold lands of Scythia where, it was hoped, a market could be found for English cloth. Chancellor himself, after an epic journey, arrived in Moscow, and was eventually welcomed by Czar Ivan the Terrible. On his return to England, the promise of trade appeared such that in 1555 the Muscovy Company was incorporated under royal charter and granted a monopoly of English trade with Russia and all areas 'northwards, northwestwards or northeastwards'.[12] But further expeditions proved disappointing and old ambitions of finding a route to Cathay were revived. Jenkinson himself apparently favoured a north-easterly path. Humphrey Gilbert inclined to an exploration of the North West Passage.

At the end of 1565, Gilbert petitioned the queen, offering to undertake 'the discovering of a passage by the North, to go to Cataia, and all other the east parts of the world'.[13] Gilbert and Jenkinson were summoned to debate their ideas before the Privy Council, but nothing, it seems, was done. Even when the two men joined forces (not without a degree of suspicion on Jenkinson's part) the government still followed a course of studious inaction. This was not altogether surprising in view of the Muscovy Company's monopoly and the fact that the schemes themselves appeared singularly far-fetched. This was certainly the view of Gilbert's older brother, since Gilbert himself now set about writing his 'Discourse of a Discovery for a New Passage to Cataia' to prove to Sir John and others that 'my hope of this discovery and passage, was not so rash, or foolish, as you heretofore have deemed'.[14]

In fact, Gilbert's plans were based on the most up to date map of the world that had then appeared: that prepared by Abraham Ortelius in 1564. This suggested that America had a northern coastline more or less on the same temperate latitude as Britain and offered harbours which were readily accessible from the Atlantic. The sea along this coast was believed to flow into the so-called Strait of Anian which in turn ran to Asia, thereby beckoning the merchant to the wealth of the East.

'A Discourse of a Discovery for a New Passage to Cataia' is a work in which, for all its practical inexperience and lapses into credulity, the expansionist energies of the Elizabethans are given eloquent expression. The discovery of a short route to Cathay, Gilbert suggested, would give the country an enormous commercial advantage over Portugal and Spain, and would in turn lead to a 'wonderful enriching to our Prince, and unspeakable commodities to all the inhabitants of Europe'.[15] Before him glowed a vision of a 'great abundance of gold, silver, precious stones, cloth of gold, silks, all manner of spices, grocery wares, and other kinds of merchandise'. Gilbert's lists has the opulent, slightly primitive delight in the physical qualities of riches so characteristic of the age. The wealth of Croesus seemed within reach, and Gilbert believed – as Ralegh would after him – that other benefits would flow from this.

By engaging in maritime exploration, for example, English ships and sailors would be increased in number without burdening the state, while 'such needy people of our country, which now trouble the commonwealth, and through want here at home, are forced to commit outrageous offences' could be put to making trifles for barter with the Indians. These natives would, in their turn, provide an excellent market for English cloth. Here was a vision of enormous future promise which Ralegh himself was greatly to develop and which was rooted in a patriotic and moral idealism he was again to make his own. 'Give me leave without offence,' Gilbert wrote at the end of his essay, 'always to live and die in this mind: that he is not worthy to live at all, that for fear, or danger of death, shunneth his country service, and his own honour, seeing that death is inevitable, and the fame of virtue immortal'.

Such high-sounding aims were frustrated all the same. Gilbert himself was obliged to spend the latter half of 1566 in Ireland and then, on his return, he petitioned the queen again. He stated this time that he was prepared to sail under the auspices of the Muscovy Company (of which he claimed, probably wrongly, that he was now a member) provided he was granted customs privileges, the governorship under the crown of such lands as he discovered and, above all, personal ownership of one-tenth of all the new territories. The Muscovy Company stood by the terms of their monopoly, however, and Gilbert's scheme for a personal empire in the East collapsed. In May 1567, the young Ralegh watched him set off again for that altogether more desperate focus of Elizabethan ambition, the wilds of Ireland.

Ralegh himself, it may be supposed, returned to his school books. His intelligence, inseparable from his superabundant energy, must have been apparent as a boy, along perhaps with that haughtiness which time was to harden into an obdurate pride. But nothing substantial is known of the boyhood of Ralegh. We may guess that just as his father and brothers probably gave him his first lessons in the affairs of the sea, so it is likely that his mother, a literate woman, taught him to read. There is no evidence to show if and where Ralegh went to school, however, nor how he laid the foundations of that prodigious process of self-education by which he became one of the leading scholars of his age. Throughout his life, scholarship and action were to go side by side, but if the origins of the former are lost, Ralegh's initial contact with the second was made when he was perilously young.

Once again, it was his mother's family who provided the initiative. Experience of warfare was considered a necessary part of the education of a gentleman, and in the latter part of the 1560s, while the Religious Wars in France were enjoying a temporary lull, some of the young men of the West sought action in other parts of Europe.

Relations between Maximilian and the Ottoman Empire had collapsed, and Suleiman the Magnificent was advancing on Vienna. Henry Champernowne, Philip Budockshide, Richard Grenville, William Gorges and others 'who, according to their innate fortitude thought themselves born to arms',[16] rode into Hungary. Here they played their part in the latter stages of the siege of Szigeth and then in the sporadic fighting that ensued.

On their return to England, they learned that the Protestant cause in France was 'now in a distressed and almost desperate condition',[17] and they at once prepared to offer their help. This turn of events was a matter of both religious and family loyalty, for Gawen Champernowne had married the daughter of the Comte de Montgomerie, one of the champions of the French Huguenots. The youths resolved to rally to his cause, and were given royal permission to raise a troop of a hundred horse and then cross into France, riding under a banner emblazoned with Montgomerie's motto *Finem det mihi virtus* – 'Let Valour End My Days'. With them rode Walter Ralegh, then barely fifteen years old.

He was riding into great danger, for if Elizabeth had given the young men permission to set out, her word could give them no protection once they were abroad. Indeed, she later protested to the French ambassador that they had crossed the Channel without her permission and that she could not be held responsible for their actions. The Catholic French responded by declaring that any captured Englishman would be hanged with a placard round his neck declaring that he had been executed 'for having come, contrary to the wish of the queen of England, to serve the Huguenots'.[18]

The little troop of West Country lads who rode out for fame at once encountered the full humiliation of defeat. The Huguenots under Admiral Coligny had been routed at the battle of Moncontour. They were now fleeing in disorder, pursued by the royalist cavalry, and all seemed lost until Ralegh saw Louis of Nassau, 'brother to the late famous Prince of Orange, make the retreat at Moncontour with so great resolution, as he saved the one half of the Protestant army, then broken and disbanded, of which myself was an eye witness; and was one of them that had cause to thank him for it'.[19]

The position of the French Protestants seemed hopeless none the less. Coligny had been twice defeated, attempts had been made on his life, and there was a reward on his head of fifty thousand crowns. The French parlement had sentenced him to be hanged, strangled, and his body to be humiliated before the Hôtel de Paris. Wounded and in agony, he snatched comfort where he could. His men intercepted royalist messengers carrying thirty thousand francs for their Swiss pikemen, seized the money and presented it to Coligny. He at once used it to pay his mercenaries. Then, as he was being carried along in his litter, an aged and wounded friend, drawing up beside him, thrust his head through the curtains and muttered 'Surely God is gentle!' This speech, it was said, 'braced him up and set him on the way to good thoughts and resolutions for the future.'[20]

Indeed, Coligny was now to find in himself a courage and resource, a sheer dogged heroism, which, triumphing over fortune, was profoundly to inspire Ralegh with an image of all a man might achieve. Taking with him Prince Henry of Navarre and the young Condé, Coligny headed south, accompanied by Ralegh and his West Country friends. Leaving his exhausted infantry at St-Jean-d'Angély, he then swept south-west, across the great rivers of the Dronne and the Lot, to Montauban. Here he arrived exhausted and with barely a horse that could put one leg before another. Having rested, his troops – Ralegh among them – ravaged the country south of the Garonne. By 3 January 1570, the West Countrymen's hero Montgomerie had joined them, and together their forces crossed the Tarn, engulfed Toulouse, and burned the houses of the members of the Parlement before advancing into the Albigeois where the German troops drank themselves stupid.

Coligny's retreat was a supreme act of will-power accompanied by the utmost moral squalor. Before the eyes of the teenage Ralegh there opened up a vista of humanity at its most courageous and depraved. While Coligny held resolute to his purpose, discipline deteriorated amid rapine and plunder. Ralegh himself was later to recall the part he played in this. When he and his colleagues reached Languedoc, for example, they chased a group of Catholics into some caves where the victims hid in fear of their lives. There was no way, it seemed, to get them out, nor, more importantly, to seize such treasure as they had taken with them. In the end, and with that gratuitous cruelty of young men exerting themselves in a war-torn foreign land, Ralegh and his companions collected bundles of straw, let these down into the caves on chains, and smoked out their victims like bees from a hive.

Ralegh was maturing in a land where all decency had collapsed. When the Catholics surrendered at Navarrens, Montgomerie slaughtered every man of them. Montluc retaliated at Mont-de-Marsan and again at Rabastens. 'The face of France is lamentable at this season', wrote a young English volunteer.[21] Last year's harvest had been eaten, next year's was left rotting on the ground. France was a land where 'murder is no cruelty', and it was commonplace to see people 'bathing one in another's blood, making it custom to despise religion and justice, or any more sacred bond, either of divine or human constitution'.

Here, while fighting in the name of organized religion, was mankind at its most brutal, and amid 'barbarous murders, devastations and other calamities',[22] Ralegh's sceptical intelligence was being shaped. As he looked at the wholesale collapse of civil order, so he came to understand that the French Wars of Religion had been 'begun and carried on by some few great men of ambition and turbulent spirits, deluding the people with the cloak and mask only of religion, to gain their assistance to what they did more specifically aim at.'[23] That aim, of course, was power.

This briefly fell to Coligny's share. Having wintered in Montauban, his troops began marching to Paris with irresistible momentum. His army won the battle of Arnay-le-Duc and, on 8 August 1570, Catherine de Medici, the Catholic queen, was obliged to sign the Peace of St Germain and grant the Huguenots territorial security, freedom of conscience, and a measure of civil liberty. To further secure this alliance between Protestant and Catholic, the king's sister, Marguerite de Valois, was to be married to Henry of Navarre, while his brother, the Duc of Anjou, was proposed as a bride for Elizabeth I.

This last arrangement the young man himself strongly resisted, believing he would be dishonoured by marriage to a woman the Catholic Church had declared a bastard. His insistence that he be allowed to worship in his own way in England effectively brought the proposal to a close. While preparations went ahead for the marriage of Marguerite de Valois, however, Franciscan friars whipped up the fury of the Parisian populace. Coligny, loathed by the Catholic aristocracy, feared for his plans in the Netherlands, and resented by many of the ordinary people, became once again the focus of political hatred. On 22 August, as he was returning from the Louvre, he was shot at and wounded in his left forearm. The grandees of the rival factions gathered round their leaders. In the palace of the Tuileries, Catherine de Medici, fearful of her involvement in the affair, manipulated the king and his council into resolving on the massacre of the entire Huguenot hierarchy. The gates of Paris were closed, the local militia armed, and Catholic loyalists ordered to wear a white scarf and wait for the great bell of the palace to toll the alarum.

Tocsin sounded on the eve of St Bartholomew's Day and, when the official business – the murder of Coligny and the dumping of his body from a window – had been done, the Catholic mob roared through the city. For three days their victims were stripped, stabbed, and their bodies dumped in the Seine. 'The greatest and most grievous calamity that can come to any state is civil war', Ralegh was later to write, 'a misery more lamentable than can be described.'[24]

Ralegh himself escaped the massacre of St Bartholomew's Day. His little troop of West Country soldiers was disbanded after the Peace of St Germain and his own immediate movements are unknown. His experiences in France were to remain indelibly impressed on his memory none the less. He had glimpsed at first hand the tyranny of princes and the squalor of anarchy. He had seen the misery inflicted by organized religion in the pursuit of power. As a consequence, he had counselled himself to 'beware of yielding hasty belief to the robes of sanctity'.[25] Experience had opened up a deep vein of scepticism that was later to expose him to the greatest danger. Now however, and still a very young man, he returned to England, there to begin fashioning for himself a role on what he was later to call 'this stage-play world'.[26]

CHAPTER TWO

Education

To enhance that role a formal education was necessary, and by 1572 Ralegh had matriculated as an undergraduate at Oriel College, Oxford. It is possible that his family funded his studies, but equally likely that he paid his own way with booty he had won in France. From a life of danger and adventure he turned to one of study. Where previously he had been woken by reveilles, the college bell now summoned him to his books.

Scholarship was increasingly being seen as a necessary accomplishment for a gentleman, and those who attended the two universities in the last quarter of the sixteenth century were offered a course of studies that combined rhetoric and logic with the aim of arriving at the truths of religion and expounding the Protestant faith. There was a distinctly conservative bias to this. Aristotle – or, more precisely, the medieval expositors of Aristotle – stood at the core of the curriculum, and the intricacies of dialectic formed the basis of the public examinations. Ralegh seems to have mastered these with his accustomed flair. Anthony à Wood recorded that 'his natural parts being strangely advanced by academical learning, under the care of an excellent tutor, he became the ornament of the juniors, and was worthily esteemed a proficient in oratory and philosophy.'[1]

To an original mind, much of this curriculum could seem wearisomely artificial, a mere playing with words and a juggling with circular arguments. Such modes of thought, the conventional intellectual lumber of schoolmasters and curates, could not satisfy Ralegh's energetic and sceptical intelligence. 'I shall never be persuaded', he later wrote, 'that God hath shut up all the light of learning within the lantern of Aristotle's brains.'[2] Throughout his life, Ralegh refused to believe the ancient philosopher provided the final answer to all man's questions, and continued, most dangerously, to ask his own.

To an eighteen-year-old who had travelled, fought and killed, university discipline must also have been singularly irksome. In principal at least undergraduates were forbidden to enter taverns or 'other dishonest places', to be 'nocturnal ramblers',[3] sleep outside their rooms or go into town without the company of a Master of Arts. To offset such restrictions, and what Aubrey alleges was his poverty, Ralegh had his friends: Arthur Gorges, a cousin from Somerset whom he was to know for the rest of his life, George Carew and Charles Champernowne from Devon, along with the Unton brothers and one Child who 'was his chamber fellow, and lent him a gown'[4] which Ralegh apparently neither gave back nor offered to pay for.

Another story, this time preserved by Francis Bacon, suggests that Ralegh the ex-soldier was also looked up to by less-experienced young men worried about points of honour. Bacon tells how a cowardly student who was deemed a good archer came to Ralegh and asked what he should do to revenge himself on a contemporary who had been abusive. 'Why,' Ralegh answered, 'challenge him to a match of "shooting".'[5] The tone of sardonic impatience is audible still.

Like many gentlemen, Ralegh left Oxford without taking a degree and gravitated to London and the Inns of Court. The register of the Middle Temple for 27 February 1575 records the admission of 'Walter Ralegh, late of Lyons Inn, Gentleman, Son of Walter Ralegh of Budleigh, County Devon'. Ralegh had by this time passed his probationary period at the Inns of Chancery and had now entered what was widely known as 'the third university of England', a stimulating place which gave young men not only a grounding in the law if they wished to avail themselves of it, but the opportunity of lively discussion on current topics, along with the chance of meeting influential contemporaries. Such companionship also offered a training in those gentlemanly refinements of behaviour and ambition which were held to suit a man to royal service and might even enable him to catch the eye of the queen.

This last was now Ralegh's principal aim, and once again the standard curriculum seems to have held little attraction for him. Those who hoped the law would provide a profitable career, along with others who could return to their counties to take up positions as deputy lieutenants or members of parliament, attended lectures, took part in moots and imparlances, and argued prepared issues before their superiors or pleaded extempore. At other times they ground away at law French and earnestly debated with the 'put-case men'[6] as they walked round the quadrangles. When in 1603, however, Ralegh was brought to trial and was required to plead for his life, he claimed he had never studied a word of the law.

The atmosphere of the Inns was conducive to the widest intellectual interests none the less, members of the Parliament or governing body of the Middle Temple encouraging young men in the learning of foreign languages and the study of history, particularly that of their own country. Legal skills may have held few attractions for Ralegh at this time, but if at his trial he was to plead ignorance of the law, he had read omnivorously in other areas, claiming that when he was a young man there was not a book published that he did not buy.

The students of the Middle Temple were supposed to live in, two men sharing a set of chambers. Because of limited space, however, many were required to reside outside, some no doubt preferring the greater freedom this gave them. By 1577, Ralegh himself was living in Islington, then an outlying rural area known for its elaborate mansions with their fine gardens and orchards stretching along Upper Street, the main thoroughfare. Here Ralegh was attended by at least two servants, and that his household was not the most orderly is suggested by the fact that in December 1577 he was obliged to attend court and stand recognizances of one hundred marks for his attendant Richard Paunsford who had been summoned 'to answer such matters as may be objected against him'.[6]

On another such occasion a few days earlier, Ralegh had signed himself 'Walter Rawley, Esq. de Curia' or 'of the Court' which may suggest that he was already an Esquire of the Body Extraordinary, or a reserve member of that pool of young gentlemen who might be called on at any time to wait upon the queen. Membership of this group could be a costly and frustrating business however, expensive appearances having to be kept up, sometimes for years on end, in the hope of one day winning royal favour. Such frustrated ambition could easily lead to outbursts of wild behaviour with wild friends. The gossiping John Aubrey reports that in his youth Ralegh's companions 'were boisterous blades, but generally those that had wit'.[7] One of these was Charles Chester: 'a perpetual talker, made a noise like a drum in a room . . . So one time in a tavern Sir Walter Ralegh beats him and seals up his mouth (i.e. his upper and nether beard) with hard wax.'

While biding his chance, Ralegh was also making more interesting friends. Among these was the soldier and writer George Gascoigne, and Gascoigne's motto – *Tam Marti quam Mercurio*, 'Dedicated to Mars and Mercury Alike' – provided Ralegh with an image he was to polish and refine throughout his career: that of the soldier who was also the poet, the man of renaissance accomplishment who could turn easily from the sword to the pen. Such versatility was highly desirable in a would-be courtier. Poetry could beat a path to the great and lay the foundations of a career. It was a form of that conspicuous display Ralegh was throughout his life to master in the pursuit of his ambitions. If, at its greatest and most mature, his verse could probe the recesses of complex desires, it was also, like a jewelled ribbon or a fine ruff, a means of showing the facility and artifice of the aristocrat.

Gascoigne himself had already secured the patronage of the queen's favourite, the Earl of Leicester, while his taste for moralizing was revealed in his *Steel Glass*, a satire designed to hold the traditional English mirror up to the traditional English vices. When *The Steel Glass* appeared in 1576 it was prefaced by Ralegh's first published poem. This was an ungainly exercise in self-publicity, but behind the heavy, awkward rhythms there are already signs of a sceptical and even cynical intelligence at work, along with a haughty contempt for the small fry:

> For whoso reaps renown above the rest,
> With heaps of hate shall surely be oppressed.[8]

Although Ralegh himself had done little at this stage to achieve 'renown', in imagination at least he had already, at twenty-two, anticipated aspects of his own future reputation. Here, in an early couplet, is a premonition of an entire career.

But the shaping of that career required more than occasional versifying, and the most influential figure from this period of Ralegh's life was his newly knighted half-brother, Sir Humphrey Gilbert. While the younger man was kicking his heels and waiting for advancement, Gilbert's study at Limehouse became his true university. Here the beliefs and ideas of the gentlemen of the West were being refashioned in a way that attempted to bear on the whole course of national policy.

On his return from Ireland, Gilbert's thoughts turned again to exploration and the enlargement of trade, to the problem of rivalry with Spain, and to fashioning a concept of the courtier in which the well-born young man of the widest education could at once display the versatility of his powers while harnessing these to a patriotic ideal of the strong nation state. This was no formal education, no picking over Aristotelian subtleties or canny hunting in the thickets of the law. It offered, rather, the constant stimulus of conversation and example and was, above all, a preparation for action.

Gilbert set down his educational ideas in a paper he entitled 'Queen Elizabeth's Academy'. In an age when the fashioning of a gentleman for courtly and public duties was one of the most intensively considered areas of secular life, Gilbert's ideas were characteristically bold and original. Above all, his proposal for an academy offers a clue to the origins of Ralegh's own conception of his future role – of the courtier who was, in Gilbert's words, 'meet for present practice both of peace and war'.[9]

Gilbert first urged that his school should teach the humanist disciplines of Greek and Latin grammar, logic and rhetoric, adding that the academy should also employ a man who could instruct the scholars in Hebrew. With that concern for rich and flexible expression which came so naturally to the Elizabethans, Gilbert further suggested how the native language would be strengthened by a training in 'the choice of words, the building of sentences, the garnishment of figures, and other beauties of oratory'. Such ideas were later to find fulfilment in one of the masterpieces of Jacobean literature – Ralegh's *History of the World*.

Gilbert realized that classical precedents of logic and history were not an end in themselves but acquisitions to be used for creating a strong nation. He therefore urged that a clear and comprehensive view of contemporary foreign governments should also be taught in his school, along with 'the distinct disciplines and kinds of arming, training and maintaining of . . . soldiers in every particular kind of service'. His pupils would thus be well fitted for the world around them, aware of the international political situation, and able to defend their country in time of war.

And to this ambitious ideal of the courtier, Gilbert added some of the special interests of the gentlemen of the West. In particular, he suggested their accumulated experience of ships and the sea should become part of every gentleman's education, a body of knowledge again to be used in the service of the nation. Astronomy and navigation should be taught, along with cartography and the handling of nautical instruments. Convinced that the future of the country lay in maritime expansion, Gilbert hoped the conventional social prestige that went with the training of a young man as a soldier could now be accompanied by a similar respect for the sea.

Gilbert's Academy never materialized, but the ideas contained in his proposal suggest the influence of the circle of intellectuals, explorers and politicians in which he and Ralegh were now moving. Among these was the great Elizabethan magus John Dee.

Dee was, besides his many other qualifications, the greatest mathematician of his day and he gave unstintingly of his expertise to ensure that his knowledge was diffused as widely as possible. In an age when the use of Arabic numerals was far from common and mathematics itself was often numbered among the black arts, this was no easy matter. However, insistent that he should reach the broadest audience, Dee began publishing mathematical works in English. These were designed for the use of builders, surveyors, lens makers and, above all, navigators. His 'Mathematical Preface' to Euclid is a paean uniting theory with practice and is a manifesto for a form of education that was deeply to impress Ralegh with its possibilities.

Dee was also a learned geographer and was in contact with most of the leading figures on the continent. This knowledge he again put at the disposal of those planning the basis of English maritime expansion, while the surviving parts of his *General and Rare Memorials Pertaining to the Perfect Art of Navigation* show that Dee was not only a man of great technical accomplishment but a political visionary whose ideas made a strong appeal to Protestant minds especially.

Basing himself on a study of the legendary history of the country, a history in which King Arthur played a prominent role, Dee became convinced that the Tudor monarchy should follow the expansionist achievements of their great alleged ancestor and revive what he considered to be their legal entitlement to an empire in North America. Drawing also on a rich tradition of political thought, he elaborated an image of Elizabeth as Astrea the Imperial Virgin who, as the embodiment of just power and the true church, should initiate a revival of political and religious rectitude in the West. This admiration for Elizabeth as the Virgin Queen, and her association with the colonization of America especially, was to be of the utmost importance to the mature Ralegh's thought. For the moment, however, he was only a very young man on the edges of this circle, and others of altogether greater importance were visiting Dee and his library at Mortlake.

The dark and subtle Sir Francis Walsingham, for example, took a regular interest in the ideas being discussed. Walsingham was one of the principal members of Elizabeth's Privy Council, a man of the severest principle, and 'a most sharp maintainer of the purer religion'.[10] He was convinced that religion rather than national rivalry was the mainspring of European disorder, and he had the imaginative flexibility to envisage America as a suitable location for those English Catholics who wished to persevere with their religion free from political interference. He was also prepared to lend his prestige to those he thought could further these purposes, and his hand can be seen behind many plans for American colonization, including those soon to be launched by Humphrey Gilbert and Ralegh himself.

Another visitor to Mortlake – and a man who was again to exercise great influence over Ralegh's career – was the queen's favourite, Robert Dudley, Earl of Leicester. In the early days of the reign, Dudley's virile energies and handsome presence had exercised so obvious an influence over Elizabeth that ambassadors referred to him as 'the king that is to be'.[11] The passion between the great courtier and his monarch had been cruelly frustrated none the less. At the deepest level of her consciousness Elizabeth was wedded unshakeably to her throne and was obliged to the recognition that her 'sweet Robin' was merely her creation, her creature even. From time to time she was forced tartly to remind him of the fact.

Leicester's immense ambitions remained unfulfilled while for two decades he danced in sterile attendance on his queen. He craved love and desperately wanted an heir to succeed to his vast estates and his family's influence at court. For the moment, his hopes had necessarily to focus on his nephew the young Philip Sidney: proud, brilliant, ardently Protestant and, to the other young men of his generation, the admired of all admirers. Sidney, too, was an enthusiastic member of the Dee circle – the magus had taught him his chemistry – while as Ralegh's exact contemporary, Sidney was an enviable example of what aspirations the lottery of birth might bring. As he was later to admit, Ralegh at the time loathed Leicester's heir apparent with all the corrosive jealousy of youth.

The maritime interests of these men – Walsingham, Leicester, Sidney, Gilbert and the young Ralegh – were now sharply focused by political considerations, in particular the deepening attrition between England and imperial Spain. This last was to provide the focus of Ralegh's political career.

There had been problems between the two countries since the 1530s when reports began to filter back to West Country ports especially of the confiscation of English goods and the maltreatment and even torture of English merchants at the hands of the Holy Office. To the Protestant gentry, this was proof of the enmity of the Catholic power and, if this seemed to justify the privateering activities of men such as the older Ralegh, further arrests made by the Spaniards both in their home ports and later in the Low Countries deepened mutual hostility.

It was in the Caribbean that the friction was felt at its most intense, for here Spain viewed every foreign ship as an interloper on her monopoly of trade granted under papal law. For their part, English merchants were reluctant to accept what they considered an arbitrary embargo on their profits, and soon after the accession of Elizabeth, John Hawkins of Plymouth began the lucrative if repulsive trade of shipping negro slaves from Africa to the Caribbean. Here, despite rulings from their government, Spanish colonists were all too ready to buy cheap labour, their own cruelty having decimated the native population.

In 1562, and 'trusting the Spaniards no further than by his own strength he was able still to master them',[12] Hawkins successfully shipped some three hundred Negroes – 'this prey'[13] as they were called – to the West Indies and returned with a handsome profit. A second and larger expedition sailed the following year, this time with financial support not just from Londoners such as Hawkins's father-in-law the Treasurer of the Navy, but the Earls of Leicester and Pembroke, and even the queen herself who contributed her seven-hundred-ton vessel the *Jesus*. On arrival in the Caribbean, a show of arms subdued any lingering doubts the Spaniards might have had over dealing with Hawkins's illicit cargo, but the might of Spain and her hatred of interlopers were real threats indeed. By August 1567, the Spaniards, still nominally allies of the English, refused to salute English ships in the Channel, and it was in the certainty that 'I know they hate me'[14] that Hawkins set out on his most famous voyage.

Sailing to Sierra Leone, he spent three months securing five hundred Negroes, some of whom were robbed from the Portuguese while others were accepted from native chiefs as payment for help in a tribal war. However, the Spanish colonists at Rio de la Hacha could only be persuaded to buy Hawkins's cargo after Hawkins himself had burnt part of their town, while those at Cartagena refused to be coerced at all. And then disaster struck. Some of the crew of the *William and John* were lost in a storm, the queen's ship was almost destroyed, and Hawkins was obliged to sail towards Vera Cruz and the port of San Juan de Ulúa. The Spaniards, thinking their own fleet had arrived, gave Hawkins entrance, panicked, and then abandoned him to his repairs.

The following morning, eleven large vessels of the Spanish plate fleet and two escorting men-of-war appeared on the horizon. The flotilla was under the command of the viceroy of New Spain, a man freshly dispatched with imperial orders to defend his master's trade from English privateers. If, as the Queen's Officer, Hawkins refused the Spaniards entry to San Juan de Ulúa, he risked provoking an international incident that might lead to war. If he allowed the Spaniards to sail into their own port, he would be wholly at their mercy.

A truce was arranged and hostages exchanged, but at ten the next morning the Spaniards opened battle at point-blank range. This was to last for six hours. Curses on the English '*Luteranos*' (to the Spaniards all Protestants were Lutherans) alternated with cries of 'God and St George!' Amid smoke, shouts and confusion, the Spanish flagship was sunk and the vice-admiral's vessel set on fire. While the Spanish guns rained down on the beleaguered English privateers, Hawkins, with that sense of drama inseparable from the Elizabethan seaman, called his page to bring him his beer in a silver cup. Having toasted his gunmen and willed them to stand by their ordnance, he drained the beaker and the empty vessel was at once shot away. The voice of the Western gentry rose confidently above the din. 'Fear nothing, for God who hath preserved me from this shot will also deliver us from these traitorous villains!'[15]

But now the *Jesus* was immobilized. The *Angel* was sunk, the *Swallow* captured, and the masts of other vessels shot away. Then, in the afternoon, the Spaniards launched their fireships. Though Hawkins himself stayed so long on the queen's ship that he was almost left behind, the *Jesus* had eventually to be abandoned. Only two English vessels remained: the *Minion* under Hawkins and the *Judith* under the young Drake who, later giving rise to misunderstanding, slipped away under cover of night.

But even then 'the miseries and troublesome affairs of this sorrowful voyage'[16] were far from over. The *Minion* was so short of food and water that a hundred of her men pleaded with Hawkins to be put ashore, preferring to surrender to the Spaniards than risk the hazards of the Atlantic. They fell, inevitably, into the hands of the Inquisition. Those more mercifully treated were sentenced to two hundred lashes and six to eight years in the galleys. Others were condemned to be strangled and burnt at the stake. The *Minion* herself limped back to Mount's Bay in January 1569, crewed, it was said, by a mere fifteen exhausted men. From now on, there was to be open and constant hatred between Spain and the gentlemen of the West.

Such incidents were to shape Ralegh's political career, to inspire some of his greatest feats and eventually cause his death. Even before reports of the Spaniards' treachery at San Juan de Ulúa reached England however, fear of an all-surrounding Catholic threat had reached crisis point. Mary, Queen of Scots, had fled to England and was the focus of constant plots and fears of insurrection. Across the Channel, the Duke of Alba had marched into the Low Countries, there to triumph over the rebellious subjects of Spain. A small Protestant neighbour, a sometime ally, and an important trading partner, the Low Countries now glittered with 50,000 armed enemy soldiers, men paid more or less regularly with money borrowed against the security of Philip II's American silver and gold. In 1568, the English ambassador in Madrid was expelled, while his Spanish counterpart in London was replaced by a series of men altogether more fanatical.

The short-term recourse was to harry Spain at her weakest point and threaten her credit by regular attacks on her bullion fleet in the Caribbean. The gentlemen of the West were prepared. An expedition under Francis Drake was dispatched by the Hawkinses to discover the secrets of the Spanish mule trains which crossed the isthmus of Panama to the Caribbean port of Nombre de Dios. These carried burdens of Peruvian silver Drake believed he could ambush. With exceptional courage in pioneering the commando techniques Ralegh was later to exploit, Drake made a night raid on Nombre de Dios and then, in partnership with a Huguenot privateer, seized a staggering hoard of booty and returned in triumph to Plymouth.

Other men followed his lead or planned enterprises of their own. In 1574, Sir Richard Grenville was ready to sail to the River Plate and on through the Strait of Magellan to the Chile coast, there to set about the conquest of the tip of South America in the belief that this region was 'by God's providence left for England'.[17] Elizabeth, altogether more cautious and wishing to foster the slight improvement in her relations with Philip II, forbade the expedition to sail. The plan was revived in 1577, however, when Drake set out on that greatest of Elizabethan sea epics, his circumnavigation of the globe. This triumph of seamanship and privateering was to have a profound effect on public opinion in England, not only by making Drake himself a national hero but by focusing a defiant Protestant nationalism against Spain and identifying this with English mastery of the sea.

It was in such an atmosphere that Gilbert too turned his attention to the strategic possibilities of a sea war. In 1577 he produced two memoranda for the queen in which he suggested ways in which she might 'annoy'[18] the king of Spain. Both papers reveal the spirit of the man: intensely patriotic, wholeheartedly Protestant, and driven by a combination of intellect and imagination at once vertiginously ambitious and little restrained by practical considerations or common sense.

Convinced that war with Spain was now inevitable, and believing it 'as lawful in Christian policy to prevent a mischief betimes as to revenge it too late',[19] Gilbert proposed a two-pronged attack of the greatest audacity. His ships would first – if necessary under the cover of a patent for discovery – sweep up to Newfoundland and seize the fishing fleets of Spain, Portugal and France. These vessels would then be brought back to England or the Netherlands and their catch disposed of. The mercantile power of the nation's rivals would be thereby much reduced.

A second fleet would then be sent out, again under the cover of a reconnaissance expedition, to join the first for a grand attack on the West Indies. Bermuda would be used as a base for capturing Spanish galleons before proceeding to San Domingo and Cuba which would be taken and made to serve as bases for harrying the Spaniards on the mainland of America. England would thus acquire new colonies, new trade, and new power. In Gilbert's words: 'This realm being an island shall be discharged from all foreign perils' while the queen herself would become mistress of 'all the northern and southern viages of the world'.[20]

Elizabeth, with characteristic sagacity, turned the plan down. The Imperial Virgin of the theoreticians was, in the deepest recesses of her being, no imperialist at all, while she was also too seasoned a politician easily to be gulled by the idea that a great power might be mortally wounded by a couple of privateering expeditions. Above all, she was appalled at the thought of open war with Spain, for she had an altogether more certain understanding of the perils to which this exposed her than the men who urged impossible schemes of conquest. This was a policy of great political wisdom which the 'men of war' – Ralegh among them – were to chafe at for being unimaginative and tame.

Frustrated in his aim of destroying Spanish power in the Atlantic, Gilbert turned his restless intelligence to plans for American colonization, thereby providing the young Ralegh with an ambition and an ideal that were to dominate his later career and draw him out of a circle of thinkers and politicians into the world of action. In June 1578, Gilbert received letters patent granting him permission to sail in search of 'remote, heathen and barbarous lands, countries and territories not actually possessed of any Christian prince'.[21] Ralegh was to accompany him.

The licence was to last for six years and, although its terms are sufficiently vague, its purpose seems to have been to authorize Gilbert to set up colonies which he and his heirs could occupy in perpetuity. These colonies were probably to be situated on the North American coastline, in latitudes above those of the Spaniards' settlement in Florida, and in an area known generally as Norumbega. Taking their cue from similar enterprises projected in Ireland, Gilbert's colonies were to be held in homage from the Crown in return for a payment of royalties on any gold and silver that might be discovered. Gilbert would, in turn, grant rights of tenure to such colonists as were allowed to leave England. He was also to protect them from intruders, frame laws in accord with those of England, and exercise jurisdiction. In such ways might a land-hungry generation hope to acquire for themselves estates greater than any England could reasonably offer.

The anti-Spanish party on the Privy Council, led by Walsingham, had some influence in granting Gilbert's patent, but despite the fact that Gilbert himself seems to have intended to finance his expedition in some degree by privateering, the document was carefully drafted to curtail his freedom to annoy Spanish shipping. It was stated that any damage Gilbert or his men might inflict would have to be made good, and failure to make restitution would result in his being put 'out of our allegiance and protection'.[22]

The precise goal of the expedition Gilbert launched none the less remains clouded in mystery. Mendoza, the Spanish ambassador, believed he was sailing for the West Indies and knew he had enlisted the services of the Portuguese pilot Simon Fernandez who was an expert in the area. Mendoza also hoped, as did the French ambassador, to plant spies amid the crew. In such an atmosphere, Gilbert himself remained extremely secretive. He was preparing late in the year to set out on a major expedition, but when he told the French ambassador he was heading South, apparently to 'Terra Australis Incognita', he was almost certainly laying a false trail. What seems most likely, especially considering the heavy armament of five hundred men and a hundred and twenty-two guns his fleet was provided with, was that, despite the explicit terms of his patent, part at least of Gilbert's plans involved sailing into the Caribbean and there founding a base which could be used for attacks on Spanish shipping.

So confident was Gilbert of his expedition's success that he invested all of his own money in the venture. He also persuaded his brothers John and Adrian to subscribe, as well as Carew and Walter Ralegh, both of whom were to sail as captains. William Hawkins also contributed, as did a number of London merchants including the greatly wealthy Thomas Smith. Among the gentlemen who lent their support were Lord North, Sir Edward Horsey, the Governor of the Isle of Wight, and Henry Knollys, the son of Elizabeth's Vice-Chamberlain, who was in command of three ships. Gilbert himself was to sail as admiral in the *Anne Aucher*. Ralegh, at last experiencing the thrill of his first command, sailed as captain of the *Falcon* with Simon Fernandez as master.

This veneer of respectability was not maintained by those who actually made up Gilbert's men, and Walter Ralegh sailed on his first seaborne expedition with some of the country's most notorious pirates. No very satisfactory machinery was yet in place to limit their activities. Such matters were still in the hands of the vice-admirals, and although since 1564 every convicted pirate was condemned to be hanged near his home port as an example to others, in the first twenty years of Elizabeth's reign only a little over a hundred men were executed for piracy. In 1578, a year in which the authorities were particularly active, of the nine hundred men brought to trial for piracy, only three were actually sentenced to death.

A fleet crewed by men used to such conditions would be almost impossible to discipline, and with a commander of Gilbert's temperament friction was inevitable. There were delays and disagreements from the start. Certain ships only made Dartmouth towards the end of August, while Henry Knollys – Gilbert's principal colleague, and a man as volatile as himself – arrived as late as 10 September. Thirteen days later, eleven ships and five hundred men were ready to set sail, and on 26 September they weighed anchor. Contrary winds at once forced them back up the Channel, Gilbert's ship being driven as far off course as the Isle of Wight. It took a fortnight for the flotilla to reform, and five days for Gilbert himself to lead them on to Plymouth.

Another attempt to sail on 29 October failed, and by 5 November tempers were so frayed that Knollys decided to quit the expedition. On 18 November, he deserted with the *Elephant*, the *Bark Denys*, and the *Francis* along with fifty-three guns and one hundred and sixty-one men. Piracy had quite simply proved too strong a temptation, and John Callice, the notorious captain of the *Elephant*, too persuasive a pirate chief. Making for Ireland, the deserters captured a Breton ship, disposed of her goods in Cork, and then, while Knollys himself returned to London, the *Francis* was despatched to Cape St Vincent for yet more lucrative privateering.

On 19 November 1578, Gilbert finally left Plymouth with seven vessels, one hundred and twenty-two guns, and a little over four hundred men. The fleet made for Ireland, but Gilbert's ambitions were again confounded. The *Hope of Greenway* sprang a leak, while the rest of the fleet was constantly driven back to the Irish coast. There was only one exception to this miserable story. Walter Ralegh, the captain of the *Falcon*, 'being desirous to do somewhat worthy of honour, took his course for the West Indies'.[23]

His ship was a vessel of about a hundred tons and was armed with some fifteen cannon and a comparable number of smaller pieces. Riding in Plymouth harbour, she had made a brave sight with coloured streamers and the flag of St George waving from her three masts: the mizzen at her stern end, her sixty-foot mainmast secured by ropes of tarred Italian hemp, and her foremast rising from the foredeck where the crew would assemble for battle. Her timbers, caulked and blackened with pitch, were, like all such vessels, brightly painted with geometric designs, a form of decoration applied with particular lavishness around her high, imposing stern. But for all her gallant appearance, the *Falcon* was a tiny vessel, probably less than seventy-five feet long at her waterline and under a hundred feet overall. Her complement of soldiers, mariners and gentlemen – the officers, master, mate, bosun, cook, pilot, skilled craftsmen, gunners and boys – numbered some seventy in all, and were packed together in conditions at once cramped and dangerous.

Privacy being the most prized commodity on such a ship, it was reserved almost entirely for the captain and his senior officers. The poop deck on the stern would probably have been regarded as Ralegh's special territory, as most certainly was the captain's cabin, the only private cabin on the ship, and a small, wedge-shaped room where charts and navigational instruments were kept. Its aura of mystery and distance were essential in the preservation of discipline.

The low, round-topped door of Ralegh's cabin led out to the half-deck from where he gave his commands and Fernandez plotted their course. Forward from this, and down a steep flight of wooden steps, was the main deck, an area barely twenty feet wide and largely covered with a hatch through which supplies and booty could be lowered. Here, at the foot of the main mainmast, might also have been found two carved wooden heads on posts. These, it was believed, brought good luck when touched and also served to keep ghosts out of the whistling rigging.

Below the half-deck was the great cabin, an area of comparative luxury for the officers. Here, a dining area, panelled and lit by leaded ports, offered a table and benches where the gentlemen could eat in that degree of state on which they insisted. Here, too, conferences could be called while, through the long and often tedious days of a voyage, these men could beguile their time with chess or reading. Ralegh himself always sailed with a chest of books. At night, those allowed into these quarters slept in the foremost part of the cabin (which also served as the armoury) in small, flimsy cabouches which could easily be dismantled when a fight with the enemy was in view. Access to such light and relative comfort provided the strongest indication of gentry status, a privilege enhanced by the fact that this was the only communal living space on the ship where a man could stand upright without fear of hitting his head.

At the opposite end of the *Falcon*, in the fo'c'sle under the bowsprit, were the quarters of the skilled mariners: the smith, carpenter and sailmaker. Dark and cramped, its planks painted blood red to disguise the mess of battle, the minimal comfort marked the divide between these valued men and the rest of the crew who were crowded some thirty at a time in the gun deck below. Here the stench and squalor, the noise, cramped conditions and risk of disease were at their worst. Light and air filtered through the hatch on the main deck above, but because it was essential to keep the *Falcon* as low in the water as possible to preserve her balance, no grown man could stand in such space as there was between the timbers and the guns themselves.

In a period before the introduction of hammocks, the crew slept – sometimes perhaps on folded sails – around the guns. These were positioned very close to the waterline, and even in a mildly rough sea, water would deluge through the ports so that the men slept in constant, skin-rotting damp. The fetid air was made worse by the fact that washing was considered a particularly dangerous activity likely to remove the luck that clung to a sailor's skin. During a long voyage, and around these already stinking bodies, others less fortunate groaned in the often fatal agonies of dysentery, typhus, beri-beri and scurvy.

To this human putrescence was added the smell of the animal droppings in the cages where the officers' fresh meat was housed, a luxury the ratings themselves rarely enjoyed at sea. Ladled into their wooden bowls and leather cups was a monotonous diet of gruel, salt-beef, putrid water, flat beer and weevil-infested biscuit brought up from the hold, an area below the gun deck ruthlessly controlled by the bosun.

The theft of food was a serious offence – the careful rationing of victuals often making for the success or failure of a voyage – and thieves would be locked in the brig until a suitable punishment had been decided. This might well consist of nailing the offender's hand to the mainmast with a marlin spike for a few hours. His screams, as the rocking ship tossed his weight against his broken bones, served as a warning to others, while, at the end of his term of punishment, the offender's ribboned hand would be cut off and the stump dipped in oil as a permanent reminder of his folly.

In such conditions as these – and as the only ship in Gilbert's fleet not ignominiously moored off the Irish coast – the young Ralegh sailed out into the Atlantic to reach the Cape Verde Islands. The hazards he faced were daunting: waves forty feet high, fogs so thick they hid the stars, storms so fierce that the mainmast was blown level with the sea. There was also the constant worry of opening timbers, the loss of the rudder or the mutinous resentment of frightened men. All that is known for certain however is that Ralegh 'passed many dangerous adventures, as well as by tempests as fights on the sea',[24] that large numbers of his company died, and that, his victuals depleted and his ship 'sore battered and disabled',[25] he eventually returned to Plymouth in May 1579.

Here, after so arduous a trial, he immediately found himself in trouble. The piracies associated with the expedition were in clear breach of Gilbert's patent, and those who sailed with him were now under suspicion. Gilbert himself protested his innocence, but the Privy Council sent word that his licence would be revoked unless he stood surety for future good behaviour. When some of his company then seized a Spanish ship loaded with oranges, an exasperated Privy Council wrote again, mentioning Gilbert and Ralegh by name, and informing Sir John Gilbert that he was 'required friendly to advise them to surcease from proceeding any further, and to remain at home'.[26] The matter of the oranges, meanwhile, was to be investigated by local officers who risked the royal anger if they allowed Gilbert, Ralegh and their associates to sail.

Gilbert himself was eventually sent to patrol the coasts of Ireland. His first seaborne expedition had been a disaster, and such hopes as the young Walter Ralegh had entertained were reduced to a discreditable mention in Privy Council correspondence and a wrangle over some oranges. This was a lesson in bitter disappointment, and he would now have to seek advancement in other ways and take on other roles.

CHAPTER THREE

The Fringes of Power

Ralegh returned to London and the expensive, quarrelsome life of a young man on the fringes of the court. On 7 February 1580, he and Sir Thomas Perrot were called before the Council 'for a fray made betwixt them'[1] and were committed to the Fleet prison for six days to cool their heels, after which they were released on promises of good behaviour. A month later, Ralegh was taken up before the Council again, this time for fighting by the tennis court at Whitehall. He was sent to the Marshalsea. Neither spell in prison was a particularly severe punishment, nor a wholly unusual one. The pride and hot-blooded enthusiasms of young courtiers often led to affrays, and gentlemen prisoners could receive friends, have meals brought to them by their servants, and even go out for occasional social engagements.

By coincidence, the day after Ralegh was committed to the Marshalsea, he was joined there by his cousin Arthur Gorges who had rashly challenged a nobleman to a duel in the Presence Chamber. Ralegh and Gorges had known each other at Oxford, and their relationship was rooted among the families of the West. The daughter of Ralegh's aunt Frances Champernowne had married Arthur's father, Sir William Gorges. While the friendship of Ralegh and Gorges looked back to their West Country origins however, it also offered an opening to some of the greatest families in the land.

Through his father, young Arthur Gorges was a great-grandson of the Howards. Charles Arundel was pleased to call him 'my cousin', and it was probably through this connection (perhaps with Walsingham, the spy-master of Elizabethan England, hovering in the background) that Ralegh briefly became attached to that volatile and dangerous group of aristocratic young Catholics who took for their leader the Earl of Oxford.

Oxford was the premier peer of England, the son-in-law of Burghley and a favourite of the queen. Among his friends and kinsmen were the Lords Charles and Thomas Howard, Windsor and Compton, as well as the Earls of Northumberland and Southampton. In addition to his immense social prestige, Oxford also claimed wide intellectual interests. He was a very considerable patron, flattered by his dependants as a man who 'doth heartily embrace all such as excel in any worthy virtue'.[2] He lent his name to protect companies of boy and adult actors, and accepted dedications from writers on religion, philosophy, music and medicine, as well as from a number of important translators. He also wrote poetry himself in a stilted, courtly manner.

But if Oxford appeared a brilliant figure for Ralegh to woo, he was radically and dangerously unstable. Left an orphan, he had been brought up as a ward in Burghley's household where, at seventeen, he murdered one of his guardian's servants and was only acquitted on a plea of self-defence through Burghley's personal intervention. Those who fell foul of him – among them his sister's fiancé Peregrine Bertie – went in fear of their lives. Nor could Oxford control his purse any better than his temper. In 1575, he set out on a grand tour of Europe. Having insisted that Burghley sell off some of his estates, he proceeded to run through £4,561 in fifteen months, while Burghley himself was left to deal with over a hundred angry tradesmen demanding the settlement of debts amounting to a quarter of that sum again.

On his return from Europe, discontented, jealous of rising new families like Burleigh's, and refusing to live with his wife (Burghley's daughter and the mother of his child) Oxford converted to Catholicism. The move was little more than the petulance of a foolish young man who now proceeded to embarrass both the French ambassador and the French king by offering to lead a Catholic revolt in the country if France would support him. Such disaffection was underpinned by little depth of religious idealism. When Ralegh, along with Henry Howard, Arundel, Francis Southwell and Lord Windsor were dining with him, they were treated to theological insights no more profound than the notion that Joseph was a cuckold and the Virgin Mary a whore. Such, it seemed, could be the tedium of dining with the great. But the very brilliance of Oxford's position inevitably drew him into political intrigue, and here, for the moment, Ralegh sensed the opportunity of being associated with the core of national policy.

In 1578, Elizabeth reopened negotiations for marriage to the Duc of Alençon, brother to King Henri III of France, in the hope of forming a political alliance with the man who was now providing troops to the beleaguered Low Countries and rejoiced in the title 'Defender of Belgian Liberty against Spanish Tyranny'. To deter Catholic Spain, Elizabeth would parley with Catholic France. Encouraged by reports from the French ambassador, who was using the young men to create a pressure group at court, Oxford and his circle saw their faction headed for success. The queen might at last marry and produce an heir while, as the Spanish ambassador later reported, they all 'desired that the match should take place, believing, like many other Catholics, that by this means they would come to hold their religion in freedom.'[3]

Such hopes were entirely misplaced. Elizabeth had no intention of marrying. She had made her status as Virgin Queen into one of her greatest political assets, and at forty-five she was not going to hazard this for a dubious alliance. None the less, in order to buy time, she would go through the exquisite movements of an international charade, playing her part so well that at times, it seems, she almost convinced herself. To Ralegh, watching from afar, it appeared his new friends might become influential men indeed – co-religionists of the future king.

At the start of 1579, the French envoy Jehan de Simier arrived to begin his master's wooing. 'A most choice courtier, exquisitely skilled in love-toys, pleasant conceits, and court dalliance',[4] he enquired of Elizabeth's doctors if she could still bear children and, receiving a favourable answer, proceeded to exercise his charms. Very soon he was her 'Monkey'. In a court where royal nicknames were a particular sign of favour, the English nobles were furious. Hatton sulked and Leicester muttered about magic, while the Monkey himself crept into the royal bedroom to steal a nightcap to send his master before being surprised in his turn by the queen herself 'with only his jerkin on'.[5]

Leicester, fearing for his own position and the well-being of the Protestant cause, remonstrated with his mistress. By now he had all but abandoned his hopes of marrying Elizabeth and was conducting clandestine affairs with various available ladies of the aristocracy. He had had a son by Lady Sheffield, a woman he claimed he never married, but when it became clear that Lettice, Countess of Essex, was pregnant by him, Leicester secretly wedded her. Sensing the force of his opposition to their plans, the French at once informed the queen of her old favourite's marriage. Elizabeth, in an excess of jealousy, ordered Leicester from the court, put him under house arrest, and only when she had been soothed by Lord Sussex agreed to save face by visiting him on what was given out to be his sickbed.

Then the Duc himself arrived. He was very small and exceedingly ugly, his large nose protruding from a pock-marked, cunning face. He wanted to see the queen at once, but 'I persuaded him to take some rest,' Simier wrote to her, 'and soon got him between the sheets, and I wish to God you were with him there as he could then with greater ease convey his thoughts to you.'⁶ The following day, the expectant couple met. The queen professed herself delighted with the young man. He was, she said, her 'Frog'.

As negotiations for the marriage appeared to become increasingly serious, so the courtiers divided themselves along party lines. Burghley, believing the queen was serious in her intentions and realizing the political advantages of the match, led the pro-marriage group, while Leicester and Walsingham headed those opposed to it. Among the latter was Philip Sidney.

Late in August 1579, Sidney was playing tennis in front of the French negotiators when Oxford appeared on the court and commanded him to leave. Sidney, as hot-blooded as all young courtiers, made an angry reply. Oxford called him 'Puppy'. Sidney asked him to repeat the gibe and Oxford did so, more loudly than before. Sidney at once gave him 'the lie direct' or the prelude to a duel, and then, after a moment of furious silence, withdrew from the tennis court.

But no challenge was forthcoming from the Earl of Oxford. Sidney angrily reminded him of his obligations to honour, and Arundel, in a paper written later and in bitterness, reported that he and Ralegh were eventually sent with the Earl's reply, adding that Oxford himself was planning to murder Sidney in his bed rather than face the duel. In the event, such cowardice was unnecessary. The Council heard of the matter and reported it to the queen who summoned

Sidney to her. With that regard for the traditional social order which ran so deep within her, Elizabeth explained that it was quite simply not the business of a man in Sidney's position to challenge one of the great peers of the realm.

But the French marriage was not only a matter of honour among courtiers. The people too were horrified, believing their queen was being 'led blindfold as a poor lamb to the slaughter'.[7] Puritan zealots added that she was old, past childbearing age, and was wrong to want to surrender her virginity to a syphilitic French Catholic. A pamphlet was issued 'letting her majesty see the sin and punishment her behaviour was provoking'.[8] Elizabeth, furious at a Puritan commoner's attempt to influence her policy, had the author John Stubbs, his printer and publisher arrested, dubiously tried, and sentenced to mutilation. When his right hand had been struck off, Stubbs 'put off his hat with his left, and cried aloud "God Save the Queen!"'[9] Then he passed out. Elizabeth muttered vindictively that he should have been hanged. Why, she asked her Council tearfully, why was she alone not allowed to marry and have children?

The Frog, meanwhile, had been recalled to France and, in November 1579, Simier followed him. The English had already twice tried to shoot him, and now the Oxford circle, exultant but wary, decided to send Ralegh across the Channel as Simier's escort. Someone (the Catholics were later to say it was Leicester) organized another bungled attempt on Simier's life. Pirates were hired to sink the ship in which the envoy made his crossing. They failed in their plans due to the presence of 'some of her Majesty's ships who to break of this designment attended by special commandment to waft him over in safety'.[10] None the less, as Ralegh himself was sailing back to England, the pirates gave him chase for four hours.

He returned to find Oxford involved in political and personal turmoil. The young Earl had quarrelled with his closest friends on a matter of family honour and was now shunned at court. Leicester, determined to crush Catholic opposition and hopes of the French marriage especially, saw his opportunity. During the Christmas festivities he made up to the young man and suggested he confess to the queen that he now recognized the error of his Catholic ways and was prepared to report his erstwhile friends as traitors. By showing so many highly placed supporters of the French marriage to be secret

Catholics, Leicester recognized he could greatly harm the negotiations. Oxford – weak, deceitful and easily led – followed his
advice. For a time, the queen was greatly distressed and imprisoned
a number of the young men while the matter was investigated.
Realizing the issue was best kept quiet, she soon set Oxford himself
at liberty. Far from leading him to power and influence, Ralegh's
friends seemed to be pushing themselves to the lunatic fringe of
Elizabethan politics.

The storm broke when the full reasons for Oxford's family quarrel
emerged. By March, the Earl was known to have got his young
kinswoman Anne Vavasour pregnant. If Elizabeth was pragmatic
about religious dissent, particularly when those involved were great
aristocrats more foolish than dangerous, she invariably responded
harshly to sexual impropriety among the women of her court. Her
ladies-in-waiting were her vestals, and seducing them merited con-
dign punishment. While Oxford prepared to flee the country, Anne
herself, having given birth to her child, was sent to the Tower.

The recriminations were bitter. Charles Arundel and Lord
Howard sided with the Vavasours against Oxford. Oxford in his turn
charged his accusers with conspiring against the Protestants and
with the possession of treasonable literature. The queen's suspicions
about the group's Catholic sympathies were re-opened, and the erstwhile friends set about a further blackening of their names. Oxford
in particular was accused of planning the deaths of Anne's uncles,
and to these charges of murder were added equally dangerous allegations of atheism and sodomy. 'I will prove him a buggerer of a
boy that is his cook,'[11] Arundel declared, adding that he had witnessed certain scenes himself.

Ralegh's supposedly powerful friends had shown their true
natures, while he himself had tried to win prominence in a political
game altogether too deep for him and one inevitably doomed to
failure. All he had achieved was to make enemies in high places. He
now resolved to change sides. Perhaps as a reward, he was offered
a minor commission in the army and told to prepare himself for
Ireland. While Oxford issued hysterical threats and boasted of 'a
brave vendetta'[12] whereby he had hired a man to kill Ralegh as soon
as he saw action, Ralegh himself shrugged the threats off. As Captain
Ralegh, marching at the head of a hundred men, he was now embark-

ing for a land whose people were as foreign to the Elizabethans as any on the most distant part of the globe.

This cultural divide had been spectacularly brought home when, in 1562, Shane O'Neill came to pay homage to the queen. The people of London watched in amazement as O'Neill processed through their streets surrounded by a bodyguard of his hired gallowglasses. Here was a great tribal chief, a man from a culture ancient and warlike, protected by followers whose terrible battleaxes belonged to the Norse societies of a forgotten past. Their long hair fell down in 'glibbs' over their foreheads (some were later to say the better to hide their lying eyes) while they were dressed in the long-sleeved saffron gowns in which they lived and fought, slept and hid their knives. When he came before the queen, O'Neill made his speech of submission in his native Erse, but to the nobility of the Elizabethan court, reared on Cicero and the precision of the law, his profession sounded like the merest 'howling'. Here was a difference of culture, a difference of time, and a chasm which was to swallow many from both sides in bloody and terrible conflict.

O'Neill himself had risen to power after a period of the wildest confusion in Ulster. He had murdered the heir to his predecessor and then claimed his position as tribal leader through the ancient Irish custom of tanistry, or the election to power of the strongest man within the ruling family. Now, despite the efforts of Lord Sussex to have him overthrown, O'Neill was creating violent disturbances. Elizabeth had been forced to compromise. O'Neill came to London on the promise of a pardon, swore his allegiance, and was rewarded with the captaincy of Tyrone. His responsibilities were now to keep the peace in Ulster as the English required. Having returned to his stronghold, however, O'Neill at once began to assert his dominance over the other local chiefs through the raiding and conquest that were the habitual occupations of his class.

The English presence in Ireland was currently restricted to a tiny area within the Pale around Dublin that was harassed on all sides. Beyond the Pale, those English people living in the chartered towns of the southern and western coasts – Waterford, Youghal, Cork, Limerick and Galway – were under constant pressure from the inhabitants of the surrounding countryside and had begun to absorb

[43]

their ways. The housewives of Cork, for example, were forbidden to talk to English soldiers in any language but Erse.

Among the Anglo-Irish of Leinster, Munster and South Connaught, this process of absorption had gone much further. Although the heads of their families held many of the great titles confirmed by Henry VIII – Ormonde, Kildare and Desmond – these people were now almost wholly native and, for all their power, were regarded as 'very patch-cocks as the wild Irish themselves'.[13] And it was the Celtic inheritance of the 'wild Irish', however primitive or anachronistic it appeared – and however doomed it was eventually to prove – that for the moment asserted its power.

Organized religion had little effect on this. The Catholic Church in Ireland had fallen to its lowest ebb, and for the moment the Popes showed small interest in her. An often barely literate priesthood were obliged to rely on the local chiefs who had in turn gladly accepted the Royal Supremacy and the dissolution of the monasteries in return for English titles which confirmed their personal possession of Church property. The ordinary Irish people, meanwhile, were left to suffer at the hands of their chiefs and their continuous tribal wars.

To the Elizabethans, this was a horrifying spectacle. Ireland, wrote Ralegh's future friend the poet Edmund Spenser, was 'a nation ever acquainted with wars, though but amongst themselves, and in their own kind of military discipline'.[14] This last had developed little since the Dark Ages. The chieftains were fighting leaders who pursued their interminable quarrels with the utmost savagery and rejoiced in their deeds being celebrated by bards in a poetry whose forms had barely changed for three centuries. Cavalrymen rode into battle without stirrups, while the terrible gallowglasses, paid by the chiefs with exactions of coign and livery inflicted on their impoverished peasants, were joined by roving redshanks for the internecine blood-lettings by which chief succeeded chief.

Surveying such conditions, the English were quick to believe the Irish represented the nadir of human existence, a rejection of the 'civil' and of civilization itself. They were a people easily to be characterized as intellectually backward, lazy and dissipated. While for much of the time they seemed content to live in the woods with their cattle, yet, recalled one observer, 'When they came to towns nothing was more frequent than to tie their cows at the doors, and never part from the taverns till they had drunk them out in sack and strong water, which they call usquebaugh; and this did not only the lords, but the common people, though half naked from want of clothes to cover them.'[15]

When the Irish were neither drunk nor fighting, then, the English liked to believe, they were busy cattle raiding. 'They account it no shame or infamy to commit robberies, which they practise everywhere with exceeding cruelty,' wrote a horrified Jesuit priest. 'When they go to rob,' he continued, 'they pour out their prayers to God "that they may meet with a booty", and they suppose that a cheat or booty is sent unto them from God as His gift; neither are they persuaded that either violence or rapine or manslaughter displeaseth God, for in no wise would He present unto them this opportunity if it were sin.'[16]

In these dangerous and unstable circumstances, Ireland became a constant subject for concern among politicians and speculators. The Elizabethans hoped to reduce the country to a 'civil' existence through methods variously short-sighted and ruthless. Aristotle had taught them that man is a creature of the community and they wished now to settle the Irish themselves in stable societies. To effect this, they sought to establish English as the sole official language of the country, to destroy the rights and privileges of the native aristocracy, and impose as uniform a system of law, taxation and administration as they could. While English troops would display their power, it was hoped that this expensive necessity could in time be replaced by groups of small, loyal and preferably English landholders. Conquest by the Crown and colonization by groups of individuals became the two cardinal points of English policy.

The progress of events determined that conquest came first. Shane O'Neill's ambitions had not been satisfied by small victories over local rivals and, by 1566, as the dominant figure between Sligo and Carrickfergus, he was being hailed by the Pope as 'prince of Ulster'. Catholicism now quickened the spirit of revolt and allied itself to the older Celtic traditions. O'Neill boasted that his Irish title made him superior in birth to any earl. He sent appeals to the king of France to help drive the Protestant English out of Ireland and carried his raids over the border of the Pale. Sir Henry Sidney, the Lord Deputy of Ireland and father of the poet, informed the queen that if she did not act resolutely she ran the danger of losing Ireland, just as her sister had lost Calais, England's last foothold in France.

Sidney was despatched from Dublin, while Humphrey Gilbert and others sailed to Carrickfergus and moved on to Derry. Here Sidney joined them, and it was probably on this occasion that Gilbert first discussed with the Lord Deputy his plans for colonization in Ireland. The situation looked propitious. Shane O'Neill was on the run, having been humiliated by the English and routed by his Irish rivals before being murdered by the Scots of Candleboy in a drunken brawl.

It was now being mooted that Gilbert himself should be appointed to an administrative post in Ireland, and a cautious interest was expressed in his plans for colonies. His uncle, Sir Arthur Champernowne, was sufficiently interested to sail to Ireland, but the position in Ulster was too unstable for colonization easily to proceed. When, in 1569, the attention of two further West Country families, the Grenvilles and the St Legers, turned to Munster, however, Sidney lent them his support.

The English settlers found themselves in a country of spectacular beauty ravaged by human suffering. Sidney himself had moved south into Munster after defeating Shane O'Neill, and he sent the queen a heart-rending report on what he found there. Famine held the land in its terrible grip, and the lives of such people as remained were a succession of 'lamentable cries and doleful complaints'.[17] Their villages and churches had been destroyed and castles thrown down. The bodies of famine victims lay in the fields beside those who had more quickly died on the edge of the sword. There were few left with the strength to bury them, and the corpses rotted until the soft rain washed their bones. Neither women nor children were spared from horror. Sidney was told how a servant of the Earl of Desmond, 'after that he had burnt sundry villages and destroyed a great piece of the country', slew a band of mothers who begged for their lives. Afterwards, he revelled in his house while their unborn babies stirred in their mothers' wombs.

And now the local militant chief Fitzmaurice was moving against the newly settled English. Their leading menfolk were all in London pressing the queen for reinforcements and positions of authority. Eventually, the Privy Council despatched orders for the English to levy four hundred soldiers, while the Lord Deputy marched from

Dublin with several hundred more. Cork was relieved, the local chiefs subdued, and order restored. Then Humphrey Gilbert arrived to pacify the province. His revenge was terrible. It was Gilbert's belief that 'no conquered nation will ever yield willingly their obedience for love but rather for fear.'[18]

In the pursuit of this aim, he instituted a six-week terror. More castles were taken, their defenders massacred, and every living creature put to the sword. Gilbert was exercising, he told Sidney, the queen's 'absolute power',[19] and for the moment it corrupted him absolutely. In the madness of his fury, the Irish became for him less than human. His mere dogs were too good to hear their barbarous speech. And in the evening, when the day's killing was done, the victims' heads were hacked from their corpses and placed in rows along the torchlit pathway to his tent while the living crawled towards him to sue for pardon. For these actions, Gilbert received his knighthood.

Such was Ralegh's inheritance in Ireland, and he would often cite Sir Humphrey Gilbert as a model for the English to follow there. In many respects he would do so himself, for soon after his arrival in Cork he revealed the ferocity that was to characterize his dealings with the Irish at this period. Sir James Fitzgerald was in the custody of Warham St Leger, and Ralegh and his kinsman immediately set about his hanging, drawing and quartering. In response, the Fitzgeralds ambushed Ralegh's cousin Sir Peter Carew and murdered him, George Carew barely escaping with his life.

Such incidents were little more than the day to day barbarity common in Ireland, a form of guerrilla warfare that, as always, was difficult to counter. Ralegh was to find the path of the English forces was constantly blocked with interlaced trees and branches, while the Irish descended and attacked only to melt away again into the bogs and hills. He also noticed that when the English broke camp, the Irish emerged to scavenge what was left. On one occasion, he asked permission to lay an ambush for them and took a number prisoner. One of the scavengers was carrying a bundle of withies and, in reply to Ralegh's question, told him they were used 'to hang English churls'.[20] He was informed they would serve just as well to hang Irish kerns, and the man was promptly executed.

But if a guerrilla war was impossible to win, the real threat appeared to lie in a proposed invasion. Since the time of the Munster troubles ten years before, Fitzmaurice had been trying to rise above his position as a mere tribal chief and present himself as a figure on the European political stage, the advocate of a Catholic Ireland united against the English Protestants. In 1569, he sent emissaries to Spain and the Pope, putting forward the bold and imaginative plan whereby Philip himself or 'any active Catholic prince of his Catholic majesty's blood' would be accepted as the legitimate ruler of Ireland.

In the 1570s, Spain was little interested in what she regarded as a barbarous country on the edge of Europe. By 1577, however, the Pope was beginning to show himself more enthusiastic and he appointed Fitzmaurice leader of a holy war against the heretical Elizabeth, 'that woman who . . . has been cut off from the church.' But the little force of eighty Spaniards and Portuguese he offered never reached Ireland. A similar project the following year also came to nothing, and in July 1579 Fitzmaurice tried a third time. He was now the military leader of what was termed 'The Catholic League' and headed a force of some three hundred Italian and Spanish soldiers paid for by the papacy and Spain. They were armed not just with weapons but with the propaganda of the Counter-Reformation. When the little army landed at Dingle in 1579, they had pikes and calviers for five thousand gallowglasses and copies of the bull of excommunication legitimizing revolt against Elizabeth.

The papal emissary, Dr Nicholas Saunders, preached on the religious aspects of the war, but less than a month after he landed, Fitzmaurice himself was killed by some fellow Irish in an incident by the Shannon. The Earl of Desmond rose reluctantly to replace him, and late in May 1580 the Pope issued Desmond with 'a plenary indulgence as conceded to Crusaders to all who take up arms against Elizabeth'. When, in September, a further papal force under Colonel San Joseph arrived in Smerwick and occupied the fort, Ralegh was part of an English army of some six hundred foot and two hundred horse led by Lord Grey of Wilton and supported by Irish forces of twice that number under Ormonde.

Grey advanced towards the fort, ordered his men to dig siege trenches, and waited for siege guns to arrive from England. When they were in place, he summoned the enemy officers to a parley. They declared they were a force serving under the Pope who had given Ireland to the king of Spain and that they were now defending the Catholic faith. Grey, a man of ruthless Protestant conviction, began the bombardment. It lasted for four days. When the walls were destroyed and the English assault was imminent, a parley was requested. Grey refused. The defeated army asked to be allowed to depart with honour. Grey again refused. If they wished to surrender, it must be unconditionally. A truce was arranged, hostages given, and the following morning, after the papal forces had hung out their white flag with cries of 'Misericordia! Misericordia!', the slaughter began.

The Irish believed Grey had promised them their lives, but the English always denied this. The massacre itself was to horrify Europe. First Captain Wingfield entered the fort and ordered the enemy troops neatly to stack their armour and pikes, then Grey sent in the two duty officers of the day: Captain Mackworth and Captain Ralegh. First they broke the arms and legs of two assistants to Dr Sanders and hanged the men. They strung up a row of women whose pregnant bellies seemed ample proof that they had pandered to the enemy's lust. Then the real work of the day began. Ralegh and Mackworth with a hundred men apiece began the systematic slaughter of the papal troops.

It was the common experience of sixteenth-century experts in such matters that massacres blunted the edges of swords, and it was recommended that, to keep their sharpness, a light stroke to the side of the neck or a jab through the belly would both preserve the weapons themselves and ensure a lingering death. Ralegh and his companions worked their way through the terrified men until there was silence. Lord Grey was well pleased by the several hundred naked corpses of 'as gallant and good personages as ever were beheld'.[21] His views were earnestly supported by Edmund Spenser who wrote of the Papal troops that 'they could not justly plead either custom of war or law of nations, for that they were not any lawful enemies.'[22] Mercy could not be shown them, both for fear that they might join with the Irish and because the Irish themselves 'were much emboldened by those foreign succours'. The massacre, Spenser argued, was the only realistic political solution.

Out of such barbarity, a reputation could be made. Sorting through the belongings of the massacred troops, Ralegh discovered letters that revealed 'some matters of secrecy'.[23] What these were remains unknown, but the papers were judged sufficiently important for Ralegh to be sent with them to London in December 1580. Here was a glorious opportunity to draw attention to himself. While his chiefs remained in Munster, he was to attend the Lords of the Privy Council and present to them matters of national security. In albeit a minor capacity, he now had the ear of Leicester, Walsingham and Burghley. He had begun to make his mark even if, sometime in late February, he was ordered back to Ireland. Now he would have to continue to ensure that his merit was recognized, his career not hidden in the obscurity of an Irish mist.

By the time of Ralegh's return, Grey's devastation of Munster had begun. English rule was to be reimposed with the utmost ferocity, and Ralegh played his part in this as the English tried to stamp out the distinguishing traits of Irish life. The wearing of the traditional saffron smocks and glibbs was forbidden, and all carroughs, bards and rhymers – the people who composed the lays extolling the deeds of the chiefs – were put in the stocks until they were ready to find more suitable employment. Above all, the English pressed ahead with legislation whereby land was held by the chiefs from the Crown rather than in trust from the tribe. The corollary was that the estates of any Irish chief who showed himself disloyal could be forfeited and redistributed to those who had shown their worth.

Ralegh found reason to doubt the loyalty of Lord Barry. Here was his chance as a land-hungry younger son to serve both English interests and his own. Ralegh knew that Lord Barry was making raids from his castle on the Great Island of Cork Harbour, and he proceeded to act with abrasive self-assertion. Ormonde had refused to do anything about the matter, and so Ralegh himself now rode to Dublin to present his case to Grey and the Irish Council. Here he not only accused Barry of treachery but declared the Earl of Ormonde to be at best incompetent, telling the leaders in a most difficult situation that their interests would be much better served if they sacked Ormonde and appointed Sir Humphrey Gilbert in his place.

Lord Grey was to find such displays from a junior officer intolerably bumptious. He none the less recognized the value of an energetic young man (as well as the fact that Ralegh had contacts with the Privy Council) and for the moment Barry Castle was made over to him. Ormonde at once got the order countermanded. Ralegh responded angrily that Ormonde himself, far from wanting to serve English interests, was an intensely ambitious and greedy man who intended that Barry Castle should fall to him. And 'I think all is too little for him.'[24] This is Ralegh's authentic tone: arrogant, quick, dismissive, the voice of a highly intelligent man too rashly opinionated for the quiet guile of politics.

Nor, in this case, was he right. Ormonde did not keep the castle for himself but gave it to Barry's mother. Barry himself was so incensed by this that he at once set about burning the castle and firing its crops. As a result, he was proclaimed a traitor and his estates forfeited to the Crown. Ralegh, meanwhile, was still hankering after the property. He wrote to tell Lord Grey that he had begun some repair work on the castle, promising that if Grey could contrive for it to be given to him then he would, at his own cost, 'build it up again and defend it for Her Majesty'.[25] Ralegh's eye was still firmly fixed on the court.

Meanwhile, he was displaying his undoubted courage. As he was returning from his mission to Grey, he was ambushed by John Fitzedmund Fitzgerald, Seneschal of Imokellie. Ralegh had forded a river ahead of his small and straggling company and was set upon by Fitzgerald and twelve of his horse. Ralegh turned, broke through his attackers, recrossed the river and rode to join his men. Henry Moyle, the head of the stragglers, now followed Ralegh back across the stream, but as Moyle's horse plunged into the water so the animal reared and threw him. Moyle called out for help, and Ralegh seized the frightened beast by its bridle and led it back to its rider. In his enthusiasm, Moyle himself vaulted clean over the horse rather than landing on it. As the animal ran off, so Moyle was left saturated and stumbling with only Ralegh to protect him from Fitzgerald's troops. With a pistol in one hand and his staff in the other, Ralegh held the twelve horsemen at bay through the sheer power of his presence. When his other men caught up with him, the Irish simply melted away.

Ralegh was coming to appreciate that subterfuge was necessary when dealing with so wily an enemy, and he clearly relished the cunning that might earn him renown. When, for example, he was ordered to bring Lord Roche before the President of Munster to answer suspicions of disloyalty, he guessed the Irish intelligence network would know of his movements and try to ambush him. Fitzgerald and David Barry had indeed moved over a thousand of their men into the area between Cork and Roche's castle.

Ralegh decided that a night's forced march of twenty miles would be the means of evading them. His men were ordered on pain of death to be ready by ten o'clock. Then, in the dark, when any whispered order or broken twig might betray them, they threaded their way through the treacherous countryside and surrounded Roche's castle. By dawn they had achieved their objective. Watchmen on the ramparts gave hurried warning to the citizens inside, and a ragged army of some five hundred townsmen quickly armed. While the English troops held them at bay, Ralegh parleyed at the gate.

Eventually he was admitted, and Roche proposed they sit, eat, and talk matters over. As the meal came to its close, Ralegh informed Roche and his wife that they must now accompany him to Cork. Roche demurred, but Ralegh told him he had no choice. While the meal had been proceeding, little groups of his men had entered the fortress. They had caused no alarm as they stealthily positioned themselves at the key points of the defences, and when Roche was shown how quietly his castle had been taken he realized he had no option but to follow his captor. Protected by a few of their own men against the possibility of an Irish ambush, the Roches made their way to Cork under Ralegh's surveillance, stumbling in the teeth of a storm and exhausted.

Such episodes took place against a background of appalling suffering. Grey pressed on ruthlessly in his determination to crush the Desmonds' power. One by one their castles were taken: Youghal, Carrigofoill, Askeaton, Ballylogh. Junior members of the family were caught. Sir John was speared in an ambush by a former servant. James was brought to Cork where he was hanged and quartered, his head being placed on a spike by the city gates. Only the Earl himself for the moment survived, a moody, depressive outlaw hiding in the woods near Tralee where, in 1583, he was at last captured and executed.

But the plight of the ordinary people was far worse. Thirty thousand died in six months of starvation, plague and the sword. Grey's secretary, the young Edmund Spenser, watched with horror as the Irish crept out of woods and glens on their hands and knees, people so weak and starving that their legs could not carry them. 'They spoke like ghosts crying out of their graves.'[26] A little plot of watercress or shamrocks was seized on as a feast, and when, in their desperation, they could not satisfy their hunger in any other way, they scraped corpses out of their shallow graves and fed on putrefying flesh. Pity, horror and ruthless cruelty: the Elizabethans were founding their empire at an appalling price. 'Certainly', Ralegh was later to write, 'the miseries of war are never so bitter and many as when a whole nation, or a great part of it, forsaking their own seats, labour to root out the established possessors of another land.'[27]

Amid this barbarity, Ralegh himself sought comfort in a woman's arms. Little is known about Alice Goold, save that she had a West Country name and perhaps came from one of the Anglo-Irish families that had been settled around Cork since the thirteenth century. How long she and Ralegh were together or exactly when they met it is impossible to say. All that is clear is that Alice Goold bore Ralegh a daughter, the love-child to whom he left five hundred marks in his will. Alice Goold herself was still alive in 1597, for that is the date of the will in which she is mentioned. Three years later, Ralegh arranged for their daughter to marry David Dumaresq, Seigneur de Saumarez, his page in Jersey. The young woman later died, it seems, in 'London or Kingston' of the plague.

Now however, amid the dreadful suffering of Munster, Alice Goold had found herself a prominent protector. By the spring of 1581, Ralegh had earned himself sufficient reputation to be nominated as one of the three deputies left to control the province while the President of the Council was in London. For a young man, this was a position of some local eminence.

But, for all that, Ralegh was increasingly dissatisfied and bored in Ireland. His critical mind began to jib at what he saw as the shortcomings of English rule. Frustrated ambition turned to carping. English soldiers, commandeered from among gaol-birds and the unemployed, were 'such poor and miserable creatures as their captains dare not lead them to serve'.[28] He also felt that Lord Grey had

[53]

not sufficiently recognized his merits, and he would not be passed over. It was essential to draw attention to himself, to remind the grandees of the Privy Council of his existence.

He began writing them letters, criticizing Grey when it served his turn. 'I have spent some time here under the deputy,' he wrote to Leicester, 'in such poor place and charge, as, were it not for that I know him to be one of yours, I would disdain it as much as to keep sheep.'[29] Surely Leicester could be made to see that Ralegh was being wasted. A great patron would promote him to better things. 'I will be found as ready, and dare do as much in your service, as any man you may command'.[30]

He wrote to Walsingham too, complaining that Ormonde was altogether too lenient. There were a thousand more traitors in Munster now, he declared, than when Ormonde took command. The queen's service was being abused. 'I will rather beg than live here to endure it.'[31] Besides, Ralegh had given serious thought to the problems of Ireland and had his own solutions to propose. He now offered himself as the soldier turned pundit, and late in 1581 the grandees resolved to hear what he had to say.

Ralegh's proposals were a shrewd revision of the methods by which the government hoped to impose its aims. He recognized the necessity of trying to reduce Ireland to manageable units and of imposing English forms of rule whereby a strong central authority devolved its power on the leading figures of the regions. He also recognized the destructive influence wielded by the great Irish nobles and the grievances of those lesser chiefs caught between Celtic traditions of tribal warfare and the insecurity and resentment caused by English attempts to revise the tenure of their lands.

Ralegh therefore suggested that if the Crown could persuade these lesser chiefs that their position was safe under the influence of Elizabeth they would offer their loyalty to her rather than to the anachronistic and destructive traditions of the past. He was proposing, in other words, a form of Irish gentry class with a vested interest in English rule. English colonists would also be able to work with such people. It was an attractive idea – 'so much that the Lords took no small mark of the man and his parts'.[32]

Ralegh also had other notions that were attractive to the queen's parsimony. Surely, he suggested, the cost of maintaining five hundred soldiers in Munster could be shifted from the Crown to the deep pockets of the Earl of Ormonde. Burghley wrote to Grey on these matters and received a peeved reply. Grey had come to find his brilliant, pushy subordinate altogether intolerable. 'I like neither his carriage nor his company,' the Deputy wrote, 'and, therefore, other than by direction or commandment, and what his right can require, he is not to expect at my hands.'[33] But Grey was in distant Ireland, and Ralegh was at the court. Above all, he had now attracted the eyes and ears of the queen. She 'began to be taken with his elocution, and loved to hear his reasons to her demands. And the truth is, she took him for a kind of oracle, which nettled them all.'[34] Walter Ralegh was the coming man, ready now to thrust himself centre stage.

CHAPTER FOUR

The Worship of the Virgin Queen

He was ideally fitted for this role. Ralegh was now approaching twenty-eight, and all eyes were suddenly on him. He was a commanding figure. At six foot, he was a head taller than most of his contemporaries, and he carried himself with a swagger that suggested natural authority and pride. Among the courtiers, such bearing was an affront, but to the queen, now forty-eight, Ralegh's youth and ambition made Leicester seem old. He had, besides, native good looks. His face was pale and refined, his forehead imposing. His hair grew abundantly, was dark and, like his beard, naturally curled. Enemies might disparage his voice, saying it was 'small',[1] but they noticed the quick intelligence of his hooded eyes. This was a new face and a threatening one. It radiated energy, boldness, cunning. From the shade into which he cast them, rivals looked on as the queen permitted herself to be intrigued.

Stories began to circulate explaining his sudden rise. There is no means of establishing the truth of these, but, because they so aptly picture the Ralegh of legend, they were still being told two generations later. The antiquarian Thomas Fuller recorded the most famous of them. 'This Captain Ralegh,' Fuller wrote, 'coming out of Ireland to the English court in good habit (his clothes then being a considerable part of his estate) found the queen walking, till, meeting with a plashy place, she seemed to scruple going thereon. Presently Ralegh cast and spread his new plush cloak on the ground; whereon the queen trod gently.'[2]

The flamboyant gesture, real or imagined, has taken its place among the nation's myths, and its combination of extravagance and deference captures exactly the relationship between a thrusting young man and his queen. So does another of Fuller's anecdotes, which may again be apocryphal. Ambition, danger and display were all aspects of royal service, along with a constant recognition of the queen's power. Knowing she would see him, Ralegh is said one day to have scratched the first line of a poem on a window-pane: 'Fain would I climb, yet fear to fall.' With that wit which was a common bond between them, Elizabeth supposedly completed the couplet: 'If thy heart fails thee, climb not at all.'[3]

Neither his courage failed him nor his invention. In such ways as these, Ralegh was now fashioning himself as the perfect Elizabethan courtier. He excelled in those little contrivances that delighted the queen's self-regard, and he could talk earnestly of politics in his strong Devon brogue when the occasion required. The accent, indeed, was part of his allure. 'Notwithstanding his so great mastership in style,' wrote John Aubrey, 'and his conversation with the learnedest and politest persons, yet he spoke broad Devonshire to his dying day.'[4] This is the man exactly: ambition and intellect driving him into company with the great and the brilliant, while his own personality and West Country loyalties asserted his individuality.

Elizabeth was determined to keep such a man by her. She wrote to Grey informing the Deputy that although it was her pleasure 'to have our servant, Walter Ralegh, trained some longer time'[5] in Irish affairs, for the moment she was content to double his pay and have him appoint a lieutenant in his place. Ralegh was to stay in England. Elizabeth hinted opaquely at 'some considerations by us excused' and left matters there. Ralegh was to remain by her side for ten years. Throughout, she kept him constantly occupied – royal favour was earned as well as won – and slowly she revealed to him the immense complexity of her existence.

Now, in 1582, the courtship of the Duc of Alençon was approaching its long delayed and extravagant conclusion. In the middle of the previous year, French emissaries had been entertained with a lavishness that impressed even the followers of the Valois. At a cost of over £1700, a huge marquee boasting three hundred windows, its roof painted with clouds and its ornamental fruit baskets sprinkled with gold, had been erected in the river garden of Whitehall Palace. Five hundred exquisitely costumed gentlemen accompanied the delegation along the Thames. A bear was baited, and dinners of fantastic expense prepared. A triumph was held in the tiltyard. The Earl of Arundel, Lord Windsor, Philip Sidney and Fulke Greville were accounted as the forces of 'Desire' and sent to attack the 'Castle of Perfect Beauty', the symbol of Elizabeth's virginity.

When, at the end of October 1581, the Frog himself came a-wooing, another pageant was played out. The queen and Alençon were walking in the gallery at Whitehall (an exasperated Leicester and Walsingham looking on) when the French ambassador entered demanding to know the queen's real intentions. With that sense of political drama that came so spontaneously to her, Elizabeth drew her pock-marked lover to her, kissed him, drew a ring from her finger and, giving it to the Duc, turned to the ambassador and told him he might write to his king informing him that Alençon would indeed be her husband. Protestant Europe was delighted – bells were rung in Antwerp – while Elizabeth, deciding the comedy should soon end, suddenly informed her Frog that, after all, she could not marry him. She was afraid she might die after the ceremony. But, of course, he would always be her friend. Alençon drew her ring from his finger, threw it to the ground and, saying he would die of shame, promptly burst into tears.

She offered him her handkerchief and £60,000 for his war against Spain in the Netherlands. Finally, on 1 February 1582, and after further fantastic and impossible demands, the Duc prepared to depart. Elizabeth, as was fitting, accompanied him as far as Canterbury. Her new favourite rode in her train and, when Elizabeth had tearfully expressed the hope of seeing her Frog once again swimming along her Thames, Ralegh and Leicester crossed with the Duc to the Netherlands. Here, William the Silent entertained the party: Philip Sidney, Fulke Greville, Lord Hunsdon, Leicester and Ralegh. And it was Ralegh that the great hero of the Protestant cause now chose as his secret emissary, begging him to tell Elizabeth: *sub umbra alarum tuarum protegimur* – 'under the shadow of thy wings we are protected'. Eighteen months before, the Alençon marriage had seen Ralegh as the messenger boy in a fracas between a great poet and a great Earl. Now, in the same issue, he was an ambassador between heads of state.

But Ralegh's involvement with Oxford was not quite over. The Earl was languishing under house arrest, and Burghley resolved to do what he could for his foolish son-in-law. If that meant asking help of Ralegh the young maverick, then so be it. Burghley approached Ralegh, and Ralegh spoke to the queen. It was a tricky situation. He was to beg mercy for a man with whom he could no longer easily be associated. For his part, Ralegh made sure Burghley understood the favour he was doing him.

Elizabeth did not, Ralegh informed the Lord Treasurer, consider this a matter 'slightly to be passed over'.[6] None the less, he boasted, he had managed to persuade his royal mistress that there was little point in reopening old wounds. Personally, he regarded the Earl of Oxford with the utmost distaste, but he would endeavour to do Burghley a good turn. Despite the Earl's erratic temper, 'I am content for your sake to lay the serpent before the fire.' Matters were slowly patched up, but this was a dangerously condescending way to address the greatest minister of the crown. The queen's new favourite was indeed 'damnable proud'.[7]

Others were soon feeling threatened by his rise. With their shared love of verbal artifice, Elizabeth had punned on Ralegh's first name and called him 'Water'. It was an apt term of affection for a West Country sailor, but others detected danger. In particular, Sir Christopher Hatton, that exemplary courtier and Elizabeth's 'Bell-wether' or 'castrated ram', was concerned about his own political future. To discover where he stood, Hatton staged with the help of his friend Sir Thomas Heneage a subtle and exquisite little charade that exactly evoked the high sophistication of Elizabeth's court.

On an October morning in 1582 when the queen was riding out to hunt, Heneage suddenly appeared before Elizabeth bearing three gifts: a bucket, a book, and a richly jewelled dagger. The bucket was a pun on how 'Water' should be contained, a theme elaborated in a letter hidden inside the book. This in turn lamented how Elizabeth, Hatton's beloved 'Shepherdess', had been paying more attention to 'Water' than to her faithful ram. The dagger was a hint that Hatton might kill himself were he to lose the royal favour. Elizabeth, who delighted in such pageants and had probably been prepared for this one, calmed her horse and then, 'with blushing cheeks',[8] read the letter through. As adept as her courtiers in the exchange of compliments, she declared she was still Hatton's true 'Shepherdess' and would now cherish him in a pasture protected with high banks 'so sure that no *water* nor floods should ever overflow them'. Hatton's slow rise, assisted by his immense charm and considerable ability, would continue. Ralegh need not be feared as a rival. The queen had other concerns for him.

In scenes like this, Elizabeth's role was gracefully but surely asserted over the competitive men about her. It was a subtle exercise in female presentation and social control, a heady combination of fact and poetic fiction, passion and politics. In pursuing such a woman, Ralegh was moving in a world where the erotic and the political coincided. The Elizabeth who appeared before him was at once an actual, ageing woman and a supposedly timeless embodiment of authority. She moved on levels at once personal and mythical.

To warm his fervour, she appeared to his imagination in a score of guises. He later wrote that he had been 'wont to behold her riding like Alexander, hunting like Diana, walking like Venus, the gentle wind blowing her fair hair about her pure cheeks, like a nymph; sometimes sitting in the shade like a Goddess; sometimes singing like an Angel; sometimes playing like Orpheus.'[9] This was a compliment of the expected high artifice. The queen's heroic qualities as a great leader of men are skilfully juxtaposed to suggestions of her fierce chastity, her desirability, and even hints of a girlish allure. The voice of a middle-aged woman is described as heavenly, while the music she plays (Elizabeth was a gifted performer) would tame, it is suggested, the wildest of hearts. She was the imperious and near mystical embodiment of a very real earthly authority.

Ralegh now worshipped this with all the force of his imagination and intellect, playing the lover in pursuit of power. This last was one of the very few roles in which a man could kneel before a woman and yet preserve his pride, while, in so abasing himself, the queen herself was exulted. In the intense, rarefied atmosphere of the court, Elizabeth could parade before her favourite as both an icon of power and the object of the heart's desire. By the time of Ralegh's appearance at court, she had long established herself as the nation's virgin goddess, and her hierophants had elaborated around her a wealth of devotional practices that Ralegh himself was greatly to extend.

Royal portraits show the ideas he was to develop, none more effectively than the great *Ermine Portrait* of 1585, painted for Burghley and now at Hatfield House. The first and abiding impression the work provides is of female authority. Elizabeth's face is frozen into an image at once mature, intelligent and self-possessed. Her fine and tapering hands of which she was so proud are posed in a way that suggests command while also displaying their beauty. Her costume is fantastically wrought with jewels. Golden clasps are set with precious stones, threads of thick gold run between rows of pearls, gold studs powder the black velvet of the dress itself. Round the queen's neck is displayed the great rope of pearls of a shade 'like that of black muscat grapes' which had once belonged to Mary, Queen of Scots, while from her jewelled collar or carcanet hangs the 'Three Brothers', a pendant of enormous rubies bought by her father from the Dukes of Burgundy. Worldly power and worldly wealth are mutually affirming and magnificent.

But the picture allows a more detailed interpretation. The sprig of laurel the queen carries in her hand, for example, suggests that she belongs to the blessed company of peacemakers, while the sword by which her other hand rests is an emblem of justice. Her rule is thus benevolent but strong, merciful but firm. The black velvet of her dress and the whiteness of her veil again allowed a contemporary viewer to look at the queen's image with wonder refined by thought – thought that would lead to an awareness of the benefits brought to the nation by Elizabeth's personal strengths. Black and white were her special colours, and with that gift for symbol which came so readily to the Elizabethan mind, onlookers would remember that black suggested her constancy, white her virginity.

Finally, and for the learned especially, the exquisite little ermine perched by her cuff prompted a wealth of ideas. It was believed, for example, that the ermine was an immaculate beast and that it would choose to die rather than let its coat become besmirched. The emblem books that circulated so widely in Elizabethan England – works in which elaborately contrived visual images prompted the mind to think of moral truths – occasionally pictured the ermine, while it also appears in one of the most illustrious of renaissance poems: Petrarch's 'Triumph of Chastity'. The portrait at Hatfield is thus a likeness of a woman and a representation of the moral and political strength that flowed from Ralegh's mistress, the Virgin Queen.

His own contribution to this cult was made the more powerful by his gifts as a poet. In the early years of Elizabeth's reign, most courtly poetry was composed to celebrate particular occasions or discuss moral issues in a way at once improving but dull. Only in the 1570s did the belief that a poem could be a beautifully wrought and inspiring artefact begin to take hold.

The Earl of Oxford had been a prime mover in this, and some of his poems to Elizabeth, written in the strains of a great courtier's flattering hyperbole, compare Elizabeth's 'face divine'[10] to that of the classical goddesses. The poet himself meanwhile is prostrated by the hopeless suffering to which his love of the queen has, in all innocence, condemned him. The tone of such work is polished, artificial and sophisticated, but under the flirtatiousness is an albeit playful recognition of the realities of power – of Elizabeth's position as queen and the courtier's dependence on this. Ralegh was now to develop such ideas in ways that were subtle, elaborate and innovative.

This last was clear from the first days of his success at court. In the early 1580s, for example, Ralegh's poem 'Farewell false love' was circulating widely in manuscript, being passed round and copied out by followers of the queen who were variously admiring or jealous of its popularity. All of them were of necessity interested in the latest fashionable toy. By 1588, 'Farewell false love' had been set to music by William Byrd, and in an age when domestic music-making was of the highest standard and the widest popularity, Ralegh's poem was sung by thousands. Some, indeed, were to hail him as a true innovator in poetry. George Puttenham, for example, in *The Art of English Poetry*, published in the same year as Byrd's setting of 'Farewell false love', declared: 'For ditty and amorous ode, I find Sir Walter Ralegh's vein most lofty, insolent, and passionate.'[11]

To advance beyond such trifling required an imaginative leap of great audacity. Searching for an image of the ideal to explain and define their elaborate worship of the queen, Ralegh and those around him began to fashion an image of the virgin Elizabeth as the moon, ruler of the seas and tides, and the chaste, all-powerful goddess Diana:

Praised be Diana's fair and harmless light,

> Praised be the dews, wherewith she moists the ground;
> Praised be her beams, the glory of the night,
> Praised be her power, by which all powers abound.[12]

Although this poem can no longer be safely attributed to Ralegh himself (when it was published in the famous anthology *England's Helicon* the bookseller pasted a cancel slip over the attribution to the pseudo-anonymous S. W. R.) it none the less develops ideas central to Ralegh's thought.

The poet's scholarly imagination has drawn on the arcane resources of renaissance philosophy and myth to fashion an image of Elizabeth in which the poet himself becomes both her loyal adherent and the embodiment of the highest reaches of human content – the worshipper of sovereign truth itself. In this he was helped by the writings of the great renaissance magus Giordano Bruno who, during the 1580s, was living in London under the protection of the French ambassador.

In his *Degli Eroici Furori*, or 'Concerning Heroic Frenzies', Bruno attempted a fresh interpretation of Plato's belief that the passions of sexual love aspire beyond bodily longing to a spiritual recognition of the divine, the supreme good. For his part, Bruno felt that wholly to cleave the body from the soul was to deny each its splendour while divorcing man himself from a full participation with the universe in which he lives. Body and spirit are not to be sundered, but must instead be brought into harmony through the benevolent exercise of reason.

When, after innumerable trials and setbacks, the truly heroic lover at last stares on his beloved with soul, sense and intellect in unison, he has achieved beatitude. Neither sensualist nor ascetic, he experiences desire without pain. He appreciates his beloved's mingled beauty, intelligence and majesty as a finite image in the natural world of the infinite divine. The beloved is a being bathed in the light of celestial truth, just as the moon is revealed by the light of the greater sun. Diana's service now becomes perfect knowledge, perfect freedom, the heroic lover's insight into the universal truth the poet hymns in his ecstasy:

> A knowledge pure it is her worth to know,
> With Circes let them dwell that think not so.[13]

'Diana's fair and harmless light' radiates softly over the universe, blessing her 'nymphs' or the ladies of the court, along with 'her knights, in whom true honour lives'. As the moon, revolving in serene, eternal change above the random and mutable earth, she is also the mistress of the tides (an image of fundamental importance to Ralegh) and an embodiment of perfection:

> In heaven queen she is among the spheres,
> In aye she mistress like makes all things pure,
> Eternity in her oft change she bears,
> She beauty is, by her the faire endure.

> Time wears her not, she doth his chariot guide,
> Mortlaity below her orb is placed,
> By her the virtues of the stars down slide,
> In her is vertue's perfect image cast.[14]

In the act of writing his poem, the courtier and poet becomes her lover and hierophant, the man raised to mortal perfection as he contemplates the physical divine. The court of Elizabeth is thus the seat of human excellence and, in Bruno's words: 'Captive though I am ... I am so greatly blessed I envy the freedom of no man nor any god.'[15]

For the moment, Ralegh himself did not chafe at such imprisonment either, although it is hardly to be supposed that a vigorous twenty-eight-year-old was entirely satisfied by acting out a role of chaste adoration to a woman twenty years his senior. While the mingling of hopes of worldly power with the erotic divine could certainly produce intense excitement – the thrill of seemingly boundless opportunity – the charade was fatally severed from more natural needs. John Aubrey, in a scabrous and far from accurate little story, gives a suggestion of how the royal favourite spent his salt hours:

> He loved a wench well and one time getting up one of the maids-of-honour up against a tree in a wood ('twas his first lady), who seemed at first boarding to be somewhat fearful of her honour

and modest, she cried 'Sweet Sir Walter, what do you me ask? Will you undo me? Nay, sweet Sir Walter!' At last, as the danger and the pleasure at the same time grew higher, she cried in ecstacy 'Swisser, Swatter! Swisser, Swatter!' She proved with child . . . [16]

In fact, Ralegh was not a virgin when he came to court, and the plight of the Earl of Oxford and others has shown the peril attendant on desecrating the royal vestals. Inaccurate as its details might be, however, Aubrey's story suggests the inevitable and dangerous obverse of the performance Ralegh mounted for his Virgin Queen.

The settings for Ralegh's relationship with Elizabeth were many and sumptuous. The queen had inherited from her father one of the finest collections of palaces in Europe, and it was in these that Ralegh now displayed his ambiguous adoration.

Hampton Court, although never Elizabeth's favourite, was perhaps the most grandly formal of her palaces. Here, surrounded by her nobles and ladies-in-waiting, by Ralegh and her attendant Esquires of the Body in Ordinary, Elizabeth received ambassadors in the Paradise Chamber where Persian hangings gave mute magnificence to a diamond studded throne. In other rooms, innumerable royal toys served to entertain: an ebony and ivory chessboard, a backgammon set with solid silver dice, a virginals with gold and silver strings.

It was at Nonesuch however that this element of the fantastic reached its height. Built by her father to rival the châteaux of the Loire, the palace rose from behind its walls, a castle apt for a fairy queen. Twin towers, five storeys high, painted and pinnacled, commanded a view of the Surrey countryside and were surmounted by exotic onion domes. Inside, fountains and clock towers punctuated the courtyards while, amid bas-reliefs of gilt and stucco, the magisterial figure of Henry VIII reigned in triumph amid a crowd of Roman emperors.

If Nonesuch showed Ralegh his queen at her most rarefied and exotic, Greenwich served to display his other great concern: Elizabeth's naval power. Here her ships assembled for her salute, given from the gallery of the gatehouse. Here, too, she journeyed on the

Thames either in her magnificent state barge, rowed by twenty oars-men, or in the smaller Greenwich barge with its satin awnings and pillows, 'cloth of gold of tissue', which conveyed the queen and her party to Windsor. Here, where the Garter ceremony elaborated yet further her political mystique, there were more trophies variously lavish and intimate: a red marble table, a bird of paradise, a unicorn's horn, a cushion worked by her own hand. Here, too, Elizabeth had built the Long Terrace for her morning walks.

But for all this magnificence, Richmond, at the other extreme of the Thames, was her favourite palace: a vast acreage of Perpendicular fan vaulting, warmer than the other residences, reasonably plumbed and cleanly watered. Here, near to where many of her courtiers also had houses, Elizabeth could most happily follow her intellectual interests, visit Walsingham and the Sidney circle at Barnes, or discuss the sciences – practical and occult – with Dr Dee at nearby Mortlake.

It was Whitehall that none the less remained the prime focus of royal splendour. Here, a vast collection of buildings, added to from the thirteenth century, formed what was probably the largest palace in Europe. Holbein's great portrait of the Tudor dynasty, showing Elizabeth herself at thirteen standing in tiny self-possession, domi-nated the Privy Chamber and those who came there for audience. Here was royalty at its most magnificent. Elsewhere around the palace, the tiltyard, tennis court, cockpit, the Sermon Court, the Ban-queting Hall and Great Hall, the Chapel Royal and the Privy Garden with its gilded heraldic beasts and elaborate sundial, suggested the multifarious activities of the royal household.

Whitehall itself was thronged with people petitioning Elizabeth for favours, and she prepared herself carefully to receive them. At the start of her day, the Gentlewomen of the Bedchamber, under the guidance of the Mistress of the Robes, attended to the long labour of dressing the queen. From her silver-gilt and porcelain lye pot they poured the mixture of wood ash and water in which they washed her hair, attended to her cosmetics, her mouthwashes, and the per-fume she had specially distilled from marjoram. They sorted through her vast collection of costumes and jewels, although on ordinary days Elizabeth was quite likely to wear simple black offset with pearls, her emblematic colours contrasting with her red-gold hair, and the whole given mystery by a diaphanous silver veil. So attired, she would hold audience with members of the Council in her Privy Chamber, the great officers of state kneeling until they were bidden to rise.

Elizabeth was also on public display at Whitehall, and Sunday was the great ceremonial day when she might be seen at her most magnificent. Surrounded by her Gentlemen Pensioners, she processed to the Chapel Royal where the service (rather too papist for some) was beautified by the boys' voices of her choir and over forty instrumentalists as they performed the anthems and motets of Tallis and Byrd to standards unrivalled in Europe. After the service, Elizabeth was again on display, though only rarely at the great ceremonies that accompanied the serving of dinner which the queen herself, ever frugal in her habits, usually ate in private. The royal virgin preserved her mystery in her Privy Chamber where only her especial favourites, Ralegh among them, might have access to her.

Elizabeth now began to inundate Ralegh with evidences of her favour. In April 1583, two leases held by All Souls College, Oxford, reverted to the Crown and were promptly given to him. Sometime in the same year he also received for the term of the royal pleasure use of the greater part of Durham House, one of the erstwhile ecclesiastical palaces that stretched along the Strand, lining the north bank of the Thames with a Venetian splendour. Ralegh was now established at the focus of power, close to Whitehall and the London homes of the great officers of state: York House, Arundel House, Leicester House, and Burleigh's mansion on the borders of Covent Garden.

Durham House itself is pictured in Norden's map of Westminster of 1593. Already two and a half centuries old, the river frontage with its watergate rose between towers joined by a magnificent crenellated wall. Behind this appeared the steep lead roof of the hall, the interior of which Norden described as 'stately and high, supported with lofty marble pillars'.[17] But it was on the apex of the roof of the garden front that the most pleasing feature of Durham House was to be found. Here was perched the exquisite lantern tower Ralegh used as his study. John Aubrey remembered that this 'looked into and over the Thames, and has the prospect which is pleasant, perhaps, as any in the world, and which not only refreshes the eye-sight but cheers the spirits, and (to my mind) I believe enlarges an ingenious man's thoughts.'[18]

Such a building also enlarged Ralegh's sense of proprietorial magnificence, and he lived at Durham House with the flamboyance becoming a renaissance grandee. In his lively letters to John Thynne, Maurice Browne wrote he had, 'heard it credibly reported that Master Rawley hath spent within this half year above 3000 pounds.'[19] Every aspect of this lavish expenditure asserted his prestige while also underlining his dependence on royal favour. It was seen, for example, that the plate of Ralegh's table was all of silver and was engraved with his coat of arms. Of the thirty of so liveried men who attended him, many had chains of gold. They moved to and fro, bearing dishes and delivering messages, in rooms furnished with dazzling splendour. The walls of Durham House were covered with arras, but the height of magnificence was revealed in Ralegh's bedroom. Here, much to his wonder, Browne found a bed covered with green velvet, beautified with silver lace, and surmounted by white, bespangled plumes.

Browne also noted Ralegh's 'very sumptuous' apparel, the flamboyance of which is underlined by the case of one 'Hugh Pewe, gentleman', brought before the Middlesex courts for robbing the royal favourite in April 1583 of 'a jewel worth £80, a hatband of pearls worth £30, and five yards of silk, called damask, worth £3'.[20] Some of these jewels were purchased from the great goldsmith and banker Peter Vanlore whose customers included the queen herself and several of the earls of England. Indeed, London was the centre of a luxury trade of the greatest opulence, and fashion – which could never be separated from the constant expression of social status – was an all-absorbing interest for the Elizabethan male. 'The English dress in elegant, light and costly garments,' wrote a foreign visitor, 'but they are very inconstant and desirous of novelties, changing their fashions every year to the astonishment of many.'[21]

The quest for pre-eminence among the courtiers was an enormous stimulus to this obsession with flamboyant clothing, and 'he that enjoys it with means', declared Ben Jonson, 'puts the world in remembrance of his means.'[22] This was precisely the point, and in fact a courtier's means were often very far stretched. It was not unknown for a man wishing to gain the royal attention to sell large parcels of his land and borrow against legacies – often at extortionate rates of interest – in the hope of making his mark. Such display was naturally a matter of keen concern to the queen, for while she took a natural delight in male display, she recognized that such magnificence not only complemented her own, but helped keep ambitious men dependent on her approval and financial favours while ensuring continuous competition among the courtiers themselves.

The Earl of Leicester had set the fashion in the 1570s, and the fabulous if disciplined ostentation of his clothes – salmon pinks slashed, padded, and woven with gold; a fine pearl hanging as a pendant from his Garter medal; his hat offset with an ostrich feather and a jewelled band – had established him as the arbiter of Elizabethan elegance. The trimming of a ruff, the cut of a cloak, the design of a jewel, were all charged with power and politics, and when Ralegh's man dressed him in the morning – first warming his embroidered shirt, helping him choose his neckwear, his doublet, hose and jerkin, threading an intricate series of 'points' through eyelet holes, and finally handing him his scented gloves – he was preparing his master for a daily battle in which the quick, competitive eyes of other courtiers, their whisperings and jealousies, were weapons in a constant campaign for pre-eminence.

This was a battle in which Ralegh's desire for display allowed him to excel. A portrait miniature by the fashionable and expensive Nicholas Hilliard shows the new favourite in his glory, the little ivory disk suggesting with exquisite care the evanescent complexities of Ralegh's image – its sexuality, its power and artifice.

The tensions within the image are especially revealing: a virile man of action is here imprisoned in a carapace of fabulous, slightly effeminizing display borrowed from the fashions of the French court. A little jewel-encrusted bonnet sits rakishly on Ralegh's dark, naturally curling hair. This last has been carefully brushed back from his forehead, while the forehead itself also gives prominence to the articulated eyebrows, the strong nose and, above all, the narrow, worldly stare which is the focus of the portrait. Ralegh's moustache and his beard, cut 'pique de vant', suggest a self-delighting sophistication and masculinity, and bring his head to a fine, tapering point.

But this love of human finery, the display that gives the courtier his prestige, is suggested above all by Ralegh's immense cartwheel

[69]

ruff. Tilted on wires, immaculate yet sensuous, its crisp pleats run outwards in rays from the neck to terminate in a fantastic haze of dentilated lace. Here is a man apparently placed beyond the mundane concerns of earning a living, dirtying his hands, or even troubling about the English weather which easily made such ruffs 'go flip flop in the wind, like rags flying abroad'.[23] Here is a Ralegh who is almost wholly the creation of an artifice in which sexuality, power and display have all been taken to their most refined even while constraining Ralegh himself within wires and drawstrings.

The young Browne was clearly impressed. Having noted the sumptuousness of Durham House and the gorgeousness of Ralegh's apparel, he felt obliged to end on a note of rhetorical excitement. 'He hath', he declared, 'all other delights and pleasure abundantly and above all he behaveth himself to the good liking of every man.'[24] Browne had clearly been dazzled by the wealth he saw, for his last point betrays an uncritical excess of enthusiasm. In fact, Ralegh was becoming intensely unpopular among both the courtiers and the ordinary people of Elizabethan England. This was a state of affairs to which he was haughtily – even dangerously – indifferent.

Among the courtiers, Ralegh's spectacular rise threatened many who thought their birth and merits had been overlooked. Sir John Harington, the queen's godson and her 'Boy Jack', looked on the new favourite's position with particular disdain. Witty, inventive, and delightful company (he was both the translator of Ariosto and the inventor of the flushing lavatory), Harrington was a lightweight of the old guard. His portrait of Ralegh as 'Paulus', however, sharp with the established nobleman's contempt for the parvenu, is shrewd and witty:

> No man more servile, no man more submiss,
> Than to our Sovereign Lady Paulus is.
> He doth extol her speech, admire her feature,
> He calls himself her vassal, and her creature.
> Thus while he daubs his speech with flattery's plaster
> And calls himself her slave, he grows our Master.[25]

Ralegh as Paulus is the flatterer whose supine and calculating subservience disgusts even as it attains its purposes.

But the established grandees had means altogether more power-ful than poetry to secure their influence. Leicester, restored to royal favour, was equally determined to promote his family's interests. If his new wife dared not show her face at court, her young son by her previous marriage was a boy attractive enough to catch the queen's eye. In 1584, Leicester brought this stepson, Robert Devereux, Earl of Essex, to Elizabeth's notice. He was just seventeen – too young, perhaps, to win the queen's immediate attention – but tall, red-haired, intelligent, volatile, and eager for advancement. He had extreme youth on his side and, far more dangerously, a place among the hereditary peerage. Very soon, he and Ralegh were to circle round their intrigued royal patron with the intense, mutual fascination of bitter rivals.

In addition to this threat of competition at court, Ralegh was now becoming loathed by the ordinary people of England who were having to fund his magnificence out of indirect taxation, in particular his exploitation of two highly lucrative monopolies given him by the queen. The first of these was the patent to license the export of quotas of woollen broadcloths, the highest-quality element in the country's staple trade and a commodity which for many years had sent men far afield in the search for markets.

At the time he acquired the monopoly, the number of cloths being exported from London was comparatively high, and the zeal with which Ralegh and his agent, the merchant William Sanderson, handled the privilege, resulted in an immense annual income in the region of £3,500. Such profits inevitably caused bad feeling. The Merchant Adventurers of Exeter were particularly vociferous in their complaints, while fluctuations in the trade generally caused by Span-ish reprisals and the unstable nature of the continental market resulted in Ralegh being made the scapegoat for criticism.

This groundswell of hatred was something Ralegh was blithely to ride for long periods of his career. To contemporaries, the degree of his indifference to ordinary opinion was a matter for comment. 'He was so far from affecting popularity', wrote one observer, 'as he seemed to take a pride in being hated of the people, either for that he thought it a point of policy, or else because he scorned the approbation of the multitude.'[36] In fact, both interpretations were correct. The wise favourite always recognized that his position rested entirely on the queen and had no basis in popular acclaim. Leicester, too, had been widely disliked, and Elizabeth had rarely seen this as a disadvantage. Indeed, his lack of broad popular support ensured that she herself remained the origin of a favourite's power and that, of necessity, he would stay deferential to her. For the sake of national unity, Elizabeth was determined to assert that the love of the people was hers alone.

This was a truth of which Ralegh was fully aware. The queen, in her turn, both rewarded such loyalty and sought to protect it. On 4 May 1584, Elizabeth granted Ralegh his second lucrative monopoly: the farm of wines. This meant that, in return for supervising the quality control and price of certain imported vintages, Ralegh had the right to charge the greater part of the country's publicans for a licence to sell them.

This was again an immensely lucrative perk and one which, in the conventional manner, Ralegh had overseen by a deputy, in this case Richard Brown who initially paid Ralegh a guaranteed flat fee in the region of £700 per annum for seven years, any remaining profits being his own. So zealous was Brown in the prosecution of his duties, however, that his income from the farm of wines convinced Ralegh that he had struck a bad bargain. He tried to renegotiate. When Brown insisted on the original terms, Ralegh, exercising his influence, returned to the queen, prevailed on her to call in the licence and then regrant it so that he could reassign it and ensure himself a better profit.

Ralegh could not always get his way so easily, however. In Cambridge, the right to issue wine licences lay with the University whose Vice-Chancellor gaoled one of Ralegh's appointed vintners after a fracas at an inn and a letter of complaint from Ralegh himself. He wrote twice more, hinting at his influence with Burghley, the Chancellor of the University, and suggesting that the behaviour of the dons had been 'a proceeding unsufferable'.[26] He declared that the gaoling of his vintner was an injustice that not only challenged his own authority under the Great Seal of England but posed a threat which 'much concerneth the validity of my patent elsewhere'.

An ancient institution was not to be cajoled by a new royal favourite however, and when the matter was finally brought to arbitration it was found that 'by usage and charter from her Majesty' the University had the right to nominate its own vintners.[27] Ralegh's man, meanwhile, languished in gaol for many months, the victim of the rapacious haste of the now greatly wealthy royal favourite.

Such wealth was enhanced by Ralegh's privateering. Throughout this period of royal favour, his activities in this area expressed his enmity towards Spain while richly lining his pockets. The profits, indeed, could be vast. Ralegh and William Sanderson had shares in £7,000 worth of prizes from one expedition, while the *Bark Burton* returned from another venture with booty valued at £10,000. Out of such profits, Ralegh could build his own fleet of privateering vessels. The *Roebuck* was named after the animal that appeared on his coat-of-arms, while the *Bark Ralegh*, frequently commanded by his admiral Jacob Whiddon, made no attempt to disguise either the ownership or the reasons for her existence.

But success was not always straightforward, and the all but invisible line between privateering and sheer piracy occasionally resulted in embarrassing complications. This was the case when Ralegh, together with Sir George Carey and others, formed a consortium to fit out the *Bark Randall* for a venture. Two ships were captured and the prizes were immense, the cargoes of pepper, cloves, mace, sugar, ivory, brazilwood and precious stones amounting to over £25,000. This was to be shared by the other ships in the flotilla: the *Riall* of Weymouth, the *Discharge* of London, and the *Samartain*. Much to the embarrassment of the government, however, the ships attacked did not belong to the enemy but had been commissioned by Italian merchants resident in Lisbon and were sailing for Florence. For all that Carey referred to them as 'Spainicised Italians', this was a clear case of piracy, and when Fillippo Corsini, acting with the support of the governments of Florence and Venice, made representations to the Admiralty Court, he obtained an order for the sequestration of the goods involved.

The order was issued to little purpose. The privateers had almost certainly been tipped off, and the goods of one of the ships had rapidly been sold on by the time the Court's officer arrived. The Privy Council put on a stern face – this could easily have become an international incident – and they wrote to Dr Julius Caesar at the Admiralty Court declaring, 'We would have this cause so uprightly used as the Duke of Florence whom the queen's Majesty favoureth greatly, may not have any just cause to complain of lack of favourable justice.'[28] Caesar, torn between profit and loyalty, declared the decision on the goods already distributed to be a fair one and that the rest should be divided between Ralegh's consortium and the Italians. Caesar was overruled by the Privy Council who set up an illustrious tribunal to consider the matter. Their judgement again favoured the Italians, but their ruling was of little help to Corsini who three years later was still complaining about the prevarications that prevented his getting hold of his fellow countrymen's goods.

Ralegh himself, however, was now enjoying the full warmth of royal favour, and the diary of Leopold von Wedel, a tourist from Pomerania, allows a rare and detailed glimpse of the queen, Ralegh and the court at dinner in Greenwich on 27 December 1584.[29]

Surrounded by the great noblemen of England – Howard, Leicester, Oxford and the rest – the queen talked almost ceaselessly as they kneeled before her. When commanded to rise, they bowed, retired, and then, when they had reached the centre of the hall, bowed again. When she herself rose, signalling that the meal was over, two bishops stepped forward to say grace. Three noblemen with a silver-gilt bowl and two more bearing a towel then knelt before her. The queen took off her ring and passed it to the Chamberlain while water was poured over her hands. For a while she chatted with 'an earl's son' in the bow window and then, her business with others being done, the dancing began.

Only those of the highest rank were permitted to perform the first dance, but, when it was over, the queen, lolling on cushions on the floor as was her habit, watched as the young men took off their rapiers and cloaks, and invited the ladies to the galliard. In her youth, Elizabeth herself had been an enthusiastic dancer. She was a connoisseur of the galliard especially, an extremely complicated dance of five steps ending with a 'caper' or a leap in the air and a beating of the feet. She danced it, people said, 'after the Florentine style, with a high magnificence that astonished beholders'.[30] She still looked on with a critical eye while other members of her court, young and old, came to chat and joke with her.

Among these people was Ralegh, to whom the queen said 'pointing with her finger at his face, that there was a smut on it, and was going to wipe it off with her handkerchief; but before she could he wiped it off himself'.[31] This is an evanescent moment of the greatest charm and intimacy, a second of casual life glimpsed against the deep-toned elegance of a consort of viols, of courtiers dancing and after-dinner ease. The friendship between Ralegh and his queen is caught in a simple, natural gesture.

Then von Wedel comes to the point of his story. 'She was said to love this gentleman beyond all the others; and this may be true, because two years ago he could scarcely keep one servant, and now with her bounty he can keep five hundred.' Like some gorgeous dragonfly, Ralegh's life was opening in the sun of royal favour, and early in 1585 he received his knighthood in recognition of the colony he hoped to found in America and which he had named Virginia in honour of his Virgin Queen.

CHAPTER FIVE

Virginia

The aim of planting colonies in North America was the most ambitious of the projects bequeathed to Ralegh by Sir Humphrey Gilbert. In the long term, its successful realization was profoundly to shape the course of world history, but in its origins the plan should be seen as only one among Ralegh's numerous ventures at this time and an initiative which for him at least was to end in disappointment.

The practical difficulties of American colonization had been made evident by Humphrey Gilbert's expedition in 1578. Despite these, Gilbert had persisted in his plans with characteristically obsessive determination. His first American venture and, even more, his subsequent activities in Ireland, had left him greatly in debt, however, and by the middle of 1581 he was complaining to Walsingham that he was 'subject to daily arrests, executions, and outlawries',[1] and pleading that he was even obliged to sell the clothes off his wife's back. The patent granted him for American discovery was due to expire early in June 1584, and the combined pressures of time and poverty were keen incentives to an imagination now wholly given over to plans for an American empire.

By the end of March 1580, Gilbert had enlisted the services of Simon Fernandez, now in Walsingham's employment, for a voyage of reconnaissance. Given the Portuguese pilot's reputation, Gilbert was obliged to enter into a bond of £500 for Fernandez' behaviour and, in particular, an agreement that he would not indulge in privateering. While to the Privy Council this might have seemed only prudent, it effectively prohibited Gilbert from financing this voyage out of anything save his own meagre resources. Fernandez' crossing was none than less a considerable feat of Elizabethan seamanship, for he was despatched in the tiny, ill-fated *Squirrel*, a ship of less than ten tons and crewed by under a dozen men. Fernandez crossed the Atlantic and returned within three months, bringing valuable information on the New England coastline.

By the first week of June 1582, Gilbert was allocating shares in a vast paper empire to Protestants such as Sir Philip Sidney (who received an assignment of three million acres) as well as to a number of Catholic gentlemen who, in a manner approved by Walsingham, hoped to live in America as loyal citizens of the Crown, free from religious intolerance. The enthusiasm of this latter group was almost immediately placed under severe restraints, however, by the hostility of the Spanish ambassador and the fact that their recusancy fines were not, after all, to be waived. In addition, the £500 either subscribed or promised by fifty citizens of Southampton was wholly insufficient for funding the expedition, and Gilbert was forced to rely on contributions from his family. Sir John Gilbert certainly offered help, but it was Walter Ralegh, now rising in the queen's favour, who contributed the largest sum. By May 1583, he had fitted out the *Bark Ralegh* for the venture at a cost of £2000.

This was a brave and generous gesture, but certainly a futile one. Even if Gilbert's expedition had been blessed with extreme good fortune, the sums he raised – small and uncertain as they were – would have been insufficient to support the colonization of a continent. But Gilbert's expedition was not so blessed, and in this, his last and most heroic venture, his habitual bad luck turned to starkest tragedy.

There was trouble from the outset. While Gilbert was maturing his plans, Walsingham, who had appeared to give him the support of the Privy Council, was involved with his stepson Christopher Carleill in a plan to include the Muscovy Company in American exploration. A prospectus was written for this and arrangements with the merchants of Bristol were also well advanced when the initiative foundered, partly because it encroached on the terms of Gilbert's patent. But if there was competition behind the scenes, there were also practical problems to face. Gilbert's ships were ready to sail from Southampton on an initial exploratory voyage in July 1582, but delays occurred and, by November, plans had to be changed. Gilbert now resolved to sail in April 1583, and to spend about eight months establishing his colony. Then, in February, while Gilbert was already frustrated in his efforts, Walsingham wrote to inform him that the queen did not wish Gilbert to sail at all, shrewdly believing he was 'a man noted of not good hap by sea'.[2]

An anguished Gilbert replied, protesting his loyalty and competence, but in the end it was Ralegh who prevailed upon the queen to change her mind. Exercising his influence in his half-brother's favour, Ralegh persuaded Elizabeth to a gesture typical of royal caprice. She sent Gilbert a jewel of 'an anchor guided by a lady',[3] a traditional symbol of hope. She also asked for his portrait and wished the expedition such safety and good luck 'as if herself were there in person'.[4] Royal favour was thus secured, and finally Gilbert's fleet of five vessels set sail from Southampton early in June 1583.

It was already late in the year for such a voyage and Gilbert's ships were, besides, poorly supplied. It was eventually decided to sail for Newfoundland, there to reprovision from the fishing fleets, and then turn south. But at midnight, on 13 June, the *Bark Ralegh* suddenly changed course and headed back to Plymouth, some alleging sickness on board, other urging 'want of victuals'.[5] Gilbert wrote an angry letter demanding 'my brother Ralegh'[6] make an example of the crew, and then sailed on, his fleet eventually regrouping in the harbour at St John's. Here, resolved to claim Newfoundland as his own under the crown and assert his authority, Gilbert requisitioned supplies, promulgated laws to the bewildered fishermen, prospected for precious metals, and began mapping out the land.

But dissension and illness were already taking their toll, and many men were now sent back to England in the *Swallow*. Trouble then broke out in the remaining ships. In the foggy and terrible conditions, disputes erupted between inexpert seamen as to their exact position and the best course to take. No sooner had this last problem been resolved than the fleet ran into shallows. The *Delight* was wrecked with the loss of over eighty men, along with Gilbert's maps and notes, and the ores he had prospected in Newfoundland. Hopelessness became epidemic. 'Our people lost courage daily,' wrote Edward Hayes, the chronicler of the voyage, and the appalling conditions made matters all the more bleak, 'the weather continuing thick and blustering, with increase of cold'.[7]

Gilbert's company now consisted merely of two tiny ships adrift in the Atlantic and dependent on a decreasing stock of provisions. Eventually, the men begged their captain to return before they all perished. They gestured pathetically to their blue and barely fed mouths, and then to their thin, ragged clothes. Gilbert, realistic and courageous, saw there was no alternative but to sail for England. Promising to 'set you forth royally next spring', he changed course for home. Amid rising winds, high waves, and the sighting of 'a monster of the sea' whose 'horrible voice' the desperate men took for a good omen, the battered fleet sailed past the scenes of previous disaster. The men, meanwhile, 'comforted each other with the hope . . . of the good to come'.

Gilbert, who had torn his foot on a nail, came aboard the *Golden Hind* to have it dressed and then returned to the *Squirrel*, bidding the crews hang out their lanterns in the terrible Atlantic night. But beneath his courage, and beneath the show of camaraderie he put on for his men, Gilbert's spirits were collapsing. He tried to keep alive his hope that he had found precious metal in Newfoundland, but the map in which he placed his trust had been left on the *Delight* by his cabin-boy and was lost with the ship. Slowly, terribly, the Atlantic was swallowing all Gilbert had striven for.

In an access of despair, he beat the lad he blamed for the loss of the treasure map. Then he began to divide up his hopes of an empire among his supporters, reserving Newfoundland and its treasures for himself. Surely, he told his men, surely there would be another expedition next spring. No man need contribute a penny to it. The queen would lend him the £1000 he required. 'We needed not to seek any further.' As if phrase-spinning could make all well, 'these last words he would often repeat'. Gilbert's disbelieving crew merely stared at him, suspicious and uncomprehending. He was, they saw, a man obsessed, sitting doggedly on his tiny ship and muttering promises that all would be well.

Then, approaching the Azores, the weather turned viler. The winds seemed to shift to all points of the compass and, as they rushed in lunatic career, so they moulded the waves into black pyramids that crashed even as they rose. Seasoned sailors 'never saw more outrageous seas', and their minds, naturally superstitious, turned to foreboding when St Elmo's fire leapt only half way across the mainyard. Gilbert, resolute, a book in his hand, called out encouragement whenever he thought he could be heard. 'We are as near to heaven by sea as by land.' But, about midnight, the lights on the *Squirrel* were suddenly extinguished. Gilbert's voice was lost, and only the watchman on the *Golden Hind* could be heard, crying out that 'the General was cast away'. The fathomless Atlantic had at last closed over Gilbert, taking his life, even as it had stripped him of his hopes.

Ralegh was the obvious successor to Gilbert's project, and by March 1584, after the various assignments agreed by his half-brother had been confirmed, he was granted a seven-year patent for North American colonization. In return for 'the fifth part of all the ore of gold and silver'[8] the colony might produce, Ralegh was given extensive rights in regions loosely and conventionally defined as 'remote, heathen and barbarous lands, countries and territories not actually possessed of any Christian prince and inhabited by Christian people'. The underlying thinking is clear: those parts of the globe where European men and European faith were absent were held to be the natural property of those English explorers who had the initiative to seize them. The assumption is wholly imperialist, the first stirrings of a theme that over the next three hundred years was progressively to dominate English ambitions and, to a large extent, the map of the world itself.

Ralegh's patent gave him immense freedoms constrained only by the proviso that the colonies themselves should be governed according to English law and the Anglican faith. Within these broad terms, Ralegh was at liberty to organize and rule his lands as circumstances dictated. Where Gilbert, always a theoretician, had planned an elaborate constitution for his empire, Ralegh's more pragmatic mind refused to be so constrained. Practical considerations were altogether more important to him. Ralegh was given the right to ship across the Atlantic any of the queen's subjects of his choosing, as well as the power to impress both ships and men from Devon, Cornwall and the city of Bristol. Once settled, his officers had authority to expel to the natural hazards of an unknown land all those who challenged his rule or believed they could set up colonies on their own account. If America was to be England in a new land, it was to be united under one man: Ralegh, the queen's representative.

What is less clear is the extent to which at this stage Ralegh's ambitions combined exploration and colonization with another altogether more tactical aim: the establishment of a strongly fortified American base for the use of English privateers operating in the

West Indies. His interest in what is now the coastline of North Carolina certainly suggests a concern with founding an English port conveniently placed to attack Spanish shipping, yet one sufficiently far from the Spanish colony in Florida to be safe from molestation.

To realize the immense potential offered by his patent required an executive mind of a high order, and sound financing was clearly essential. Gilbert, for all his ambition, had been forced to tack and veer with every circumstance, to improvise and, eventually, to expose himself to the greatest hazard. Ralegh was quick to learn the lesson. He would ensure that his own expeditions were securely financed, properly trained, adequately provisioned and, above all, given a clear intellectual basis which would allow for genuine efforts at reconnaissance. To further these aims, his magnificent Thameside palace became one of the great centres of practical enquiry in England. Far removed from the Aristotelian niceties of Oxford and Cambridge, and funded by Ralegh's own resources, Durham House was turned into an unofficial technological university and a focus for some of the most brilliant minds of his age.

The influence of the circle gathered round John Dee is clear in this. Ralegh himself remained on friendly terms with the great magus, and Dee recorded in his diary for 18 April, 1583 that 'the queen went from Richmond towards Greenwich, and at her going on horseback, being new up, she called for me by Mr Ralegh, his putting her in mind, and she said; *"Quod defertur non aufertur"*, and gave me her right hand to kiss.' "What is deferred is not put off for ever."[9] Ralegh was clearly trying to help a respected friend, but the queen's response – encouragement without a concrete reward – illustrates her parsimony. In the event, royal reward was so long delayed that by September 1583 Dee had turned to seek his fortunes on the continent. Here he was to remain for six years until Elizabeth summoned him home. Ralegh in the meantime had employed at Durham House one of the greatest mathematicians of his day, Thomas Harriot.

The range of Harriot's interests is remarkable. If Ralegh's was the imagination that could envisage the setting up of colonies in a new world, Harriot's was the intellect that helped make these dreams a practical reality. He was born in Oxford in 1560. He matriculated at St Mary's Hall (an independent establishment later connected to

Ralegh's old college, Oriel) from where, three years later, he gradu-
ated as a Bachelor of Arts. Drawn to those London circles interested
in American discovery and the problems of navigation, Harriot was
a member of Ralegh's household by late 1582 or early 1583.

Here, as scientist, mathematics tutor and expert in navigation,
he was at the centre of an intellectual enterprise of the greatest
importance: the application of scientific method to the practical problems raised by the new discoveries and sea voyages. Ralegh's place
as the patron of this initiative was one of the greatest importance,
and his role was recognized by the younger Richard Hakluyt (himself
soon to be a member of the Durham House circle) when he wrote a
Latin dedication to Ralegh extolling the fact that

> by your experience in navigation you saw clearly that our highest
> glory as an island kingdom would be built up to its greatest
> splendour on the firm foundation of the mathematical sciences,
> and so for a long time you have nourished in your household,
> with a most liberal salary, a young man well trained in those
> studies, Thomas Harriot; so that under his guidance you might
> in spare hours learn those noble sciences and your collaborating
> sea captains, who are many, might very profitably unite theory
> with practice, not without almost incredible results.[10]

The younger Hakluyt's praise of Ralegh's uniting theory with practice and the attainment of 'almost incredible results' aptly character-
izes the excitement that drew men to Durham House and Ralegh's
invigorating presence.

Formal training was becoming ever more essential if ships were
to sail beyond their home waters or the old familiar trade routes. All
the time sailors remained tied to these, a comparatively rudimentary
knowledge of the stars and, near to the coasts, the use of soundings
made with a lead-weighted line, were sufficiently accurate for most
estimates of a ship's position. Printed handbooks or 'rutters' helped
to publicize such accumulated local knowledge, but with ships
launched on the full expanse of the Atlantic and headed for coastlines
all but unknown, a range of new and improved techniques was
urgently called for.

It was essential, first of all, that sailors should have precise ideas about the location of the lands they were sailing to. This, in turn, necessitated the drawing of accurate maps as well as familiarity with the mathematics involved in determining latitude from the meridian altitude of the sun or a star. Longitude (an altogether more difficult problem in the absence of accurate clocks) was estimated through a process of dead reckoning which again required a knowledge of maps and the compass, as well as familiarity with a ship's 'way' or the knots at which it was travelling with respect to winds and currents. Harriot was to make important contributions in all these areas and, in order to instruct his classes at Durham House, he compiled a textbook he called the *Arcticon*. Regrettably, this work has been lost, but it is clear that Ralegh himself regarded the fruits of such research as his own property. The charts, tables and instruments made by Harriot were reserved for Ralegh's own use and that of his associates.

While Harriot was involved in mathematics and navigation, another of the men gathered at Durham House was made responsible for a detailed visual record of Ralegh's American expeditions. This was the artist John White. The presence of such a man on Ralegh's staff suggests the continuing influence of Gilbert on Ralegh's think- ing, since Gilbert had suggested that an 'observer' be employed on his own voyages to 'draw to life one of each kind of thing that is strange to us in England'. These subjects included flora and fauna as well as 'the figures and shapes of men and women in their apparel as also their manner of weapons in every place as you shall find them differing'.

White himself had already sailed on Frobisher's second expedition to Baffin Island in 1577. He had made a lively study of an encounter between Frobisher's men and Eskimo kayaks as well as a sensitive and delightful study of an Eskimo woman clad in furs, the head of her baby just peeping out from the side of her hood. The accuracy of these studies was no doubt in large part responsible for recommending White to Ralegh, and theirs was a relationship that was later to have considerable consequences for the colonizing of America.

Having gathered about him men of this calibre and trained others in the most advanced skills of navigation, Ralegh was now able to launch a preliminary reconnoitring voyage. Simon Fernandez was inevitably appointed master, but the two leaders of the expedition are men altogether less distinct. Philip Amadas – referred to somewhat disparagingly as 'little Amadas' – was a member of a well-known West Country family who appears to have served both at sea and in the army where, it is to be presumed, he picked up his knowledge of fortification. Ralegh's other choice as leader was Arthur Barlowe, a man who had already served with him in Ireland and had probably been a member of Ralegh's household for some time. Barlowe appears to have made a voyage to the eastern Mediterranean, but his distinction lay above all in the powers of description revealed by his journal of the expedition on which he was now sent. This was later to serve as the basis for the report that was published as part of Ralegh's propaganda for his American venture.

By 10 May 1584, Amadas and Barlowe (possibly accompanied by Harriot and White) reached the Canaries. From there, borne by favourable currents and a trade wind, their two ships made a rapid crossing of the Atlantic. By 2 July, as they coasted Florida, they were greeted by the welcome smell of land breezes, and two days later they glimpsed land itself. Encouraged by this, they cruised northwards along the barrier islands of the Carolina coast and finally dropped anchor off the north tip of what was known to the natives as Hatarask. Having given thanks to God, the leaders of the expedition went ashore on Hatarask Island to claim the land for the queen and Ralegh, probably erecting a post emblazoned with the royal arms as a sign of possession.

Recording this historic moment after his return to England, Barlowe felt that he and Ralegh's men had landed in a paradise, a Utopia of warmth and fecundity. Grapes grew down to the edge of the shore, so close to the waves indeed that in a beautiful passage Barlowe tells how 'the very beating, and surge of the sea overflowed them'.[11] Climbing to higher ground, the Englishmen noted 'valleys replenished with goodly cedar trees', trees redder than those anywhere else in the world and of finer quality than any Barlowe had seen before. Deer and rabbits bounded through the woods, while, when the sailors discharged their guns, a flock of sandhill cranes 'arose under us, with such a cry redoubled by many echoes, as if an army of men had shouted altogether.' Surely here, Barlowe seems to

[84]

imply, in this earthly paradise, might be found the inhabitants of the Golden Age.

Eventually three Indians approached in their canoes and began to call to the Englishmen who had now returned to their ships. Friendly overtures were made, and an Indian was welcomed on to one of the English vessels where he was given a hat, a shirt, and his first taste of European wine. Tribal custom required an exchange of gifts, and the lone Indian returned to the shore and then, with his associates, came back with a great catch of fish. This, he indicated, was to be divided between the two English crews.

Having established that these strangers were friendly, the Indians resolved to send a larger delegation to greet them. Their chief, Wingina, had recently been wounded in a local skirmish, and in his place, and at the head of a party of forty or fifty men, came his brother Granganimeo. The warriors were all, Barlowe noted, men of the greatest dignity and deportment: 'Very handsome, and goodly people, and in their behaviour as mannerly, and civil, as any of Europe.' When compared to Elizabethan views of the Irish, Barlowe's description of the American Indians emerges as an adroit piece of propaganda for the new continent – an invention in which America becomes the promised land.

As the acting chief of his people, Granganimeo presented himself to the Englishmen in some state. Servants spread a long mat on the ground on one end of which he sat accompanied by four warriors while the others stood some way off. As Ralegh's men approached him, Granganimeo, completely confident, begged them to come and sit by him. 'And being sat,' Barlowe continued, 'he makes all sign of joy, and welcome, striking on his head, and his breast, and afterwards on ours to show we were all one, smiling, and making show of the best he could, of all love, and familiarity.' These gestures again suggest a rational and humane being, but such sign language could lead to confusion. When the English tried to discover what the natives called their country, they received the answer 'Windgandcon', a name that stuck until it was discovered that the phrase meant 'What fine clothes you are wearing!'

Difficulties of communication apart, further gifts were now exchanged and trading relations established. A few days later the Indians returned with skins, Granganimeo exchanging twenty of these for a tin dish he wished to wear at his throat as a sign of rank. To the Englishmen, such trading was both profitable and harmless, but when the Indians began to cast glances at the strangers' axes, their knives and, above all, their swords, they refused to barter them, unsure what the future might bring.

Both sides were careful to avoid mutual suspicion. Granganimeo sent the English daily gifts of food and lit fires on the shore to tell Barlowe, Amadas and their men how many of their canoes to expect. Trading in 'leather, coral and divers kinds of dyes' continued daily, the less important Indians giving way to Granganimeo and his elders or 'weroances' when, distinguished by their copper gorgets, they appeared on the scene. Granganimeo himself paid further visits to the English ships and, on one occasion, brought with him his wife and small children.

The woman, Barlowe noticed, was comparatively short of stature and very shy. He continues with a passage of exact and delightful description: 'She had on her back a long cloak of leather, with the fur side next to her body, and before her a piece of the same: about her forehead she had a broad band of white coral, and so had her husband many times: in her ears she had bracelets of pearls, hanging down to her middle (whereof we delivered your worship a little bracelet) and those were of the bigness of good peas.' The link between these Indian tribal aristocrats and the English courtier is a telling touch, and in such details Ralegh's presence is felt as his men carried out his orders half a world away.

At some point – it is not clear when – Amadas and the larger of the two vessels sailed away from the area, perhaps going north to Chesapeake Bay and thence more certainly to Bermuda in pursuit of Spanish treasure ships. This suggests how important a part the proposed colony was to play as a base for Ralegh's privateering plans. However, Amadas himself captured no prizes off Bermuda and was equally unsuccessful in the six weeks he spent sailing round the Azores. Eventually, when his stores began to run low, he returned to England, reaching landfall by November. Barlowe and his men meanwhile were experiencing more of Indian life.

With seven of his men rowing the pinnace, Barlowe crossed the Sound to make a first landing on Roanoke Island, a name which was soon to echo through all Ralegh's dealings with North America.

Having landed on the island and found Granganimeo's palisaded village, Barlowe's party was welcomed by the acting chief's wife who took their clothes, washed and dried them, bathed the men's feet in warm water, and then prepared a meal of boiled corn, fish, squid, venison, roots and fruits. Although Barlowe was wary and insisted, much to his hostess's distress, that he and his men sleep on board their boat, he was clearly impressed by the hospitality he received and was determined to create in English minds a similarly favourable impression.

Here were a people capable of a settled and civil existence, different in their outward appearance from Englishmen to be sure, yet enjoying refined and generous manners. 'We were entertained with all love and kindness, and with as much bounty, after their manner, as they could possibly devise,' Barlowe wrote. Then, rising to the height of his theme, he declared: 'We found the people most gentle, loving and faithful, void of all guile and treason, and such as lived after the manner of the Golden Age'. Here indeed was an Eden where 'the earth bringeth forth all things in abundance, as in the first Creation without toil or labour.'

But Barlowe had been employed to note facts as well as spin fantasies. He was keen to observe the Indians' weapons, for example, and he noted how Granganimeo's village of nine log cabins was defended by a palisade of cedar trunks. As a military man, he recorded how 'the entrance into it made it like a turnpike' – something altogether feeble when compared to a European fort. Boat building too came under his scrutiny, and Barlowe describes how 'they burn down some great tree, or take such as are windfallen, and putting myrrh and rosin upon one side thereof, they set fire into it, when it hath burnt it hollow, they cut out the coal with their shells, and ever where they would burn it deeper or wider, they lay on their gums, which burneth away the timber, and by this means they fashion very fine boats, and such as will transport twenty men.'

This suggestion of innocence and ingenuity is an aspect of Barlowe's general approach to his subject. None the less, with his conjuring up of a picture of these canoes, it is impossible to forget his own ship riding at anchor off Hatarask, its iron anchor rooted in the sand and its cannon pointing out of the sides of one of the most efficient engines of war European man had yet devised. The fantasy of a golden age could easily be destroyed by the men who had dreamed it – men who, besides, believed that they were cherished in the hand of an omnipotent God.

With respect to the Indians' own religious beliefs, Barlowe noted that 'within the place where they feed, was their lodging, and within that their Idol, which they worship.' Concerning this idol, he declared, 'they speak incredible things', meaning by this things not to be believed – mere superstitious idolatry. He also recorded that the Indians carried their totem to war with them, adding that they asked counsel of the figure 'as the Romans were wont of the Oracle of Apollo'. Here were a people ripe for conversion.

Other members of Barlowe's crew meanwhile were making a reconnaissance of the immediate area. Precisely what this entailed is unclear, but in some undisclosed manner they managed to take on board two Indians: Manteo and Wanchese, men whom they were determined to bring back to England. Wanchese was a warrior from Granganimeo's tribe, while Manteo was a leader of a Croatian people ruled over by his mother. How voluntary Wanchese's departure was when, after a month or so, Barlowe and his men prepared to depart, is unclear. Manteo however was obviously taken with all things European, and by the middle of September, and after a safe and rapid voyage, both men were disembarked in England. Ralegh immediately set to work developing his ideas for his new enterprise.

To this end, he employed the experts gathered about him in Durham House. Harriot began familiarizing himself with Manteo and Wanchese's Algonquian tongue (he was at some point to work out a phonetic alphabet for this), while the two Indians themselves likewise began to acquire fluency in English. By the middle of October, both men were living in Ralegh's household, and by the end of the year they were being spoken of as the people who had revealed to him the 'singular great commodities'[12] of the New World. As this process of mutual acquaintance developed, so more valuable information came to light and was inserted into Barlowe's narrative. Meanwhile, and largely at Ralegh's instigation, further experts had been employed to work on the cause of North American plantation.

In 1585, the elder Richard Hakluyt issued a pamphlet entitled *Induce-*

ments to the Liking of the Voyage Intended Towards Virginia. This was written to encourage the commercial potential of Ralegh's scheme for North American colonization, and Hakluyt here describes his vision of an agricultural community in North America based, as the latitude of Virginia suggested, on the growing of such Mediterranean staples as sugar, olives, vines, oranges and figs. He further suggested that buffalo hides, brine, timber and fish would provide an immediate source of profit while the colonists themselves were preparing the ground for agriculture.

Hakluyt was also insistent on a number of the general principles that repeatedly surface in Elizabethan plans for colonization. Chief among those for Hakluyt himself was a mercantilist vision of the nation's future. Imports from foreign powers, he argued, should be reduced to a minimum, and England's own colonies should satisfy the nation's demand for those luxury goods she herself could not produce. In addition, exports should be maximized to secure a highly lucrative balance of trade. Trade would thus follow the flag, while Hakluyt hoped religion would follow them both.

Hakluyt was insistent on this last, convinced as he was that the moral teachings of Protestant Christianity provided the essential basis for his hopes of economic development. Noting the deep resentment inspired in native people by the barbarous dealings of the Spaniards, Hakluyt wrote that 'a gentle course without cruelty and tyranny best answereth the profession of a Christian, best planteth Christian religion; maketh our seating most void of blood, most profitable in the trade of merchandise, most firm and stable, and least subject to remove by practice of enemies.'[13]

The older Hakluyt was no wide-eyed innocent, however, and he wished 'that some ancient captains of mild disposition and great judgement be sent thither with men most skilful in the art of fortification'. A secure base was considered essential both for protection and as a centre from which map-makers could survey the territory and discover those 'gates and entries' which could then be defended against an enemy. Such ideas were the fruit of many years' thought and enquiry, and Ralegh and his colonists were to act on much of the older Hakluyt's advice.

However, the most important of the documents concerned with Ralegh's first major colonizing endeavour was the work of the younger Richard Hakluyt, a cousin of the lawyer, and a man whose great energies were given throughout an entire career to the cause of English expansion overseas. Even before the return of Barlowe and Amadas, Hakluyt had, at Ralegh's request, digested his great wealth of ideas and knowledge into a document now known as the *Discourse of Western Planting*. This is the most comprehensive expression of the Elizabethan colonizing ideal and a work intended for Ralegh, Walsingham and the queen alone.

In asking Hakluyt to prepare it, Ralegh had once again attracted to himself a man of the highest calibre. If the Virginia colony was to give Ralegh an empire in the New World, Hakluyt's memorandum provided the essential foundation of ideas on which such ambitions could be raised. Thus, with one exception, the *Discourse* is not a profoundly original document, rather it is a full, clear and logical exposition of the expansionist hopes of a generation. What gives the *Discourse* authority is the weight of accumulated thought and detail that lie behind it. Ralegh's wish to plant colonies in America, we are made to feel, is propelled by the full and various forces of national self-consciousness, a momentum that is irresistible.

To ensure this impression, Hakluyt first drew attention to the religious initiatives of the Anglican church, suggesting that its missionary work was sluggish in comparison to what had been achieved by the Roman Catholics of Spain and Portugal. 'The people of America cry out unto us their next neighbours to come and help them, and bring unto them the glad tidings of the Gospel,' he declared,[14] citing St Paul to his purpose along with the queen's duties as Defender of the Faith and the chief among the princes of the reformed religion. Having established this primary goal, he then turned to the natural resources to be found in the territory.

For Hakluyt, America was a promised land of Biblical plenty which offered 'honey, venison, palm trees, cedars, cypresses, vines', twice-yearly harvests, 'sassafras' (which was believed to be a cure for the epidemic of venereal disease sweeping Europe), 'gold and red copper', and a wide variety of 'things incident to a navy'. Hakluyt then rehearsed the familiar argument 'that this enterprise will be for manifold employment of numbers of idle men.' The Elizabethan belief that unemployment, being the fault of the unemployed, was an offence worthy of punishment, is here joined to the contemporary fear of the threat posed by 'multitudes of loiterers and idle vagabonds'. Hakluyt sees America as the panacea for such ills. The prisons can be emptied of petty criminals who, rather than being left to 'pitifully pine away', can be sentenced instead to a variety of useful labours in the New World.

Having dealt with religion, commerce and social questions, Hakluyt turned to the political and strategic reasons for encouraging American colonies. Here the profound loathing of Spain he shared with Ralegh verges on hysteria. 'That this voyage will be a great bridle' to Spanish ambitions is a major concern and, over the course of six chapters, Hakluyt offered a vivid picture of a corrupt and mighty empire tottering towards inevitable decline. Hakluyt itemized especially the evils caused by the influx of gold and silver into Spain. Spanish treasure, he insisted, has been used 'to the afflicting and oppressing of most of the great estates of Christendom'. Ranging over Portugal, the Low Countries, France, Scotland and Ireland, he painted a threatening picture of 'the sons of Belial' undermining European stability with their imported bullion.

He also insisted that the barbarious treatment meted out to the natives by their Spanish conquerors has greatly weakened the enemy in those places where they supposed themselves to be master. Taking the information provided not just by Protestant sources but by the great Spanish bishop Bartholomew de las Casas (a cleric whose publications resulted in one of the earliest and most sophisticated debates on human rights) Hakluyt proceeded to suggest that the Spaniards in the Americas had adopted a policy of genocide towards the Indians. They 'neither yet do at this present ought else than tear them in pieces, kill them, martyr them, afflict them, torment them and destroy them by strange sorts of cruelties'. Carried away by his genuine outrage, Hakluyt first wrote and then crossed out a paragraph in which he suggested that if the queen were to 'assist the revolted Indians' then 'great matters may be brought about.'

Ralegh was later to be much influenced by this idea, while Hakluyt's broader arguments – his presentation of the dangers inflicted by Spanish silver and gold, and his belief in the weakness of the enemy's position especially – were both widely influential on the policies of the great Elizabethan seamen. Most important of all however, both Ralegh and Hakluyt believed that state involvement was essential if England were to secure these advantages, and the closing sections of the *Discourse*, the twentieth chapter in particular, are addressed to Elizabeth herself. Re-employing the arguments of the Dee circle, Hakluyt established the queen's legal right to her American colonies and then proceeded to contrast Spanish tyranny with something altogether more glorious.

'Whensoever the queen of England, a prince of such clemency, shall seat upon that form of America, and shall be reported throughout all that tract to use the natural people there with all humanity, courtesy, and freedom, they will yield themselves to her government and revolt clean from the Spaniard.' The vision is of Elizabeth as the imperial British Virgin and of a colonial policy addressed to a kingdom. Written 'to enduce her Majesty to . . . take in hand the western voyage and the planting there,' the *Discourse* is a comprehensive statement of Ralegh's belief that North American colonization ought to be a matter for the English state rather than being left merely to the hazards of private enterprise.

This was not a policy with which the queen herself agreed, but by the closing months of 1584, Ralegh's initiatives had raised English plans for American colonization to new levels. He had gathered together a remarkable company of experts, and the result of their joint efforts was a great enhancement of the knowledge required for exploration.

Hakluyt had provided him with a document which, intended as a contribution to national policy, had brought together many years' thinking on English colonial expansion and united around the cause of American plantation the various strands of commerce, foreign policy and religion. With the return of Barlowe and Amadas, knowledge of the eastern American seaboard itself and of its people especially had increased. Now, while Harriot was gaining fluency in the Algonquian dialect and was learning from Manteo and Wanchese yet more information to be included in Barlowe's report, so both that report and the two Indians themselves could serve Ralegh's purpose of kindling interest in the cause of American colonization.

In October 1584, the two warriors were presented at court. Here they were observed by the industrious Leopold von Wedel. 'He allowed us to see them,' von Wedel wrote of Manteo and Wanchese.

'In face and figure they were like white Moors. Normally they wear no shirt, just a wild animal skin across the shoulders, and a piece of fur over the privies, but now they were dressed in brown taffeta.'[15] For von Wedel, these two men from an all but undiscovered continent were worth no more than a cursory and patronizing glance. 'No one could understand what they said,' he continued, 'and altogether they looked very childish and uncouth.' Others were more favourably impressed, especially by the opportunities for American trade the two warriors appeared to represent. Thomas Harvey, citizen of London and member of the Grocers' Company, was among those who listened to reports derived from the 'two strangers' and, in the hope of profit, he not only sank into Ralegh's second American expedition 'the greatest part of his own wealth . . . but also borrowed divers sums of money of others for his better expedition therein.'[16]

It was just such backers Ralegh was seeking, and to further the appeal of his new expedition he sought, as the newly elected Member of Parliament for Devon, to pass a private bill through the Commons confirming his title to those American lands so far possessed under his patent. The bill was presented on 14 December and, after its second reading, when it was much 'argued upon', it was passed to a committee. This was packed with Members known for their interest in colonization, many of whom also represented West Country constituencies and were to offer Ralegh their practical support. The older Hakluyt's *Inducements* (and possibly a printed or manuscript version of Barlowe's report) further encouraged their enthusiasm.

Among the committee men were Sir Francis Walsingham, a longtime supporter of American colonization, who was now to subscribe to Ralegh's venture, as well as sending on it a number of his servants. Sir Philip Sidney was a member, although his chief concern was with the plans of yet another member, Sir Francis Drake, whose proposed raid on the Spanish Indies was probably intended to dovetail with Ralegh's hopes of finding a deep-water harbour on the eastern American seaboard. Sir William Courteny, co-member for Devonshire along with Ralegh himself, Sir William Mohun and Sir Richard Grenville, Members for Cornwall, sat on the committee, as almost certainly did two men who were actually to sail on the expedition, Anthony Rowse and Thomas Cavendish.

In spite of the packed committee there were two objections to

Ralegh's bill and after its subsequent readings in the Commons it was presented to the Lords with the provisos that Ralegh should not be allowed either to press ships for his expedition or sail with criminals and debtors aboard. The result was that, after its first reading in the Lords, the bill was dropped. Ralegh's patent had initially been granted under the royal prerogative, and Elizabeth, ever keen to protect the Crown's privileges from parliamentary encroachment, would not allow her will to be crossed in this way.

She sought instead to help her favourite by other and more practical means. She permitted him to obtain over £400 worth of gunpowder from the Tower of London and placed her ship the *Tiger* at his disposal. So much she would do to help her newly knighted courtier in his attempt to found the colony he had named after her. She would not, however, let Ralegh himself sail on the expedition. He was to remain in England by his queen. The entrepreneur of colonization was to stay at home, fettered by the golden chain of royal favour.

CHAPTER SIX

The Royal Servant

While preparing his American expedition, Ralegh was also acquiring considerable public responsibilities. The profits received from his monopolies had not been granted to him merely to fund a life of luxurious idleness, and for all that Jesuit agents might carp at his status as 'the darling of the English Cleopatra',[1] his new wealth was intended primarily to establish him as a grandee and so give him the means and status to fulfil his potential as a servant of the Crown. He was an excellent choice for this role. Ralegh could indeed 'toil terribly',[2] and it was reported by a seventeenth-century observer that he was constantly active, allowing a mere five hours to sleep and two to conversation, while reserving four hours for his reading and the rest of the day for business.

Ralegh's administrative posts were designed in particular to make him the Crown's great servant in the West. In a remarkably short space of time, this youngest son of a small tenant farmer acquired many of the great regional offices of state. Ralegh thereby became both an important official and the representative at court of the aspirations of his locality, his family and kin. Already, in 1584, he had been elected a junior Member of Parliament for Devon. The following year he was appointed Vice-Admiral of the West and successor to the deceased Earl of Bedford as Lord Lieutenant of Cornwall and Lord Warden of the Stannaries.

This last appointment was particularly suited to Ralegh's maverick talent and suggests the intense regional differences with which the ambitious courtier had to be familiar. The Stannaries were the administrative units of the West Country tin mines, an industry that yielded valuable tax revenues to the Crown but existed under ancient and fiercely independent laws and customs. A contemporary, carping at Ralegh's appointment, described the tinners themselves as 'so rough and mutinous a multitude, 10,000 or 12,000, the most strong men of England',[3] and he doubted Ralegh's ability to control them. In fact, for all the unpopularity his pride and the exploitation of his monopolies caused elsewhere in the country, Ralegh commanded passionate respect in the West. His overriding political concern (as it was again to be in the later Elizabethan parliaments) was to secure the loyalty of ordinary people to the Crown in the wider interests of national unity. His imaginative sympathy with the plight of the poor has nothing of the democrat about it. It was, rather, a further aspect of his intense devotion to the queen as the fountain of authority.

And his efforts to this end were widely appreciated. It was not idle flattery when Richard Carew, dedicating his *Survey of Cornwall* to Ralegh, declared: 'Your ears and mouth have ever been open to hear and deliver our grievances, and your feet and hands ready to go and work their redress, and that, not only always as a magistrate, of yourself, but also very often as a suitor and solicitor of others of the highest place.'[4] In other words, Ralegh could and did discuss the tinners' troubles with the queen. Nor was this concern shown just in large issues. With that interest in petty detail so important for winning local support, Ralegh is found writing to some Devonian Justices of the Peace asking them not to insist on a contribution from the tinners to a private bridge, the cost of which would be, he declared: 'overburdensome to poor men in regard to their daily travail and disbursements'.[5]

This comment goes some way to suggest that the conditions under which the tinners of Devon and Cornwall lived were appalling in the extreme. An account of the Stannaries written in 1586 reveals that these men were earning wages barely sufficient to sustain life, that many were deeply in debt, and that by being paid at least partly in kind they were cruelly subject to fluctuations in the price of tin and the taxes levied on it.

The work itself was extremely hard, a four-hour shift in the ill-ventilated shafts being the maximum most miners could endure. Housing conditions were notoriously squalid, and heavy drinking was the almost inevitable panacea for wretchedness. Furthermore, many of the mines themselves had been sunk so deep that difficulties with drainage made them impractical to operate. The result, in a time of widespread financial depression, was a decline in the annual production of tin. As Lord Warden, Ralegh had the essential problem, in a period of mounting threat from Spain, of maintaining for the queen the loyalty of a fiercely independent but impoverished people living in a remote area of great strategic importance.

This required political skill and considerable force of personality. Over many centuries, the Stannaries had come to enjoy a remarkable degree of autonomy in matters of administration and justice. Charters of 1201 and 1305 constituted the two corporations of the Stannaries of Cornwall and the Stannaries of Devon, and each possessed courts where, except in the most serious of criminal matters and in civil suits, the tinners were subject to their own laws. It was these courts whose functions had also been developed into the tinners' parliaments. Such assemblies were summoned by the Lord Warden whose speech was read at their opening. The Lord Warden then approved the election of a speaker and his clerks before withdrawing while the debates themselves were held. Issues pertaining 'to the prejudice of any tinner, or other person having to do with black or white tin' were discussed, enactments being subject to the signature of the Lord Warden himself.

In his role as Lord Warden of the Stannaries Ralegh was also responsible for mustering the West Country tinners for the army while, as Lord Lieutenant, it was his duty to supervise the military training of the remaining able-bodied men of Cornwall between the ages of sixteen and sixty. Ralegh's combination of these roles in a time of gathering threat from Spain suggests the considerable trust placed in him by the queen. He was playing an important part in the defence of the realm, and the result was a growing burden of administration.

Forts and coastal defences had to be looked to, in addition to the supervision of supplies of armour and horses, the mustering of men and training in the new standards of continental warfare with its increased use of firepower. Poor communications, regional loyalties, a fair measure of Falstaffian dishonesty and arguments over the social standing of officers added to these difficulties and illustrate clearly the problems faced by the Elizabethan government when trying to impose nationwide policies. The energy and competence of a man like Ralegh, and the power of his local influence especially, were of exceptional importance in readying the country for its defence.

The musters reveal the chain of command under Ralegh's super-vision and suggest the startling inefficiency of Elizabethan bureau-cracy. Ralegh's deputies, the most prominent gentlemen of the county, received the orders he passed on from the Privy Council. The deputies would then make arrangements with the local Justices of the Peace and issue orders to the high constables concerning the time and place of the muster. These orders, along with assessments for money and equipment, were then handed down to the parish constables who were all too often men of small ability wished by their betters into a trying role.

If the chain of command often proved inefficient, the fiercely individualistic nature and local loyalty of Elizabethan Englishmen added to the confusion. Prior to 1588 when the rule was changed, they all knew that they were not liable for service beyond their county borders. Large-scale manoeuvres were thus all but impossible to train for. Since the majority of those called up were engaged in agriculture, the timing of musters was severely restricted by the demands of the farming year.

There were also disputes as to whether armour should be stored centrally or in the various houses of wealthy men, those arguing for the latter hinting at the chaos caused when soldiers ran to a common armoury 'and there in hubbledehuffe disorderly ... arm them-selves'.[6] A picture at once comic and alarming was painted of little men putting on the armour of tall men and the general pande-monium of running matters 'according to the old saying, first come, first served'.[7] Even when the men were finally on parade there were difficulties. In a period when numeracy was rare, the muster certificates were notoriously unreliable. Ralegh himself was to become so irked by this that the Privy Council eventually answered his complaints by assuring him that they had resolved to enforce the use of standard issue certificates.

Under such conditions, disciplined training was hard to achieve. English writers on military affairs looked anxiously at the serried ranks of Spain and lamented how English officers were more con-cerned to train their horses than their men. They also worried about the small amount of time given to military practice. 'How barbarous that common opinion is', lamented Thomas Digges, 'that an English-man will be trained in a few weeks into a perfect soldier.'[8] Nor was there any agreement as to what a perfect soldier should be proficient at. In Cornwall, it had been considered that soldiers be trained merely in marching, charging, guard duty and understanding the various drum taps.

And then there was always the weather. Training of men in the maritime counties had been proceeding with particular urgency since 1583, but two years later when, after much haggling over money and numbers, Ralegh issued orders for a muster, it had to be postponed because of the rain. His role as the Lord Lieutenant of Cornwall was made easier however by his careful choice of subordinates. The discreet and expert Captain Horde, being popular with his men, had 'won them generally to such a willingness to be employed and trained that they that erst were abashed, yea and as would have given good sums of money to have been excepted from the service, rejoice in that they have profited by this training.' Indeed, they were clamouring for more. It is one of the indications of Ralegh's great administrative ability that he could find men of high calibre to whom he was prepared to delegate.

Ralegh's offices had given him overall responsibility for the land and sea defences of an area of vital strategic importance. He was indeed one of the greatest gentlemen of the West. His position was anomalous even so. He was a Lord Lieutenant but not a peer, a grandee with no patrimony. His father had died in 1581, but as a younger son there was little for Ralegh to inherit. To establish his position in the West, particularly after receiving his knighthood, he needed both a substantial house in the region and some aura of old gentility to offset his very obvious position as a parvenu. He set the local antiquary to research into his family origins. Hooker duly discovered that a Sir John de Ralegh had married the daughter of D'Amerie Clare, a descendant of Henry I. A remote trace of Plantagenet blood thus ran – or was alleged to run – in Ralegh's veins.

Ralegh also tried to purchase Hayes Barton, the house in which he had spent his boyhood. 'I will most willingly give whatever in your conscience you shall deem it worth,' he wrote to the landlord, Richard Duke.[9] Duke was impressed neither by this nor by offers of the services of 'a thankful friend' at court. He would not sell, and

Ralegh was obliged to establish himself in other ways, ways that point once again to his dependence on royal favour and his involvement in the most modern forms of enterprise. His ambitions once more turned to Ireland.

The colonization of Munster had now become a matter of state policy. It appeared essential to secure the devastated province against the possibility of future invasion while also converting the huge and confiscated estates of the Desmonds into an enclave of English influence. The country offered many advantages. Land was cheap and plentiful. The surplus of English overpopulation could here be gainfully employed, while younger sons of gentry families might find work suitable to their status. In an age much influenced by classical precedent, it was known that the Romans had appreciated the benefits accruing from colonization, a view reinforced by Machiavelli. Burghley was a prime mover in this and the result of his involvement, along with that of the queen and such figures as Walsingham, the Irish Secretary of State, the Attorney-General and others, was a high level of bureaucratic interest.

Plans were worked out in detail between the end of 1585 and the middle of 1587. On paper at least, every contingency appeared to have been foreseen, while the government was also prepared to recognize the importance of advertising its aims. Officials were despatched round England to expound the benefits of Irish colonization and the fact that smallholdings and estates could be bought from between £6 and £300. The government would pay for civil administration and military protection (to start with, at least), while for the first five years rates would be waived. An Elizabethan enterprise zone was to be set up, and the involvement of such glamorous names as Sir Walter Ralegh would hopefully attract interest. In June 1586, Ralegh, as one of the chief 'undertakers' in the scheme, was granted 12,000 acres in Ireland. He was the senior partner in a West Country consortium that also included Sir John Clifton and Sir John Stowell. Sir Richard Grenville and Sir Warham St Leger were later to join them.

They were to transplant whole sections of English society to lands that had, it was said, been surveyed, allocated, and prepared for them. In fact, as was so frequently the case, bureaucratic hopes vastly outstripped bureaucratic achievement. The map was incomplete, there were wrangles between the English and the Irish, and even between the settlers themselves. Clifton and Stowell eventually returned exasperated to England. A man of altogether greater administrative ability was needed, someone who could be relied on to get things done. By the close of February 1587, and contrary to the original limits proposed for undertakers, Walter Ralegh was granted under the warrant of the Privy Seal 42,000 acres of reasonably mapped, cultivatable land at a cheap fixed annual rate. He had sought an estate and won himself what was virtually a kingdom.

The queen was determined her royal favourite should succeed, and she granted him further help in the project. Extra troops were sent over at her expense, along with an agent who, if picked by Ralegh, again showed his skill in selecting the right man for the job and the shrewdness with which he delegated authority. Largely through the competence of Richard Colthurst, 144 men were settled within two years, nearly all of them from the West Country and half of them accompanied by their families. The essentials of village life were also shipped over – tools and cattle, a miller, a baker and a blacksmith. Half of what Ralegh had promised to achieve was soon fulfilled, and while his colonizers settled in, Colthurst began adding status to Ralegh's domain. The beautiful castle at Lismore was bought with a view to making it the seat of power in the province, while the college at Youghal was converted into the administrative centre.

The confiscated estates of the Desmonds gave Ralegh vast estates in Ireland, while those of another traitor were now also to fall into his hands. By 1586, the tragedy of Mary, Queen of Scots, was moving towards its crisis. After twenty years of imprisonment, Mary was still plotting to murder Elizabeth and assume the English throne with the help of Spanish arms, a project to which Philip II was lending an increasingly open ear. The leading members of the Privy Council – Burghley and Walsingham especially – had resolved on Mary's death however, and with quiet, ruthless efficiency were directing matters so that a reluctant Elizabeth would eventually be forced to comply with her rival's execution.

Walsingham's spy network was put into action. Double agents in both the French embassy and at Chartley where Mary was held a prisoner ensured that her most secret correspondence was intercepted by the government. Walsingham then arranged that Anthony Babington, a hot-headed young Catholic who was one of Mary's most ardent supporters, was brought into contact with the Scots queen. Babington's letters soon revealed how he and six supporters were plotting to murder Elizabeth. Ralegh himself was privy to at least part of this.

As one of the most influential men in England, he felt obliged to have his own secret sources of information, and with that relish for political intrigue which was a strong and ultimately disastrous element in his personality, he allowed William Langhorne, his Catholic secretary, to approach Mary's agent Thomas Morgan. A somewhat amateur version of Walsingham's espionage system was set up. By means of this, Ralegh would be well informed on matters of the greatest secrecy and have a clear knowledge of the motives behind the leading members of the Privy Council. Secondly, in the unlikely event of Mary's plot succeeding, he would have allies close and apparently loyal to the new focus of power.

But it was Walsingham who was the chief player in this dangerous game. When he had gathered sufficient information, he had Babington arrested, brought before the Lord Chancellor and others, and heard his full confession. In the forlorn hope that Ralegh might be able to use his influence, Babington wrote offering him £1000 if he could obtain the queen's pardon for him. Nothing was further from Elizabeth's mind. Believing that the execution of Babington might satisfy a people baying for Mary's death (a prospect she looked on with abject horror), Elizabeth ordered Babington and his fellow conspirators be executed with the utmost cruelty.

They were taken to Tyburn, hanged until they were almost dead, cut down, emasculated, eviscerated, and made to watch as their intestines and private parts were burnt before them. Even the bloodthirsty crowd was revolted. As a convicted traitor, however, Babington forfeited his estates in Lincolnshire, Derbyshire and Nottinghamshire to the Crown. Elizabeth, moving in moral agony towards the recognition that Mary too must die, reserved for herself 'a certain curious clock' from among Babington's possessions. The rest she gave to Ralegh.

And now, as the threat from Spain mounted, so Ralegh tried to involve himself more deeply in schemes of international espionage. In 1586, two of his privateering vessels, sent down to the Azores, returned to Southampton with prizes that included Don Pedro Sarmiento de Gamboa, governor of the Spanish territories in Patagonia. Ralegh at once hurried to the port to greet a man who was in several respects his Spanish equivalent. There were possibilities of a large ransom, but also the more subtle political opportunities to be gained from contact with an important figure in the Spanish imperial drive to exploit the natural resources of Central and South America.

Sarmiento de Gamboa had been a commander in the campaign to capture Tupac Amaru, the last of the Inca warriors. He was, too, a man of intellectual interests and a respected historian of the Spanish involvement in Peru. He could provide first-hand accounts of the fabulous wealth and civilization his countrymen had so ruthlessly crushed. He could perhaps also be induced to provide information on the exploitation and shipment of the gold and silver that were flooding Philip's treasury and helping to finance both his army in the Netherlands and his massive fleet. As a man who had fought as an admiral against Drake and then been appointed governor of a Spanish expedition to colonize the Straits of Magellan, Sarmiento de Gamboa was knowledgeable about naval tactics, geography and Spanish expansionist aims, all of which could be of prime importance. He and Ralegh were men of a kind, and his captive soon fell under Ralegh's spell.

This last was dangerous to both men, and Ralegh's handling of Sarmiento de Gamboa reveals something of the weakness that lay deep in the character of the royal favourite. He had now, through the sheer force of his abilities, raised himself to remarkable eminence. Wealth, power and prestige had come to him as if commanded by his presence. The force of his personality, it seemed, had created him in splendour, and with this went a pride that believed it could carry all before it by the energy of its own magnificence.

But in the court of Elizabeth, Ralegh remained a man with no allies and few if any friends. Superb, imperious and sophisticated, he was, by contrast, a loner, a maverick, a man who seemed to be the author of himself and the prisoner of his own vanity. Rightly convinced of his merits, he had a fatal disinclination to see the facts of political life with a cold and calculating eye. He had, besides, a shallow relish for intrigue – a lethal quality in an imaginative man.

In particular, he now convinced Sarmiento that he wished to work as a double agent. His plan was not an original one, but Ralegh succeeded in making parts of it at least sound plausible.

Some years before, John Hawkins had informed King Philip that he was no longer satisfied in the service of Elizabeth and could be persuaded for an adequate reward to work against her in the interests of Spain. The queen and the Privy Council were fully aware of Hawkins's activities and were happy that a useful man of ardent Protestant convictions should enrich himself in the service of the enemy while providing them with such information as he might obtain. This, in the event, seems to have been comparatively little. Deep in the recesses of the Escorial, however, an irate Philip, toiling over the endless memoranda by which he hoped to rule the greater part of the known world, took to scribbling expletives in the margins of such papers as referred to the perfidious 'Achines'.

Ralegh now suggested he play a similar role. He convinced Sarmiento of the precariousness of royal favour and let him see that a Spanish pension had obvious attractions for a man in his position. His extravagant lifestyle required all the support he could find. Being in the pay of Spain would help keep him at the centre of English political life. Philip's interests would apparently be served while, as Sarmiento himself explained: 'Your Majesty's support, when occasion arose, might prevent him from falling.'

The hook was then more alluringly baited. First, Ralegh suggested to Sarmiento that he could use his influence at court to ensure as little as possible would be done to further the interests of Dom Antonio, the pretender to the throne of Portugal. Ralegh then made an offer which seemed to reinforce both what he had suggested was his relative financial insecurity as well as his apparent wish to betray his country's secrets. He offered to sell the King of Spain two ships from his fleet.

This was, perhaps, slightly less incredible than appears. Trading with the enemy was a recognized if disreputable part of sixteenth-century warfare. It was impossible wholly to prevent when national security was so dependent on free enterprise, and even the Spanish Armada was in part supplied with English cannon. The offer was, none the less, rash and essentially unrealistic. It suggests a melodramatic extreme of imagination that unsuited Ralegh to high politics and ensured that Elizabeth, in the ripeness of her judgement, never appointed him to a place on the Privy Council.

Nor was King Philip any more impressed. Even when Sarmiento was arrested by Protestants in France and was freed by Ralegh's influence, his view of his offer did not change. His ambassador's enthusiasm for the man likewise failed to move him. Mendoza reported to Madrid that Ralegh was now 'very cold' about England's preparations against the Armada 'and is secretly trying to dissuade the queen from them'.[10] Philip did not believe a word of it. Both Sarmiento and Mendoza may have thought they had secured a great prize for their master, but their vision had been distorted by Ralegh's glamour.

The King of Spain, seated at his remote desk in the Escorial, was more practised in such matters and altogether more circumspect about the promises of the would-be double agent. His reply to his ambassador is a masterly example of a great politician's scornful commonsense. 'As for [Ralegh] sending for sale the two ships he mentions,' Philip wrote, 'that is out of the question, in the first place to avoid being looked upon with suspicion in his own country . . . and secondly, to guard ourselves against the coming of the ships under this pretext being a feint or trick upon us (which is far from being improbable). But you need only mention the first reason to him.'[11]

Ralegh had handled the whole business very inexpertly. He had not secured a Spanish pension, while he had also let Sarmiento go without a ransom. What he had salvaged from this ineptitude, however, was something altogether more fantastic – something altogether more akin to the true workings of his imagination: a dream that was ultimately to contribute to his ruin.

'Many years since,' he was to write in 1596, 'I had knowledge by relation, of that mighty, rich and beautiful Empire of Guiana [supposedly present-day Venezuela], and of that great and golden city, which the Spaniards call El Dorado and the naturals Manoa.'[12] Sarmiento de Gamboa was the most likely source for this story. He had been among the conquistadors sent to capture Tupac Amaru, and he may well have given Ralegh the idea that the last of the Incas had taken refuge in a great, golden empire in equatorial America. Both men were probably influenced by the idea that gold, being the colour of the sun and supreme among metals, 'grew' more abundantly near the equator where the sun itself is closest to the earth. Sarmiento would also have known something of the many expeditions at once heroic and vile that the Spaniards had launched against the lands of the devastated Indians. Most dangerously of all, Ralegh could have heard from him the legend, first hatched in Quito during the 1540s, of El Dorado himself – the Golden One who lived in an as yet undiscovered empire of fabulous wealth.

The glittering figure of El Dorado was the product of the collective imagination of tough and desperate men, many of them illiterate, all of them superstitious, who had been drawn across half a world to lands where reality sometimes matched their most rapacious dreams. If El Dorado himself did not exist, he was easy to invent – even easier to believe in – and Sarmiento's description was doubtless close to that of the careful historian Fernandez de Oviedo who made plain he was only reporting the common talk in Quito.

Here men fired their imaginations with stories of a great prince living somewhere on the equatorial band that runs east through dense forests to the then unknown lands between the Orinoco and the Amazon. He went about, this prince, covered in gold dust fine as ground salt, his noble body otherwise naked and yet 'resplendent as a gold object worked by the hand of a great artist'.[13] He lived far exalted above the common lot of kings, the aesthete of his own perfection who felt 'it would be crude and common to put on armour plate of hammered or stamped gold, for other rich lords wear these when they wish.' To powder oneself with gold by contrast, 'is something exotic, unusual, novel, and more costly' – these are the dreams of an intensely aristocratic society – while with that effortlessness and abundance that lie at the heart of wish-fulfilment, El Dorado bathed himself nightly, washing away his wealth confident that in the morning his attendants would bathe him again in unguents and shower him with a limitless supply of gold.

'I would rather', de Oviedo added, 'have the sweepings of the chamber of this prince than the great meltings of gold there have been in Peru or that there could be anywhere on earth!' For such a dream men would cross oceans and traverse forests, unaware that their true goal lay at the dangerous jungle in their own minds. To be trapped there was to be lost indeed, and for the moment Ralegh himself sorted the fantasy away and employed his energies on seizing wealth through the more traditional means of privateering.

Privateering had assumed a renewed importance in the state of undeclared war that now existed between England and Spain. The official grant of letters of reprisal had become at best a formality. Gentlemen, merchants and pirates 'weary of their former trade' were all involved in an activity to which the Crown, when not actually concerned in person, was more than willing to turn a blind eye. This was an attitude particularly encouraged when Drake's triumphant return from his circumnavigation of the globe suggested how nationalism and enterprise could be blessed with spectacular rewards. At least a hundred vessels a year now became involved in a business that was 'grown a common traffic', and by 1590, Dr Julius Caesar, the judge of the Admiralty Court, felt able to declare 'that her Majesty hath gotten and saved by these reprisals since they began above two hundred thousand pounds.'

Caesar was referring, of course, only to such declared sums as went to the Exchequer. Private and undisclosed profits greatly exceeded this amount, and Ralegh's involvement in privateering placed him in the forefront of what was both a major industry and, as he was repeatedly to emphasize, an activity that kept English ships and crews alert and readied for any seaborne attack launched by Spain. As Vice-Admiral of the West, this was a major concern. Meanwhile, in the days before the sailing of the Armada itself, Ralegh's ships were conducting their own war against Spain. The report by John Evesham of the privateering expedition that captured Sarmiento da Gamboa provides a vivid account of what sailing on one of Ralegh's privateering missions involved.

Evesham and his fellow crewmen set sail from Plymouth during June 1586 in two of Ralegh's pinnaces: the tiny *Serpent* of thirty-five tons, and the delightfully named *Mary Sparke* of fifty tons. Evesham's account tells how, approaching the Azores, Ralegh's flotilla seized a small bark laden with 'sumacke' or dye and other commodities as well as taking prisoner the governor of 'St Michael's Island' and his retinue of Spaniards and Portuguese.[15] Flushed with this success, Ralegh's ships then sailed round to Graciosa and thence to the west of Terciera where they descried another likely prize.

Evesham describes events with beguiling frankness. 'Bearing with her', he declares, 'we found her to be a Spaniard; but at the first not greatly respecting whom we took, so that we might have enriched ourselves, which was the cause of this our travail, and for that we would not be known of what nation we were, we displayed a white silk ensign in our main top, which they seeing, made accompt that we had been some of the king of Spain's Armadas, lying in wait for English men of war.' By means of this ruse, Evesham and the rest of the crew managed to sail within gunshot distance of the Spaniards before their spurious white flag was suddenly hauled down and the red cross of St George run up in its place. The sight of this, Evesham declared, 'made them to fly as fast as they might, but all their haste was in vain, for our ships were swifter of sail than they.' No doubt on the orders of the hapless Sarmiento who was on board the Spanish ship, the crew cast ordinance, letters 'and the draft of the Straits of Magellan' into the sea. In the face of inevitable capture, Sarmiento ensured that at least the enemy English would not profit from the King of Spain's secrets.

More prizes were to follow. Two likely ships were seen which were chased to Graciosa where they anchored in the protection of the fort, hoping that contrary winds would keep the English away. Not so, as Evesham shows. 'We having a small boat, which we called a light horseman, wherein myself was, being a musketeer, and four more with calviers, and four that rowed, came near unto the shore against the wind.' The alarmed Spanish crew began hastily to transfer their cargo on to dry land and, as soon as the English came within musket shot, fired at them. The enemy's fire was returned. The English then boarded one of the Spanish ships which they found to be deserted and 'so we cut her cables, hoist her sails, and sent her away with two of our men.' The remainder of the English then rowed closer to the shore and boarded the second ship which they found to have 'only one Negro therein'.

The Spaniards began to hurl stones at them. Daunted neither by this nor by the fact that the wind had now dropped, Evesham and his men cut the cables of the second ship, hoisted her sails, and began to tow her out of the harbour behind their own little boat, 'the fort still shooting at us, and the people on land with muskets and calviers, to the number of one hundred and fifty or thereabout'. Evesham then describes his own piece of good luck. As the English privateers were towing their prize out of the harbour, he noticed the gunman on the enemy fort 'giving level to one of his great pieces'. The English were an easy target. Evesham at once aimed, fired, and 'the shot of my musket being a crossbow shot happened to strike the gunman of the fort to death.' They escaped without the loss of a single man. Then, in relative safety, and having taken a Spanish mainmast to replace the one lost by the *Mary Sparke*, they sorted away their prizes before letting the captured ships and the greater part of their crews go, 'leaving them all within sight of land, with bread and water sufficient for ten days if need were'.

The English crew had now got what they sought. For the ordinary Elizabethan privateer, boarding a prize was one of the highlights of an expedition, the golden moment when there fell to his share the various fruits of pillage. 'There is nothing that more bewitcheth them', wrote a contemporary, 'nor anything wherein they promise to themselves so loudly nor delight in more mainly.'[16] By custom if not in fact, anything found above deck, along with the personal belongings of the passengers and crew, were theirs provided that (with the exception of clothing) this did not exceed £2 in value. The rules also laid down that all such treasures – buckles, golden chains, small change, weapons and so on – should be placed round the mainmast and shared out according to rank. There was little hope of this among undisciplined, desperate men. If they had united to defeat the enemy, they now divided, each in the hope of doing better than his fellow. Brawling and turmoil were inevitable.

Evesham does not detail how the small profits were shared out on this expedition. He had greater excitements to report. The ships now turned for England, but in their passage home they came across a sight to set the pulses of any privateer racing. The man in the crow's-nest 'descried a sail, then ten sail, then fifteen' – a Spanish treasure fleet, in fact. The *Serpent* and the *Mary Sparke* turned to face what proved to be an armada of twenty-four enemy vessels, two of them over a thousand tons, and all 'laden with treasure, spice, and sugars'. Evesham and his companions gave chase for thirty-two hours, 'continually fighting with them and they with us'. The Spaniards covered themselves so well, however, that the English, eventually running low on powder, 'were forced to give them over against our wills, for all that we were all wholly bent to the gaining of some of them, but necessity compelling us, and that only for want of powder, without loss of any of our men, (which was a thing to be wondered at considering the inequality of number) at length we gave them over.'

They returned to a hero's welcome. In Evesham's phrase, 'We were received with triumphant joy.' Salutes were fired from land and sea. The quays of Plymouth were crowded, ringing loud with greetings from 'the willing hearts of all the people of the town, and of the country thereabout'. More guns were fired and more answered as they sailed to Southampton. They had secured for England an important Spanish prisoner and, for themselves, prizes of 'sugars, elephants' teeth, wax, hides, rice, brasill and Cuser'. Eventually they docked at Southampton 'where Sir Walter Ralegh, being our owner, rewarded us with our shares.'

While Ralegh's privateers were enjoying such spectacular success, his responsibilities as Lord Warden of the Stannaries were placing him in an extremely difficult position. An incident from 1586 – the year after Ralegh's appointment – illustrates clearly how the local duties of a great Elizabethan magnate could rapidly connect him to the savage competition of life at court and the more terrible threats posed by the international situation.

The position in the Netherlands had been rapidly deteriorating. Despite gifts and further supplements, Alençon had proved himself as incompetent as a commander as he had been supine as a lover. An attack launched against Dutch towns at the opening of 1583 had obliged him to flee disgraced to France where, eighteen months later, he died. Elizabeth considered it her duty to put on a show of mourning, but a few weeks later came altogether more grievous news: William the Silent, Prince of Orange, the great defender of Protestant liberty, had fallen victim to Spanish assassins. 'Under the shadow of thy wings we are protected,' he had whispered to Ralegh for the ears of the queen. Now Elizabeth was the sole great representative of the European Protestant cause.

It was a desperate role. She was a monarch threatened in the West by instability in Catholic Ireland, in the North by the claims of Mary, Queen of Scots, and across the Channel by a political situation which neither her inclinations nor her finances allowed her whole-heartedly to resolve. To support the Dutch, which she was morally and strategically obliged to do, made it appear that Elizabeth was prepared to defend the albeit legitimate rights of a people rebelling against an anointed king – Philip II, her greatest enemy. As always, Elizabeth played for time. Knowing the danger and recognizing the expense of involvement, she prevaricated until the arguments of the more ardent Protestants on the Council were reinforced by the actions of Philip himself. In April 1585, he seized English ships in Spanish harbours, tortured their crews, and made inevitable a terrible if undeclared war. Nearly seven thousand men were despatched to the Netherlands under the command of the Earl of Leicester.

Freed from the immediate and restraining influence of his patron-ess, Leicester crossed to the Netherlands with an entourage befitting a king. Here, despite orders, he accepted the title of Governor-General and revelled in the splendour of fireworks and triumphal arches, the gifts of jewels and the 'subtleties' of spun sugar that were loaded on to his banqueting tables. Elizabeth, when she discovered, was furious. The cost of her army was a terrible drain on her finances. The Dutch only reluctantly repaid their loans, and waste, incompetence and sheer dishonesty beggared the ordinary soldiers. The royal anger could barely be kept within bounds. 'Our express pleasure and commandment is that, all delays and excuses laid apart, you do presently, upon the duty of your allegiance, obey and fulfil whatso-ever the bearer hereof shall direct you to do in our name: whereof fail you not, or you will answer the contrary at your uttermost peril.'[17]

Leicester trembled, as he was meant to, and cast around for excuses. The campaign – insofar as it had achieved anything at all – had been hampered by those at home, he declared. In particular, the Lord Warden of the Stannaries had failed to send the contingents of West Country miners so essential for throwing up fortifications. The implication was that Ralegh, left behind in England when so great a part of the court had come abroad, was plotting Leicester's fall. Ralegh tried to placate the great, ageing grandee. 'You wrote unto me in your last letters for pioneers to be sent over; whereupon I moved her Majesty, and found her very willing, in so much as order was given for a commission; but since, the matter is stayed. I know not for what cause.'[18]

The most likely reason was that Elizabeth was desperately trying to economize, but Ralegh was well aware of the dangerous position in which he had been placed. His letter is a skilful example of his diplomacy. He had, first of all, to convince a great rival of his friendliness and trustworthiness, and so he was pleased to tell Leicester that he had arranged for one of the Earl's clients to be appointed to the office of the royal bakehouse. After this small gesture, Ralegh went on to assure Leicester that 'I have been of late very pestilent reported,' and he begged the Earl to ignore any 'poetical' or lying writer who tried to persuade him that Ralegh was concerned with anything other than 'to perform all offices of love, honour and service to you'.

Having established this point, Ralegh turned to squash an altogether more insidious idea: the notion that the failure to send men from the Stannaries somehow suggested he was a traitor in league with the enemy. 'Your Lordship doth well understand my affection towards Spain, and how I have consumed the best part of my fortune, hating the tyrannous prosperity of that estate, and it were strange and monstrous that I should become an enemy to my country and conscience.' Since any letters between the grandees of England were likely to be publicly shown or read by Walsingham's secret service, this was a judicious flourish on Ralegh's part, and a wholly honest one.

He had shown himself to Leicester as friendly, helpful and patriotic. Now he had to suggest quite the degree of influence he enjoyed as a royal favourite and appear a peacemaker. Ralegh added a postscript to his letter. 'The queen is in very good terms with you, and thanks be to God, well pacified; and you are again her "Sweet Robin".' This was the name Elizabeth had given Leicester in the years when it seemed she might marry him. Ralegh's use of it here suggests all is well while hinting at his own intimate knowledge of the queen's affections. The letter as a whole shows Ralegh doing what he could to resolve a tricky situation, but writing the letter was all he was allowed to do. Elizabeth would not let him go in person to the Netherlands to make his peace with the Earl. Rather, and in a time of national crisis, she prevailed on Walsingham to assure his fellow Privy Councillor that the royal favourite had spoken up for the Earl as enthusiastically as any of Leicester's known friends.

Ralegh appeared to have secured his position through elaborate paper diplomacy, but in fact Leicester's expedition had planted an altogether more dangerous threat to his security. At a wretched skirmish along the Yssel, near Zutphen, Sir Philip Sidney was struck in the thigh by a musket ball. He was carried back to his tent where he lay dying amid the sweet, putrescent smell of gangrene. The nation, when it heard the news, went into mourning, for Sidney had been the embodiment of the Elizabethan ideal: a poet, a warrior, a courtier and a devout Protestant. Three months after his death, when his father-in-law Walsingham had paid off his immense debts, his cortege made its slow way to St Paul's Cathedral. The whole of London turned out to watch, 'of which great multitude there were few or none that shed not some tears as the corpse passed them by'.[19]

Even Ralegh was moved to write an epitaph – the finest of his early poems. He paid lavish tribute to Sidney's virtues and then, with an honesty not always to be found in such works, confessed that only now, when Sidney's death had set him free, could he admit to the envy he had felt for the young man while he was living:

> To praise thy life, or wail thy worthy death,
> And want thy wit, thy wit high, pure, divine,
> Is far beyond the power of mortal line,
> Nor any one hath worth that draweth breath.
>
> Yet rich in zeal, though poor in learning's lore,
> And friendly care obscured in secret breast,
> And love that envy in thy life suppressed,
> Thy dear life done, and death hath doubled more.
>
> And I, that in thy time and living state,
> Did only praise thy virtues in my thought,
> As one that seld the rising sun hath sought,
> With words and tears now wail they timeless fate,[20]

But, in truth, Ralegh was not free from Sidney's influence, for in his will the dying hero had made a particular bequest: 'I give to my beloved and much honoured lord, the Earl of Essex, my best sword.'[21] In spirit at least, Essex was to be Sidney's heir, the new embodiment of the Elizabethan ideal, the great courtly aristocrat of the younger generation. Such a role and such ambitions posed a grave threat to the queen's favourite. For the moment however these were no more than a cloud on the horizon. Ralegh had other concerns, in particular his plans for a settlement in America.

CHAPTER SEVEN

Ralph Lane's Colony

Since the queen kept him in England busy with responsibilities, it was essential Ralegh find a leader for his second expedition to the New World. He turned naturally to his kinsmen among the West Country gentry. Sir Richard Grenville, eager to overcome the disappointment of Elizabeth's refusal to let him sail for South America, and out of the 'love he bore unto Sir Walter Ralegh, together with a disposition that he had to attempt honourable actions worthy of honour', accepted the post.[1] Although this was Grenville's first maritime command, Ralegh had once again called on the talents of an impressive figure.

Observed by the Spanish secret service, Grenville set sail from Portsmouth on 9 April 1585. He was the commander of a fleet of five ships and two pinnaces, and the fact that half the complement of six hundred men were soldiers suggests that the chief purpose of the venture was detailed reconnaissance and the establishment of a military base rather than permanent agricultural settlement. Such dangers as were envisaged came not from the natives but from the Spaniards, and this tends to confirm the impression that the chief concern of both Ralegh and Grenville was to create a strong base at a reasonable distance from Spanish Florida, a base that was sufficiently well equipped to protect vessels involved with privateering in the West Indies.

Grenville himself sailed on the queen's ship, the *Tiger*, which also carried the bulk of the supplies. Simon Fernandez inevitably accompanied him as pilot, while also on board were Philip Amadas and Ralph Lane, the latter an equerry of the queen's newly released from service in Ireland and now in command of the soldiers. This last appointment was perhaps an unfortunate one, for if Grenville had more than his share of arrogance, Lane too was to show himself as a hot-tempered and sometimes narrow man.

Nor was the crossing itself an easy one. Having passed the

Channel in safety, the fleet encountered so ferocious a storm off Portugal that one of the pinnaces was sunk and the fleet itself scattered. The *Tiger*, now on her own, made a rapid passage of less than a month, sighting Dominica on 7 May. Four days later, and clearly by pre-arrangement, Grenville dropped anchor off the south-west coast of Puerto Rico. Here, mindful of the Spanish presence, he built a camp for his men in which they would wait for the rest of the fleet.

The Spaniards themselves kept a wary eye on these proceedings and, after some days, sent out a troop of twenty horse. Grenville at once despatched twenty of his own men. The Spanish waved a white flag and a parley was arranged. It was a difficult encounter none the less. The English explained that they were only looking for water and victuals, and that they would prefer to set about this in a friendly way rather than with their swords. The Spanish 'yielded to our requests with large promises of all courtesy',[2] but when, two days later, Grenville marched out to their agreed meeting place, the Spaniards 'keeping their old custom for perjury and breach of promise, came not, whereupon our General fired the woods.'[3] Grenville then burned the fort he had built and readied his men to sail the next morning.

Piracy had been an important element in the expedition from the start. Among the stragglers in Grenville's fleet, the *Red Lion* seems to have been looking for prizes, while Grenville himself, having failed to obtain supplies from the Spaniards on Puerto Rico, set out to capture some Spanish vessels with which to augment his fleet. Having captured two of these, stripped the larger of its goods and then ransomed the crew, he sent Lane in the smaller Spanish ship to bring salt from a nearby bay. Lane discovered two mounds of this vital commodity lying in the sun, but when he began removing them he was approached by a force of Spaniards. Although these men did not attack, Lane was clearly shaken by the danger in which he had been placed, and when he returned to the *Tiger* he protested violently to Grenville. This was the first of a series of quarrels between the two men that was severely to threaten the well-being of the expedition.

Now re-equipped, Grenville headed for Hispaniola. Here, such were the ambiguous relations between England and Spain in the period immediately before the outbreak of war, that the governor treated him with the utmost courtesy. While the Spaniards them-

The 'Ermine Portrait' of Elizabeth I

Ralegh and his son Wat

Bess Throckmorton, Lady Ralegh

Top left: Robert Dudley, Earl of Leicester. *Top right:* The only alleged likeness of
Thomas Hariot. The identity of the sitter is not certain however.
Above left: Sir Richard Grenville. *Above right:* Robert Devereux, 2nd Earl of Essex

Above: Ralegh's birthplace, Hayes
Barton in Devon

Left: Elizabeth II: a reconstruction
of the three-masted ship familiar to
Ralegh

An engraving by Crispin de Passe celebrating victory over the Armada

Top left: John White's portrait of a Carolina Algonquian in body paint

Top right: A chief's wife with a young girl

Left: Native Americans eating

Top: Theodore de Bry's engraving of El Dorado being powdered with gold
Above: Ralegh and the aged Topiawari

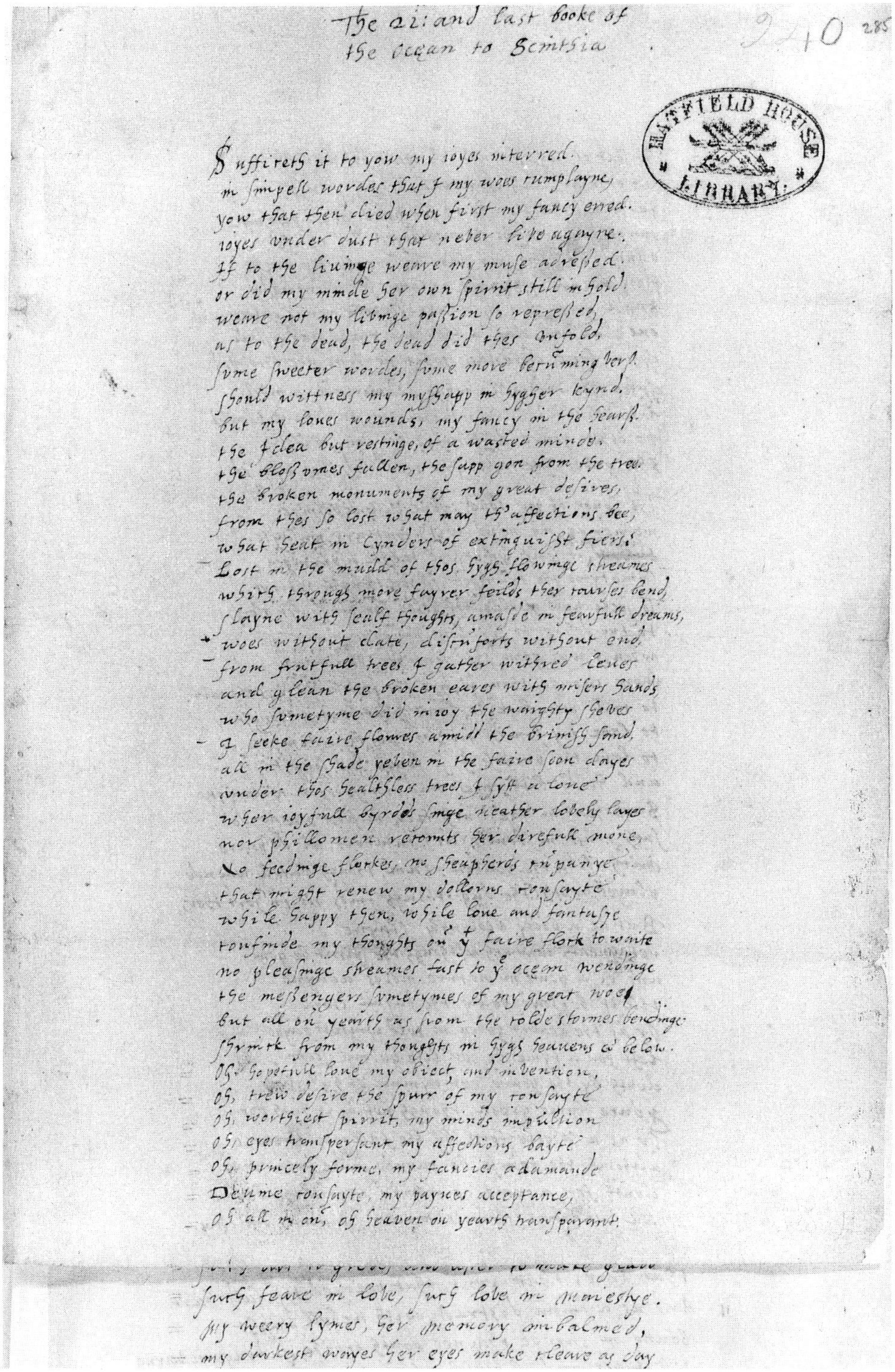

The 21: and last booke of
the Ocean to Scinthia

240 285

Sufficeth it to yow my ioyes interred,
in simpell wordes that I my woes cumplayne,
yow that then died when first my fancy erred,
ioyes under dust that never live agayne.
If to the livinge weare my muse adressed,
or did my minde her own spirit still inhold,
weare not my livinge passion so repressed,
as to the dead, the dead did thes unfold,
sume sweeter wordes, sume more becumming vers,
should wittness my myshapp in hygher kynd,
but my loves wounds, my fancy in the hearse,
the Idea but restinge, of a wasted minde,
the blossumes fallen, the sapp gon from the tree,
the broken monuments of my great desires,
from thes so lost what may th'affections bee,
what heat in Cynders of extinguisht fiers?
Lost in the mudd of thos hygh flowinge streames
which through more fayrer feilds ther courses bend,
slayne with sealf thoughts, amasde in fearfull dreams,
woes without date, discumforts without end,
from frutfull trees I gather withred leves
and glean the broken eares with misers hands
who sumetyme did inioy the waighty sheves
I seeke faire floures amidd the brinish sand.
all in the shade yeven in the faire soon dayes
under thos healthless trees I sytt alone
wher ioyfull byrdds singe neather lovely layes
nor Phillomen recounts her direfull mone,
No feedinge flockes, no sheapherds cumpunye
that might renew my dollorus consayte
while happy then, while love and fantasye
confinde my thoughts onn that faire flock to wayte
no pleasinge streames fast to the ocean wendinge
the messengers sumetymes of my great woes
but all onn yearth as from the colde stormes bendinge
shrinck from my thoughts in hygh heavens and below.
Oh hopefull love my object, and invention,
Oh, trew desire the spurr of my consayte
Oh, worthiest spirit, my minds impulsion
Oh, eyes transpersant my affections bayte
Oh, princely forme, my fancies adamande
Devine consayte, my paynes acceptance,
Oh all in on, oh heaven on yearth transparant.
[illegible]
such feare in love, such love in maiestye.
My weery lymes, her memory imbalmed,
my darkest wayes her eyes make cleare as day

Manuscript of 'The Ocean to Cynthia'

selves offered lavish hospitality, 'our men provided two banqueting houses covered with green boughs, the one for the gentlemen, the other for the servants, and a sumptuous banquet was brought in served by us all in plate, with the sound of trumpets, and consort of music, wherewith the Spaniards were more than delighted.'[4] It was a glorious occasion enjoyed by both sides and enlivened perhaps by Grenville performing his party piece, for it was reported that 'while at dinner or supper, he would carouse three or four glasses of wine, and in a bravery take the glasses between his teeth and crash them in pieces and swallow them down, so often times the blood ran out of his mouth without any harm at all unto him.'[5] Only when the English had departed with the commodities they needed, did the Spanish write to King Philip urging the dangers they saw to the homebound treasure fleet.

Grenville now sailed on past the Bahamas and up the Florida Channel. When he was preparing to anchor off the inlet by Wococon, however, disaster struck. As the *Tiger* was being brought through the difficult inlet in the Sound, she grounded in heavy seas. Here was a first indication that the length of coastline chosen by Ralegh's explorers was wholly unsuited for the type of ships he was proposing to send. Indeed, the area was later to be called the graveyard of the Atlantic.

This was an unfortunate beginning. In addition, valuable time had been lost in the West Indies, much of the stores had been spoiled, and it was now too late to sow crops. Harriot thought there was sufficient food for a mere twenty days and, realizing they would have to live off the land, lamented the 'want of English means for the taking of beasts, fish and fowl'.[6]

Furthermore, there was still trouble between various members of the expedition itself. Grenville in particular bitterly resented the accidents of Fernandez' pilotage, while Lane became the Portuguese's warm supporter. Indeed, Lane's hatred of Grenville was eventually to reach boiling point and he was to give vent to this in 'an ample discourse of the whole voyage'[7] presented to Ralegh. The document no longer exists, but the frayed nerves and wounded pride, the venomous resentments which the cramped conditions of a long voyage could inspire, are clear from a letter Lane wrote to Walsingham in which he begged to be excused from taking any office where Grenville himself was in overall command. His 'intolerable pride, and unsatiable ambition'[8] clearly drove Lane to the limits of his patience.

On 11 July Grenville led a party to the mainland. His purpose may well have been to search out a possible location for a second expedition due to be despatched under Amyas Preston and Bernard Drake. Grenville and his company were victualled for eight days, and they spent a week exploring the country round the mouth of the Pamlico River. Whatever its strategic purpose, their visits to a number of native settlements gave Grenville and his men a valuable insight into the Indians' way of life, and this last was beautifully recorded in John White's drawings.

White's portraits of Indian men and women show his observant and sympathetic eye for character and the nuances of tribal life. His studies inevitably reveal the influence of the north European mannerist school from which White had learned so much, but if this makes the artist a man of his time, the enduring value of his work lies in his depicting a wholly unfamiliar way of life without either exaggeration or condescension. To achieve such effects, he almost certainly worked by preparing a quick pencil sketch and marking this with notes on the colours he would use when developing his preliminary study into a completed watercolour. In this way, he could preserve something of the freshness of his initial observations while adding to them his accumulated knowledge of tribal dress and gesture. The results would help greatly in Ralegh's appreciation of the indigenous peoples of his territories and eventually to the European discovery of America itself.

White's drawings of Indian women were especially sympathetic. Harriot noted their 'small eyes, plain and flat noses, narrow foreheads and broad mouths',[9] and these are features White reproduced without reducing them to a stereotype. His drawing of the wife of a chief of Secoton shows her in a characteristic pose with her arms crossed in front of her. Her hair has been cut in a fringe over her forehead, the rest hanging in wisps around her ears and down her neck. As with many of the Indian women, her face, forehead, arms and calves have been tattooed with geometric patterns, while her neck has also been decorated with similar designs. She wears a double apron skirt fringed and ornamented with rows of beads that may perhaps be pearls.

Such costumes were worn by all girls above the age of about ten, female children younger than this wearing in the summer months only a little pad of moss over the divide of the legs which was supported by leather strings. In White's delightful drawing of 'a chief Herowans' wife of Pomeioc and her daughter', the little girl is shown carrying a doll dressed in Elizabethan costume, a touch that suggests the sympathy with which gifts for the natives were sometimes chosen.

White's drawings also portray a variety of males. An elderly man of Pomeioc, for example, is shown in his winter garment, standing with a large skin tied over one shoulder. This hangs down over his left arm to his knee, while his right arm emerges freely. Such skins were skilfully dressed 'with the hair on, and lined with other furred skins'[10] to protect against the cold. The man's hair has been shaved on both sides of his head to leave a crest down the centre of his skull, while, as a conventional sign of age, his thin beard has been allowed to grow.

Among the most vivid of White's studies of Indian men is his sketch of one showing 'the manner of their attire and painting themselves when they go to their . . . huntings or at their solemn feasts'. The figure who makes up this composition is posed in a position of authority reminiscent of European depictions of the aristocracy. The man stands with one arm raised and the other bent in such a way that the back of his hand rests against his hip. In his raised hand he supports a six-foot bow, his forearm protected by a bracer. A reed quiver is swung from his back, supported by what is probably a puma's tail. His hair, although cut like that of the other warriors White depicted, has been decorated with feathers. His body-painting is made up of lines and circles of red ochre.

One of White's most pleasing drawings shows an Indian couple eating. The sense of a relationship between the two people is suggested by the woman's confident smile and the man's alert, slightly questioning gaze. They are dressed in skins and are seated on a reed mat while their knees are drawn up level with their chests. Between them is a round, communal dish filled with what are probably maize kernels swollen by soaking and boiling. Although maize was the

Indians' staple diet, it was supplemented by the hunting of wild animals. Deer and rabbit were plentiful in season, and Harriot knew that the Indians hunted bears as well as living off a variety of wild fowl. Many of these last were skilfully drawn by White, as were the fish and crustaceans which supplemented the natives' diet.

Being coastal dwellers, the Indians were adept at setting wires to catch these harvests, and White's drawing of Indians fishing is one of his most interesting works. It provides information on the animals familiar to him from the area, the Indians' techniques for catching food, and his own particular methods of working up composite pictures from individual sketches. Swans and a flight of duck can be discerned in the sky, while the water is crowded with catfish, sharks and two types of crab.

The communal aspects of Indian life are best seen in White's drawings of two villages: Pomeioc and Secoton. The houses in both are of similar construction, although in Pomeioc they are carefully arranged within a circular palisade, while in Secoton they are arranged along a central thoroughfare. In both cases the houses are of pole and mat construction which, as Harriot noted, was 'used in many arbours in our gardens of England'.[11] To build them, long thin poles were inserted into the ground at intervals and then arched over and secured in the earth opposite to provide a curved roof. Cross-pieces were then secured along the length of the tunnel thus formed and the whole was covered with woven mats or bark which made up the walls and roofing. For the most part, the only permanent furnishings these houses contained were benches for sleeping, Indian life being largely led in the open air.

White's drawing of Secoton, again a composite work, reveals this clearly. The tribespeople are shown going about their daily activities around their thirteen longhouses. In particular, the various seasons of the maize harvest are shown: 'corn newly sprung' and green corn are growing in the fields nearest to the spectator, while in a third field is the ripe corn planted in May and ready for harvest by mid July. This has grown to a height of ten feet. Such a field would clearly be a great temptation to birds, and Harriot tells how a scaffold was erected amid the harvest on which was placed a little booth where one of the villagers sat to scare the birds away. Harriot adds picturesquely: 'for which cause the watchman maketh continual cries and noise'.[12]

[120]

Such detail brings the scene alive, while de Bry's engraving adds details omitted in White's surviving drawing. Sunflowers and pumpkins, for example, flourish abundantly, as does the indigenous *nicotiana rustica*, a plant different from the more famous *nicotiana tabacum*. Harriot himself described tobacco as 'an herb . . . the leaves thereof being dried and brought into powder, they [i.e. the Indians] used to take the fume or smoke thereof by sucking it through pipes made of clay into their stomach and head.'[13] Herein, for the Elizabethans, lay the novelty.

Tobacco itself had in fact been known to the English for its alleged medical properties for some years. Indeed, it had even been grown in England on a small scale since 1565. It was rarely smoked however, and while the story of Ralegh introducing tobacco to the country is a myth, what he did do was to make tobacco smoking a fashionable activity among courtiers and thus, in time, with the rest of the population. By the late 1590s, Londoners were alleged to be constantly smoking, and by early in the next century tobacco had become one of England's major imports and re-exports.

As the popularizer of a substance that was to achieve such commercial importance, Ralegh inevitably became linked to stories about tobacco. The anecdote of the surprised servant who poured a mug of ale (in some versions a pail of water) as he sat smoking is variously assigned to his periods of residence in England and Ireland. Another tale, and one which more interestingly reflects Ralegh's experimental mind, concerns the queen herself whom he had persuaded to take some puffs from his silver pipe.

As he boasted he could weigh the smoke thus exhaled, Elizabeth challenged him to do so. Ralegh, it is said, took some fresh tobacco from his pouch, weighed it, smoked it, placed the ashes back on the scales and subtracted the second reading from the first. Elizabeth, delighted by his ingenuity (if not by the fact that she had to pay up for the wager) allegedly replied that she had heard of men 'who turned gold into smoke, but Ralegh was the first who had turned smoke into gold.'[14] The incident is witty enough, but others were to pay the terrible price of the addiction Ralegh had popularized. Thomas Harriot, convinced of the medical advantages of smoking though he was, became one of the first victims of tobacco, eventually dying from a cancerous tumour of the nose.

For the Indians, tobacco had an important place in their religious rites, and White's drawing of Secoton shows a number of these ceremonies taking place. They appear to represent the cycle from birth to death. In the foreground of the left-hand side stands a longhouse 'wherein are the tombs of their kings and princes'.[15] A more detailed study shows the interior. Ten corpses have been laid side by side on a platform. White's accompanying inscription describes the process whereby their flesh had been removed, dried in the sun, and placed in the large matting baskets at the far end of the longhouse. The skeletons themselves had then been recovered in their original skin, stuffed with leather, and the whole rejoined to their mummified heads. Besides these mummies, although none too clearly drawn, is the god Kywash 'which is an image of wood keeping the dead'.[16] The area below the platform provided lodging for the priest who 'mumbleth his prayers night and day, and hath charge of the corpses.'[17].

In the foreground on the right-hand side of the drawing, by contrast, is the place where 'they meet with their neighbours to celebrate their chief solemn feasts.'[18] Here, in a detail clearly taken from another study, ten men and seven women are shown dancing anti-clockwise round a circle of posts topped with carvings of human faces. Many of the dancers carry either twigs or gourd rattles, while their skins have been heavily decorated. Two lines of squatting figures complete the scene which may well represent a corn ceremony.

Once the Europeans had arrived, such a way of life could not long go uncontaminated. Contact brought its own perils. On 13 July, Grenville's expedition moved up the river towards the village of Aquascogoc. While their reception here was not hostile, it does not seem to have been sufficiently encouraging for White to make any drawings. More importantly, while the Englishmen were on land, some of the more curious among the Indians came to examine their boats. Searching through the contents, they found a silver cup which seems to have belonged to Grenville himself. Its shine was irresistible, and they stole it.

The English party, unaware of what had happened, moved back to the Pamlico River and proceeded in the direction of Secoton. Here, a more friendly reception allowed White to make sketches. By 16 July however, when Grenville decided to turn back in the direction of Wococon, he discovered the loss of his cup. Amadas and his men were at once despatched to Aquascogoc to reclaim it. The local chief made some vague excuses, but the cup itself was not produced. In stupid revenge, Amadas and his men put the village and its crops to the torch. Violence had been introduced into what had once seemed an earthly paradise.

When Grenville returned from his expedition his men began to build their settlement on Roanoke Island. A visit from Granganimeo, again acting as Wingina's envoy, appears to have raised no objections to this (news of the devastation wrought to Aquascogoc appears not to have reached him) and the laborious process of preparing the site began. While trees were being felled and fortifications raised, Lane, keen to emphasize the benefits of settling the area, wrote glowing accounts to Hakluyt and Walsingham.

It had been decided to settle a little over a hundred men, and when, on 25 August, Grenville himself left, his task in Virginia appeared completed. Lane was clearly relieved to be free of him, but Grenville believed he could congratulate himself on the successful accomplishment of his mission. 'I have, God be thanked, performed the action whereunto I was directed as fully as the time wherein I have been absent from hence and all possibilities would permit me,' he later wrote.[19] Now he could sail home in the expectation of capturing prizes. Success in this would go a long way to proving that Walter Ralegh's settlement in Virginia was not only viable in itself but also provided an excellent base for privateering. A further rich prize to add to those taken on the passage out would indeed be a crowning achievement.

Grenville directed the *Tiger* in the usual track of the Spanish treasure fleet. The flotilla of thirty-three ships that had left Havana in July was now beyond his reach, but lagging in their wake rode the *Santa Maria*, newly out of San Domingo and poorly armed. Grenville chased her in the direction of Bermuda and then successfully attacked, according to one account boarding her 'with a boat made with boards of chests, which fell asunder, and sank at the ship's side as soon as ever he and his men were out of it.'[20] While the money and jewellery of those on board were handed over, Grenville himself investigated the cargo. To his immense delight he found the holds of the *Santa Maria* stuffed with gold, silver and pearls, sugar and spices. Grenville at once laid claim to these and then, transferring half the Spanish crew to the *Tiger*, proceeded to sail home in triumph, eventually docking at Plymouth.

Here Ralegh hastened to greet him. His American adventure, it seemed, had brought undreamed success. Rumours of a million ducats in prizes echoed round the port. For the queen, in whose name the settlement had been founded, there was an entire cabinet of pearls. Other investors, Grenville assured Walsingham, would get back their money with profit. Ralegh's enterprise had more than paid for itself, and with success like this, new investors could easily be found. Virginia seemed a promised land. The English had a toe-hold in the New World, and Ralegh's initiative, it appeared, had set the country's future on a new and prosperous course.

Such optimism was not so easily maintained behind the protective earthen banks of the fort on Roanoke. Here, in the seventy-foot square invisible from the sea, Lane and his 107 men had thrown up the buildings required for their settlement. Rush-roofed cottages were erected for the leading members of the party, while barrack-like structures had been built for the soldiers. There was a gaol equipped with leg-irons and a primitive form of handcuffs, as well as a store, an armoury, a treasury and a forge. Cooking was probably done communally. Such conditions implied a spartan, pioneering existence, and Lane, a strict disciplinarian and a man inured to the difficulties of life in Ireland, showed himself an effective leader in difficult circumstances. Only four of his men had died on the voyage out (a remarkably low figure for the time) while throughout the hard months on Roanoke itself he was to lose only four more.

He was in charge of a heterodox community. The greater part were in effect servants of Ralegh's who were paid a standard wage. They lived under Lane's military command and had no financial share in the expedition itself. Many of these men were soldiers, but a number of craftsmen were also essential to the settlement. These included carpenters, smiths, armourers, cooks, a baker and a brewer. Administrative staff were also required, especially the master of the stores who was responsible for victualling the company. In addition, there were the gentlemen who had sailed on the expedition, fifteen of whom made up an informal council Lane could consult when the need arose.

Many of these gentlemen had come in the hope of finding gold and silver. When such treasure was not immediately forthcoming, they began to grow sullen and resentful. Harriot's quick intelligence turned to sarcasm in the face of such behaviour. On his return to England, he was to write caustically that 'because there were not to be found any English cities, nor such fair houses, nor at their own wish any of their old accustomed dainty food, nor any soft beds of down or feathers, the country was to them miserable.'[21] Such words were intended to warn off dilettante colonists. American exploration was an arduous business, only to be undertaken by those of the strongest constitution.

From the start Lane's community faced a number of urgent problems. The first of these was the provision of food. The range of fruits and plants the settlers had brought with them from the West Indies failed for the most part to survive the voyage, while the seed corn they had carried from England went musty after the *Tiger* ran aground. Nor were soldiers used to a settled, agrarian way of life. Nothing was done during the early autumn months to provision the settlement from its own resources, with the result that, apart from such animals as they were able to hunt or trap, the English were dependent on the Indians for food.

This was clearly a dangerous position, and the tension it created between the two communities was, in the end, disastrously to affect their relations. For the moment, however, Wingina became the settlement's chief victualler. In the early months, he was ready to supply the English with quantities of maize and other food in return for the copper he and his people so prized. Under such conditions, Lane's men seem to have acquired sufficient food to tide them over the winter, even if their rations were spare and monotonous. The turn of the year and early spring, however, would see the position change.

Lane's second problem was to counter the growing disillusion that had set in and which he himself was beginning to share. There were mutterings of discontent, and Lane felt obliged to write that only 'the discovery of a good mine . . . or a passage to the South Sea, or some way to it, and nothing else can bring this country in request to be inhabited by our nation.'[22] He began to focus his energies on exploration. Late in 1585, he despatched a party north some 130 miles from Roanoke in the direction of Chesapeake Bay.

The expedition, which included Harriot and White as cartographers, set out in the pinnace and a number of canoes under the leadership of an unnamed captain. Harriot was later to recall that 'in all our travels, which were the most special and often in the time of winter, our lodging was in the open air upon the ground.'[23] They were sleeping rough in the previously unexplored country of the Chesapian Indians and, despite the hardships, its fertility delighted them. As Lane later wrote: 'The territory and soil of the Chespeans . . . for pleasantness of seat, for temperature of climate, for fertility of soil, and for the commodity of the sea, besides multitudes of bears (being an excellent good victual, with great woods of sassafras and walnut trees) is not to be excelled by any other whatsoever.'[24]

In this pleasant region, the explorers set up camp, siting themselves in a village situated some ten miles west of Cape Henry. Here they remained for some time, creating great interest among the local Indians, many of whom came to visit them and provided further information on Chesapeake Bay, on the Hampden Roads and the James River. This in turn was to stimulate interest in the vital matter of a deep-water harbour, while the expedition itself is important as the first recorded visit to what is now Virginia proper.

The map of the region drawn by Harriot and White was the first surveyed record of any part of North America, and was one of the colony's most significant achievements. The task, being a considerable one and subject to the most detailed instructions, occupied the two men from July 1585 to June 1586. They travelled widely in the area, White making his preliminary sketches both for the map and of the local peoples, while Harriot, accompanied by the two assistants who carried his equipment, plotted the details of his survey. The Englishmen seem to have encountered little if any opposition from the native Indians, mutual curiosity apparently marking their dealings. Harriot's ability to converse in Algonquinian dialect greatly helped in this, and his *Brief and True Report* is a most interesting account of contact between peoples.

The *Report* is marked throughout by high intelligence and optimism. Harriot first of all outlined the crops that might be grown in the region, its flora, fauna, and the natural resources future colonists might exploit. His most interesting discussion, however, is reserved

[126]

for 'the nature and manners of the people'.[24] Thus, while White portrayed their physical life, Harriot explored their ideas, beliefs, and responses to European culture.

Such an approach is characteristic of the Ralegh circle as a whole: questioning, curious and open-minded, yet constantly underscored by the notion that the centralized Protestant state was superior in achievements to native societies. These last would, in their turn, allegedly benefit from their contact with the Europeans, just as the colonists themselves would profit from their American discoveries. The purpose of the *Report* was to propagandize such a view and reinforce the aspirations of the Durham House group by recording Indian life in such a way 'that you may know how that they in respect of troubling our inhabiting and planting, are not to be feared.' Harriot's message is essentially one of benevolent paternalism secured by confidence in English military superiority.

Harriot was at pains to point out the relative feebleness of Indian armaments, the small size of their settlements, and the weakness of their political alliances. The advantage given by English firearms 'may be easily imagined', and Harriot illustrated this by mentioning that for the Indians 'the turning up of their heels against us in running away was their best defence.' He was keen to suggest that these people, although comparatively backward and easily subdued, are innately 'very ingenious' and 'show excellency of wit'. As a result, they would be all the more willing to submit amicably to the settlers: 'Whereby may be hoped if means of good government be used, that they may in short time be brought to civility, and the embracing of true religion.' Thus, while reserving the ability to conquer them by force, the English were to try to woo the Indians with the sweets of reason and the truths of their revealed faith.

Harriot carefully prepared the ground for this last and, for the Elizabethans, vitally important point. His analysis of the Indians' beliefs was not an objective description but an attempt to show how far these people had developed towards virtue by the force of natural reason. He suggests that although believing in the existence of a large pantheon of 'petty gods' who had fashioned from the waters 'all diversity of creatures that are visible or invisible', Indian thought had advanced sufficiently to recognize 'one only chief and great God, which hath been from all eternity'. Such monotheism was intended as both a tribute to the Indian intellect and an advantage to the missionary.

So too was another tenet of their faith which it is just possible they had derived from earlier contact with the Spaniards. Harriot writes thus: 'They believe also in the immortality of the soul, that after this life as soon as the soul is departed from the body, according to the works it hath done, it is either carried to heaven the habitacle of gods, there to enjoy perpetual bliss and happiness, or else to a great pit or hole, which they think to be in the furthest parts of their part of the world towards the sun set, there to burn continually: the place they call Popogusso.' Although insufficient wholly to root out criminal behaviour, 'this opinion worketh so much in many of the common and simple sort of people that it maketh them have great respect to their Governors.' This was a view that would be well received both in Durham House and the court.

Having prepared the ground for a favourable opinion of the Indians, Harriot went on to portray an altogether more subtle and personal version of an Elizabethan Englishman's first contact with an unknown culture. Harriot mentions in particular his 'special familiarity with some of their priests', one of whom White had painted in his characteristic 'short cloak made of fine hares' skins quilted with the hair outward'.[26] Harriot claimed that his probing revealed the priests' own doubts about their traditions and that this led them to seeing how their beliefs 'were not so sure grounded' as they had previously thought.

By the same token, Harriot declared that such conversations on religion led to the Indians having 'no small admiration of ours, with earnest desire in many, to learn more than we had means for want of utterance in their language to express'. But if this form of conversation was frustrated by problems with language, the mathematical instruments Harriot had brought with him seemed to provide a strong persuasion to believe in the Englishmen's God. This was a daring argument to propose, for while many in England itself looked on scientific enquiry as sinful – a Faustian pact – the faith of the Indians seemed to be enhanced by 'the virtue of the loadstone in drawing iron ... books, writing and reading, spring clocks that seemed to go off by themselves, and many other things we had.'

As a result of this kindling of Christian belief, Harriot says he felt able to preach the gospel 'many times and in every town where I came'. This is the earliest account of English missionary endeavour in North America, and Harriot supports his claim for success with some anecdotes that reveal the close and trusting relationship he built up with the natives. He tells that Wingina, for example, 'would be glad many times to be with us at our prayers, and many times call upon us both in our town as also in others wither he sometimes accompanied us, to pray and sing psalms.' Furthermore, when Wingina himself was 'so grievously sick that he was like to die', he 'sent for some of us to pray and be a means to our God that it would please him either that he might live, or after death dwell with him in bliss.'

This spreading of disease was as mysterious to the Elizabethans as it was to the Indians, and the fact that the colonists were immune to illnesses that proved fatal to the natives was a cause of wonderment on both sides. Harriot himself seems sincerely to have believed that such diseases only struck Indian villages that had proved themselves to be untrustworthy, while Wingina, thinking that this power to strike down enemies 'was the work of our God', begged Harriot to intercede with his deity so that he might punish the Indians' enemies.

Harriot urged that what his God truly wanted was that all men should live in harmony and forgiveness. None the less, when by coincidence Wingina's enemies did indeed fall victim to the white men's diseases, awe of the Englishmen was greatly enhanced. 'This marvellous accident', Harriot declared, 'wrought so strange opinion of us, that some people could not tell whether to think us gods or men, and the rather because that all the space of their sickness, there was no man of ours known to die, or that was specially sick.'

Because of this power to bring fatal sickness and the fact that 'we had no women amongst us', Harriot saw how some of the Indians 'were of the opinion that we were not born of women, and therefore not mortal, but that we were men of an old generation many years past there risen again to immortality.' Others believed more Englishmen, hovering for the moment as invisible spirits in the air, would reincarnate themselves in the bodies of dead Indians.

Harriot dutifully recorded these ideas, but in the end his true purpose was to urge Ralegh's colonization of America, and at the close of his work he turned the superstition of the Indians to the

[129]

political advantage of the English, urging that 'there is good hope they may be brought through discreet dealing and government to the embracing of the truth, and consequently to honour, obey, fear and love us.' For all his scientific curiosity and undoubted sympathy for the native peoples, the illusion of benevolent imperialism was never far from Harriot's thought.

Lane too was determined to advance English interests, but where Harriot's approach was that of a humane intellectual, Lane's plans reveal him as a purely militaristic colonizer. By the time Harriot, White and the northern reconnaissance party had returned to Roanoke in the late February or early March of 1586, Lane had become attracted to various plans of exploration, in particular the possibilities opened up by the broad, deep waters of the Albermarle Sound into which the Chowan River flowed. He had learned from the local Indians about the Chowan tribe and their famous leader Menatonon, and he was now determined to penetrate far into Chowanak territory.

Although relations between him and Wingina were more strained than he realized, he confided his plans to the chief who promptly lent him guides. Taking the pinnace and a couple of wherries, Lane proceeded with a number of his men up the Chowan River to where it 'groweth to be as narrow as the Thames between Westminster and Lambeth'.[27] Having arrived at the Chowanak village, Lane burst in on the assembly of Indians he found gathered there. Unknown to him, Wingina, increasingly frustrated by the pressures placed on him by the colonists, was now arranging in secret for a confederacy of the neighbouring tribes to attack and destroy the English. It may have been that representatives of the Weapemeoc and Moratuc tribes were now conferring with Menatonon about this alliance. Certainly, a meeting was in progress. Lane, nothing daunted, at once seized the crippled chief and clapped handcuffs on him. Eventually, and probably through the efforts of Manteo acting as interpreter, the two men reached some sort of understanding.

Menatonon was, according to Lane, 'a very grave and wise man, and of a very singular good discourse in matters concerning the state, not only of his own country . . . but also of his neighbours round about him as well far as near'.[28] Lane and the Indian chief held long conversations over several days, and by the end of these the Englishman's imagination had been fired by two new projects. The first concerned a great ruler, rich in pearls, who was said to live on an island by the sea, an island that could be reached after a seven-day journey by boat and on foot. To prove his existence, Menatonon presented Lane with a rope of fire-blackened pearls he claimed to have traded for a quantity of copper. Lane believed the chief was directing him towards Chesapeake Bay, and he resolved to follow up his suggestion when English reinforcements arrived.

Meanwhile, another opportunity seemed altogether more alluring. Menatonon confirmed that far up the Roanoke River there was a tribe of Mangoak peoples so rich in copper that they beautified their houses with the metal. In addition, thirty or forty days' canoe journey beyond this place, Lane would come to the head of a great river flowing into the sea. It was from this region, Menatonon declared, that the Mangoaks obtained a copper that was 'soft and pale' and altogether unlike the metal familiar to the English. To Lane's excited imagination, this sounded like gold. Furthermore, Menatonon's description of a great sea raised hopes that a passage might here be found to the Pacific. If men could cross from one ocean to another by traversing the narrow isthmus of Panama, why could they not do so here? Unaware of the vast landmass of the American continent, Lane felt that Roanoke might be an outpost on the route to the East. Here, surely, was the promise of rich rewards for Ralegh's expedition, and these possibilities he would now explore.

Lane admired Menatonon but he did not trust him. So powerful a tribal leader could easily wipe out his own settlement and he therefore decided to take the chief's son Skiko as a hostage for his father's good behaviour. The young man was sent back in the pinnace to Roanoke while Lane himself conferred with his men about exploring further along the river. Having resolved that 'whilst there was left one half pint of corn for a man' they would not turn back, thirty armed soldiers, accompanied by two powerful mastiffs, rowed their way against the strong and unknown currents of the Roanoke River in a desperate search for gold.

Two or three days upstream, exhausted and hungry, their mission had to be abandoned. Possibly forewarned by Wingina that Lane meant them harm, the Indian peoples off whom the Englishmen had hoped to live disappeared along with their supplies. War cries echoed eerily from the distant forest and a hail of arrows was released by an invisible foe. Having pitched camp for the night, the Englishmen resolved to return to Roanoke. Only the leaves of the sassafras tree offered them sustenance – those and the two mastiffs which were now butchered for their meat.

Lane returned to Roanoke embittered and convinced that Wingina had double-crossed him. The disaffection between the two peoples was approaching its crisis. Wingina himself was growing increasingly exasperated by the settlers' constant demands for food, and he began to spread rumours that Lane and his men had died of starvation on their expedition. He also began talking ominously of deserting Roanoke itself and so leaving the rest of the English colony to starve. Who, he asked, was this Christian God who could not save his followers from such a fate?

The sudden return of Lane seemed to Wingina almost miraculous, and the horrified chief realized that he had been proved disastrously wrong. The elders of his tribe began to whisper that the English must be dead men come back to live on earth awhile. They were spirits who must be served since they could not be destroyed. The guides Wingina had sent with Lane also told him of the Englishman's strength and skill, the authority he wielded. Then, as if to confirm these, Menatonon himself sent Lane a gift of pearls in the hope of ransoming his son, escorting his offering with twenty-four braves and a tribal chief whom he commanded 'to yield himself servant and homager to the great Weroanza of England and after her Sir Walter Ralegh'. Half a world away – invisible and unknown – Ralegh and his queen were honoured as powers to be propitiated and perhaps even feared. Momentarily cowed, Wingina agreed to set traps for fish around Roanoke Island, while at the end of April he sowed the ground with sufficient corn to last the English settlers a year. Such actions, Lane declared, 'put us in marvellous comfort'.

Their ease was short-lived. Spring and early summer were invariably difficult times for the Indians, their stores of maize having run low. The presence of a hundred Englishmen 'daily sending to him for supply of victual' made intolerable demands, and Wingina rightly believed that Lane would use force if necessary to feed his men. He knew that his chief responsibility was to his tribe and not to these cormorant aliens, much as his elders had cautioned him to revere their power. Desperate to preserve his people, Wingina laid plans which Menatonon's son, still in captivity, betrayed to Lane.

Skiko told him how Wingina, who had now withdrawn to the mainland, was declaring himself sufficiently rich in the copper traded by the settlers to bribe the local tribes to rally to his cause and join him in his village under the pretext of a religious ceremony. Having assembled such forces, he would then launch a combined attack on the English. Wingina himself would arrange some excuse for his men to row across to Roanoke where, having arrived, they would wait for nightfall when a score of braves would fire the settlers' buildings, murder their occupants, and signal the remaining braves to cross and overwhelm the colony entirely.

Lane decided to take the initiative. He despatched half his settlers over the area, apparently to search for food and keep a watch for the arrival of English reinforcements. Then, with his defences seemingly weakened, he sent word to Wingina that he wished to discuss the purchase of provisions and the loan of some guides for foraging expeditions. Apparently playing into the chief's hands, Lane resolved on a daring night attack. His remaining men, the white tails of their shirts hanging out to identify them in the dark, stole across to the mainland to seize the Indians' canoes. But the plan misfired. One of the Indian crews resisted and two of its men were killed. Shots rang out and, the English attack having been surprised, the Indians themselves melted into the darkness.

Lane, determined to assert his authority, changed his tactics. The following morning he boldly crossed over to Wingina's camp and began to complain of the previous night's events, claiming it was he who had been attacked. When he had stormed to the middle of the surprised Indian group, he suddenly shouted his watchword: 'Christ our victory!' Twenty-seven English guns were fired at the braves. Wingina himself was injured and, as he crawled away towards the trees, so Lane's boy fired on him again, this time hitting him in the buttocks. The wounded chief eventually disappeared into the woods where he was pursued by one Edward Nugent and a colleague. After a long pause, the Englishmen reappeared carrying the chief's severed head. The godlike visitors had finally proved their power.

With the Indian threat apparently contained, the Englishmen waited anxiously for reinforcements. Ralegh had indeed planned to send such a relief expedition, but the accidents that befell it and the events surrounding the final departure of Lane and his company from Roanoke show the immense difficulties, both practical and political, which for the moment stood in the way of American colonization.

By June 1585, Bernard Drake was ready to sail for Roanoke in the *Golden Royal* with supplies and reinforcements. The unofficial outbreak of hostilities with Spain in that year, however, meant he was needed for matters altogether more urgent. Drake was suddenly ordered to Newfoundland, there to warn the English fishing fleet not to sail with their catch to Spanish ports. Ralegh also victualled another ship intending that she should sail for Roanoke with all manner of provisions for the supply and relief of his colonists. Although she was supposed to reach Roanoke by the beginning of April 1586, the ship actually arrived much later, delayed perhaps by a call in the West Indies.

Finally, a large-scale expedition was planned under the leadership of Sir Richard Grenville. This was intended, among other things, to raise the number of colonists to over three hundred. Grenville's voyage was an unlucky one, however, further delayed by his privateering activities. When finally he dropped anchor off Roanoke itself, Grenville found neither the supply ship sent by Ralegh nor the colonists themselves. It was a moment of intense worry and disappointment. He did what he could, travelling up country to search for his fellow Englishmen. Finding the region deserted, but unwilling to abandon English claims over it, he left fifteen of his own men and a supply of stores on Roanoke 'and so departed to England'.

But what had happened to the colonists on Roanoke? The truth was they had taken the first opportunity that presented itself of leaving the island and, in so doing, had become involved with the greatest of Elizabethan seamen, Sir Francis Drake. With the fierce increase in hostilities between England and Spain widening to an open Atlantic war, Drake had been sent on the long-planned expedition against Spanish bastions in the West Indies and North America. Learning that the Spaniards intended to attack the English in Virginia, he resolved to bombard their base in Florida and then leave many of his captives with Lane to reinforce his settlement. On 8 June, Drake's ships were sighted by one of Lane's men. A great bonfire was lit to advise Drake of the colony's whereabouts, and Drake himself sent out a skiff to establish contact.

Now, to his great surprise, Drake learned of the failure of any of Ralegh's relief expeditions to arrive. He at once wrote to Lane generously offering his full support both in the supply of provisions and ships. Eventually, on 11 June, the two men met, and Drake was immediately apprised of the disheartening condition to which the colonists had been reduced. Here were men enfeebled, short of food, disappointed at their failure to discover gold, and reduced to the sort of menial life they could have enjoyed in England with far greater security.

Lane himself evidently wanted to return home, but did not wish to appear to have abandoned his post. He agreed with Drake, however, that 'a number of weak and unfit men' should be sent back to England. He also arranged with his great visitor that sufficient sailors, craftsmen, shipping and victuals should be left to support the proposed expedition to Chesapeake Bay. Drake generously lent Lane his own ship the *Francis* for this purpose and, on 13 June, a number of Lane's men boarded the *Francis* to help with the transfer of supplies.

Suddenly a tremendous storm broke. Thunder and rain, along with 'hailstones as big as hen's eggs', fell from the skies. For three days the water-spouts that rose on the sea were so great that it appeared 'as though heaven and earth would have met'. Many of the smaller boats in Drake's fleet were smashed on the Banks, while it seemed that the anchors of his bigger vessels might not hold. The ships were consequently forced to put out to sea. Three days later, when this unnaturally early hurricane had passed, all the larger ships save one returned. The *Francis* however, along with some twenty of Lane's men, had sailed far away.

With this desertion, a change of plan became essential, and Lane gratefully accepted Drake's offer that he and the remaining colonists on Roanoke should be shipped home. The men, relieved that their ordeal would soon be over, evacuated the settlement with unseemly haste. Harriot and White gathered together the voluminous records they had made of their journeys, but many of their bundles were thrown overboard by sailors caring more to make space for their fellow men than for the writings of a couple of intellectuals. In the scrimmage, the string of pearls Menatonon had given Lane was also lost. Worst of all, three men were left behind by accident. Of the remaining colonists, some were placed aboard the *Primrose*, and others on the *Elizabeth Bonaventure* which eventually docked at Plymouth on 28 July 1586. Ralegh's Roanoke adventure, it seemed, had collapsed amid desperation and sheer bad luck.

CHAPTER EIGHT

'The Best Hated Man in the World'

To his intense disappointment over the failure of the Roanoke colony was added the loathing in which Ralegh was now held by the greater part of the population at home. His exploitation of his monopolies, his bearing and his conspicuous wealth were making him, as one observer reported: 'the best hated man in the world'.[1] Others swelled this chorus. One of Burghley's informants wrote of Ralegh: 'No man is more hated than him; none cursed more daily by the poor of whom infinite numbers are brought to extreme poverty by the gift of cloth to him.'[2] The monopoly rankled. So, too, did Ralegh's arrogance. The biographer Thomas Fuller gives a suggestion of what this last was like when he claimed that Ralegh was wont to say: 'If any man accuseth me to my face, I will answer him with my mouth; but my tail is good enough to return an answer to such who traduceth me behind my back.'[3] John Aubrey noted Ralegh's 'awfulness and ascendancy in his aspect over other mortals'[4] and claimed he would make a prince cower. Tarelton the jester, pointing to Ralegh and Elizabeth as they sat watching a play, exclaimed: 'See, the knave commands the queen!'[5]

In this he was wrong. Ralegh depended entirely on the royal favour (it was the obverse of his pride) and Elizabeth's bounty was still showered on him. In the same year as he received the Babington lands, she appointed him Captain of her Guard. This was an honorary position of great prestige, carrying with it a uniform allowance of 'six yards of tawny medley at thirteen shillings and fourpence a yard, with a fur of black budge, rated at £10'.[6] So attired, Ralegh was in charge of that corps of handsome young men who, carrying their gilded battleaxes, escorted the queen to chapel and surrounded her on great public occasions. They served her food, delivered her messages, and delighted her eye.

Good looks, indeed, were an essential qualification, and the story was told of a father who wished to place his eighteen-year-old son in the corps. 'I put in no boys,' Ralegh replied.[7] The father none the less insisted Ralegh see the youth, and so handsome was he that 'Sir Walter Ralegh swears him immediately, and ordered him to carry up the first dish at dinner, where the queen beheld him with admiration, as if a beautiful young giant had stalked in with the service.' But there was far more to the post than the arrangement of such royal pleasures as these. The Captaincy of the Guard gave Ralegh ready access to the queen – a better access, he was to say, than some councillors enjoyed – while he was also the man in whom Elizabeth vested her personal safety. The post was a token of her highest esteem.

1587 also saw the launching of a great new vessel, the *Ark Ralegh*. She was one of the largest and most advanced ships of her day. Unlike the swift and tough little privateering vessels, the *Ark Ralegh* was an imposing ship designed so that she 'should carry such grace and countenance as to terrorize the enemy'.[8] She had three banks of guns, four masts instead of the usual three, and additional sails or 'topgallants' made after the new pattern recently introduced by Sir John Hawkins. Her name proclaimed her owner's ambition, for Ralegh was later to write of Noah's ark that there was never a ship 'so capacious nor so strong to defend itself . . . as the ark of Noah, the invention of God himself'.[9] In such ways as this, Ralegh remained the great courtly actor, the improviser of renaissance magnificence, his immense range of activities serving his queen while exulting his own status.

Such a role was underscored by insecurities both private and political. The tragedy of Mary, Queen of Scots, was nearing its climax. Walsingham's espionage had brought matters to the state where this feckless woman would have to stand trial. But the execution of a sovereign placed the severest strain on Elizabeth herself. She had hoped the deaths of Babington and his associates might have appeased public opinion, but once Parliament became involved, Mary's execution was inevitable. Elizabeth insisted on supervising every detail of her trial, much to Walsingham's irritation, and when sentence at Fotheringay had been delivered he wrote with great satisfaction that the judges had unanimously found Mary guilty of conspiracy and condemned her as 'an imaginer . . . of her Majesty's destruction'.[10]

Elizabeth was thrown into personal agony and indecision. Parliament urged the machinery of execution into motion and, after a two-day debate, resolved on Mary's death. The queen was petitioned to sign the warrant, twenty peers and forty MPs presenting their request at the palace of Richmond. Elizabeth delivered them a speech in which she claimed she would willingly forgive Mary's crimes. She had the prerogative of mercy, and her personal tone gave her words the appearance of sincerity. 'I have had good experience and trial of this world,' she declared. 'I know what it is to be a subject, what to be a sovereign, what to have good neighbours and sometimes to meet evil-willers.'[11] She was deeply conscious, too, of her public responsibilities. 'We princes are set on stages, in the sight and view of all the world duly observed . . . It behoveth us to be careful that our proceedings be just and honourable.'

On the terrible stage of Elizabethan politics, the queen was the greatest actress. But still she prevaricated. Was there, she asked Parliament, no alternative to the execution? She was again petitioned by the Members, and again she tried to delay. The formal proclamation of the sentence was written and rewritten. Parliament was adjourned for ten weeks during which Elizabeth steeled herself finally to putting her name to the warrant. When execution had been done and was announced by the pealing of church bells, she broke down. For several days she had neither eaten nor slept. Hatton and Walsingham were refused her presence. Burghley was in disgrace and terrified by the wildness of the queen's thoughts as she reacted to the crisis. She vowed to execute Secretary Davison who had seen that the warrant was carried out.

And now Essex, impulsive and quixotic, tried to intervene on Davison's behalf, thereby revealing that lack of political judgement which, in the end, was to ruin him. He wrote to Mary's son, the Scots King James, begging him to take up Davison's case. But James was too canny to involve himself, especially at the behest of a young man who, for the moment, had no political influence. Elizabeth herself, however, was almost certainly aware of these proceedings, and she was prepared to forgive them as a young man's indiscretion.

Amid so much strain and the sheer relentless gravity of high politics, Essex's impetuosity was delightful to her, a token of pleasure in the world. By the spring of 1587, she was stretching out her hands to warm them at his youth. She made him Master of Horse, a post worth £1500 a year. The young man accepted with alacrity. His charms might yet win him a fortune. He plied them remorselessly, and the queen was willing to be beguiled. 'When she is abroad, nobody near her but my Lord of Essex and, at night, my Lord is at cards, or one game or another with her, that he cometh not to his own lodging till the birds sing in the morning.'[12] In 1587, Elizabeth was fifty-four, Essex just twenty.

Ralegh was acutely aware of the threat so suddenly posed to him:

> Fortune hath taken thee away, my love,
> My life's joy and my soul's heaven above;
> Fortune hath taken thee away my princess,
> My world's delight and my true fancy's mistress.[13]

In the treacherous game of courtly passion, the worshipper of the Virgin Queen stood bereft. Essex, blessed by Fortune's gifts of birth and youth, was usurping his place and, as a poet, Ralegh felt he could only turn aside from such worldliness and haughtily proclaim his moral superiority. The role is the measure of the man, and Ralegh's poem is a sharp, elegant trifle in a game of deadly seriousness.

The position was indeed becoming intolerable, and in July 1587, when Elizabeth was on her annual summer progress and had reached North Hall, the seat of the Earl of Warwick, matters came to their first crisis. Essex informed the queen that his sister Dorothy was staying there. As Dorothy Devereux, she had, some years before, contracted a runaway marriage with Sir Thomas Perrot. Elizabeth strongly disapproved of such proceedings. The moral tone of her court was a matter of the utmost importance to her, and hasty alliances made without her consent invariably resulted in punishment. Elizabeth now ordered the woman be confined to her room.

Without any grounds for the accusation, Essex blamed his great rival for this insult. He rounded on the queen, accusing her of punishing his sister 'only to please that knave Ralegh'.[14] The Captain of the Guard, meanwhile, stood silently by the door, watching the young earl make a fool of himself. 'It seemed she would not well endure anything to be spoken against him,' an outraged Essex wrote, 'and taking hold of one word, "disdain", she said there was no such cause why I should disdain him.' This response made Essex so angry that, as the queen sat impassively, enjoying his tantrum, he proceeded to pour out a torrent of abuse.

Asserting his rank as a hereditary earl, Essex reminded Elizabeth that Ralegh was a mere commoner. Here, surely, was a reason for Essex 'to disdain his competition of love'. Furthermore, he wondered if he could easily bring himself to pay court to a woman 'that was in awe of such a man'. Knowing perfectly well that Ralegh could hear him, and assuming his anger would impress his listener as much as it clearly did himself, Essex continued, 'I spake, what of grief, and choler, as much against him as I could'. Then, rising to a climax of petulance: 'I told her . . . I had no joy to be in any place but loathe to be near about her when I knew my affection so much thrown down, and such a wretch as Ralegh highly esteemed of her.'

By now Elizabeth had had enough. Essex might very well disdain Ralegh for his humble origins, but the stripling earl would do well to look to his own forbears. Was not his mother that 'she wolf' Lettice Knollys who had secretly married Elizabeth's beloved Leicester and who was a woman the queen had vowed would never show her face in the court again? Essex, cowed by the queen's fury, began to mumble his apologies. His inconvenient sister could, of course, be sent away. But if she were, he declared, his anger again getting the better of him, family honour required that he go with her.

He sent his servants to pack his sister's belongings, and while the great trunks were being carried through the darkness of the night-time countryside, the young earl himself hurried past on his horse. He was upset, angry. He would make for the Low Countries and prove himself a hero on the field of battle. He was all for death or glory now. 'If I return, I will be welcomed home; if not *una bella morire* is better than a disquiet life.' He stopped overnight in London and then made for the Kent coast. On his way to Sandwich, he was overtaken by Robert Carew with a message from the queen. He was forgiven and was to return to court. There would be a tender reconciliation. He accepted. 'But if the queen try to drive me to be friends with Ralegh,' she would fail. Any efforts in that direction 'rather shall drive me to many other extremities'.

But now, as the year wore on, there were problems to face altogether more grave than the petulance of a favoured young earl. The sea war with Spain that had been mounting in ferocity since 1585 was about to reach its crisis. The great battle which would decide who had control of the Atlantic was imminent.

Walsingham's spy network had long been informed of the preparations being made by Philip for the invasion of England, and in the spring of 1587 Sir Francis Drake was despatched to Cadiz, there to destroy the royal flagship – an enormous vessel of 1500 tons – along with twenty-three other ships great and small, as well as the coopers' stores in which water and essential provisions were carried. It was a devastating blow to Philip's schemes, but it did not blunt his purpose. He had, along with the Marquis of Santa Cruz, planned a fleet totalling 77,000 tons which would carry an army of 60,000 to head the invasion.

But in February 1588, Santa Cruz died and was replaced by the Duke of Medinia Sidonia who modestly claimed that he had 'neither aptitude, ability, health nor fortune for the expedition'.[15] Both men, however, regarded the Armada primarily as a military matter, and by 5 May 1588, 130 ships had been collected to transport 19,290 troops. Twenty of these ships were galleons, and four immense armed merchantmen. They were crewed by 8,350 sailors and 2,080 galley slaves. They were armed with 2,630 guns. They made up the largest fleet Europe had ever seen.

Once launched, it was planned the Armada would meet at sea with Parma's crack troops from the Low Countries (there was no adequate deep-water port available) and prepare to invade. Ralegh regarded such strategic thinking with contempt. 'To invade by sea upon a perilous coast, being neither in possession of any port, nor succoured by any party, may better fit a prince presuming on his fortune than enriched by understanding,' he wrote. Such an ability to cut to the heart of the enemy's weakness made Ralegh welcome when he attended the Council of War.

Present were Lord Grey, Sir Richard Grenville, Ralph Lane (who had been appointed Muster General of the Forces) along with the Governors of Guernsey and the Isle of Wight. Many of these men had been involved with Ralegh both in privateering and his Roanoke expeditions, and to their expertise was now added that of two mighty Elizabethan soldiers: Sir Roger Williams and 'Black John' Norris, a man from a family long favoured by the queen and a warrior in whose defence Ralegh had spoken when Norris had fallen out with Leicester. Their discussion centred principally on the military defence of the realm, and it is in this role – and as the leading grandee of the West Country – that Ralegh was to play his most important part in the Armada terror.

He laboured with tireless energy. Two areas required his special attention. Parma's troops in the Low Countries might have landed on the east coast, and Ralegh travelled from the maritime towns of Essex to King's Lynn surveying the fortifications, noting where more would have to be done, and advising the leaders of Norfolk on the defence of their beaches. Given the urgency of the situation, the paucity of supplies and, above all, the immense difficulties of communication in Elizabethan England, Ralegh gave priority to defending the country's deep water harbours. Turning his attention to the West, he then begged the Privy Council for cannon to defend Portland and Weymouth.

Ralegh set up his own headquarters in Plymouth where he could command authority as the Vice-Admiral, and began his preparations for the mustering of several thousand men. Despite the intensity of the national crisis, he met with the old problem of deeply entrenched local loyalties, the reluctance of the regions to support the realm. Ralegh described his problems in a memorandum to Burghley, telling him he had:

> attended the Earl of Bath and confered with the deputies of Devon and Cornwall for the drawing together of two thousand foot and two hundred horse, and I find great differences of opinion among them. Some are of the opinion that this burden will be grievous unto the country standing at this time void of all traffic, the subsidy not being yet gathered and the past musters having been very chargeable. Sir John Gilbert, Sir Richard Grenville and the Earl himself being more zealous both in

religion and her Majesty's service, who have always found a
ready disposition in their divisions and willingness to bear whatsoever shall be thought meet for Majesty's service by their
people, are of opinion that the matter and service will be very
feasible.[17]

Employing his relations in this way, and by dint of cajoling, detailed
administration and sheer hard work, the required quantities of men
were assembled. By January 1588, Ralegh, as Lord Lieutenant of
Cornwall and Lord Warden of the Stannaries, had mustered the
largest army these counties had ever raised: 5,560 men, 1,395 shot,
633 corslets, 1,956 bills and halberds, 1,528 bows, 4 lances and 96
light horse.

Meanwhile, the English navy was assembling, and leading it was
the great *Ark Ralegh*, newly named the *Ark Royal*, the first of that
glorious line. 'I think her', wrote Admiral Lord Howard of
Effingham, 'the odd [best] ship in the world for all conditions: and
truly I think there can be no great ship make me change and go out
of her.'[18] It was a tremendous compliment. Ralegh's vessel was leading the defence of the realm in her hour of peril and, by the afternoon
of 19 July 1588, the great Armada itself had been sighted and the
beacons lit, light answering light as the terrible message of peril was
flashed to where the queen kept her state at Richmond. The Spaniards advanced in a slow crescent up the entrance to the Channel,
English ships firing on its horns. This was a tactic later to be condemned by some, but it was part of a deeply considered plan and
Ralegh was to extol its wisdom.

He realized that the disadvantage for the enemy galleons lay in
their enormous size and consequent slow manoeuvrability. 'We find
by experience that the greatest ships are the least serviceable,' he
wrote. They sailed 'very deep to water', and an altogether smaller
ship 'will turn her broadsides twice before the greater one can wind
once.'[19] To grapple with the Spanish galleons would have been foolhardiness, and Ralegh knew that Lord Effingham and his advisers –
Drake and Hawkins especially – appreciated this. 'The Spaniards
had an army aboard them and he had none; they had more ships
than he had, and of higher building and charging; so that, had he
entangled himself with those great and powerful vessels, he had
gravely endangered the kingdom of England.'[20]

Instead, the kingdom had to watch as the galleons continued their passage up the Channel, harried by the swifter English ships. Victory would lie in initial piecemeal successes. 'We pluck their feathers little by little,' Effingham wrote.[21] The Armada's treasure ship, the *San Salvador*, was badly holed. The *Rosario* collided with another galleon and was obliged to fall back. On 23 July, there was a more general engagement off Portland Bill. Two days later, while the nation still watched, the *Santa Anna* had her rigging shot away and was left to drift to her destruction on the French coast. The remaining enemy ships meanwhile made for the Calais roads, there to rendezvous with Parma's forces.

The danger to the West Country had passed, and Ralegh was now able to join the fleet. On Sunday 28 July, he boarded the *Ark Royal*. Here decisive action seemed imperative. Supplies and ammunition were running low. To blockade Calais was to run too great a risk, and Effingham called a hurried council. A fireship attack was prepared for that Sunday night. The pitch waiting at Dover would have to remain where it was. Something more immediate, something calling for greater nerve, was required.

It was the high moment of the nation's crisis. Drake and Hawkins at once offered to sacrifice their own ships, and other commanders followed suit. To save their country, the English officers would send their own navy burning among the enemy galleons. The English vessels were emptied of their stores and men. All that would burn was then loaded aboard. The guns were primed to bursting, and then these lethal carcasses of a navy were manoeuvred into position, lit, and released into the darkness and the mercy of the wind. Discipline on the galleons collapsed as the terrified enemy saw bearing down on them not the little fishing vessels for which they were prepared but a high, full masted fleet, stealthy and terrible with resistless fire.

Behind them waited the English vessels manned and ready to destroy the Spanish pinnaces. They watched as the fireships drifted closer to the galleons waiting in hapless and impotent pomp. The moment was coming when, out of the sheer heat engendered in their holds, the unmanned English guns would explode. The curtain of galleons drew back in terror and the fireships sailed into their heart. In the pandemonium, the Spaniards cut their own cables. Orders were shouted to sail out, to meet off Dunkirk, to save the royal fleet at any cost. Galleons collided or ran aground in a darkness lit only by the fireships as they exploded their terrible cargoes.

The following day, off Gravelines, the Spanish fleet was holed, sunk or scattered. Its pride was broken and its will destroyed. Its survivors headed out into the North Sea, pursued as far as the Firth of Forth where conditions could be trusted to do their worst. Ralegh himself provided the most vivid description of this:

> their navy which they termed invincible, consisting of two hundred forty sail of ships, not only of their own kingdom, but strengthened with the greatest argosies, Portugal carracks, Florentines, and huge hulks of other countries: were by thirty of her Majesty's own ships of war, and a few of our own Merchants, by the wise, valiant, and most advantageous conduction of the Lord Charles Howard, High Admiral of England, beaten and shuffled together; even from the Lizard in Cornwall: first to Portland, where they shamefully left Don Pedro de Valdes, with his mighty ship: from Portland to Calais, where they lost Hugo de Moncado, with the Galeas of which he was captain, and from Calais, driven with squibs from their anchors: were chased out of the sight of England, round about Scotland and Ireland. Where for the sympathy of their barbarous religion, hoping to find succour and assistance: a great part of them were crushed against the rocks, and those other that landed, being very many in number, were not withstanding broken, slain, and taken, and so sent from village to village coupled in halters to be shipped into England. Where her Majesty, of her princely and invincible disposition, disdaining to put them to death, and scorning either to retain or entertain them: were all sent back again to their countries, to witness and recount the worthy achievements of their invincible and dreadful navy. Of which the number of soldiers, the fearful burden of their ships, the commanders names of every squadron, with all other their magazines and provisions were put in print as an army and a navy unresistable, and disdaining prevention. With all which so great and terrible an ostentation, they did not in all their sailing round about England, so much as sink or take one ship, bark, pinnace, or cock-boat of ours: or ever burnt so much as one sheepcote of this land.[22]

These final stages of the defeat were observed by Ralegh himself. On 14 September, when it was known that the stragglers from the Armada were rounding the coast of Ireland, the Council resolved to send a small squadron of ships from Devon and Cornwall to observe and harry their passage. Grenville was commander and Ralegh was to assist him by staying the English ships required to transport the seven hundred soldiers deemed necessary for the enterprise. Fireships were again to be used. The Mayor of Bristol was ordered to provide fifty barrels of tar, along with brimstone, pitch and pitch boards. With these, the flotilla sailed into the Irish Sea and watched as twenty Spanish ships were driven on to the rocks while their crews died in their hundreds.

The defeat of the Spanish Armada was a victory that profoundly influenced the course of national thinking. The image of the queen was exalted to new heights, and in an engraving, possibly by Crispin de Passe, Elizabeth is shown in all the magnificence of state, bearing her orb and sceptre. Behind her, cannon fire on the fleeing remnants of the Armada, while on either side of her stand two columns. On one of these, above the royal coat of arms, a pelican feeds her young from the blood of her own breast, an ancient emblem of power mercifully succouring her people. On the other column is a phoenix rising from its flames. This suggests how, under a unique and self-perpetuating ruler, the period of spiritual renewal has arrived.

The columns themselves further this idea of benevolent and divine rule, for they may be taken to represent the Pillars of Hercules, the geographical limits of the Roman Empire in the West. Now, with her victory over the Spanish Armada, Elizabeth could truly be seen as the Imperial Virgin who might step beyond these ancient confines and assert her just rule over the New World. She was, in the words of the Latin inscription: 'Queen, by the Grace of God, of England, France, Ireland and Virginia'.

Ralegh had contributed as much as any man to this image, and a portrait from the Armada year shows him aged about thirty-four. The gaudy young man of the Hilliard miniature has grown into a figure altogether more mature. The elegant little French bonnet has been cast aside. Ralegh's beard is longer and has the effect of heightening his broad forehead from which the hair has been brushed back to accentuate its authority. The face is more restrained, more tranquil. The intelligence behind the gaze has been tempered by an experienced wariness. But the fabulous pearls hanging in his ear still hint at the deep and mysterious sexual vitality devoted to the queen whose virginity they symbolize.

Ralegh indeed is presented as her admirer, and his costume is her livery of black and white. The colour contrast is emphasized by the pale pink of Ralegh's simple collar and the brown fur of the luxurious velvet cloak on which handfuls of pearls have been sewn in heraldic imitation of the rays of the moon. The cloak is thus a sumptuous declaration of his allegiance, as is Ralegh's white silk doublet, opalescent like the carapace of some fabulous creature of the seas. One elegant hand is displayed to reveal a bracelet of pearls, perhaps that brought back from Virginia by Barlowe and Amadas. High above, remote even from the motto *amor et virtute*, floats a crescent moon, emblem of the quasi-divine virgin of imperial power celebrated in de Passe's engraving.

But this triumphalist image disguised a reality altogether more bitter and dangerous. The defeat of the Armada was not the final victory in the sea war with Spain but rather a campaign which served to mask its intensification. The destruction of huge quantities of enemy shipping might have suggested that the English had the upper hand and could force Spain into ever more expensive ways of protecting her trade. In fact, the overall strategic position had not been radically changed. The vast military resources of the enemy were still marshalled in the Low Countries, a substantial core of the Spanish fleet was still in existence, while the resolution of Philip II had only been hardened by defeat. He still commanded the resources to build further Armadas.

Elizabeth by contrast did not, and she was well aware of the fact. While the 'men of war' – Ralegh, Drake, Hawkins and, increasingly, the Earl of Essex – urged expansionist policies, believing dreams of imperialist enterprise could readily be given flesh in the world after 1588, Elizabeth was altogether more circumspect and less inclined to aggrandizement. Her pragmatism was a growing source of friction and, after her death, Ralegh was to give forcible expression to this:

> If the late queen would have believed her men of war as she did

her scribes, we had in her time beaten that great empire in pieces and made their kings kings of figs and oranges as in old times. But her Majesty did all by halves and by petty invasions taught the Spaniard how to defend himself, and to see his own weakness which, till our attempts taught him, was hardly known to himself.[23]

Here was a divide in policy that was to colour the rest of Ralegh's career and compound with other dangers now threatening him at court.

For Leicester, despite his proven military incompetence, had been appointed to supreme military command during the Armada crisis. On 8 August, he allowed Elizabeth to visit his camp at Tilbury. Dressed in virgin white, bareheaded, her silver helmet carried before her by a handsome page, she had inspected her militia. She was surrounded by a guard of honour consisting of the Earl of Ormonde, Sir John Norris, Essex her newly appointed Master of the Horse, and Leicester himself. Now, with the crisis over, she wanted to shower honours on these men. Leicester in particular was to be fantastically rewarded by being created Lieutenant-General of England and Ireland. But Leicester was dying. He was already in agony from cancer of the stomach and was now making his slow way to Buxton in Derbyshire by way of Rycote, near Thame, with its lovely chapel. From there he wrote Elizabeth his last letter which she kept to the day of her death in a jewel box in her bedroom.

She mourned, but she also insisted Leicester's hated wife be punished by the settlement of his vast debts. Then she turned to the one living vestige of him that remained. Essex was to take over Leicester's lodging at St James's Palace and, a short while later, Elizabeth rewarded him with the Garter.

The competition between Ralegh and the new favourite became ever more intense. Obliged to meet regularly at court, the tempers of the two men often flared. As early as August 1587, the queen had been forced to intervene personally to reconcile them after a quarrel in which Essex boxed Ralegh's ears. In the last months of 1588, matters had reached such a crisis that Essex challenged Ralegh to a duel – a potential catastrophe to both men – which was only avoided by the strenuous intervention of some of the other courtiers.

[149]

Elizabeth herself meanwhile fuelled the fire by favouring both sides. As she did so, she began inevitably to bring into the open the altogether more serious issues that surrounded the conflict: the lethal rivalry and mutual dependence of two vain and headstrong men which was to result eventually in tragedy.

Although divided by intense mutual loathing, Ralegh and Essex found themselves thrust uneasily into the same political camp. Here Essex was beginning to conduct himself in a manner that showed the measure of his ambitions. With the death of Leicester, the last vestiges of the older generation's aristocratic military glamour appeared to have faded. Essex would revive them in his own person. He aspired to be commander-in-chief to the nation, to hold the sword where Elizabeth held the sceptre. His radiant charm and his cunning furthered his strongest claim to power: his position as a great if impoverished hereditary aristocrat. The hopes of a younger generation of men – men who had never known the rule of any save Essex's ageing mistress – could radiate around a figure like this. The much-hated Ralegh, by contrast, could focus their loathing for a parvenu, a man manifestly out for himself. By August 1589, they could claim a major tactical victory. 'My Lord of Essex', wrote one of his supporters, 'hath chased Mr Ralegh from court and hath confined him into Ireland'.[24]

Ralegh hotly disputed that anything of the sort had occurred. He wrote to his cousin Sir George Carew, newly appointed Master of the Ordinance in Ireland: 'For my retreat from court it was upon good cause to take order for my prize.'[25] By this he may have been referring to the privateering spoils recently awarded to him by the Council. What is certain is that his estates in Ireland required a more active hand than that of an absentee landlord.

Ralegh had first viewed his Irish estates when despatched with Grenville to observe the homeward course of the remnants of the Armada. He stayed for three months. He accepted the mayorality of Youghal for the year 1588–9, began the conversion of the Warden's House of the college there, set about the conversion of Lismore Castle, and held meetings with his agents Andrew Colthurst and Richard Maule. His estates in Munster were of very considerable extent, running east and west of the Blackwater River as it turned due south from Capoquin to follow a valley to the sea at Youghal. The region comprised six castles and the decaying town of Tallow, while Ralegh's domains to the north of the river extended as far as the Knockmealdown Mountains. On the whole the soil was good but, 'long overgrown with deep grass, and in most places with heath, brambles and furze'.[26] In addition, the region was 'so barren, both of man and beast, that whosoever did travel . . . should not meet man, woman, or child, saving in cities or towns, nor yet see any beast, save foxes, wolves, or other ravening creatures.'

Ralegh's properties were officially handed over to him in the spring of 1589, but for nearly two years he had been shipping settlers over and encouraging them to repair the lands and properties. By 12 May 1589 Ralegh had settled some 144 men, thereby making up an English community of three to four hundred. The work that faced these people was arduous as, often enough, were the terms of their leases. For example, one John Clever, a gentleman of London, leased four hundred acres from Ralegh in Inchiquin, the barony lying to the west of Youghal in County Cork. The term of the lease was one hundred years, for which, after the first five years, Clever was obliged to pay £110 per acre with four capons. In addition, he was responsible for providing an armed rider for the defence of the region, to build 'one mansion or dwelling house',[27] and to enclose one hundred acres of his property with a good, well-maintained quick-set hedge.

Legal problems and rivalries inevitably arose. There was continuous friction with Sir William Fitzwilliam, the Lord Deputy, especially. By the early 1590s this was becoming acrimonious, for Fitzwilliam, immured in Ireland, was embittered by courtiers and mistrustful of them. Already, in 1589, he believed that Ralegh was in some sort of disgrace and hoped to exploit this to his advantage. Such attitudes brought out the extremes of Ralegh's pride and resentment. In his letter to George Carew he insisted that those who thought they could get the better of him 'much deceive themselves'.[28] Hoping to make those in authority clear of his power, Ralegh added: 'I am in place to be believed not inferior to any man, to pleasure or displeasure the greatest; and my opinion is so received and believed as I can anger the best of them.' Fitzwilliam should beware of Ralegh using such influence.

[151]

In the end, Ralegh was obliged to show his hand. A complication over the lease of Lismore resulted in a situation whereby the lands were claimed by the wife of a traitor. The Privy Council were, on the face of the evidence presented to them, sympathetic to her case and had referred the matter to Fitzwilliam's predecessor for an opinion. Ralegh was determined to show the new Lord Deputy that a royal favourite – albeit one in remote Ireland – had influence still. 'For the suit of Lismore', he declared, 'I will shortly send over order from the queen for a dismiss of their "cavelacions".'[29] He was as good as his word. Early in 1590, Fitzwilliam received instructions that he was not to continue with the matter for the term of the royal pleasure. Nothing more was heard of threats to Ralegh's possession of Lismore. The favourite was powerful still. He could get his way, if needs be by appearing to override the due forms of law, a convenience made use of again when Ralegh turned to exploit the natural resources of his estates.

In 1589, and in partnership with two Englishmen and Veronio Martens from the Low Countries, Ralegh obtained a royal licence to export goods from Munster regardless of pre-existing legal restrictions. He used this favour to develop the sales of timber from his lands. Large areas of his estates were covered by forests, and such natural resources were potentially very profitable. Placing one of his partners, Henry Pyne, in the castle at Mogeely, Ralegh and his associates invested £5,000 in sawmills and then persuaded nearly two hundred mainly English workers to man these. Vast quantities of timber were felled, sawn and carried by horses for transport by river to Youghal. From here, in the form of barrel staves and ships' timbers, this Irish timber was exported not only to England but to the Canaries, Madeira, and even (with later embarrassing consequences) to Spain.

Perhaps because of such intense local activity and his distance from great affairs, the court and its factions continued to preoccupy Ralegh. Remoteness gave him moments of an exile's self-obsession and he turned again to poetry, finding in his craft a new depth:

> Like truthless dreams, are all my joys expired,
> And past return are all my dandled days,

My love misled, and fancy quite retired:
Of all which past the sorrow only stays.[30]

This poem was almost certainly intended for Elizabeth, and was part of the continuing struggle with Essex, but its mainspring is altogether more potent. It is Ralegh's recognition of encroaching middle age. He was now about thirty-five in a period when men rarely exceeded their allotted biblical span. Behind him, Ralegh suggests, lay a brittle mess of disappointed hope, its outlines all the sharper for his physical remoteness in Ireland and his being left to meditate 'alone in unknown ways'. The collapse of worldly hope – the apparent loss of the regard of the Virgin Queen – leads to a melancholy that is at once as oppressive and repetitive as the poem's refrain: 'the sorrow only stays'.

The worship of Elizabeth required something altogether more substantial than a sonnet, however, and from this time – and quite possibly from these months in Ireland – there are indications that Ralegh was working on a more ambitious poem in which the Virgin Queen is presented in her mystical role as Cynthia, the immaculate goddess of the moon. These early versions of what was soon to become Ralegh's most substantial poetic achievement have largely been lost, and all that remains is a brief passage of quotation in a later work where Ralegh describes having hymned his goddess in terms at once conventional but rapturous. Elizabeth is:

> nature's wonder, virtue's choice,
> The only paragon of time's begetting,
> Divine in words, angelical in voice,
> That spring of joys, that flower of loves own setting,
>
> Th' Idea remaining of those golden ages,
> That beauty braving heavens, and earth embalming
> Which after worthless worlds but play on stages . . .[31]

But Ireland, and the presence there of the great Elizabethan poet Edmund Spenser especially, were now to have considerable consequences for the history of English literature. Ralegh and Spenser had perhaps known each other since the close of the 1570s when they were moving in the circles gathered around Leicester and Sidney.

[153]

Both men were also probably present at the Smerwick massacre, but it was only now that their friendship flourished.

It is likely that sections of Spenser's great poem *The Faerie Queene* had been circulating in manuscript, and Ralegh may have read these loose sheets along with Spenser's earlier work. However, Spenser was now also Clerk to the Council of Munster and one of that small band of hardy English undertakers who were colonizing the devastated province. He was settled on some three thousand acres that ran up the slopes of the Ballyhoura Hills and was living, in all likelihood, in the forty-foot peel tower whose ruins still stand in the centre of his domain. This estate was thirty miles from Ralegh's own, and it was now that the two poets met to discuss the problems of their art. Spenser recorded the occasion in *Colin Clout's Come Home Again*, picturing the scene as an encounter between two poetical shepherds rather than two ardent colonialists:

> One day (quoth he) I sat, (as was my trade)
> Under the foot of *Mole* that mountaine hore,
> Keeping my sheepe amongst the cooly shade,
> Of the greene alders by the *Mullaes* shore:
> There a straunge shepherd chaunst to find me out,
> Whether allured with my pipes delight,
> Whose pleasing sound yshrilled far about,
> Or thither led by chaunce, I know not right,
> Whom when I asked from what place he came,
> And how he hight, himselfe he did ycleepe,
> The shepheard of the Ocean by name,
> And said he came far from the main-sea deepe.
> He sitting me beside in that same shade,
> Provoked me to plaie some pleasant fit,
> And when he heard the musike which I made,
> He found himselfe full greatly pleasd at it:
> Yet aemuling my pipe, he tooke in hond
> My pipe before that aemuled of many,
> And plaid theron; (for well that skill he cond)
> Himselfe as skilfull in that art as any.
> He pip'd, I sung; and when he sung, I piped,
> By chaunge of turnes, each making other mery,

Neither envying other, nor envied,
So piped we, untill we both were weary.[32]

This was all sufficiently charming and a welcome relief no doubt from the managerial and legal problems with which both men were beset. It was *The Faerie Queene*, however, that was of the greatest interest to Ralegh, for here, in a poem written in one of the furthest and most desolate regions of the kingdom, was a celebration of the Virgin Queen of fantastic richness. With Spenser's erstwhile benefactors Leicester and Sidney both dead, Ralegh took on the mantle of their patronage and presented Elizabeth with a work of exceptional literary importance. In order to achieve this, he urged Spenser no longer to hide himself away on his Irish estates, 'that waste where I was quite forgot',[33] but rather to sail with him for the court of Cynthia herself, there to receive her bounty and the honours that were his due. Spenser was ready to comply. A deputy was found for his Munster clerkship, his huge and priceless manuscript was readied for its journey, and the two men set sail across an Irish Sea:

Rolling like mountaines in wide wildernesse,
Horrible, hideous, roaring with hoarse crie.[34]

Such a heaving passage gave (or, in Spenser's poetic evocation, it was presumed to give) the opportunity for Ralegh to expatiate on his maritime ambitions. 'The Shepherd of the Ocean'[35] explains to his fellow poet how Cynthia the moon goddess has by natural right the government of the seas. In a beautiful and subtle image that was soon to be of great importance to Ralegh himself, geography and politics merge. Just as the moon, moving through the purity of the heavens, draws after her the tides by a mystic power, so Elizabeth as Cynthia, the goddess of the moon, holds political sway over the seas around her kingdom and draws into her service both its ancient gods and more humble modern shepherds. Ralegh in particular can boast that his goddess has 'in the Ocean charge to me assigned'.[36] His maritime and colonizing ambitions have become one with his poetic adoration.

When the two men arrived in London, the machinery of patronage was set in motion. To ensure its smooth running Spenser wrote

a series of dedicatory sonnets, addressing himself to that constel-
lation of names who made up the great of the Elizabethan court.
Among these, naturally enough, was Ralegh himself who is hailed as
'the summer's nightingale'[37] and as the author of the still-mysterious
poem written in Cynthia's praise. Ralegh replied in what is one of
his finest works, a sonnet in which he praises Spenser for having
surpassed Petrarch in poetic achievement:

> Methought I saw the grave, where Laura lay,
> Within that temple, where the vestal flame
> Was wont to burn, and passing by that way,
> To see that buried dust of living fame,
> Whose tomb fair love and fairer virtue kept:
> All suddenly I saw the Fairy Queene:
> At whose approach the soul of Petrarch wept,
> And from thenceforth those graces were not seen.
> For they this Queen attended, in whose stead
> Oblivion laid him down on Laura's hearse:
> Hereat the hardest stones were seen to bleed,
> And groans of buried ghosts the heavens did pierce.
> > Where Homer's spright did tremble all for grief,
> > And curst th'acess of that celestial thief.[38]

Ralegh was also the recipient of the 'Letter' written by Spenser to
explain the technique of his great poem. Here Spenser announces
his most deeply considered purposes. *The Faerie Queene* is an epic
poem designed 'to fashion a gentleman or noble person in virtuous
and gentle discipline'.[39] It is thus an analysis of all that went – or
should have gone – into the making of a courtier like Ralegh himself.
Sweetening this ambitious moral purpose with the pleasures of 'an
historical fiction', the poem presents a series of aristocrats riding out
to perform various feats of derring-do at the behest of their mistress,
the Faerie Queene. Among these heroes is one who can be seen as a
partial image of Ralegh himself.

No contemporary offered a more refined analysis of Ralegh's current
predicament than Spenser in portraying his patron as Timias, the
'honoured' or 'dear' one. *The Faerie Queene* returns Ralegh to the

political and psychological perils of the Elizabethan court – or, rather, to the dark wood that lay at its allegorical heart.

Here Timias has become separated from Prince Arthur, Spenser's image of man at his best and greatest: active, moral, his powers integrated and harmonious. As befits a chivalric romance, Arthur and Timias have been busy about avenging a wronged woman, and Timias himself has ridden deep into the wood in pursuit of the foul forester who has presumed to assault her. The speed and cunning of the man have been such, however, that he has eluded Timias and joined forces with his two equally repulsive brothers. Girding their instruments of 'spoyle and murder',[40] these men now resolve to ambush Timias at a ford and kill him. Nothing happens in the narrative world of *The Faerie Queene* however that does not have a moral interpretation, and these three ugly brothers can be seen in conventional terms as 'the lust of the flesh, the lust of the eyes, and the pride of life'.[41]

It is also likely that they have a more particular application to Ralegh himself. As the embodiments of the barbaric and the sub-human, as creatures who can melt into the woods only to reappear and launch a surprise attack, the brothers are strongly reminiscent of the recalcitrant Irish. Indeed, as three 'ungracious children of one graceless sire',[42] they carry with them suggestions of the Desmonds, suggestions reinforced by the fact that they plan to ambush Timias at a ford, just as the Seneschal of Imokellie had when young Captain Ralegh was seeking to make his way during the period of the Desmond revolt. That episode had recently come back into prominence with the publication of Holinshed's *Chronicles*, and Sir Walter Ralegh now found his youthful heroism memorialized in the great, quasi-official record of the country's history, a record of which he was now patron.

Spenser proceeded to give the incident a bolder interpretation, lavishing on it his powers of description. When two of the evil brothers have been killed, for example, the third is mortally wounded by Timias:

> With that he would have fled into the wood;
>   But *Timias* him lightly overhent,
>   Right as he entering was into the flood,

[157]

> And strooke at him with force so violent,
> That headlesse him into the foord he sent:
> The carkas with the streame was carried downe,
> But th'head fell backeward on the Continent.
> So mischief fel upon the meaners crown;
> They three be dead with shame, the Squire lives with renowne.[43]

But if Timias has overcome, 'the pride of life' and the Catholic Desmonds, thereby winning the honour which his name implies is his true essence, he also been wounded by the very forces he has been opposing and he now lies in a pool of his own blood. If honour is not to pass into oblivion, he must be rescued, restored and raised to an altogether higher level of awareness. Such matters, Spenser believed, were in the hands of God, and it is Providence who now arranges for the arrival of his rescuer. 'Belphoebe was her name.'[44] It is a name suggestive of beauty, purity and the moon. As such, Belphoebe is, of course, a manifestation of Elizabeth: Elizabeth seen not in her political role but in her personal, womanly existence. On the moral plane, Belphoebe represents that gracious outgoing of non-sexual love which binds the world in community and which Spenser called Chastity.

Accompanied by her ladies, Belphoebe escorts Timias to her seat, an aristocratic earthly paradise and the place of mortal and religious love which serves as a representation of the court. Here she sets about Timias's cure through her knowledge of herbs and 'divine *Tobaco*',[45] a reference which points clearly to Ralegh. She also plies him with 'costly Cordialles' which suggest Elizabeth's gift of lucrative monopolies. Such love has nothing of the erotic about it however. Lovely, unique and virginal, the 'fruit of all honour and all chaste desire',[46] Belphoebe is the embodiment of the highest ideal of womanhood and a lady to whom Timias is naturally drawn since, in the words of a contemporary moralist: 'It appeareth that men of wit and complement are drawn with nothing more than with honour.'[47]

But for a lesser mortal like Timias to be attracted to such a paragon inevitably raises the clouding energies of an altogether more human desire. Lust, albeit at its most refined, intrudes its presence. The wound inflicted by the forester is healed only to be replaced by a more subtle wound to the heart. Timias's need is now for that sweetest of all salves, the sexual response which by her very nature is irrelevant to Belphoebe's being. Timias's emotions are rendered an agony, and death seems the only answer to his troubles.

What Spenser is here suggesting are the contradictions and human waste inherent in the cult of the Virgin Queen when taken to excess. There is no doubt that such love can be ennobling, and it takes a truly honourable man like Timias to experience it and worship the embodiment of female excellence. This is a short-circuited passion none the less, since it is one to whose satisfaction. Elizabeth as Belphoebe is immune. Such devotion, Spenser implies, can lead neither to further spiritual advance nor to bodily satisfaction. It thus defeats the greatest aims of man. It keeps Timias from Arthur and, by implication, Ralegh from true magnificence and right action in the world: the renaissance ideal of military prowess combined with patriotism.

In offering this picture of his patron, Spenser rightly indicated the grave dangers in Ralegh's ostentatious but ultimately sterile dance of attendance on Elizabeth. For his own part, Spenser believed 'the Shepherd of the Ocean' should give his genius to roles altogether more fulfilling. One of these was Ralegh's continuing concern with founding a settlement in America.

CHAPTER NINE

The Lost Colony

I f Ralegh's first attempt to settle Roanoke had proved a failure, there was much that could be salvaged and much too that had been learnt. Harriot's transatlantic crossings had been of the greatest importance in refining and correcting older navigational practices, as well as in inspiring a new generation to learn what was now becoming a fashionable art. His studies of American botany, geography and ethnography were of immense interest, as were White's illustrations and the map on which both men had worked. Here was the first scientific indication in English of a vast new empire that was at once a landmass to colonize and a kingdom of the mind. In the face of others' discouragement, it was essential to think again how America might be peopled by Englishmen.

Before Grenville's return, and while White was piecing his and Harriot's map into a general picture of the Virginian coastline, Ralegh was in communication with the indefatigable Hakluyt who had now returned to Paris. Hakluyt himself was busy with Spanish accounts of western North America, translating reports that spoke of rich silver mines and arranging for the copying of maps of the area. Now he was briefed on what Lane, Harriot and White had discovered on the opposite coast and was asked in particular for his view on the possibilities of further expeditions to the region around Chesapeake Bay.

His reply, carefully indicating what he believed was England's legal right to the area, suggested that Ralegh's 'best planting' would indeed be close to 'the bay of the Chesapians'.[1] Even the Spaniards admitted that Sebastian Cabot – 'our Cabot' – had been the first European to land in this region, thereby giving England the prior claim. Furthermore, and because, like Harriot and White, Hakluyt was unaware of the vast landmass of America, he believed Chesapeake Bay might be close to the area where the Spanish explorers he was studying had told of rich mines of silver. The possibility of such wealth being found close to a deep-water harbour was another incentive for exploration. But it was the enthusiasm of John White that now provided the focus for Ralegh's developing plans. Of all the men who had returned from Roanoke, White was the most dedicated 'American'. The draughtsman had conceived a passion for becoming a pioneer, and the Chesapeake region took on for him some of the qualities of a promised land. Changes would have to be made, however, to the form that colonization would take.

The unhappy conclusion to Ralegh's first American settlement had shown that a colony based on military lines was unlikely to succeed since few if any of the settlers had either a personal or a financial interest in the venture. Ralegh's plantation of Ireland, by contrast, suggested that there were in England sufficient numbers of families and landless younger sons prepared to uproot themselves and so make the transportation of whole communities a viable proposition. While many of these people had volunteered for Ireland itself, there were, especially amid the burgeoning population of London, some who were plucky enough to think of selling their possessions and then trying their chances in a largely independent and self-sufficient community half a world away. Ralegh could transship them and offer a measure of protection, but the fact that these colonists would pay their own passage, fend for themselves on arrival, and perhaps form a market for the exchange of goods, appealed both to Ralegh's entrepreneurial spirit and his continuing need to assert his presence in his American domains. By the close of 1586, White was busy gathering recruits for a projected 'City of Ralegh' in Virginia.

Ralegh himself meanwhile was establishing the legal and business foundations of the enterprise. Up to 150 colonists would receive five hundred acres with additional land in proportion to the size of their investment. Part of this money would be left with representatives in England who would undertake to keep the colonists supplied until they were fully established. The deed for establishing the City of Ralegh, drawn up and signed on 7 February 1587, no longer exists, but it appears that by it Ralegh released a portion of his claim on America to a syndicate having corporate status, a body of men who could exercise rights of self-government under their own officials. These men included White himself, whom Ralegh appointed

Governor, while among White's twelve assistants were Simon Fernandez (whose commitment to the project was far from wholehearted) and White's recently acquired son-in-law Ananias Dare.

To give these men the authority necessary to their position, Ralegh arranged that they should each be granted a coat of arms and so be accorded gentry status. By these means, Ralegh hoped to delegate responsibility while holding on to his own ultimate control of the colony as well as his rights to invest and draw a portion of such profits as might be made. The combination of national expansion and private enterprise in the scheme is aptly suggested by the arms of the City of Ralegh itself: the red cross of St George quartering Ralegh's own emblem of the roebuck.

By 8 May over one hundred settlers had sailed from Plymouth in a flotilla of three ships. The *Lion*, a vessel of 160 tons commanded by Simon Fernandez, carried the bulk of the emigrants and also acted as flagship. She was accompanied by a fly-boat which transported the supplies and a pinnace which, it was intended, should be left behind with the colonists. Ralegh had provided written instructions for them which laid down that the company should first make its way to the West Indies where they were to take on water, plants and livestock. After this, the expedition was to head for Roanoke, make contact with the men left there by Grenville, and install Manteo (now converted to Christianity) as lord of the region and Ralegh's representative. Having done this, the colonists were to sail to Chesapeake Bay and there found the port and settlement which would be the origins of the City of Ralegh.

These clear and careful plans were under threat from the moment of the expedition's first setting out. A May departure was late for people hoping to establish a colony, while the flotilla's slow passage up the Channel was probably due to adverse conditions. Nine days out to sea, the friction between White and Fernandez that was to dog the expedition became manifest. As White recorded in his diary, the only record of the voyage: 'Simon Ferdinando master of our admiral, lewdly forsook our fly-boat, leaving her distressed in the Bay of Portugal.'[2] Fernandez, an inveterate pirate, was almost certainly looking for prizes, and the fact that he could so soon and so blatantly disregard Ralegh's instructions and White's authority illustrates what was soon to become ever more obvious: White's position was merely a paper command. Fernandez' experience, personality and influence over the crew ensured that the expedition was effectively in his hands. White was bitterly to resent this, and with good reason.

The plan to take on supplies in the West Indies, for example, was hampered both by bad luck and Fernandez' truculent conduct. After he had temporarily absconded off Portugal, the *Lion* sailed on for Dominica where, two days after landfall, Fernandez joined her in his errant pinnace. When the colonists went ashore, relieved by the chance of at least a temporary respite from their monotonous ship's diet, they fell greedily on the first fruit that came to hand. This was the manchineel of which Columbus had warned. The results of eating it were immediate and frightening. Mouths felt as if they were burning, and some of the colonists' tongues swelled up so greatly that they were unable to speak. White recorded in his diary the grotesque moment when a child, breast-feeding from a mother who had eaten a manchineel, 'had at that instant his mouth sent on such a burning that it was strange to see how the infant was tormented for the time'.

Such symptoms disappeared after twenty-four hours, but the colonists' further efforts at gaining supplies were constantly frustrated. The only standing water found was so contaminated it made them sick. Fernandez despatched the pinnace in search of fresh meat, but none of the promised sheep were found. Water was eventually discovered on Puerto Rico, but White noted bitterly that it was taken on board in direct relation to the amount of beer the men consumed. The colonists also failed to discover salt, and although Fernandez told of the fruits that grew on the western part of Puerto Rico, he refused to let the colonists land there, insisting instead that they make for Hispaniola. It is clear that by this time he was on the lookout for prizes and was quite prepared to fool and bully White in his pursuit of them.

Eventually, with relations between White and Fernandez getting ever more strained, the flotilla turned north in the direction of the Florida channel. White's resentment was turning to paranoia, and every mishap was blamed on Fernandez. Land was sighted on 16 July, and Fernandez wrongly informed the expedition that they were off Croatoan when in fact they were still in the dangerous region of

Cape Fear. Here, 'such was the ignorance of our master', that they almost ran aground. White's loathing of the Portuguese was now at such a pitch he could not bring himself even to write Fernandez name, and when, on 22 July, Port Ferdinando itself was at last reached, White insisted on calling it by its old name, declaring that the *Lion* and her pinnace had finally 'arrived safe at "Hataraske" '.

Here the final blow fell. In compliance with Ralegh's orders, White and forty of his best men boarded the pinnace and headed for Roanoke. Here they were to install Manteo as chief and reconnoitre, as they supposed, with Grenville's fifteen men. As they made their way across the water however, a voice from the *Lion* 'called to the sailors in the pinnace, charging them not to bring any of the planters back again, but to leave them on the island'. White and his people were to remain on Roanoke.

Fernandez' countermanding Ralegh's instructions in this way amounted to mutiny. Excusing himself by 'saying that the summer was far spent', he refused to make for Chesapeake Bay and would only allow White to return to the *Lion* with a handful of his men to supervise the disembarkation of the rest. White's powerlessness in the face of the pirate's authority was absolute. The main purpose of the new colony – the founding of the City of Ralegh by the deep waters of Chesapeake Bay – had been betrayed. Fernandez and his men could do, it seemed, what they liked, and White wrote bitterly in his diary, 'it booted not the Governor to contend with them'. His weakness was now clear for all to see, and the colonists would have to survive on Roanoke as best they could.

This was a bad beginning to a fateful episode. White and his colonists had no alternative but to cross to Roanoke Island. Here, desolation greeted them. Few traces of the men left by Grenville could be found save 'the bones of one of those fifteen which the savages had slain long before'. Lane's fort was in ruins, while melon plants had forced their way into many of the first settlers' cottages and were being grazed on by deer. Even the Indians it had once been White's pleasure to draw had retreated. Roanoke was silent, abandoned. But at least it was familiar territory. White set the colonists to repairing such buildings as they could and to erecting 'other new cottages for such as should need'. No doubt these activities offered some relief of spirits, and when the fly-boat eventually arrived on 25 July and the full company of colonists was reunited, there was 'great joy and comfort' among them all.

Such joy was short-lived. A few days after landing, George Howe, one of White's assistants, was killed while catching crabs in a pool. The Indians, wary now of the presence of any Europeans, brought him down with sixteen arrows and then battered his skull with wooden clubs. Alarm spread, and White decided to cross the Sound to Croatoan with Manteo, there to consult with the Indian's mother. After initial hostility, their reception was cordial, but the tribesmen remained aware of the pressure a company of colonists could put them under. They embraced White and Manteo in friendship, but requested them 'not to gather or spill any of their corn'. Memories of Lane's demands were still fresh in the Indians' minds. They also told White how the remainder of Grenville's men had been wiped out by a posse that included braves from Wingina's tribe. White himself, sensing danger and increasingly anxious to place his relations with the Indians on a secure footing, suggested a meeting with all the local chiefs.

Unfettered by European notions of time, the men failed to turn up on the arranged day. White feared the worst. His suspicion that the tribes were in alliance against him seemed confirmed, and he was mindful too that the deaths of Howe and Grenville's men demanded revenge. He therefore resolved to attack the Indians, and organized a pre-emptive strike against the peoples living on the mainland village of Dasemunkepuec. This was a disastrous exercise. The tribesman who had murdered Howe had fled, and Dasemunkepuec itself was now occupied by a friendly party of Croatoans who were scavenging for food. Unaware of this, White's night raiders surrounded the village, burst in upon it, and shot one of the Indians before realizing their mistake. White and Manteo tried to patch matters up as best they could and then returned quickly to their settlement. Here, on 13 August, 'our savage, Manteo, by the commandment of Sir Walter Ralegh was christened in Roanoke, and called Lord thereof and of Dasemunkepuec in reward of his faithful service.'

Other events also called for celebration. Five days after Manteo's christening, White's daughter gave birth to a girl. She was the first English child to be born in America and was called Virginia in honour of Ralegh's colony and its queen. But if some sort of domestic life was now being established on Roanoke, there was growing apprehension. The 'goods and victuals of the planters' had been safely landed, and Fernandez was now eager to depart on a privateering expedition. It appeared however that the stores themselves were insufficient. There was neither livestock nor salt. Although the colonists had been assured that further supplies would be sent from England, they realized these would be taken to Chesapeake Bay where they themselves were supposed to be. The party had already resolved to move there as soon as they felt able, but they were rightly worried that they might not reach their destination by the time the supply ship arrived. They now considered it vital that their colleagues back in England be given precise information on the true state of affairs.

At first they thought two colonists should return, but they later decided that only a certain Christopher Cooper should be sent. Cooper was soon persuaded to remain on Roanoke, however, for it was gradually becoming clear that, in the end, there was only one man with the status, knowledge and personal incentive to do all that was required. John White alone could adequately represent the colonists' case back home and, after the birth of Virginia Dare especially, he was morally bound to return to America with the supplies that would ensure the continuing survival of his family.

White tried to excuse himself in any way he could. He urged that his reputation would be ruined if he were seen to return to England so soon. He was also concerned, especially after a small outbreak of pilfering that had occurred during his visit to the mainland, that more of his goods might be stolen in his absence. Such petty concerns were now uppermost in his mind, and only after a fresh deputation had presented him with signed promises that both his goods and his reputation were safe, did White agree to go. With only half a day in which to prepare himself, he eventually departed, leaving the colony as he thought adequately protected by 'a high palisade of great trees, with curtains and flankers, very fort-like'. He also agreed with the colonists that, in the event of their moving on, they would leave the name of their destination carved on a tree, following this with a Maltese cross if their departure had been forced on them by the Indians. Then, with a mere fifteen men in the fly-boat, White set sail for England and an audience with Ralegh.

His crossing was a tale of unrelieved disaster. When the fly-boat's crew tried to weigh anchor, one of the capstan spars broke and sent the others spinning so violently that several of the crew were permanently injured. Incredibly, this happened a second time and, in the end, the men were forced to cut the cable and so lose their anchor. They then sailed for twenty days with continuously slackening winds and constantly leaking water barrels. By the time they reached the Azores, only five of the crew were able to sail the ship. Then, having met up briefly with the *Lion*, a great storm blew the fly-boat off course for six days. It took a further thirteen days to right her course, and she eventually arrived, broken and famished, at the port of Smerwick. Here, three more of the crew died. Eventually, White himself set sail in a fresh boat and, arriving at Southampton early in November, learned that the *Lion* had put in before him, prizeless and so enfeebled that her men had to be helped ashore.

The timing of White's return could scarcely have been less opportune. Although both Hakluyt and Harriot were busied about preparing their material on American discovery for the press, Ralegh himself was preoccupied with his Irish plantations and the readying of the nation for the imminent crisis of the Spanish Armada. The chances of organizing a relief party were slim indeed. On 9 October 1587, a royal order had been issued prohibiting all vessels from sailing from English ports, and only Ralegh's influence could evade this. Certainly, Sir Richard Grenville was waiting in Bideford with ships that were probably intended for Chesapeake Bay. But if White and the handful of new colonists he had gathered hoped to sail at once, they waited at Bideford in vain. Both the season and the danger from Spain militated against a small boat crossing the Atlantic at this time. When, in March, Grenville declared himself ready to sail, contrary winds held him up long enough for an order to come requiring that he abandon the voyage altogether and dispatch his ships to meet Drake and the Lord High Admiral at Plymouth for the defence of the realm.

In this time of national crisis, virtually every ship was needed, and only two from among Grenville's flotilla were considered unsuitable: the *Brave*, a bark of thirty tons, and the *Roe*, a vessel of twenty-five tons rated as a pinnace. Even to free these boats for an Atlantic crossing was a difficult matter, and it required all Ralegh's guile to achieve it. In a letter to his half-brother Sir John Gilbert in which he urged that great care should be taken to see that ships were not leaving West Country ports without permission, he added a post-script in which he hinted that Gilbert should allow the *Brave* and the *Roe* to sail. On 22 April 1588, White's new recruits set out for Virginia with stores and a letter from Ralegh promising 'that with all convenient speed he would prepare a good supply of shipping and men with sufficience of all things needful, which he intended, God willing, should be with them the summer following'.[3]

To the captains of the *Brave* and the *Roe*, such promises were of even less interest than the colonists they had aboard. Their one concern was privateering, and to this end they began indiscriminately to attack any ships they encountered. But their luck was less than their foolhardiness. When the *Brave* was attacked by two vessels out of La Rochelle, many of her complement were wounded. These included White himself who was twice struck on the head 'and hurt also in the side of the buttock with a shot'.[4] The *Brave* was then looted of virtually everything save a few biscuits, and she limped chastened back to port, 'God justly punishing our former thieving'.[5] A few weeks later, the *Roe* also returned 'without performing our intended voyage for the relief of the planters in Virginia, which were thereby not a little distressed'.[6]

Such haphazard and piecemeal efforts were clearly unsatisfactory, and by the start of 1589 (perhaps indeed several months earlier) it was becoming clear to Ralegh that projects for the colonization of America could no longer be supported either by privateering or by the sort of company that had been set up to fund the first expedition made under White's leadership. Hakluyt had long urged that state contributions were essential, but, since these were not forthcoming, other means of financing American colonization would have to be found. Ralegh turned to his friends among the City merchants, people who had much experience of the administrative and practical problems of financing voyages of exploration as well as the resources to fund them. This was a move indicative of larger developments to come.

By 1589, a corporation of these wealthy men was set up in the hope of ensuring the development of White's colony. William

Sanderson, who had already sunk over £1000 in the venture, acted with Hakluyt as Ralegh's link with the City. Others involved included the two Thomas Smiths, father and son, the elder of whom headed the City men. The younger Smith was later to prove himself a major figure in English mercantile expansion, becoming a member both of the Levant Company and, in time, a founder of the great East India Company. The Smiths' assistant Richard Wright was also involved, as was the mathematician Thomas Hood.

In return for a grant of seven years' freedom of trade in Ralegh's American possessions and an exemption from dues and taxes accruing, these men promised to adventure capital, shipping and victuals. Both commercial and technical expertise were now being brought together on a large scale, and Ralegh himself made a number of provisions to help this. Sanderson and Hakluyt, for example, were released from the corporation of the City of Ralegh in order to share in the rights of the new group to trade in the lands covered by Ralegh's patent. Ralegh reserved for himself and his heirs a fifth of any bullion profits that might accrue from the venture. He also undertook to obtain a royal charter for the corporation and presented it with a token sum of £100 out of his 'especial regard and zeal of planting the Christian religion, in and amongst the said barbarous and heathen countries, and for the advancement of and preferrment of the same, and the common utility and profit of the inhabitants therein'.[7]

But still, months after White's return, nothing was being done to help the settlers on Roanoke. White persisted in his efforts and eventually, in 1590, appeared to succeed. Ralegh brought pressure to bear on William Sanderson who commissioned the eighty-ton *Moonlight* captained by Edward Spicer. Against a background of the altogether more frantic and profitable rush of privateering that followed in the wake of the defeat of the Spanish Armada, the *Moonlight* was fitted out, crewed with forty men, and provided with cannon and a quantity of supplies. So tiny a ship would also need protection, and eventually, after royal influence had been applied, John Watts, the leader of one of London's most active privateering syndicates and one in which Ralegh himself later had a share, agreed that his 150 ton *Hopewell* would accompany the *Moonlight*, Abraham Cocke sailing as captain.

When, in February 1590, White and his new settlers prepared at last to sail, Cocke was adamant that only White himself should make the voyage. There was no opportunity of gainsaying him. Privateering on the high seas had now reached such a pitch that to sail with a band of inexperienced colonists was simply too dangerous. Besides, Cocke and his men were determined to seek prizes for themselves. From late March to the end of July, the *Hopewell* and the *Moonlight* scoured the West Indies for this purpose and only when they had achieved considerable success (success that was to lead to an exceptionally complex legal wrangle between the parties involved) did they finally sail for Virginia. They at once ran into storms off the Florida coast. Undeterred, they sailed on and, by 3 August, had sighted Wococon. It was six days, however, before they could put into the shore and another nine before they dropped anchor.

White saw distant columns of smoke rising in the direction of Roanoke. This was, perhaps, an optimistic sign, and the next day, he and the two captains led out a landing party. Further columns of smoke were now seen rising from Hatarask and the boats turned aside to investigate. No settlers were found, however, and at nightfall the men returned to their ships. They woke to find a strong northeasterly wind had blown up, creating dangerous waves on the ebb tide. White and the two captains were determined to pull out in the direction of Roanoke none the less, but Spicer's boat was overturned and he and six of his rowers were drowned. Only four of the crew survived and, not unnaturally, the men on Cocke's boat 'were all of one mind not to go any further to seek the planters'.[8]

It was only with the greatest difficulty that Cocke convinced them otherwise. As darkness fell, they eventually made for the north point of Roanoke. A fire was burning in the woodland, fanned by the winds. No settlers could be seen, however, and White's own simple words best recapture the pathos of the occasion. 'We let fall our grapnel near the shore,' he recounted, 'and sounded with a trumpet and call, and afterwards many familiar English tunes of songs, and called to them friendly. But we had no answer.' White and his men eventually returned to their boat where they spent the night.

The following day showed that the fire on Roanoke was no more than a spontaneous combustion in the scrub. As the company moved round the north point of the island and approached near where White had left the colonists in 1587, they spotted Indian footprints in the sand. They then came to a forested dune where, looking up to the top of one of the trees, White saw 'curiously carved these fair Roman letters CRO'. The inscription was a hurried effort, incomplete, a cause for worry. As White approached the settlement itself, he noticed that 'one of the chief trees or posts at the right side of the entrance had the bark taken off and five feet from the ground in fair capital letters was graven CROATOAN without any cross or sign of distress.' The settlers had moved on, and White comforted himself with the thought that he had 'found a certain token of their safe being at Croatoan, which is the place where Manteo was born, and the savages of the islands our friends.'

The houses of the settlement itself had been stripped and left to collapse. Bars of iron, four light cannon, some shot and other heavy items lay overgrown with grass and weeds. As White was staring at these melancholy remains, some of the oarsmen ran across and reported how they 'had found where divers chests had been hidden and long since digged up again and broken up, and much of the goods in them spoiled and scattered about but nothing left of such things as the savages knew any use of undefaced.' Five of these chests were found, and White, a man proud and careful of his possessions, recorded bitterly: 'Of the same chests three were my own, and about the place many of my things spoiled and broken, and books torn from their covers, the frames of some of my pictures and maps rotten and spoiled with rain, and my armour almost eaten through with rust.' He felt a stab of resentment as he thought of Wingina's former followers who, he believed, 'had watched the departure of our men to Croatoan, and as soon as they were departed digged up every place where they suspected anything to be buried.'

But by now the weather was fast deteriorating. A 'foul and stormy night' was predicted and the boats made a troubled passage back to the *Hopewell* and the *Moonlight*. For the moment there was nothing more White could do except fix his hopes on Croatoan while the wind raged. The following morning it was still blowing, and as the crew assembled round the *Hopewell*'s capstan and strained against the spars, the cable broke and an anchor was lost. The wind then blew the *Hopewell* herself landwards, and only the chance of her running into a deep channel saved her from wreck. A landing on Croatoan was now out of the question. While the crew of the *Moonlight* set sail for England in 'their weak and leak ship', Cocke resolved to make for the Caribbean. Here he would resupply and go privateering before making 'our return to visit our countrymen at Virginia'. White had no option but to agree.

Eventually, and after yet another change of plan had been forced on them by contrary winds, the *Hopewell* joined a fleet of the queen's ships off the Azores. Here Sir John Hawkins was in command and privateering was uppermost in every man's mind. All ideas of returning to Virginia were put aside, and on 24 October 'we came in safety, God be thanked,' White wrote, 'to an anchor in Plymouth.' All he could later bring himself to say of his expedition suggests the resignation of a defeated man who had committed 'the relief of my discomfortable company the planters in Virginia, to the merciful help of the Almighty'.

It remains to try to piece together the fate of the lost colonists themselves. A party of perhaps a dozen may have been left on Roanoke to guard the island in anticipation of White's return. Eventually despairing of seeing him again, they probably abandoned the site for Croatoan. Their subsequent fate is unknown, but they may have tried to make for the rest of the colonists who had by now probably moved off in the direction of Chesapeake Bay. A Spanish expedition failed to find traces of them there, although it did discover 'a slipway for small vessels' on the outer banks of the Sound, along with a quantity of English barrels and debris.

Subsequent English expeditions sent by Ralegh himself appear to have been equally unsuccessful, despite the fact that there were persistent rumours about the fate of the settlers circulating in London. In September 1605, for example, a character called Captain Seagull in Ben Jonson's play *Eastward Ho!* spoke of Virginia saying: 'A whole country of English is there man, bred of those that were left there in '70 [sic]; they have married with the Indians and made them bring forth as beautiful faces as any we have in England.'[9] Perhaps the colonists had indeed settled in peaceful co-existence with the Indians around Chesapeake Bay, even if less successfully than Seagull implies.

[172]

By April 1607 however, the local Indian leader Powhatan was asserting his power. Determined to rebut the prophecies of his priests that 'from the Chesapeake Bay, a nation should arise which would dissolve and give an end to his empire', Powhatan attacked the local Indians and wiped them out with ruthless force. Their villages and crops were burnt, the inhabitants massacred. Ralegh's colonists most probably died with them. Certainly, by 1612, it was an accepted fact that 'the men, women, and children of the first plantation at Roanoke were by the practice and commandment of Powhatan . . . miserably slaughtered.' Stories of a handful of survivors continued to be told, but these increasingly belonged to fantasy. Ralegh himself had lost £40,000 in these plans for American colonization. 'Private purses,' he declared bitterly, 'are cold comfort to adventurers.'[10]

CHAPTER TEN

The Favourite's Fall

The worship of the Virgin Queen meanwhile continued in all its fantastic elaboration. Some time before the close of 1592, Ralegh presented Elizabeth with one of the expensive gifts she regarded as her due. What this present might have been is no longer certain, but Ralegh accompanied his offering with a song. Divided into parts for the voices that were to perform it, the work apostrophizes Elizabeth as Cynthia the goddess of the moon, as Phoebe, Diana, Flora and the spirit of the dawn. She is the archetype of beauty:

> A flower of love's own planting
> A pattern kept by nature
> For beauty, form, and stature,
> When she would frame a darling.[1]

Eternally renewing herself, Elizabeth is a beauty beyond the reach of time and, although the object of 'virtue's true desire', mere mortals cannot draw close to her as she rides the heavens aloof in divine isolation. The poet needs a quill 'drawn from an angel's wing' properly to describe her nature. Lacking this, he must experience his hopeless love turning to all too immediate sorrow. The old song is here raised to new heights of exaggeration, and perhaps only two people who heard its first performance detected the false notes amid its elegant trifling. The first of these was Ralegh himself, the second a woman who had come to court in 1584 and now numbered herself among Elizabeth's Maids of the Privy Chamber.

Bess Throckmorton was not quite twenty when she first appeared among that galaxy of vestals who surrounded the queen, their lesser beauties allegedly throwing hers into relief while they attended to the monarch's necessities or beguiled such leisure as she had with music and conversation. This was a position of prestige for an unmarried woman, and Bess Throckmorton aspired to it by virtue of her family connections. Her father, Sir Nicholas Throckmorton, who died when she was a child of six, had served as Elizabeth's first ambassador in Paris. Her brother, whose diary provides one of the most valuable and intimate records of the life of a leading Elizabethan gentleman, was a courtier faithful both to his queen and his sister. Despite the involvement of his cousin Francis in a Catholic conspiracy to place Mary, Queen of Scots, on the throne, Elizabeth recognized the loyalty of other members of the Throckmorton family, and Arthur laboured hard to advance his sister's interests.

This was both a brotherly duty and a necessity. The small portion left to Bess by her father had been alienated through a bad investment, and the young woman was dependent for her dowry on a farm in Mitcham. When her mother died, she was left merely some tapestry and bedhangings along with clothes and jewellery. By placing her among the Maids of the Privy Chamber, Arthur would be freed of the responsibility of keeping her – Bess would become a charge on the royal household – while she would also be in a position to attract the notice of the leading men of the day. She might even, subject to the iron discipline with which the queen governed her maids, find herself a husband.

Placing Bess in the royal household was a matter requiring some tact and persistence, but by 8 November 1584, Arthur could record in his diary: 'I came and dined at Hampton Court. My sister was sworn of the Privy Chamber.'[2] He had done his duty. Now his sister, unconventionally beautiful with her high forehead, characterful nose and berry-bright eyes, would have to find her own way in the world. Her greatest asset and her gravest danger lay in the strength of her personality. Bess Throckmorton was intelligent (if but lightly educated) forthright, passionate and courageous.

It was these characteristics that attracted Ralegh, challenging and even, on occasions, intimidating him. He was approaching his early forties, a mature man for whom the occasional delights of 'swisser-swattering' could no longer provide the emotional nourishment he needed. Nor could the feigned worship of the Virgin Queen. While Cynthia circled in the heavens above, untouchable and unmoved, Bess Throckmorton stirred the deepest sources of his being. Between the man and the woman, both of them from comparatively modest backgrounds and both wholly dependent on the queen, hovered an atmosphere at once mysterious and specific:

> Her eyes he would should be of light,
>   A violet breath and lips of jelly,
> Her hair not black, nor over-bright,
>   And of the softest down her belly.[3]

The passion between them was urgent and desperately dangerous. He was one of the queen's favourites, a man who had grounded his fortune on an elaborate public fiction of chaste desire for the all-powerful goddess of the moon. Bess Throckmorton was as dependent as a schoolgirl on her spinsterly mistress's whim. For both of them, there were examples enough of what might happen were they to break free of these constraints.

Early in the reign, when the positions of their respective families still posed a genuine threat to the security of the crown, Lady Catherine Grey and the Earl of Hertford had contracted a secret marriage. Both were sent to the Tower and then released into the custody of their separate families. The young people died without ever seeing each other again. Even relatively unimportant couples who dared to marry without permission were punished. When it was discovered that Mary Shelton had secretly married James Scudamore, the queen was so furious with her maid and attacked her with such fury that she broke her finger. When the members of the Leicester family contracted secret marriages her wrath was yet more terrible. The young Earl of Essex was painfully aware of the vengeance visited on his mother and sister, and when, in 1590, he himself married Sir Philip Sidney's widow, the mild daughter of Sir Francis Walsingham, Elizabeth's anger knew no bounds. The couple were banished from the court until the queen recovered from the sense of betrayal.

In a court crackling with gossip, Ralegh and Bess had to seize their secret pleasures and nurture their relationship as they could. The deepest unfolding of their personalities took place amid danger and intrigue, the risks at which they connived giving an edge to their passion and revealing to Ralegh himself the subtlety of the chains with which he was bound, constrictions that tied him not just to an ever more factitious relationship to his queen, but to a pleasure whose very intensity suggested less the comforts of domestic habit than the more abject intuition of his mortality. The poem in which he urged his mistress to the moist and melting intimacies of the body reserves its fullest power for an ancient intuition:

> O cruel Time which takes in trust
> Our youth, our joys, and all we have,
> And pays us but with age and dust;
> Who in the dark and silent grave,
> When we have wandered all our ways,
> Shuts up the story of our days.[4]

On the last night of his life, when Ralegh was a prisoner in the Tower, he was to return to this stanza, copying it out and adding a couplet expressing his hope of salvation. But now, in 1591, his passion was reaching its first inevitable climax. Sometime in the summer of that year Bess discovered she was pregnant, and then – if not before – the couple were secretly married. They were together in the shadow of immanent catastrophe.

While they lived thus, Ralegh was pursuing his public career with ever greater ambition. Although he had worked with tireless energy as the Crown's great representative in the West and shown the entrepreneurial skills with which he had launched expeditions to the New World, he had as yet to be trusted by the queen with a high command that led to action. In the summer of 1591, it seemed his chance had come.

The year after the Armada had limped back to a heartbroken Spain, the 'men of war' in England had persuaded Elizabeth to a three-pronged attack designed to destroy those elements of the enemy's shipping that were being refitted in Santander. This was a move the strategic sense of which the queen fully appreciated. However, with the naval threat removed, it was planned that the English fleet was to capture Lisbon and restore the pretender Dom Antonio to his throne. Having succeeded in this unlikely mission, they were then to complete the campaign by seizing a base in the Azores from which to ravage Spain's merchant shipping and her treasure fleet.

Ambition so overextended could only result in failure, and Drake was obliged to shoulder the blame while a major reappraisal of English strategy was undertaken.

The altogether more modest policies proposed by Sir John Hawkins were adopted. The aim of these was to blockade the Azores with a small but powerful fleet that was to be replaced every four months with a fresh squadron from England. Although even this degree of administration proved difficult to achieve, the sea war against Spain had entered a new phase. While the bulk of the navy was held back to defend the Channel, small squadrons of the royal fleet, equipped and furnished on a joint-stock basis, were to join with the great numbers of privateers operating in the Atlantic and the West Indies, and there to seize Spanish prizes.

In 1591 the queen, Ralegh and Lord Howard of Effingham raised the money to finance one such expedition under the command of Effingham's kinsman the young Lord Thomas Howard. Ralegh invested £5,000 of his own money in the venture and had every reason to think he would sail as Vice-Admiral of the fleet on the *Revenge*. Suddenly however, in March 1591, his hopes were dashed and he was remanded in England for duties altogether more pressing.

The ambitions of Philip, supported by the immense resources of his American silver mines, had led to a revival of Spain's maritime power. The failure to destroy his fleet while it was being refitted in Santander had indeed been a strategic blunder. Now the king began to reinforce the vessels that remained to him with the famous 'Twelve Apostles'. These vast ships were to be further supplemented with a number of smaller, swifter vessels, the *zabras* in particular. Despite chronic shortages of men and materials, the great engine of Spanish bureaucracy was put into action under Don Alonso de Bazan. By 27 May, six of the Apostles were ready or nearing completion and, in July, fifty-nine ships were riding in the harbour of Ferrol. Thirty of these were men-of-war, seventeen galleons, while the rest ranged from vessels of 1500 tons to the little *zabras*. Deficient though it was in munitions, this fleet was now to sail at the king's command for Flores in the Azores, there to rid the sea of pirates and escort home an Indies fleet swollen to twice its usual size.

'The King of Spain's treasure comes unto him as our salads to us – when we have eat all, we fetch more out of our gardens; so doth he fetch his treasure out of the ground after spending all that is coined.'⁵ Thus wrote one Elizabethan of the ease with which Spain seemed to replenish her limitless wealth. To ensure the regular supply of this treasure, two fleets were despatched each year between April and July, one sailing to the Mexican port of Vera Cruz, the other to collect Peruvian silver from Nombre de Dios. Spanish exports were sold in the Americas over the winter months and then, when fully laden with treasure, the two fleets departed, reconnoitring in Havana before sailing in convoy for Spain.

Heavy defence was essential, but so too was speed, and it was the *zabras* which so frustrated the efforts of the privateers. Nevertheless, the threat posed by the English round the waters of Havana was such that, in 1590, the Mexican fleet was forced to wait overlong for the remainder of the convoy. When this finally arrived, it was deemed too late to sail and, calling a hurried meeting, the Spanish captains 'resolved that we winter here because the margin of time allowed us in which to get away is so short.'⁶ News of this delay caused intense excitement in England. Ralegh, it seemed, was about to sail on the richest privateering expedition ever mounted.

But English intelligence had provided more worrying reports. Spies told of the massive build-up of shipping in Ferrol, and a dismayed Privy Council was obliged to realize that, the defeat of the 1588 Armada notwithstanding, Spain was now able to mobilize vast forces that posed a threat altogether too serious to be ignored. But the intelligence was contradictory. Were these ships to be used to reinforce Spain's interference in France and so prepare for an attack on England or – as one report coming from Lisbon via Dublin intimated – were five hundred ships being readied for an outright attack on the realm itself?

An English expeditionary force of 8,000 men was sent under Sir John Norris to support the Huguenots in France, while orders were sent to the Lords Lieutenant to muster the trained bands and ready the beacons on the hills. Alarming reports were now circulating that the Spaniards had occupied or were about to occupy the Scillies, and Sir Walter Ralegh was despatched to Plymouth 'to take up ships and men there to save Scilly if it be not taken and to defend the coast of Cornwall and Devon.'⁷ Once again, he was to attend

[179]

to the defence of the realm, his only contact with Lord Howard's great expedition now being to provide news and victuals.

While Ralegh was thus busied on land, his place as Vice-Admiral on the *Revenge* was taken by Sir Richard Grenville. Grenville himself – Don Ricardo de Campoverde as his name appeared Hispanizied in reports to Philip – had acquired largely in Ralegh's service his reputation as 'a great sailor and pirate and a great heretic and persecutor of Catholics'.[8] Now even in Spanish eyes, he was to gain his apotheosis as a hero, the last fight of the *Revenge* and Grenville's death being the purple patch in the history of Elizabethan privateering. This was an episode at once epic and foolhardy to which Ralegh, albeit anonymously, gave enduring fame in *A Report of The Truth of the Fight about the Isles of Azores, this last Summer betwixt the* Revenge, *one of her Majesty's Ships and an Armada of the King of Spain.*

Great story-teller that he was, Ralegh began the narrative part of his account *in medias res*: 'The Lord Thomas Howard, with six of her Majesty's ships, six victuallers of London, the bark *Ralegh* and two or three pinnaces riding at anchor near unto Flores, one of the westerly islands of the Azores, the last of August in the afternoon, had intelligence of one Captain Middleton of the approach of the Spanish Armada.'[9] The emotionless factual tone contrasts powerfully with the effect of impending terror as does Ralegh's careful description of half the English being laid low with disease while the remainder were busied 'providing ballast for their ships; others filling of water and refreshing themselves from the land with such things as they could either for money, or by force recover.'

This impression of factual accuracy is enhanced by Ralegh's references to the eye-witness accounts he used and by his employment of nautical terms such as his description of the moment when Grenville's ship, being the last to leave, turned to face the enemy 'who as the mariners term it sprang their luff and fell under the lee of the *Revenge*'. The other English ships had already slipped through the horns of the Spanish navy, and battle was now about to be engaged between Grenville's solitary vessel and the might of Spain.

This was a moment of tremendous drama and Ralegh is wholly convincing in his portrayal of Grenville's patriotic heroism: 'Sir Richard utterly refused to turn from the enemy, alleging that he would rather choose to die, than to dishonour himself, his country, and her Majesty's ship, persuading his company that he would pass through the two squadrons, in despite of them: and enforce those of Seville to give him way.' This was sheer recklessness, as Ralegh well knew, and he wins our confidence by confessing as much. Grenville, he suggests, would have been much wiser to follow his master mariner's advice and let the *Revenge* sail out of enemy range. 'Notwithstanding out of the greatness of his mind, he could not be persuaded.' This is do-or-die heroism, and we are in the hand of a master propagandist.

And it was propaganda that was both Ralegh's subject and his real purpose. He had to turn the one great English defeat in the sea war against Spain into an appearance of triumph: a triumph that would exalt his kinsman and so kindle the patriotic fervour of his readers that duplicitous Spain would be laughed to scorn and offer no temptation to wavering English loyalty. This last was a matter of grave concern to the government, especially in the years around the Armada peril. The papal bull of excommunication had legitimized Catholic revolt, and fears had been deepened by the arrival in the country of Jesuit priests enthused by the ardour of the Counter-Reformation and, in many cases, hungry for martyrdom.

Legislation branded such men traitors. It was held that their principal aim was to undermine the queen's subjects from their natural allegiance and thereby create sedition in order to overthrow the state. Doctrine was wholly subsumed in politics. As Burleigh declared, the issue was not the Mass and transubstantiation but treason. Seen against this background, Ralegh's *Report* is an attempt to counter the Catholic and, more specifically, the Spanish menace, with an image of English Protestantism that is heroic, patriotic, humane and all-embracing.

To achieve this required the skills of a great orator or actor, a man who could hold the attention of his audience as he led them deftly to accept his interpretation of events. This was a role to which Ralegh was ideally suited, and the *Report* allows the reader to feel Ralegh's pleasure in the exercise of his skill. Few passages in the work are more adroit than the opening paragraph. Here Ralegh ridicules the 'vainglorious vaunts' of Spanish writers who had prematurely boasted of the success of the 1588 Armada only to find themselves 'shamefully beaten and dishonoured'. All this is to Ralegh's purpose: the Spaniards are boastful, foolish and defeatable, ridiculous as a nation and fallible as an enemy. The English, both by implication and explicit statement, are altogether more modest and successful, lovers – like the narrator – of truth and accuracy, men at once pragmatic, patriotic and, in Grenville's case, heroic.

Laid bare in this way, the bones of the *Report* are crude nationalism. It is Ralegh's artifice, the quicksilver changes of what always appears as an urgent and natural voice, that makes his role so convincing – that and an ability to describe action previously unmatched in English prose. This is Ralegh's account of the last moments of the battle:

All the powder of the *Revenge* to the last barrel was now spent, all her pikes broken, forty of her best men slain, and the most part of the rest hurt. In the beginning of the fight she had but one hundred free from sickness, and fourscore and ten sick, laid in hold upon the ballast. A small troop to man such a ship, and a weak garrison to resist so mighty an army. By those hundred all was sustained, the volleys, boarding, and enterings of fifteen ships of war, besides those which beat her at large. On the contrary, the Spanish were always supplied with soldiers brought from every squadron: all manner of arms and powder at will. Unto ours there remained no comfort at all, no hope, no supply either of ships, men, or weapons: the masts all beaten overboard: all her tackle cut asunder, her upper work altogether razed, and in effect evened she was with the water, but the very foundation or bottom of a ship, nothing being left over head either for flight or defence. Sir *Richard* finding himself in this distress, and unable any longer to make resistance, having endured in this fifteen hour fight, the assault of fifteen several Armados, all by turns aboard him, and by estimation eight hundred shot of great artillery, besides many assaults and entries. And that himself and the ship must needs be possessed by the enemy, who were now all cast in a ring about him; the *Revenge* not able to move one way or other, but as she was moved with the waves and billow of the sea: commanded the master gunner, whom he knew to be a most resolute man, to split and sink the ship; that thereby

nothing might remain of glory or victory to the Spaniards: seeing
in so many hours fight, and with so great a Navy they were not
able to take her, having had fifteen hours time, fifteen thousand
men, and fifty and three sail of men of war to perform it
withal.[10]

Grenville now tried to persuade the company 'to yield themselves
unto God' and die for their country and their religion. Ralegh carefully turns the fact that numbers of the men refused this order to his
advantage. The voices of 'the Captain and the Master' urging on
Grenville the notion that while the *Revenge* herself was already lost,
many of the men were still alive and able to fight another day,
suggests pragmatism and common sense. Vainglorious heroism is
tempered by something altogether more humane, but without that
heroism itself being diminished. And it is the actions of the Spaniards
that emphasize this. Sir Richard's conduct was such that the enemy
general agreed with the English Master: 'That all the lives should be
saved, the company sent for England, and the better sort to pay such
reasonable ransom as their estates would bear.'

As everyone in England knew, such magnanimity was wholly
untypical of the Spaniards, and Ralegh makes clear that such exceptional behaviour has been inspired by Grenville's courage. In tribute
to this, the Spanish general 'used Sir Richard with all humanity, and
left nothing unattempted that tendered to his recovery.' But the
position was hopeless in any case, and 'Sir Richard died as it is said,
the second or third day aboard the General and was by them greatly
bewailed.' The Protestant English hero had won a moral victory and
'ended his life honourably in respect of the reputation won to his
nation and country, and of the same to his posterity, and that being
dead he hath not outlived his own honour.'

Such honour, Ralegh implies, can only belong to the Protestant
English, and his propaganda purpose emerges fully at the end of
the *Report* when he portrays a relation of the Irish Desmonds trying
to persuade the English mariners on the Spanish ships to desert to
Philip's cause. Treachery, it seems, is everywhere, and Ralegh's anti-
Catholic satire is ruthless as he offers an account of the papists'
broken promises, which is clearly aimed at any Englishmen wavering
in their allegiance. 'What man can be so blockishly ignorant ever to

expect place or honour from a foreign king, having no other argument or persuasion than his own disloyalty?' he asks. Treachery unerringly brings self-destruction, and the fate of the Desmonds themselves – their power squandered and their family destroyed – is held up as an example to all who might be tempted by it.

Having established this point, Ralegh returned to his abiding theme, his loathing of Spain and all her works. His final portrayal of the Catholic enemy is a picture of moral anarchy, a perilous morass threatening all aspects of human life. Spain's much-vaunted papist religion, for example, is mere hypocrisy, a 'veil of piety' thrown over the ugly face of political ambition. All Spain really wants, Ralegh suggests, is the worldly power she assumes is her right, 'as if the Kings of Castile were the natural heirs of all the world'. Reminding his readers of the threat the English government felt was posed by Jesuit missionaries, Ralegh describes how the Spaniards support these priests 'and have by that mean ruined many noble houses and others in this land.' Only look around Europe, Ralegh urges, and the damage done by this unholy alliance is palpable: Portugal, Sicily, Naples, Milan and the Low Countries have all been persecuted, while in the New World the suffering inflicted on the Indians is notorious. Now this evil is directed against the English themselves, Spain 'thereby hoping in time to bring us to slavery and subjection'.

This suggestion of all-encompassing threat is the necessary prelude to the last and most ardent of the voices through which Ralegh explores his role. He is, in the end, the loyal servant of his Protestant queen, a patriot doing the will of God and preserving his integrity by preserving his country:

> To conclude, it hath ever to this day pleased God, to prosper and defend her Majesty, to break the purposes of malicious enemies, of forsworn traitors, and of unjust practices and invasions. She hath even been honoured of the worthiest kings, served by faithful subjects, and shall by the favour of God, resist, repel, and confound all whatsoever attempts against her sacred Person or kingdom. In the meantime, let the Spaniard and traitor vaunt of their successes; and we her true and obedient vassals guided by the shining light of her virtues, shall always love her, serve her, and obey her to the end of our lives.[11]

The service of the Virgin Queen becomes, at the close, the means by which all Englishmen can live a fully humane life in which their spiritual, political and moral selves are integrated and harmonious. Ralegh's final role in the *Report* is thus the patriotic and orthodox Protestant, a man helping to bind his nation together through the logic and fervour of his beliefs.

This was not a role that went unchallenged. In October 1591, Elizabeth issued 'A Declaration of great troubles pretended against the realm by a number of seminary priests and Jesuits, sent, and very secretly dispersed in the same, to work great treasons under a false pretence of religion'. Rigorous searches were ordered to be made for recusants, and instructions were sent out informing the local commissioners how they were to conduct their inquiries. The machinery of Elizabethan state repression was set in motion while, on the mainland of Europe, the Jesuits responded with propaganda, professional book-runners carrying to London and elsewhere volumes illicitly landed on deserted coasts. Among these books was a Latin *Responsio* to Elizabeth's declaration published under the pseudonym 'Andreas Philopater'.

Andreas Philopater was the arch-Jesuit Robert Parsons and the scabrous brilliance of his work (which caused much distress to those Catholics who hoped quietly to worship in their own way) ensured that the book went through eight editions in four languages within two years. Answering Elizabeth's proclamation point by point, Parsons indicted most of the major figures of the court with a range of vices that suggested the country was rushing headlong into moral anarchy while the supposedly great and good 'live as mere atheists ... laughing at other men's simplicity in that behalf'.[12] The devout Burleigh, 'that malignant and wrangling worm', was a principal object of attack, but Ralegh also merited a paragraph.

Parsons charged him with wishing to set up an 'atheist commonwealth' in which denial of the existence of God would become a cardinal point of law. If Ralegh were invited on to the Privy Council, Parsons warns, then the nation could expect the promulgation of an edict altogether more dreadful than Elizabeth's against the Jesuits. Published in the queen's name, Ralegh's edict would outlaw as traitors all those who failed to be seduced by his 'libertinism', by that free-thinking and immorality which denied God and the immortality of the soul in the heedless search for pleasure, power, and the corruption of the young. Anticipating the talents of the gutter press, Parsons wrote 'of Sir Walter Ralegh's school of atheism, by the way; and of the conjuror that is master thereof; and of the diligence used to get young gentlemen to this school,wherein both Moses and the Saviour, the Old and the New Testament, are jested at, and the scholars taught among other things to spell God backward.'

This was mud-slinging, but Parsons had the great controversialist's exaggerated and deadly aim. While his other victims could shrug off the *Responsio*, its accusations of Ralegh's atheism were to sully his name and eventually place him in the gravest danger. For 'atheism' was a 'snarl word', a term at once loose, emotive and potentially lethal. Under its commonplace abusiveness seethed those forces which, it was supposed, would bring decent society to its knees.

The atheist first of all, of course, denied the existence of God whose substance united the three persons of the Trinity. Denying God, he necessarily denied that God created the world in time and that the earth had either a beginning or, more importantly perhaps, an end when judgement would be meted out on the wicked. All that happened, the atheist believed, came to pass through the operation of fate or chance rather than by divine providence. While it was universally acknowledged that man had a soul, the atheist refused to believe that this enigmatic essence was immortal. Nor did he consider that the Scriptures, supposedly the Word of God, were an unimpeachable source of authority to be believed rather than questioned. Arguing such points in the pride of their intellect, these 'English Italianate and devils incarnate do hold these damnable opinions: that there was no creation of the world, that there shall be no day of judgement, no resurrection, no immortality of the soul, no hell: they dispute against the Bible, reckon up genealogies more ancient than Adam, allege arguments to prove that the story of Noah his Ark and the Deluge were fables.'[13]

Such was the 'outward atheist' of the Elizabethans' fears, but a figure altogether more insidious was the 'inward atheist', the man (it was usually a man) who recognized that the forms of Christian worship were a useful means of social control and so 'turned Moses into Machiavel'. This loathed figure believed in his heart 'that the

Scriptures were devised by men, only for policy sake to maintain peace in states and kingdoms, to keep subjects in obedience to laws and loyalty to magistrates, by thus terrifying them from enormities when their consciences are possessed with an opinion of hell fire, and alluring them to subjection by hope of eternal life.'[14]

Here, in brief, were the fears of the timidly traditionalist. The men gathered in Durham House were altogether more sceptical, more alert and, in the end, more truthful. 'It is the part of an honest and valiant man', Ralegh wrote, 'to do what reason willeth, not what opinion expecteth, and to measure honour or dishonour by the assurance of his well-informed conscience, rather than by the malicious report and censure of others.'[15] By following this strenuous ideal, the men surrounding Ralegh in his London palace became leaders of that profound shift in human consciousness which, recognizing that matters of the spirit must be left to faith, determined to examine nature free from the intellectual lumber of the past. This was the tone of critical enquiry which, in the words of George Peele:

> Leaving our schoolmen's vulgar trodden paths
> And, following the ancient reverend steps
> Of Trismegistus and Pythagoras
> Through uncouth ways and inaccessible,
> Dost pass into the spacious pleasant fields
> Of divine science and philosophy.[16]

These lines point to the continuing influence of the great renaissance magus Giordano Bruno.

During his two-year stay in England, Bruno had done far more than provide the psychological and philosophic basis for the worship of Elizabeth as the goddess of the moon. He had, much to Walsingham's intense suspicion, come as the albeit secret spokesman of the moderating religious policies of King Henri III of France. While the zealous Secretary looked on these views askance, he recognized that Bruno's being protected by the French Ambassador gave the man an excellent cover as a spy. Passing not altogether convincingly as a Frenchman, and operating under the code-name 'Henry Faggot', it was Bruno's intelligence work which led to the uncovering of the plot against

Elizabeth headed by Bess Throckmorton's cousin. But Bruno had other roles to play, in particular that of a guest lecturer at Oxford.

He was not a great success. 'Stripping up his sleeves like some juggler', Bruno presented himself as 'the man who has pierced the air and penetrated the sky, wended his way amongst the stars and overpassed the margins of the world.'[17] This was not the sort of thing that went down well with a complacent elite of Aristotelians. The diminutive Italian was, besides, promoting absurd modern views. 'He undertook among very many other matters to set on foot the opinion of Copernicus, that the earth did go round and the heavens did stand still, whereas in truth it was his own head which rather did run round and his brains did not stand still.'[18]

This remark has the authentic superciliousness of the Senior Common Room, and such attacks confirmed Bruno's dismay at the intellectual poverty of those 'grammarian pedants' who were content *'vivere e morire per Aristoteles'*. In London, Leicester and the Sidney circle were a little more accessible to his ideas but, before his return to the mainland of Europe, Bruno made an altogether more profound impact on a man who was potentially one of the most powerful in the kingdom: Henry Percy, 9th Earl of Northumberland. Now, while Bruno trod his slow way to the Inquisitor's bonfire on the Campo dei Fiori, the 'Wizard Earl' gathered his more abstruse manuscripts together in his great libraries at Syon House and Petworth.

Ralegh had carefully cultivated Northumberland's friendship since the late 1580s. The young Earl was an immensely wealthy man, and with Ralegh himself earning huge profits from his monopolies and privateering enterprises, a lavish exchange of gifts took place between them. Northumberland's household account books record his presentation to Ralegh of a straw-coloured velvet saddle and the receipt of 'a bed of cedar or cypress'.[19] Northumberland bought a diamond jewel from Ralegh for £800, a price so great that even the Earl was obliged to pay for it in instalments, while Ralegh also won £10 off the younger man at the gaming tables.

Northumberland himself had travelled widely while, being the Protestant heir to one of the greatest Catholic families in the country he had – particularly after the suspicious circumstances surrounding the death of his traitor father – become an object both of Catholic hopes and government surveillance. He was temperamentally disinclined to conspiracy however, preferring to spend his time in the pursuit of 'this infinite, worthy mistress knowledge'.[20] Poetry, gardening, mathematics and the occult all came under his gaze, and Northumberland gained a reputation as a 'favourer of all good learning, and Maecenas of learned men'.[21] Mildly impeded by a stutter, intelligent, generous and perhaps a little reserved, he was clearly a delightful companion for Ralegh's more scholarly hours.

A further bond between the two men was their regard for the intellect of Thomas Harriot, and it was Harriot who had built on the foundations provided among others by Giordano Bruno. In particular, Harriot had adopted Bruno's belief in an infinite, heliocentric universe where matter was made up from atoms. Such beliefs were at once ancient and on the dangerous edge of contemporary scientific thought. Among the Greek philosophers, Democritus had posited the notion of a universe infinitely extended in time and space, where everything material, although subject to change and decay, was constructed from minute particles that could be neither created nor destroyed. Some Elizabethans also believed that the ancients had anticipated the belief that the earth moves round the sun, this notion being, according to one, the 'most ancient doctrine of the Pythagoreans, lately revived by Copernicus'.[22]

Bruno had invigorated such notions with his own fervour. Inspired by the so-called Orphic Hymns and the philosophic and religious tradition associated with Hermes Trismegistus (a tradition whose sacred texts were soon to be shown as entirely spurious) Bruno had declared the infinite material world to be penetrated with the divine energy whose power and goodness brought into being all that had a possibility of existence. Atoms – hard, eternal and unchangeable – were forever being wrought into new combinations of matter as the form-giving soul of the divine intelligence revealed its omnipotence. To the learned, this philosophy offered a vision at once intellectual and mystical, religious and scientific, through which it was possible to experience the presence of God.

As a result, when Harriot went up to the lantern of Durham House to observe the stars (his later correspondence with Kepler shows him to have been an important pioneer in the use of the telescope) he was surveying a universe he could believe was uniform, homogenous and everywhere operating according to the same physical laws. It thereby became possible to note its movements in mathematical terms, and Harriot himself was to make significant contributions to algebra, among the more accessible of which was his invention of the signs for 'greater than' and 'less than'.

But this scrupulous scientific reconstruction of the universe, this re-ordering of the old relationship between the heavens and the earth, was fraught with danger. The primitive, the narrow and the merely prejudiced perceived only a wicked combination of ideas that dared to contradict the literal word of God. Such beliefs were, they said, a denial of Genesis and an inspiration for people to believe the world was eternal rather than a finite substance created in six days out of nothing. It was whispered of Harriot himself that 'he did not like (or valued not) the old story of the creation of the world. He could not believe the old position; he would say *ex nihilo nihil fit.'*[23] Indeed, one of his recorded remarks was: 'Out of nothing comes nothing.'[24]

It was possible none the less for a refined intelligence to entertain such ideas while still believing in the fundamental tenets of Protestant Christianity – to doubt some of the dogma of the Church while revering its spirit. And this was Harriot's position. His critical mind drove him beyond the closed world of the traditionalists, and his refusal to give credence to the literal word of Genesis may well have caused him to be one of those who asked awkward questions about the chronology of the world. In spite of this, Harriot himself was no atheist and, on his deathbed, he was to write movingly of his belief in a natural order and man's duty of submission to the divine word. He was after all the person who had sung psalms with Wingina and hoped to convert the Indians through the marvels of science. Now he was also the man whom Parsons characterized as Ralegh's 'conjuror'. In the popular mind at least, Harriot was an atheist. And, as was Harriot, so, by implication, was his master.

This dangerous reputation for atheism was enhanced by association with one of the most notorious figures of the day, the poet and playwright Christopher Marlowe. Already, in 1592, the nature of Marlowe's views (or what were said to be Marlowe's views) were furnishing copy for the hacks. In the summer of 1592, the dying Robert Greene was preparing for the press his *Groatsworth of Wit Bought with a Million of Repentance*. Here he refers to his own atheism and then, addressing the 'famous gracer of tragedies' who everyone in the know realized was Marlowe, declared that he 'hath said, with thee, like the fool in his heart: There is no God.'[25] Greene's deathbed confession was published in September 1592, and in the same month that Elizabethan *manqué* Gabriel Harvey issued his *Four Letters* in which he ridiculed Marlowe under the name of the notorious Italian atheist Aretino, claiming he was a man whose practice it was to 'domineer in taverns and stationers' shops' and frighten ordinary people with his 'scoffing and girding' at the received verities.[26] In the tense religious atmosphere of the 1590s, these were dangerous allegations likely to sully the reputation of all associated with them.

The precise degree of Ralegh's association with Marlowe cannot now be ascertained. What their relationship was claimed to be about the time of Marlowe's murder is an altogether different matter. Then the machinery of insinuation would be set in motion in an attempt to blacken Ralegh's reputation with accusations of atheism altogether more terribly intentioned than the slurs of Parsons. Then the spy Richard Cholmeley would assert 'that Marlowe told him he hath read the atheist lecture to Sir Walter Ralegh and others'.[27] For the moment, however, before this web of insinuation had been spun, the only recorded connection between Ralegh and Marlowe was the fact that Ralegh replied to Marlowe's exquisitely erotic lyric 'Come live with me and be my love'.

Marlowe's poem offers the allurements of a carefree life of pleasure in a pastoral landscape where:

> we will sit upon the rocks,
> And see the shepherds feed their flocks
> By shallow rivers, to whose falls
> Melodious birds sing madrigals.[28]

All is pretty and innocent paganism, a renaissance promise of unabashed delight. Ralegh's response, his 'Nymph's Reply', refutes the arguments of Marlowe's shepherd with a deep awareness of time, mortality and human frailty. The poem suggests that broken promises, care, sorrow and vanity make even the hope of pleasure an illusion, the shepherd boy's harmless fictions a lie:

> could youth last, and love still breed,
> Had joys no date, nor age no need,

Then these delights my mind may move,
To live with thee, and be thy love.[29]

This response is no prudishness. The objections of Ralegh's nymph are not in any obvious sense moral. They spring rather from an awareness that time destroys all things and that death cancels out any trust we may put in pleasure. This was to become a theme central to the mature Ralegh's philosophy, and even here the pessimism under the surface of his elegant poem is genuine and surprisingly profound.

But in the 1590s, religious belief was hardening to religious bigotry. While the Jesuit missions appeared to pose a threat from without (a threat increasingly resented by a conspicuously loyal Catholic gentry), Puritan voices mounted a threat from within. Ralegh's contact with both groups was affected by his experiences of the Religious Wars in France, by the sceptical intelligence of the Durham House group, and his deep political conviction that loyalty to the queen as the supreme governor of the church in England was the foundation of national security.

The Puritans, however, were loud in reviling the many obvious abuses in the Church, using both pulpit and pamphlet to denounce what they saw as the complacent ignorance of its 'drunk dogs, unskilfully sacrificing priests, destroying drones, or rather caterpillars of the world'.[30] The virulence of the so-called 'Martin Marprelate' tracts raised such abuse to levels that worried even Walsingham, while Archbishop Whitgift was insistent that ecclesiastical criticism might well lead to censure on the governor of the Church herself. Elizabeth moved to suppress the danger. In February 1589, she issued a proclamation against the Puritans, characterizing them as subversives whose doctrinal zeal was a hazard to the state. Among those imprisoned was John Udall, compiler of the first Hebrew grammar in English and author of the opprobrious *Demonstration of Discipline which Christ hath prescribed in his Word for the Government of the Church, in all times and places, until the World's end.* This title is but a pale indication of the dogmatism within.

The Earl of Essex, who personally favoured the Puritans as a source of political support and theological enlightenment, had resolved to protect these men, and he now tried to persuade Ralegh to 'join him as an instrument from them to the queen upon any particular occasion of relieving them'.[31] Ralegh saw this as a possible means of binding a fractious minority to the crown, and proceeded to engineer an 'occasion' to relieve the wretched Udall. The imprisoned grammarian received a letter suggesting that exaggerated accounts of his opinions had misled the queen and that 'if you will write half a dozen lines to Sir Walter Ralegh, concerning those opinions ... he may show it to Her Majesty.'[32] Udall replied protesting his devotion to the queen and begging his punishment be commuted from death to banishment. While the bishops squabbled over the exercise of mercy, arrangements were made for Udall to be sent to Africa. But Udall, precise to the last, quibbled over the terms and, while waiting for an outcome, solved his problem by dying of gaol fever.

The end for others came less easily. Among Ralegh's official duties was the requirement to attend the executions of Catholic priests condemned for treason. Their treatment while in prison was invariably barbarous. Richard Topcliffe, the queen's enforcement agent against the Jesuits, was a man who hid limitless sadism under the torturer's mask of duty. The refinements he invented for 'scraping the conscience' may be relegated to their proper infamy by the simple comment of one who faced them. Robert Southwell, declared by Topcliffe to be a priest and traitor, replied: 'It is neither priest nor treason that you seek for, but only blood.'[33] This was a poet's intuition in the torture chamber, but now Topcliffe had another victim: Oliver Plasden, aged twenty-nine. His martyrdom was recorded by Father James Young.[34]

Others in the batch of victims had already been hanged when Plasden was forced up into the cart below the gallows. Here, in his last seconds of life, he began to pray for the queen and realm. Ralegh, attentive to the man rather than dulled by anticipation of his fate, interrupted the proceedings.

'What,' he said, 'doest thou think as thou prayest.'

Plasden replied that to do otherwise would be to lose all hope of salvation.

'Then thou doest acknowledge her for thy lawful queen?' Ralegh asked.

'I do sincerely.'

[193]

'Would'st thou defend her', he continued, 'against all her foreign and domestical enemies, if so thou were able?'

'I would', said Plasden, 'to the uttermost of my power, and so I would counsel all men who would be persuaded by me.'

The crowd began to mutter among themselves. The unexpected interruption, the clean, sincere words cutting the Tyburn air, had made them think. The priest's evident patriotism stirred their own. No man would lie thus at the point of death. Plasden was too honest a man to die. Ralegh addressed him again. Had Plasden spoken like this before his judges yesterday, he said, he would not be here now, and he might yet be saved and the mercy of the queen shown.

'I know, good people,' Ralegh said, turning himself, 'her Majesty desireth no more at these men's hands, than that which this man hath now confessed. Mister Sheriff,' he continued, 'I will presently go to the Court, let him be stayed.'

But Topcliffe was getting restless. Would Plasden, he asked, take up arms against the Pope or the King of Spain if they invaded the country?

'I am a priest,' he said, 'and therefore may not fight.'

It was a good answer.

Would Plasden then encourage others to fight and defend the queen? The priest replied that he would counsel all men to maintain the rights of their princes.

'He saith marvellous well,' Ralegh declared. 'No more. I will presently post to the queen. I know she will be glad of this plain dealing.'

But Topcliffe was less pleased. He had another question to pose, and Ralegh allowed him to ask it. Did Plasden think the queen had the right to maintain the Protestant religion and forbid his?

'No,' said the priest.

So would he then defend the queen against the armies of the Pope if he marched to re-establish Catholicism in England? 'What sayest thou to this? I charge thee before God.'

'I am a Catholic priest,' Plasden replied, 'therefore I would never fight nor counsel others to fight against my religion, for that were to deny my faith. Oh Christ,' he added, looking up to heaven and kissing the rope, 'I will never deny thee for a thousand lives.'

The crowd muttered and Topcliffe had his victim. Ralegh the

royal favourite, the sceptic of Durham House, had tried and failed in his attempts at reason. Now he must show himself a loyal servant of his queen. The cart was jerked away from under Plasden's feet, and 'he by the word of Ralegh was suffered to hang until he was dead: then he was drawn and quartered after their custom.'

Such fidelity continued to be rewarded, and the queen was now working to satisfy her favourite's long-felt need for a house in the country suitable to his status. For some years – certainly since 1589 when he first failed to secure it for himself – Ralegh had had his eye on the fine old castle at Sherborne in Dorset, a possession of the See of Salisbury. The castle lay very conveniently on the road between London and the ports of the southwest. In a biblical parallel that has the ring of a much-told story, Ralegh 'cast such an eye upon it as Ahab did upon Naboth's vineyard.'[35]

Indeed the castle at Sherborne became an obsession with him, a place as yet beyond his reach but where his imagination could unfold ideas of how his life might be extended and new roles found. He even became something of a bore about the place: 'And once above the rest being talking of it, of the commodiousness of the place, and how easily it might be got from the bishopric, suddenly over and over came his horse, that his very face, which was thought a very good face, ploughed up the earth where he fell.'[36] Ralegh was not the man to laugh such an incident off – his pride reached into the smallest details of his life – and it required the tact of his half-brother, the astrologer Adrian Gilbert, to suggest that such rapid contact with the ground of the castle was a sign that Ralegh would soon possess it.

The queen meanwhile bided her time. For Elizabeth, simony was among the minor political sins, but it was a matter to be handled with adroit chicanery. Her Church should only be mulcted under an appearance of legality, and for three years she left the See of Salisbury vacant until a candidate sufficiently supine offered himself. Eventually, after the gift of an elaborate jewel, Elizabeth was persuaded to appoint her favourite's client Doctor Cotton who in turn agreed to surrender the lease of Sherborne. But Ralegh was also avid for more church lands in the area, and when the ageing Bishop of Bath and Wells made the blunder of getting married, Elizabeth demanded the surrender of prosperous Willscombe Manor, which again fell into Ralegh's hands. Together, the estates made up a perfect domain for her great officer in the West. On the surface, all seemed well.

Now, however, in the closing months of 1591, Bess's pregnancy could no longer be kept a secret. Her brother Arthur recorded in his diary that 19 November was 'le jour quand je savoye le marriage de ma soeur'.[37] He too was being drawn into the circle of love and anxiety, one of three people waiting for the wrath of the moon goddess to strike.

Ralegh was determined to deflect this in the best way he knew. Down in Chatham, a great naval expedition was being prepared. The queen had contributed money and two ships, while that spectacular privateer the Earl of Cumberland was offering to victual no fewer than six vessels. The merchants of London were to equip two more, Ralegh and his brother Carew one each. To show the sincerity of his commitment, Ralegh also sank a large part of his capital in the venture and raised a loan for a further £10,000. So urgent was his need for money that he was even obliged to petition the government to pay him for the *Ark Ralegh*. He was eventually reimbursed with £5,000.

This and the conspicuous efforts Ralegh was making in the dock-yards as the flotilla was readied were the means by which he hoped to draw attention to himself as the great entrepreneur and patriot, the man who was now to lead an expedition to seize the argosies of Spain and sack her settlements on Panama. While his wife in secret was giving birth to his child, far out at sea Ralegh would be avenging the death of Sir Richard Grenville and the loss of the *Revenge*. He was gambling on being the hero of the hour.

Christmas came, and Arthur realized he too must secure his favour with the queen. Earlier that month he had quarrelled with a cousin and been taken up before the Lord Chamberlain on the matter. Perhaps the strain was beginning to tell. On Christmas Day, Arthur presented the queen with a waistcoat valued at £9. On New Year's Eve he made a further gift of two ruffs. Having done all he could in that quarter, he retreated to his hen house, taking comfort in the warm feathery cluckings and noting how, on 13 January, his white hen laid an egg at night in the sign of Pisces. The following night his dun hen laid an egg in Scorpio. Perhaps these activities would give a presage of the aspects of the moon. He waited, and at the close of February recorded how 'my sister came hither to lie here'.[38] Bess was now all too visibly pregnant and needed to hide with Arthur at Mile End.

By this time, Ralegh himself was ready to sail, but contrary winds held him back and he was thrown into despondency as he was obliged to 'row up and down with every tide from Gravesend to London'. He was 'more grieved', he added, 'than ever I was in anything of this world for this cross weather.'[39] And then the queen changed her mind. She decided Ralegh was too valuable to sail as Admiral on so dangerous an expedition and she insisted on a change of leadership. 'I have promised Her Majesty', Ralegh wrote, 'that if I can persuade the companies to follow Sir Martin Frobisher, I will without fail return.'[40] He was to escort the flotilla out to sea some 'fifty or threescore leagues and no further'. Elizabeth was insistent. She had 'many times bid me remember her will, which God willing, if I can persuade the companies, I mean to perform; though I dare not be acknown therein to any creature.'

His grand plan was in ruins and, in panic and dismay, he continued his letter to Sir Robert Cecil with a lie so blatant as almost to give the game away:

> I mean not to come away, as they say I will, for fear of a marriage, and I know not what. If any such thing were, I would have imparted it unto yourself before any man living; and, therefore, I pray believe it not, and I beseech you to suppress, what you can, any such malicious report. For I protest before God, there is no one, on the face of the earth, that I would be fastened unto.[41]

Tongues had been wagging. Bess's absence had no doubt been noted. Quick, envious wits were totting up the evidence against him, and allies were essential. Sir Robert Cecil, ageing Burghley's son, would be among the most useful of these. He was one of the stars of the younger generation. Brilliant, hunchbacked, indefatigable, Cecil had been groomed by his father to extend the family's dominance over English affairs for another generation. But where Burghley was severe, humourless even, Cecil was vivacious, a lover of poetry, dinner parties and the theatre. He was an immensely perceptive man and wholly, chillingly, ruthless. The favourite's letter gave him a valuable insight into the ways of the older generation.

But now Bess's time had come. On 29 March, Arthur wrote in his diary: 'my sister was delivered of a boy between 2 and 3 in the afternoon. I writ to Sir Walter Ralegh, and sent Dick the footman to whom I gave him 10s.'[42] Twelve days later, Arthur made another surprising diary entry. Ralegh's son was to be given the name of his great Plantagenet ancestor and was to have one wholly unexpected godfather. 'Damerei Ralegh', Arthur recorded, 'was baptized by Robert, Earl of Essex and Arthur Throckmorton and Anna Throckmorton.' Secrecy there may have been, but no modesty. The Raleghs had named their child after a royal forebear and called as their witness the most popular hero of his generation. They would not be cowed. Little Damerei was put out to a wet-nurse and then, on 27 April 1592, Lady Ralegh resumed her place among the maids of the Privy Chamber as plain Bess Throckmorton. It was an act of staggering impudence.

By the first week of the following month the winds had changed and Ralegh's flotilla set sail from Falmouth. Sir Martin Frobisher followed hard behind with the queen's peremptory order that Ralegh should at once resign his post and return to London. His 'crime' was now in the open, but he refused to damage the chances of the great expedition in which he had invested so much. Storms had already delayed him off Finisterre, and it was getting too late for the attempt on Panama. A sudden, swift revision of plans was necessary. Asserting his authority, Ralegh divided the flotilla in two. While half was to 'amuse' the Spanish home fleet by cruising off its coast, the other, under the command of Sir John Borough, was to sail for the Azores and there plunder the treasure ships. With these orders issued, Ralegh sailed for England.

Arthur was told of his landing and busied himself about domestic necessities. He 'paid the nurse one four weeks' wages come Monday next, 28s',[43] saw to it that his sister's marriage settlement was properly witnessed, and then, on 21 May, summoned the nurse to bring Damerei to Mile End. A week later, when Ralegh himself arrived in London, the child and the nurse went to Durham House. There were a few days of fatherly pride and pleasure before the official inquiry was set in motion.

This was altogether quieter than might have been expected. While Court and City pullulated with gossip, and wits and wiseacres deliberated on the favourite's fall, Arthur's sister Anna, Damerei's godmother, was required to make a statement to the Lord Chamberlain. On 31 May, Cecil was ordered to take Ralegh into custody, returning him to Durham House where Sir George Carew kept him under arrest. On 3 June, Lady Ralegh was summoned before the Lord Chamberlain. A week later, Arthur Throckmorton was asked for a statement. Elizabeth, it seemed, was mild, aloof even. Ralegh dared to write to her. Ireland had been the theme with which he had first won her ear and become her 'oracle'. Now he warned her of the danger of further rebellions there, but 'she made a scorn at my conceit'.[44] What was this man's advice? He was merely as he described himself to Cecil, 'a fish cast on dry land, gasping for breath, with lame legs and lamer lungs'.

Elizabeth would not, however, let him die so. She had raised him to be her great servant in the West and he had fulfilled his duties with exemplary competence. This was a role in which he was still needed. Through the long weeks of her seeming indifference Elizabeth saw that Ralegh's position there was firmly established. On 27 June, the lease on Sherborne Castle was confirmed. Then she waited, waited not as his lover, nor as the mystic goddess of the moon, but as a friend whom he had sorely, deeply wounded. Above all, she waited as his queen.

It was for Ralegh and his wife to come and sue for pardon, to confess and beg her mercy. There was no other suitable decorum. Elizabeth had screamed at Essex when he betrayed her, banished him and then forgiven him because her emotions were involved. Besides, for political reasons the farce of their noble love had to be maintained. With Ralegh, this was not so. He was not a great peer with a following that could prove a threat. He was a great servant and a foolish one. His proper role was contrition, and he refused to play it. His pride would not be humbled. Nor was Bess any less resolute. She had stolen a favourite from under the queen's nose and her womanly triumph was exhilarating to her. She had gained the love of one of the country's most outstanding men and borne his child. She was not the woman to pretend she was ashamed of such things. Matching his resolution, challenging him even, she would exert a hold over her husband altogether more powerful than that of the ageing spinster of Whitehall.

But Ralegh's pride made the silence of royal disregard intolerable. In the imprisoning emptiness of Durham House, as week after week passed, his mind began to be invaded with shrill and desperate uncertainty. Half maddened indeed, he seized upon the one part he could still play, calculating that he might win back favour by acting the royal favourite's extreme role: he would become the lover driven insane by his mistress's cruel indifference. In this state, Ralegh planned a scene of pathetic desperation.

Hearing one July day that the queen was about to land at Blackfriars, he went up to the lantern on the roof of Durham House. Here, with Harriot, he had watched the cold and mathematical motion of the stars. Here too he had read, studied, thought and planned. Here maps of the New World had been unrolled, discussions held, ships designed and plans laid. Now the room was to be his stage, and George Carew and Arthur Gorges his audience. As he spied the royal party, Ralegh struck the pose of the melancholy lover and 'having gazed and sighed a long time at his study window, from whence he might discern the barges and boats about the Blackfriars Stairs, suddenly he break out into a great distemper and swore that his enemies had of purpose brought Her Majesty thither, to break his gall asunder.'[45]

Warming to his role, he turned to Carew and vowed 'he would disguise himself and get a pair of oars to ease his mind but with a sight of the queen; or else, he protested, his heart would break.' Carew restrained him. Words flew and there was a struggling at the doors. Carew's wig was snatched off. Daggers were drawn. Arthur Gorges realized he must intervene, and so 'I played the stickler between them, and so purchased such a wrap on the knuckles as I wished both their pates broken.' Only the sight of blood dripping from his fingers eventually stopped Ralegh and Carew fighting.

Or so Gorges alleges. His account was written for Sir Robert Cecil in the hope of proving 'Sir W. Ralegh will shortly grow to be Orlando Furioso if the bright Angelica preserve against him for a little longer.' The reference was to Ariosto's poem in Sir John Harington's translation of the previous year. The whole scene was a literary fabrication, a patent and pathetic device which Gorges himself betrayed when he fixed a slip of paper to his letter in which he suggested that Cecil might, 'as you think good', let the queen know what was going on. It was desperation indeed to think that the shrewdest ruler in Europe would ever be won over with a charade.

Besides, her patience was running out. The courtiers were well aware of the fact and were now sniggering behind their jewelled fingers:

> S. W. R., as it seemeth, hath been too inward with one of Her Majesty's maids . . . All think the Tower will be his dwelling, like hermit poor in pensive place, where he may spend his endless days in doubt. It is affirmed that they are married; but the queen is most fiercely incensed, and, as the bruit goes, threateneth the most bitter punishment to both the offenders. S. W. R. will lose, it is thought, all his places and preferments at court, with the queen's favour; such will be the end of his speedy rising, and, now he must fall as low as he was high, at the which many will rejoice. I can write no more at this time, and do not care to send this, only you will hear it from others. All is alarm and confusion at this discovery of the discoverer, and not indeed of a new continent, but of a new incontinent.[46]

And the gossips were right. On 7 August 1592, Arthur Throckmorton recorded in his diary: 'Ma Soeur s'en alla à la tour et Sir W. Ralegh.'[47] The favourite had fallen into the five long years of his disgrace.

CHAPTER ELEVEN

The Years of Disgrace

Elizabeth went on a royal progress while her prisoner took up his pen. 'My heart was never broken to this day, that I hear the queen goes away so far off whom I have followed so many years with so great love and desire, in so many journeys, and am now left behind her, in a dark prison all alone.'[1] The hysterical charade at Durham House had been replaced by the accents of the melancholy lover.

This was a part Ralegh might still hope to act before his queen. But it is unlikely that Cecil, to whom these lines were ostensibly addressed, showed them to her. He noted rather the self-abasement – that perennial obverse of Ralegh's pride – with which the fallen favourite described his plight. 'She is gone in whom I trusted, and of me hath not one thought of mercy, nor any respect of that that was.' This refusal by Elizabeth to forgive his marriage by acknowledging his former services was a source of great bitterness to Ralegh. The feeling was to last many months and to be made more acid by events. For the moment however he signed himself to Cecil: 'Yours, not worthy of any name or title'. The royal prisoner presented himself as a nameless thing, a man who claimed to feel that he lived without a self or even, in the last analysis, a role.

Cecil was too shrewd a politician to alienate Ralegh in this period of misfortune. He was never the man to stretch out the frank hand of friendship, but he could at least appear an ally. Factional rivalry required limitless dexterity if a man were long to survive and, for the moment, Cecil could allow Ralegh to believe he still had a means of gaining the queen's ear. In such ways, the younger generation were establishing themselves in the ageing Elizabeth's court.

The queen herself had been more merciful in these first days of Ralegh's imprisonment than she might have appeared. Durham House was still his, and she had confirmed rather than revoked the lease on Sherborne. Furthermore, the immense profits from Ralegh's monopolies still accrued to him. He had been humiliated but not ruined, and for the private man there was one deep consolation. A letter from this time, written from the Tower in Bess's erratically extrovert spelling, is a measure of the woman. 'I am dayly put in hope of my delivery,' she began, but, 'I assur you trewly I never desiared nor never wolde desiar my lebbarti with out the good likeking ne advising of Sur W. R.'[2] She was understandably concerned about what might happen in the future – 'who knooeth what will be com of me when I am out' – but for the moment Bess was confident. In the flat vowel sounds of an Elizabethan gentlewoman, she declared: 'Wee ar trew with in ourselfes I can assur you. Towar, ever asureedly yours in frinshep. E. R.'

'We are true in ourselves I can assure you.' There is no reason to doubt this. But for Ralegh, imprisoned amid the wreckage of his hopes, there were inevitably more bitter emotions:

> My body in walls captived
> Feels not the wounds of spightful envy.
> But my thralled mind, of liberty deprived,
> Fast fettered in her ancient memory.
> Doth naught behold but sorrow's dying face.
> Such prison erst was so delightful
> As it desired no other dwelling place,
> But time's effects, and destinies despiteful
> Hath changed both my keeper and my fare.
> Love's fire and beauty's light I then had store,
> But now close-kept, as captives wonted are,
> That food, that heat, that night I find no more.
> Despair bolts up my doors, and I alone
> Speak to dead walls, but those hear not my moan.

The glad imprisonment of royal favour has given way to the desperate captivity of disgrace. There is not the slightest suggestion of guilt or repentance here, an acknowledgement that Ralegh had been at the very least foolish. Rather, the lines are constructed out of his pride, his defiance and self-pity. And it was from these that he was now to fashion the greatest of his poetic achievements: the twenty-first and fragmentary twenty-second books of a work entitled

The Ocean to Cynthia. Here, in one of the major if unfinished works of English renaissance literature, Ralegh created an exceptional response to catastrophe.

The Ocean to Cynthia is inevitably an act of self-dramatization, a poem in which Ralegh fashioned himself as the central figure in a play of passion. With the liberty of the dramatist, he recast the historical facts of his plight into a plea for favour wholly characteristic of his pride. Rather than repent, the poet and soldier resolved that attack was the best means of defence.

Ralegh's marriage to Bess is presented merely as a minor slip, an 'error' which the poet believes can scarcely be held to have besmirched his chaste adoration for his sacred lady. Indeed, it is Cynthia herself, the imperious and inconstant moon, who is the figure Ralegh presents as most grievously at fault in his work. Much of the poem challenges his goddess to reveal a constancy as great as his. *The Ocean to Cynthia* is very far from being the spontaneous overflow of powerful feelings – no renaissance literature was that – and is rather a calculated, rhetorical attempt at persuasion. It is Ralegh's means of presenting himself as the desolate hero, his means of acting out the role with all the force of his emotions and intellect. The calculated histrionics of the work are the measure of the man.

The poem opens in the waste land of a winter pastoral, and the devastated landscape is at one with the bereft shepherd's distress. Forced by sheer loneliness into the desperate position of being obliged to address his dead sorrows, the poet contrasts past happiness and present misery:

> From fruitful trees I gather withered leaves
> And glean the broken ears with miser's hands,
> Who sometime did enjoy the weighty sheaves . . .[3]

The poem will throughout build on strong emotional contrasts, the effect of these violent swings of feeling suggesting Ralegh's conflict of emotions, the turbulence of his mind.

Having established his role as the anguished lover, Ralegh begins to present his apparent defeat in his twelve years' 'war' with his imperious mistress, contrasting his own wholehearted commitment to Cynthia's inconstancy. Passages of rapturous adoration alternate with lines of bitter personal reflection. Some of the incidents are taken from Ralegh's immediate experience. Elizabeth's refusal to allow him to sail on the expedition he had recently prepared, for example, still rankled, and Ralegh's expression of this suggests at once the scale of his imaginative vision and the professed depths of his love. The verses also show his mistress's apparently gratuitous exercise of her power:

> To seek new worlds, for gold, for praise, for glory,
> To try desire, to try love severed far,
> When I was gone she sent her memory
> More strong than were ten thousand ships of war
>
> To call me back, to leave great honour's thought,
> To leave my friends, my fortune, my attempt,
> To leave the purpose I so long had sought,
> And hold both cares and comforts in contempt.[4]

It is such contrariety that makes Cynthia the image of the cruel mistress of those poets who followed the tradition of Petrarch. The ambiguous nature of her emotions – 'such heat in ice, such fire in frost' – necessarily appears as a rebuff to the purity of his own feelings. In the end, Cynthia's swinging between cruelty and kindness leads to the poet's exhaustion and defeat:

> Twelve years entire I wasted in this war,
> Twelve years of my most happy younger days,
> But I in them, and they now wasted are,
> Of all which past the sorrow only stays.[5]

To those like Elizabeth herself, who were familiar with Ralegh's poetry, the repetition in the last line of the refrain from an earlier lament reinforces the awareness of emotional exhaustion, the ultimately debilitating cycle of 'woe to wrath, from wrath return to woe'. In this state, the poet is forced to recognize that while Cynthia is 'a vestal fire that burns but never wasteth', she is not the immaculate goddess of his imagining:

> So hath perfection which begat her mind
> Added thereto a change of fantasy,
> And left her the affections of her kind,
> Yet free from every evil but cruelty.[6]

Cynthia is seen as being as fickle as all women. If she rises superior to most, she is not free from 'evil'. She is cruel. In the context of the veneration of Elizabeth elaborated by so many poets, this criticism is a sharp and even shocking stab.

Having gone so far and dared to criticize the Virgin Queen, the second half of Ralegh's poem opens with an altogether more oppressive sense of desolation. Once again, he is obsessed by the idea that his immense labours in the royal service have been for naught and, in his despair, he imagines himself inhabiting a parched and darkened landscape. Tokens of his past enjoyments are sterile. Others now enjoy Cynthia's favours – the abiding jealousy of Essex is clear at this point – while Ralegh begins to suggest that his own passion is something superior, something permanent and spiritual, a force not to be extinguished simply because the object that inspired it has proved to be fickle.

It is this high devotion – the very essence of the poet's being – that Cynthia has betrayed and, with it, Ralegh suggests, the glorious fiction they both created of Elizabeth as a divine being. By bringing his minor transgression into the open and untying 'the gentle chains of love', Elizabeth has punished him unjustly and shown herself as an overweening ruler. Most cruel of all, Cynthia's indifference makes Ralegh's lament – poetry itself – a pointless exercise, words spoken into a void. Without an audience, the actor may as well be dumb. His solitary anguish only confirms the eternal but hopeless nature of his passion.

The poet at last realizes he must suffer lifelong punishment and anguish in an unjust world where a ruthless and inconstant mistress refuses to acknowledge the love that is his whole being. In the end, he can play the amorous shepherd no more:

> Unfold thy flocks and leave them to the fields
> To feed on hills, or dales, where likes them best,
> Of what the summer or the spring time yields,

For love, and time, hath given thee leave to rest.

Thy heart which was their fold, now in decay
By often storms and winter's many blasts
All torn and rent, becomes misfortune's prey,
False hope, my shepherd's staff now age hath brast

My pipe, which love's own hand, have my desire
To sing her praises and my woe upon,
Despair hath often threatened to the fire
As vain to keep now all the rest are gone.[7]

As for his soul:

To God I leave it who first gave it me,
And I her gave, and she returned again.
As it was hers, so let His mercies be,
Of my last comforts the essential mean.
But be it so, or not, th'effects are past:
Her love hath end, my woe must ever last.[8]

Perhaps even divine mercy cannot save him from an eternity of pain.

It is unlikely that Elizabeth ever received this turbulent portrayal of her erstwhile favourite's feelings. The only version in which the poem survives is an autograph manuscript that long remained undiscovered among the Cecil papers at Hatfield House. However, while Ralegh was pining at the desolation wrought to his service of the Virgin Queen, he was also chafing at other matters. His imprisonment in the Tower forebade him exercising the great energies he had given to his activities as a crown servant and privateer, and a letter to Effingham, the Lord High Admiral, expresses his annoyance at being restricted in these spheres.

Ralegh describes in particular the incompetence by which a boat in which he had an interest had been forced to abandon her voyage with the consequent loss to English prestige at sea. Frustration is clear in this, and Ralegh went on to itemize other matters that needed his attention such as the plight of the discontented mariners who 'run up and down exclaiming for pay'.⁹ In addition, the fact that the Channel fleet was being used to transship men to the mainland of Europe rather than defending the seas irked him, and he was careful to suggest in his letter a patriot's exasperation. 'We are so much busied with the affairs of other nations (of whose mangled troubles there will never be an end), that we forget our own affairs, our profit, and our honour.' His imprisonment, Ralegh implies, is having a deleterious effect on the safety of the realm.

But now his earlier initiatives were coming to sudden and unexpected prominence. The squadron of ships Ralegh had despatched to the Azores under the command of Sir John Borough had no sooner reconnoitred with two London privateers off Flores than an immense Portuguese carrack hove into view, pursued by one of the Earl of Cumberland's vessels. Both the captain of the Earl's ship and Borough, who was aboard Ralegh's *Roebuck*, prepared to engage her when a sudden storm blew up. The captain of the Portuguese ship, realizing escape was impossible, resolved to obey his master's orders by setting fire to his vessel. Borough's anger was only relieved when he learned from one of the enemy crew that other more richly laden ships were making for the port, there to meet their Spanish escort.

On 3 August a lookout spied a vast enemy vessel: the *Madre de Dios*. She was a floating castle of sixteen hundred tons with seven decks manned by eight hundred crew. Battle was engaged from ten in the morning until after midnight when, despite the fractious behaviour of Cumberland's men who boarded the ship and began to loot her, Borough asserted his command. 'I have now,' he wrote back to London, 'taken possession of the carrack in Her Majesty's name and right, and I hope, for all the spoil that has been made, her Majesty shall receive more profit by her than by any ship that ever came into England.'¹⁰ After a stormy passage, the *Madre de Dios* was brought to Dartmouth and Borough's boast was shown to be justified. The expedition prepared by Sir Walter Ralegh had captured the richest prize of the entire privateering war.

In the vast holds of the ship were discovered 537 tons of spices. The value of the pepper alone was estimated at £120,000, while the cloves, cinnamon, mace, nutmeg and other commodities greatly augmented this sum. There were also jewels, pearls, amber and musk which the disconsolate Spaniards reckoned 'to the value of 400,000 crusados'.[11] Glittering among these were 'two great crosses and one other great jewel of diamonds which the Viceroy sent for a present to the King'. Sir John Hawkins, wildly overestimating a total haul of half a million pounds, wrote desperately to Burleigh, begging that help be despatched to the West Country.

For the wafting of the fragrant spices made Dartmouth seem like Zanzibar. The promise of limitless wealth drifted over the surrounding countryside and was carried as far as London by the exclamations of the looters. Merchants and courtiers, tradesmen and profiteers, converged on the port to buy for a trifle the treasures looted by the seamen, in some cases reselling these for five times what they paid without even having to leave town. If such fabulous wealth were not to be lost in an orgy of looting, authority had to be restored. Burghley despatched Cecil in an attempt to impose order, and the young man's letters back to his father offer vivid pictures of the chaos.

Cecil wrote of men arrested, of trunks searched, and of a bag of seed pearls discovered in the lodgings of a London agent. 'I found besides, in this unlooked-for search, an amulet of gold [and] a fork and spoon of crystal with rubies, which I reserve for the queen.'[12] He realized that if he had arrived a week earlier he might have saved Elizabeth £20,000, but 'I fear that the birds be flown.' For the bureaucratic Cecil, this was an all but impossible situation to control. 'Fouler ways, desperater ways, nor more obstinate people, did I never meet with.' Someone of altogether more commanding presence was needed, and Hawkins eventually petitioned for the release of Sir Walter Ralegh, declaring him to be 'the especial man'.[13]

Ralegh arrived in Dartmouth under the surveillance of a royal guard. Sir John Gilbert greeted him in tears and clasped him to his chest, but whenever people came up to Ralegh, offering their congratulations on his being set at liberty, he turned a sad face to them: 'No: I am still the queen of England's poor captive.'[14] This was an act clearly calculated to win sympathy, and Cecil noted that Ralegh was 'marvellous greedy to do any thing to recover the conceit of his brutish offence'.[15] Indeed, on his way to the West, Ralegh made clear that he was determined to use the situation to win back what favour he could. The rioters must be stopped. 'If I meet any of them coming up,' he swore, 'if it be upon the wildest heath in all the way,

I mean to strip them as naked as ever they were born. For it is infinite that Her Majesty has been robbed, and that of the most rare things.'[16] He did not mention that he too, as one of the investors in the expedition, had been robbed as well. The recovery of royal favour was all.

Arrived in Dartmouth, Ralegh was among his own people and could exploit their loyalty and sympathy. Cecil was aware of the effect his presence had. 'I assure you, Sir, his poor servants to the number of a hundred and forty goodly men, and all the mariners, came to him with such shouts of joy, as I never saw a man more troubled to quiet them in my life. But his heart is broken; for he is very extreme pensive longer than he is busied, in which he can toil terribly.'[17] The manic activity and the bouts of depression are wholly characteristic.

The sharing out of the spoils, the recovery of the mariners' depredations, the paying of wages and the assessment of the true value of the cargo, were the work of many months. Both Cecil and Ralegh were careful to ensure each other's good report. Ralegh wrote to Burghley: 'I dare give the queen ten thousand pounds sterling for that which is gained by Sir Robert Cecil's coming down.'[18] Ralegh's local prestige, Cecil conceded, 'is greater among the mariners than I thought for'. Ralegh himself now estimated the value of the haul at approximately £200,000 and concluded, 'Her Majesty's adventure will come but to the tenth part.' But he had every reason to fear that matters would not be dealt with on an equitable basis. He was a prisoner, a man with few rights, and he tried to proceed with their greatest delicacy. 'I know her Majesty', he hinted to Burghley, 'will not take the right of her subjects from them.'[19]

The Chancellor of the Exchequer, Sir John Fortesque, realized the political importance of dealing fairly with the treasure, and wrote to Burghley: 'It were utterly to overthrow all service, if due regard were not had of my Lord of Cumberland and Sir Walter Ralegh, with the rest of the Adventurers, who would never be induced to further adventure, if they were not princely considered of; and I herein found Her Majesty very princely disposed.'[20] But Fortesque was too easily taken in. Elizabeth, desperate as always for money, was fully aware of those with whom she should deal reasonably and those who might yet be punished – and punished hard – in their pockets.

When it came to dividing up the spoils of the *Madre de Dios*, the Earl of Cumberland was rewarded with £36,000 on his investment of £19,000. He had, besides, unloaded many of his other prizes at harbours where he could easily escape the royal tax gatherers. The City merchants, who had been obliged to subscribe £6,000 to the expedition, received twice as much in return – a pleasing profit to bind them to the crown. The disgraced Ralegh, who had invested his ship, his time and initiative, who had made the crucial decision to divide the flotilla between the Spanish coast and the Azores rather than sending it to Panama, received a mere £2,000 return. Elizabeth, who had ventured only two ships and £1,800, allocated herself a profit of £80,000. She had punished Ralegh by depriving him of a fortune. Only at the close of the year did she begin to relent. On 22 December, Arthur Throckmorton recorded in his diary: 'My sister was delivered from the Tower.'[21]

Ralegh and Bess began to build a new life for themselves at Sherborne, an intimate, country existence in which for the first time they could come to know each other as man and wife. Exiled from the court, they were free from the envious glances of the Virgin Queen, and free too from the oppressive and competitive world that surrounded her. Damerei, the first child of their love, is not heard of any more. It must be presumed the infant died. By the early months of 1593, however, Bess was pregnant again, and their new son was christened on All Saints Day in the nearby church of Lillington. There were no more attempts to suggest a royal lineage. The boy was named after his father and grandfather, and became known to his parents as Wat.

The castle at Sherborne was the ancient fortress of a medieval bishop, a building of note to antiquarians but hardly the place for a modern family to live. In 1593, Ralegh began building a new home to the south of the property on the site of a disused hunting lodge. His half-brother Adrian Gilbert acted as surveyor, and the house itself was a fine example of late Elizabethan domestic architecture. A central cube of brick construction, three floors high and generously pierced with mullion windows, was surmounted on each face with the generous curves of a double gable containing more windows. From the corners of this central pile projected hexagonal buttress towers designed perhaps to echo the lines of the old castle but suggesting less defence than proprietorial magnificence. This was an impression heightened by the fantastication of chimneys and carved heraldic beasts that stared out over the surrounding countryside. In all this, Sherborne was an early example of a substantial, non-courtier type of house, an elegant statement of an influential ideal.

The gardens, too, were remarkable, running across a little valley to join the old house to the new. Adrian Gilbert was again responsible for 'making and planting' them, and he so inspired Cecil with his abilities that he was later employed by Cecil at his mansion at Theobalds. In the delightful setting of Sherborne meanwhile, Ralegh took pleasure in rearing the rare species of flowers and trees brought back by his sailors and showing these off to his friends – Harriot among them – who remained from the days of his magnificence. His brother Carew also became a close companion, and the social life of a country gentleman was broadened by acquaintance with such neighbours as Sir George Trenchard and Sir Ralph Horsey, the deputy lieutenants of the county, John Fitzjames and Charles Thynne from nearby Longleat.

There were irksome difficulties none the less. For the moment, John Meere, the reeve Ralegh had inherited from the Bishop of Salisbury, was co-operative. The ecclesiastical authorities, however, were being awkward. The new bishop claimed that Ralegh was not honouring the terms of his lease and was delaying the payment of his dues. 'The evil reports that I bear for him,' the prelate wrote, 'and his evil usage of me, do make me in good faith weary of all.'[22] An intricate series of exchanges resulted, Ralegh finally writing to Cecil with the unscrupulous suggestion that matters might be so arranged with the queen that when the grant appeared to have been settled 'perchance master Attorney will find a way'[23] to frustrate the intentions of Ralegh's enemies.

Regaining the favour of the queen was still a principal necessity, and the parliament called for 19 February 1593 gave Ralegh the opportunity of appearing as the spokesman of her policies. He was returned as the member for the small and unimportant borough of St Michael in Cornwall. He was no longer a county representative, and his new status reflected his disgrace.

The Elizabethan parliaments met in the Chapel of St Stephen in the precincts of the Palace of Westminster. Some four hundred men were cramped into the small medieval building. They had to make do with a single committee room, and were further inconvenienced by their numerous servants jostling on the stairs that led to the chamber itself. This was, as one member described it, 'framed and made like unto a theatre, being four rows of seats one above another, round about the house'.[32] The Speaker – in the parliament of 1593 Sir Edward Coke – occupied a raised chair at the upper end. Below him the Under Clerk of Parliament sat at a table. Those members of the Privy Council who were not peers occupied the front benches around the Speaker, as did the representatives of London and York. The rest placed themselves where they could. Each 'sitteth where they cometh, no difference being held there of any degree, because each man in that place is of like calling.'[25]

Strenuous efforts were made to preserve a harmonious relationship with the crown. The greater part of the members accepted that parliament was a valuable means of communication between Elizabeth and her governing classes, that she alone had the right to summon members, and that their principal functions were to vote money, pass laws and offer advice, particularly on matters of religion and national security. Policy, however, was recognized as the prerogative of the crown, and objections, by and large, were expressed less through confrontation than by lobbying and putting pressure on members of the Privy Council. The Privy Counsellors indeed were the powerful monitors of the House's business, Burleigh and later Cecil nominating members through an intricate system of patronage which tried to ensure that the House was representative of their views. Other grandees – Essex especially – also had their placemen, and to a considerable extent the Commons became a reflection of the factional divisions within the Privy Council which itself remained the supremely powerful institution of government under the crown.

Absenteeism, a fair measure of inefficiency, and a lack of experience in matters of procedure among the numerous new men, were among the problems facing those who managed parliamentary business, a surprising amount of which was of merely parochial interest: private squabbles over land and employment, or matters of civic importance. Such business could create a serious log-jam, and the Elizabethan House of Commons was continuously working to improve its institutional procedures, a development to which Ralegh was to contribute in the parliament of 1593.

Parliamentarians also had their privileges, rights which had again emerged from attempts to tighten up procedure. Members were, for example, immune from arrest when parliament was actually sitting, but it is suggestive of the members' pragmatism that when, in 1593, Thomas Fitzherbert was arrested by the crown for substantial debt, they neither protested nor pursued the matter. Again, in the crucial matter of freedom of speech, very few members saw this as an opportunity to discuss any matters they chose. Freedom of speech was interpreted as the right to discuss issues without fear of reprisal from the crown. And it was the crown that decided what might be discussed. Religion, foreign policy, the royal marriage and, later, the royal succession, were, in the queen's view, all prerogative matters, and her sharpest rhetoric was reserved for ruling these issues *ultra vires*. In the parliament of 1593 however, Peter Wentworth was resolved to move for a settlement of the succession. Elizabeth had her own means of dealing with such men, and while Wentworth and his allies were arrested, Ralegh saw his chance of springing to the queen's defence.

He wrote a paper on the succession, hoping Cecil would pass on his expression of loyalty to the queen. The tract is now missing its concluding paragraphs, but the sheets that remain show the poet of *The Ocean to Cynthia* applying his mind to matters of state in the hope of regaining favour. Ralegh was careful to portray the pain of a fallen favourite. 'Your Majesty having left me, I am left all alone in the world.'[26] He lamented that Elizabeth's refusal to pardon him made it seem that his 'errors are eternal'. The only light by which he can now live, he opined, is 'the memory of those celestial beauties' emanating from his beloved Cynthia herself.

But if the succession tract drew on the role of the despairing lover, it juxtaposed this to more forthright energies. Ralegh's sarcasm as he ridiculed 'these great patriots' who dare to touch on a matter far above their heads is extremely effective, and gains power from the logical rigour with which Ralegh argued from historical precedent to affirm the queen's wisdom in ruling that the succession was not a matter for public debate. In so doing, Ralegh was bringing his extensive knowledge of the past to bear upon the present, a technique of great importance to the future author of the *History of the World*.

It is Ralegh's professed love of Elizabeth herself that is his strongest suit however. Praising the great care for her people she has shown throughout her reign and citing as a blessing her protection of the Protestant faith especially, Ralegh argued that for her subjects to doubt her future care for them was wholly unjustified. Besides, such people could not appreciate what damage might be done were Elizabeth to name her heir. Not only would interest and loyalty inevitably be deflected to her successor, thereby damaging her prestige, but such discussions failed to take into account the very real shortcomings of all the likely candidates. With singularly ill-advised enthusiasm, Ralegh chose to question the suitability of the man who was, in the end, to succeed Elizabeth: James VI of Scotland. Obsessed by what he saw as the peril posed to the country by Roman Catholicism and the Spaniard-backed Jesuits especially, Ralegh claimed that to nominate James to the throne might well be to encourage him to join in a league with Spain in order to bring about the succession with unnatural speed.

Chief among the issues facing the 1593 parliament, however, was the necessity of raising money for the continuing sea war against Spain. This was a subject to which Ralegh could again warm with genuine enthusiasm. On the afternoon of 7 March 1593, he rose to address the House. Speaking 'not only to please the queen, to whom he was infinitely bound above his deserts, but for the necessity he both saw and knew',[27] Ralegh offered the members a disturbing impression of Spain's power, of ships being supplied to her by Norway and Denmark, and of ports being found for these in France, the Netherlands and, through the duplicity of papist sympathizers, in Scotland as well. He alleged that sixty Spanish galleons were prepared, and as always he urged offensive action. For purposes of national security, a grant of money was an unquestionable necessity:

> I can see no reason that the suspicion of discontentment should cross the provision for the present danger. The time is now more dangerous than it was in '88, for then the Spaniard which came

from Spain was to pass dangerous seas, and had no place of retreat of relief if he failed. But now he hath in Brittany great store of shipping, a landing place in Scotland, and men and horses there as good as we have any. But for the difficulty in getting the subsidy, I think it seems more difficult by speaking than it would be in gathering.[28]

Partly swayed by such feelings, the Commons had resolved to repeat the exceptional grant it had made in 1589 and vote the crown a double subsidy.

Such a sum, as Lord Treasurer Burghley knew, was insufficient, and he now requested a joint conference of the two Houses at which he could argue for a triple subsidy. A furious debate ensued. Burghley's request was an infringement of the Commons' liberty to determine the size of taxes. Besides, although the Lords was acknowledged as the institutional equal of the Lower House, its prestige and superior efficiency were widely feared. The peers were responsible for placing many of the members in the Commons, and when their clients were summoned to them – standing bare-headed before the seated delegates of the hereditary peerage – they felt keenly disadvantaged. Francis Bacon declared that Burleigh's invitation must be refused on principle.

The two Houses seemed set on a confrontation of the utmost seriousness. Some administrative procedure had to be found which, while neither breaking with precedent nor eroding the liberties of the Lower House, would yet allow the matter to be resolved. Ralegh, with that independence of mind and genuine administrative ability which were among his greatest assets, proposed that the two sides meet to discuss the question of the Spanish danger and the subsidy generally. The question of who could command whom was thus neatly avoided.

In the hubbub caused by members angrily discussing Burghley's invitation, Ralegh's light voice could not easily be heard. He was asked to repeat his proposal. Having done so, the members happily adopted his innovation and, after their meeting with the Lords, voted the crown the exceptional sum it needed. Ralegh had helped to win a victory for his own cause while simultaneously bringing himself to prominence as a parliamentarian. The queen might indeed be prevailed to look kindly on the man who could so ably resolve so difficult a situation.

Ralegh's value, however, lay not only in his adroit display of loyalty but in his genuine powers of criticism. A second speech in the parliament of 1593 illustrates this. In the furtherance of the crown's mounting campaign against Puritan sects, Elizabeth's 'little black husband', the zealous disciplinarian Archbishop Whitgift, was proposing to amend the 'Act to retain the queen's Majesty's subjects within their due obedience'. Originally passed as an anti-Catholic measure, it was now proposed to use it against the Brownists, a sect who wished to sunder Church from State and who urged the merits of holy ignorance and divine inspiration. 'In my conceit', Ralegh declared, 'the Brownists are worthy to be rooted out of the Commonwealth; but what danger may grow to ourselves if this law pass, it were fit to be considered.'[29]

He feared, first of all, that the law might be used arbitrarily, and that 'men not guilty' might be punished by it. He also argued that it was extremely dangerous to suppose a jury could establish the nature of religious inclination, especially where the punishment proposed was death or banishment. And it was the idea of banishment that particularly attracted Ralegh's attention. No one knew better than he the extreme practical difficulties this would entail. With the experience of Roanoke behind him, he was well placed to ask a series of questions whose purpose was clearly to save the queen from unforeseen embarrassment. 'If two or three thousand Brownists meet at the seaside,' he asked, 'at whose charge should they be transported? Or wither will you send them? I am sorry for it: I am afraid there is near twenty thousand of them in England and when they be gone who shall maintain their wives and children?'[30]

But while enforced emigration appeared to create problems rather than providing a solution, the existence of a large number of foreigners in London was causing serious friction with the indigenous citizens of the capital. Plague, poor trade and the threat of increased taxation led to the need for scapegoats. Protestant refugees from the Low Countries were an easily identifiable racial minority on which to pick. If they spoke English at all, it was with a marked accent. They had their own exclusive churches and, not content merely with manufacturing goods, they 'would keep shops and retail all manner of goods'.[31] The 'Netherlanders' were a classic target for prejudice. The government, however, ignored petitions made against them and resolved instead that as they were true Protestants and conspicuous creaters of wealth, their privileges as resident aliens should be reinforced. One parliamentary voice alone spoke out against this.

'Whereas it is pretended that for strangers it is against charity, against honour, against profit to expel them,' Ralegh declared, 'in my opinion it is no matter of charity to relieve them.'[32] These people had deserted their rightful king and merely exchanged one Protestant land for another. Ralegh's principal objections, however, were less political and religious than economic. Despite his monopolies, he now spoke as a man firmly opposed to protectionism and the centralized control of trade. Looking at what the Dutch were beginning to achieve in their own country through low customs and the encouragement of trade, he became convinced it was the government's duty 'to allure and encourage the people for their private gain to be all workers and erectors of a commonwealth'.

Such progress would not be achieved by extending privileges to rivals. Besides, the process was not even reciprocal. 'In Antwerp where our intercourse was most', Ralegh declared, 'we were never suffered to have a tailor or a shoemaker to dwell there.' He offered the House a vivid description of the threat posed to English trade and security by commercial expansion in the Netherlands. 'The Dutchman by his policy hath gotten trading with all the world in his hands, yea he is now entering into the trade of Scarborough fishing and the fishing of the Newfound-lands, which is the stay of the West Counties.' Dutch commercial expansion, it seemed, was threatening even Ralegh's kinsmen and the region where he was born. Most worryingly of all, such wealth ensured that the Dutch 'are the people that maintain the King of Spain in his greatness.' He could therefore see 'no matter of honour, no matter of charity, no profit in relieving them.'

Although the House disregarded his criticisms, Ralegh had made a considerable contribution to the parliament of 1593, voicing his opinion on a wide range of issues in the hope of drawing attention to himself as a loyal and useful servant of the crown. He had written on the succession problem, urged the raising of taxes for the sea war against Spain, contributed to parliamentary procedure, saved the queen from potential embarrassment in her government's handling of the Puritans, and sounded a note of economic warning which prefigured the fierce competition between Dutch and English merchants that sixty years later would lead to war. Now, when parliament was prorogued on 10 April, he was tired and, before returning to Sherborne, he decided to take the waters at Bath. This was apparently to little purpose. 'I am worse for the Bath, not the better,' he wrote despondently.[33]

While Elizabeth noted Ralegh's contributions to her parliament, she did not consider these a sufficient reason for pardoning him. His rivals, however – Essex especially – were concerned by his performance. While in the Tower, Ralegh was no danger, but on the floor of the House of Commons his abilities posed a threat. Essex was determined to blacken Ralegh's reputation in any way he could, and his spy ring was ordered to fabricate a situation which might destroy Ralegh's name for good.

The plan adopted was to revive the allegations of atheism first made by Robert Persons and then give these substance, if necessary by manufacturing the evidence. An oblique approach was called for, and Essex's agents decided that the best means of proceeding was first to play on Ralegh's association with the notorious atheist Christopher Marlowe. In the days between the proroguing of parliament and the Easter of 1593, placards appeared across London threatening civil disorder. These placards were the work of Essex's men, and they threatened in particular that the apprentices would rise up and 'attempt some violence on the strangers'[34] – in other words the Low Country refugees whose presence in the city Ralegh had so vehemently criticized in the House of Commons. This was the first step in a campaign by which Ralegh would come to be presented as the parliamentary spokesman of the mob.

A worried Privy Council wrote to the Lord Mayor demanding he investigate. They were fearful of 'further mischief', and rightly so. More inflammatory placards appeared, and the Privy Council now set up a commission to 'examine by secret means who may be the authors of the said libels.'[35] In addition, a census was made of the terrified refugees themselves, some of whom were preparing to flee. Then, on Sunday 5 May, in this atmosphere of mounting suspicion, the most vitriolic of the placards was 'set upon the wall of the Dutch churchyard'.[36]

This time the message of crude racism was shot through with references to that great and novel source of metropolitan excitement, Marlowe's plays. Both *The Jew of Malta* and *The Massacre at Paris* were alluded to. Most blatantly of all, the Dutch Church libel was signed with the name of Marlowe's most famous hero 'Tamberlaine'. The implication was clear. Whoever was behind this rabble-rousing wished to be associated with a crude interpretation of Marlowe's dramas, with Machiavellian intrigue, sedition and atheism. This personified everything the authorities most feared, and officers of the Privy Council were at once ordered to arrest suspects and search their 'chambers, studies, chests or other like places, for all manner of writing and papers that may give you light for the discovery of the libellers.'[37]

Marlowe himself was out of town, but among those immediately rounded up was his fellow dramatist Thomas Kyd. Kyd was at once interrogated and almost certainly tortured. He confessed to the necessary information. Marlowe, he averred, was in the habit of calling Christ a homosexual and hinting that his affection for St John in particular was 'an extraordinary love'.[38] Various other insignificant remarks were also alleged. Altogether more damagingly, Kyd said that it was Marlowe's 'custom in table talk or otherwise, to jest at the divine scriptures, gibe at prayers and strive in argument to frustrate and confute what hath been spoken or writ by prophets and such holy men.' In addition, a brief document which, taken out of context, appeared heretical had been found (it was most probably planted) and attributed to Marlowe's hand. This was sufficient. One of the queen's messengers was instructed 'to repair to the house of Mr Thomas Walsingham in Kent, or to any other place where he shall understand Christopher Marlowe to be remaining and by virtue hereof to apprehend and bring him to the court in his company.'[39] On 20 May, Marlowe appeared before the Privy Council.

The Essex faction was no doubt jubilant. It was only a matter of time before Marlowe himself would be pushed into the torture chamber where, threatened or even interrogated on the rack, he would confess not just to his own atheism but to the whole blasphemous culture of Durham House. The existence of a school of atheism would be proved, Ralegh's reputation destroyed, and the opportunity of power denied him for ever.

But Marlowe was not imprisoned. He was unexpectedly placed on bail and commanded to remain at the Privy Council's disposal. The reasons for this turn of events are obscure, but they most probably derive from Marlowe's activities as a spy. He was by far the most brilliant of that sordid collection of hacks and double agents who populated the Elizabethan underworld. If Marlowe was a poet and playwright of genius, his existence was also that of a man of many masks operating in a mirror maze of lies. As such, he had powerful protectors. Sir Robert Cecil, for example, had employed him in espionage work and was probably aware of the frame-up in which his agent was now being trapped. Certainly, Cecil had the authority to ensure Marlowe was released on bail. He also had personal reasons to see this happened. It was quite possible that once in the torture chamber Marlowe might confess to clandestine operations on which Cecil himself had sent him.

Essex's men were suddenly faced with the need to produce something more substantial if they were to achieve their purpose of blackening Ralegh's reputation through the destruction of Marlowe. Their evidence so far was tenuous at best: Kyd's confession, which was not yet written down; and a paragraph in an informer's report entitled 'Remembrances of Words and Matter against Ric[hard] Cholmeley'. In this labyrinthine world of deceit, Cholmeley was a pseudo-atheist attached to the Essex circle. One of the accusations in the 'Remembrances' was that he 'sayeth and verily believeth that one Marlowe is able to show more sound reasons for atheism than any divine in England is able to give to prove divinity, and that Marlowe told him, he hath read the atheist lecture to Sir Walter Ralegh and others.' Such innuendo had not led Marlowe to the torture chamber however, and something more concrete was needed.

The Essex faction hoped it was provided when they managed to present a document entitled 'A note containing the opinion of one Christopher Marly, concerning his damnable judgement of religion and scorn of God's word'. The author of this was yet another shady figure from the Elizabethan underworld, Richard Baines. Baines was, in all probability, an Essex man who had been involved in the plot for some time and was now trying to bring it to a climax. The 'Note' itself was a sworn statement, its nineteen allegations of heresy and other matters being attested 'by mine oath and the testimony of many honest men'. The contents are a crude misrepresentation of what may have been Marlowe's views. Among his recorded comments are 'all Protestants are hypocritical asses'; that 'the first beginning of religion was only to keep men in awe'; and that 'St John the Evangelist was bedfellow to Christ and used him as the sinners of Sodoma.'

Baines's allegations, if in a somewhat censored form – Marlowe's joke about all those who love not tobacco and boys being fools was crossed out – was eventually 'delivered to Her Highness'. Elizabeth ordered that it should be 'prosecuted to the full'. But in front of the Privy Council (and protected perhaps by Cecil) Marlowe could simply deny all the charges and claim they were a cover, one of his roles in the drama of espionage. In such ways as this, he was slowly slipping from the grasp of Essex's men and was perhaps even becoming a danger to them. If this were to continue, the campaign against Ralegh would falter. Marlowe would now have to be persuaded either to give evidence against Ralegh or be silenced.

On 30 May 1593, he was invited to a 'feast' at Deptford by one of Essex's agents, Ingram Frizer. The occasion seems to have been a desperate meeting in a safe house. Present in addition to Marlowe and Frizer were Nicholas Skeres, a servant of Essex and, hurriedly recalled from the Low Countries, Robert Poley who was one of Cecil's men. Their conversation lasted for eight hours. In the end, 'divers malicious words'[40] were spoken as Skeres appeared to fail in his attempt to persuade Marlowe to turn evidence against Ralegh. A blade was drawn. It pierced Marlowe's flesh just above the right eyeball and tore at his brain. He died instantly and, as his body grew cold, so Frizer, Skeres and Poley agreed between them that the incident was a hotheaded accident, a matter of self-defence when a row had broken out over the bill. A full inquest was held and found that Ingram Frizer had indeed killed Marlowe 'in the defence and saving of his own life'.[41] One of the greatest English renaissance poets had thus been murdered in a futile attempt to blacken Sir Walter Ralegh's reputation.

Ralegh himself meanwhile was writing letters to one of the great invisible players in this tragedy. The political situation in Ireland was causing him grave concern and although, the previous year, the queen had scorned his advice, Ralegh continued to warn Cecil of the danger he foresaw. In July 1592 he heard 'that there are three thousand of the Burkes in arms and young O'Donnell and the sons of Shane O'Neil.' These dangers had not decreased by May the following year. Lamenting that he was merely a disregarded prophet, Ralegh suggested that the Earl of Argyll should have been sent to keep the peace in Ulster. Ireland, he lamented, was a treacherous, expensive, 'accursed kingdom'.[42] It was not only the machinations of the King of Spain in fermenting rebellion there that inclined Ralegh to this view however. He was now having serious difficulties with his own plantations.

Sir William Fitzwilliam – 'that wise governor' as Ralegh scornfully referred to him[43] – was persisting in his campaign to thwart the Munster colony. He regarded the size of Ralegh's holding as illegal and this probably underlay the various actions he took to damage the venture. In 1592, for example, Fitzwilliam wrongly demanded payment of an alleged debt of £400 due to the crown and sent in the sherrif to distrain Ralegh's settlers. 'All Munster', Ralegh declared, 'hath scarce so much money in it: the debt was indeed but fifty marks, which was paid.' None the less, the sheriff 'did as he was commanded and took away five hundred milch kine from the poor people: some had but two, and some three, to relieve their poor wives and children, and in a strange country newly set down to build and plant.' Such actions as these were driving Ralegh's tenants away. 'It will be', he warned, 'no small weakening of the queen in those parts, and no small comfort to the ill-affected Irish to have the English inhabitants driven out of the country.'[44] But where, in the days of favour, Ralegh could bring a deputy to heel by a nod from the queen, now he had to fight his own corner as best he could.

This was starkly brought home when Fitzwilliam alleged that timber suitable for shipbuilding was being exported from Munster to Spain and her colonies and that Ralegh's agent Henry Pyne was the communication link between the Irish Catholics and their co-religionists in Spain. Timber exports were stopped at Fitzwilliam's command, while Pyne was arrested and taken to London, there to be interrogated as a traitor by the Privy Council. Ralegh vehemently denied the charges while admitting to the export of barrel staves to the Spanish islands.

It was precisely this sort of business initiative the Irish plantations were set up to encourage. The Privy Council eventually agreed. Charges against Pyne were dropped and the export of barrel staves to France and the islands was permitted, but not to Spain herself. The following year, and in an effort to exploit further the resources of Munster, Ralegh sent fifty of his Cornish miners to his plantations in order to excavate the iron ore that had been discovered there, following up this enterprise with the building of iron mills which would be fuelled by timber from his estates. Although Irish development was costly, difficult and frequently threatened – not least by the men and institutions who were supposed to help it – for the moment Ralegh did not abandon his initiatives. He remained the tough, entrepreneurial businessman.

He also, and more dangerously, remained a committed sceptic. Sometime in the summer of 1593, while Bess was pregnant with Wat and work was continuing on his new house, Ralegh and his brother Carew were invited to dinner by Sir George Trenchard at Wolfeton. A number of other local dignitaries were also present: Sir Ralph Horsey, John Fitzjames, and two ministers, a Mr Whittle and Ralph Ironside, vicar of Winterborne. The occasion was clearly a convivial one, and as the meal came to a close, Carew Ralegh began talking rather loosely. Horsey tried tactfully to steady him with a Latin tag: *colloquia prava corrumpunt bonos mores* – 'evil words corrupt good morals'. Carew, who had perhaps drunk sufficient to derive amusement from baiting a rustic parson, looked across at Ironside and asked him what dangers such talk as his might incur. 'The wages of sin', the vicar declared, 'is death.'[45]

Carew made light of this, pointing out the fact that death is common to all, sinner and righteous alike. The Reverend Ironside, feeling the dignity of his profession threatened, 'inferred further that as that life which is the gift of God through Jesus Christ is life eternal, so that death which is properly the wages of sin is death eternal, both of the body and of the soul also.'

'Soul!' returned Carew. 'What is that?' This was a dangerous question to blurt out over a dining table, and Ironside moved to close the conversation with a pious warning. 'Better it were . . . that we would be careful how the souls might be saved than to be curious in finding out their essence.'

Ralegh, irked by the vagueness of this, and offended perhaps that his brother had been reprimanded, requested that 'for their instruction' the Reverend Ironside should answer his brother's question. Asserting his dominance and moving the conversation on to an altogether higher plane, Ralegh declared: 'I have been . . . a scholar some time in Oxford, I have answered under a Bachelor of Arts, and have had talk with divers, yet hereunto in this point (to wit, what the reasonable soul of man is) have I never by any been resolved.' He then tried to give Ironside an opening. 'They tell us', he said, that the soul is *'primus motor*, the first mover, in a man.'

Ironside gave a meaningless reply and was again urged to show his opinion. Feeling cornered, and hoping to flatter Ralegh's academic distinction, the vicar decided jargon was his best defence. 'I cited the general definition of *anima* out of Aristotle 2 *de Anima* cap. 1, and thence *a subiecto proprio* deduced a specific definition of the soul reasonable, that it was *actus primus corporis organici animantis humani vitam habentis in potentia.*' The soul was the initial driving force of the organic matter of a human being having potential for life. It was just such sterile verbalism against which Ralegh invariably set his face, and the definition 'was misliked . . . as obscure and intricate'.

Ironside demurred. However, having failed with jargon the vicar now tried to be patronizing. He would produce a definition of the soul that all those round the table could understand. 'The reasonable soul is a spiritual and immortal substance breathed into man by God, whereby he lives and moves and understandeth, and so is distinguished from other creatures,' he suggested.

'Yes, but what is that spiritual and immortal substance breathed into men, et cetera?' Ralegh asked.

'The soul,' replied the desperate cleric.

One can see Ralegh's lips pleating in exasperation at this circular argument, and Ironside now laboured to prove that it was 'in such disputes as these, usual and necessary to run *in circulum*'. Ralegh had not finished however. 'But we have principles in our mathematics,' he began, and cited the axiom that the whole is greater than the sum of the parts. Ironside acidly replied 'that such demonstrations as that were against the nature of a man's soul.' He had clearly heard rumours about this metropolitan atheist, and he now summoned St Paul to his aid: 'For as things being sensible were subject to the sense, so man's soul being insensible was to be discerned by the spirit,' he declared.

Ironside was clearly getting rattled. 'Nothing more certain in the world than that there is a God,' he added. But Ralegh was now wading in deeply. 'These two be alike,' he declared, 'for neither could I learn hitherto what God is.' This was altogether too dangerous. Fitzjames interjected with a definition from Aristotle and Ironside welcomed the proffered help. God was now *ens entium*, 'a thing of things, having being of himself, and giving being to all his creatures.' This 'was most certain, and confirmed by God himself unto Moses.'

'Yea, but what is this *ens entium*?'

'It is God.'

Ralegh, claiming to be exasperated, wished the conversation to be given over and grace said in its place. 'For that,' quoth he, 'is better than this disputation.'

He had won his point. By claiming to explain the inexplicable, Ironside had made a fool of himself, while Ralegh, offering praise to the divine, had shown his devotion, the faith that underlay his scepticism. The vicar decided he had better make a record of his conversation with this dangerous man.

The conversation had no doubt been imprudent, an instance of that refusal to be browbeaten by nonsense which was so dangerous to Ralegh's reputation. But his scepticism had its altogether more bitter and disillusioned side. It was one thing to beguile an evening by allowing a local vicar to get entangled in a web of words, it was quite another to think of all mankind as gulled by their own foolish energies. The conversation over Trenchard's dinner table could be seen, in the iron hours of Ralegh's deepest cynicism, as a particular instance of universal folly:

> Tell wit how much it wrangles
>   in tickle points of niceness,
> Tell wisdom she entangles

> herself in over-niceness
> And when they do reply
> straight give them both the lie.[46]

This poem almost certainly dates from Ralegh's years of disgrace when, in moments of despondency and impotence, a heavy-handed cynicism was natural to him. In these circumstances, the hope that 'the truth shall be thy warrant' was more a means of braving things out than an example of the nimble-minded scepticism of the Durham House group. The poem indeed is a reflection of Ralegh in his role as Misanthropos, a man casting a jaundiced eye on every institution:

> Say to the Court it glows
> and shines like rotten wood,
> Say to the Church it shows
> what's good, and doth no good.
> If Church and Court reply,
> then give them both the lie.

> Tell Potentates they live
> acting by others' action,
> Not loved unless they give,
> not strong but by affection.
> If Potentates reply,
> give Potentates the lie.[47]

'Potentates' – the bitterness of the word is striking – 'potentates' like the Virgin Queen can only exist by battening on those who serve them, and the only aims these servants have in mind is ambition.

This last was a truth Ralegh had tested on his own pulses, but now his poem begins to degenerate into an inverted sentimentality, a list of platitudinous cynicism: love is merely lust (to rhyme with flesh which 'is but dust'), honour is inconstant, beauty fleeting and so on. This is the numbing cliché of embittered fatigue. Only at the close, when the whole world has been scorned, can Ralegh suggest a final and chilly certainty in the immortality of the soul:

> So when thou hast as I
> commanded thee, done blabbing,

Because to give the lie,
    deserves no less than stabbing,
Stab at thee he that will,
    no stab thy soul can kill.[48]

Others denied he believed even this. By March 1594 the Court of High Commission under Thomas Viscount Bindon was in session at nearby Cerne Abbas, preparing to inquire into heresies among the people of Dorset. Sitting with Bindon were the sheriff, the vice-admiral of Dorset, an ecclesiastical official, and Sir Ralph Horsey who had been present at what had now become Sir George Trenchard's notorious dinner party. The industrious Ironside made notes on the witnesses' depositions. Just over a dozen were called – they were for most part local vicars and churchwardens – and they were encouraged to answer on nine points prepared by the Commissioners. The first and most inclusive of these read: 'Whom do you know, or have heard to be suspected of atheism, or apostasy? and in what manner do you know or have heard the same? and what other notice can you give thereof?'[49]

The witnesses declared they knew nothing at all. John Davis, the curate of Motcombe, said 'he hath heard Sir Walter Ralegh by general report hath had some reasoning against the deity of God, and his omnipotency.' He had also heard the same about Carew Ralegh, 'but not so directly'. Nicholas Jefferys had heard that Ralegh and his associates 'are generally suspected of atheism', and included the colourful Thomas Allen, the Lieutenant of Portland Castle and an associate of Ralegh's from Ireland, in the charge. Allen, it was said, tore pages out of his bible to dry his tobacco on, while one of his servants had shocked the sensibilities of two local matrons by drunkenly informing them that Moses kept a harem.

Jefferys had also heard about the talk at the dinner party but, like the deposition of William Arnold, the vicar of Blandford, all this was merely hearsay. The only detailed evidence submitted to the commission was Ironside's account of his being worsted at the dinner table. Ironside, however, had been advised that gossiping about 'uncertain report' placed him 'in danger to be punished', and he decided not to testify in person. The Commissioners themselves, naturally enough, could find nothing of substance in this vindictive charade, and no charges were brought against Ralegh.

It was an unpleasant business all the same, and in the following month the opportunity was found whereby Ralegh could once again prove his Protestant loyalty. He wrote to Cecil: 'This night the 13th of April, we have taken a notable Jesuit in the Lady Storton's house – wife to old Sir John Arundell, with his copes and bulls.'[50] Ralegh was keen to underline the importance of this action. 'There hath been kept in this house, as I have formerly informed you, above thirty recusants.' He was also concerned to emphasize the part played in this arrest by his friends Sir George Trenchard and Sir Ralph Horsey, both of whom had 'used great diligence in the finding of this notable knave.' Both men had also, of course, been present at the infamous dinner party, and there is every suggestion here of the local squirearchy trying to clear their names.

The priest himself, the half Cornish and half Irish Father Cornelius, was a mystic Celt much given to thoughts of martyrdom. Ralegh informed Cecil that he, along with Trenchard and Horsey, were 'now riding to take his examination'. Whatever part the others played in the inquisition of this 'notable stout villain', Ralegh himself, in a manner wholly characteristic, 'passed the whole night with him alone that he might have certain doubts resolved.' By the time dawn broke, the exhausted men had achieved some degree of mutual understanding. Ralegh 'was so pleased with the Father's conviction and reasoning and with his modest and courteous manner' that he offered to do all he could in London for his liberation, and this although 'the Father had gently reproved him for his mode of life and conversation.'[51]

But Ralegh the disgraced favourite had little influence now. Cornelius was sent to London, racked, returned to Dorchester, tried, found guilty and sentenced. Ralegh was put in charge of his execution. There could be no subtle midnight conversations now. Nor did Cornelius wish there to be. His last moments on earth were his great chance to propagandize. Ralegh several times intervened to silence him, but to no effect. Before the priest could finish his prayer for the conversion of the queen, Ralegh ordered the ladder to be jerked from under him. Cornelius was partly strangled in mid sentence and, as he died, he was cut down, disembowelled, castrated and dismembered. Ralegh then ordered his severed head to be stuck on the pinnacle of St Peter's church in Dorchester High Street. In such ways, the disgraced favourite could reveal his loyalty. He was, however, no nearer to regaining Elizabeth's favour.

CHAPTER TWELVE

The Pursuit of El Dorado

elease from the Tower had given Ralegh his physical freedom, while marriage to Bess, the birth of Wat, and the
building of Sherborne offered domestic distractions during
his years of disgrace. Exile from the queen's favour was
bitter none the less, and the fact that his past efforts were disregarded
continued to rankle. He had organized the most spectacularly successful privateering expedition of the war, and Elizabeth had
snatched his profits from him. He had written verses and memoranda expressing his love, his desolation and his loyalty, but she had
ignored him. He had defended her policies in the House of Commons, and his efforts had gone unrewarded. Despite his labours,
Ralegh remained a fallen favourite, a man trapped in the cruellest
of prisons: lack of opportunity. In these years, and in 'the darkest
shadow of adversity',[1] his thoughts turned increasingly to something
which, in the days of his success, he had been able largely to disregard: the lethal glitter of El Dorado and the golden, fantastic king
supposedly hidden in a remote South American empire.

To capture this man and possess his kingdom was a dream to
solve many problems. Untold wealth might ensue. The planning of
such an expedition would strain Ralegh's ingenuity and employ his
great administrative abilities. His imagination, intellect and courage
would all be used. More dangerously, while the energies of the
private man were thus exploited, the thoughts of the would-be public
figure – the patriot – stretched out in the effort to bind the illusion
of El Dorado to politics and the future well-being of the state. A
personal obsession was interpreted as a matter of national policy,
and from this misalliance much wretchedness would flow.

The public strategy was clearly argued. Everyone knew that the
waters off the Caribbean coast of South America were swarming
with English privateers. At least seventy-seven ships had sailed for
the area between 1589 and 1595 and there were probably more.

Drake's sacking of San Domingo and Cartagena had exposed the weakness of Spain in the region and, as a result of this raid, Philip's standing in Europe and even his credit with his bankers were severely shaken.

Hurried and expensive preparations were made to protect the bullion fleet and defend the Caribbean against pirates, but the sheer scale and cost of this operation meant that only the most strategically vital areas could receive imperial attention. Those parts of the Caribbean that were difficult to defend and which were of comparatively small commercial importance were left exposed. The sugar and pearls produced in Hispaniola and Venezuela, for example, were declining and these areas would largely have to fend for themselves. Inevitably they fell prey to privateers, while the most remote regions of all were largely abandoned to their native populations. In this situation, repeated and often small-scale raids inflicted considerable damage and continued to weaken Spain's grip.

But Ralegh, who had profited from these enterprises, was now becoming convinced that piecemeal raids on Spanish shipping were insufficient to counter the might of Spain. He began to frame an altogether more grandiose strategy, a strategy which in part drew on the ideas put forward by Richard Hakluyt a decade before in his *Discourse of Western Planting*. Here, Hakluyt had drawn attention to 'all that part of America eastward from Cumana unto the river of St Augustine'. This was a coastline of over 2,000 miles 'in which compass and tract', Hakluyt pointed out, 'there is neither Spaniard, Portingale not any Christian man but only Caribs, Indians and savages.'[2] The opportunity for the missionary was emphasized, as were the immense commercial opportunities of the area. Not only was the northern coast of South America allegedly free from rivals, but there was to be found there 'great plenty of gold, pearl and precious stones'.

These were an obvious lure but, so far, privateering had been the dominant commercial activity for Englishmen in the region, and Ralegh considered an altogether broader approach was required if England was to establish a foothold on the continent. This last he considered a matter of national importance. English possession of the lands that produced the riches of which Hakluyt had written was essential if Spain was to be finally undermined. Philip's wealth might be depleted by privateering, but what was really needed was an original fount of resources which would be an effective challenge to the damage wrought by the power of the Spanish treasury.

Ralegh offered a frightening picture of this last which was of a piece with his abiding concern with the all-encompassing threat posed by Spain. 'It is his Indian gold that endangereth and disturbeth all the nations of Europe,' he wrote. 'It purchaseth intelligence, creepeth into councils, and setteth bound loyalty at liberty, in the greatest monarchies of Europe.'³ Such power not only threatened the English state but hindered her trade. Once again, Ralegh preached his familiar lesson: an active anti-Spanish policy must be followed. War should be waged on Spain, while every effort should be made 'to advance all those attempts that might either promise return of profit to ourselves, or at least be a let and impeachment to the quiet course and plentiful trades of the Spanish nation.'⁴ The lands of the fabled El Dorado were an ideal base for this purpose. They were, it was believed, not only productive of fabulous wealth, but their coastlines and islands offered an ideal anchorage from which to raid the Spanish fleets.

By 1593, the idea had become an obsession. Information was gathered and talks with potential backers were held. Bess, anxious that Ralegh's bid to re-establish himself might be achieved in more conventional ways, wrote a worried letter to Cecil. 'I hope you will rather draw Sir Walter towards the east [i.e. London] than help him forward towards the sunset, if any respect to me, or love to him, be not forgotten.'⁵ Bess's feeling was that the quest for El Dorado posed a threat to the happiness she had so bravely struggled for. But Cecil did not choose to exert his influence on her behalf. Ralegh's presence in the Caribbean was a useful means of establishing English power. His expedition might also be a profitable one, and Cecil went so far as to invest in it himself. Besides, urging Ralegh in the direction of El Dorado and its dangers was an altogether shrewder policy than labouring to get the erstwhile favourite a place in government. Everything, it seemed, conspired to shackle Ralegh to his illusion.

In 1594, a reconnaissance mission was sent to Guiana under the command of Jacob Whiddon, the captain who eight years earlier had seized Sarmiento de Gamboa, the Spanish aristocrat who had first told Ralegh about El Dorado. Whatever the state of the myth when Sarmiento reported, however, Ralegh was now to learn the most up to date version of the story from Whiddon's efforts and a wholly unlooked for piece of good luck.

Anchoring off Trinidad, Whiddon asked the governor of the island for permission to gather wood and water. The suspicious old man agreed, while such information as could be gathered on El Dorado was supplemented by Whiddon's contacts among the native Caciques. These people were, he discovered, by and large hostile to the Spaniards because of the habitual and infamous treatment meted out to them by the invaders. They could none the less still be employed by the Spaniards for a ruse. The governor of Trinidad sent out a party of them to ask the English to go hunting. Eight men agreed to take part, but when they reached the shore they were ambushed and slaughtered. To the embittered governor, Don Antonio de Berrio, this incident was so trivial as to be barely worth recording in his frequent letters to Spain. A handful of Englishmen was a slight inconvenience compared to the treachery he was enduring at the hands of his countrymen.

Berrio was now seventy-four, a man at the close of his career and very close also to the end of his tether. His first sixty years had made him a veteran of the Spanish military machine. He had fought for Charles V against the French, taken part in the blockade of Sienna, sacked pirate fortresses along the Barbary coast, and been with Alva in the Netherlands. He had played a distinguished role in campaigns against the Moriscoes of Granada, and fought a guerrilla war in the Alpujana Mountains. Then, at an age when other men might have been content to retire, Berrio had married Donna Maria, niece of the Adelantado Gonzalo Ximenies de Quesado, on whose death he inherited vast estates in South America along with a sacred trust. Don Gonzalo's will made it incumbent on Berrio that he devote himself to the search for El Dorado in which Quesado himself had spent his declining years.

Having arrived in Bogota and with his energies undiminished, Berrio raised 40,000 ducats, a force of two hundred soldiers, horses, ammunition and stores. For more than forty years men from the Spanish empire had pursued the fantastic Golden Man from the western coasts to the innumerable tributaries of the Amazon. Now a soldier of sixty, Berrio was traversing the swamps of the upper Meta and on into the Ilanos where 'by the grace of God and his glorious Mother, and on Palm Sunday in the year '84, I discovered the cordillera on the other side of the plains.'[6] This was a moment of exultation. According to his best information, the very real presence of these mountains proved to Berrio that he had at last reached the territory of the mythical El Dorado. Halted for four months by the winter, he learned from captured Indians what he wanted to hear. In the mountains, they said, there was a very large 'laguna', and on the other side great towns and a vast population rich with gold and precious stones.

Berrio's first expedition was obliged to turn back, but by the summer of 1585, and now the reckless victim of his own obsession, he prepared a second journey down the Orinoco and into the heartland of Guiana. The journey lasted for two and a half years and was eventually halted by mutiny. Berrio returned to his estates in New Granada, where he learned that a commission had arrived appointing him governor of the province of El Dorado. His fantasy now had royal sanction, and the following year, aged seventy, he assembled a large force of men and supplies for his third and greatest expedition.

While a portion of this force took a land route under the command of his loyal lieutenant Alvaro Jorge, Berrio himself led seventy men in boats down the Orinoco, pursuing its course for over a year but failing to find a way through the mountains. His men deserted and died, the boats were lost and starvation threatened. Immense powers of leadership were required to keep the expedition together and urge it on down a tributary of the Orinoco and thus into the lands of a chief named Morequito where 'the mountains ended and the provinces of Guiana began, behind which in turn came those of Manoa and El Dorado.'[7]

Relations with the Indians deteriorated and men continued to die. Standing, as he believed, on the very edge of his long-sought paradise of gold, Berrio was forced yet again to turn back, landing on Trinidad and surveying the strategic possibilities of the island on his way. All his expedition had achieved was to fix more precisely the supposed location of El Dorado and rouse the jealousy of his fellow-countrymen. The governor of Margarita clearly wished to inveigle his way into the project now that there was more certain information as to the whereabouts of the fabulous kingdom. Berrio was obliged to join with the brilliant but unstable Domingo de Vera Ybarguen who was now despatched to beg for reinforcements from the Governor of Venezuela. When these were forthcoming, de Vera himself was sent to occupy Trinidad and there found a base at San Joseph for future expeditions.

On Christmas Eve, Francisco de Vides arrived as the new Governor of Cumana. Berrio, sensing competition, at once hastened to secure Trinidad for himself and, the following spring, despatched de Vera and thirty-five men down the Orinoco in the direction of the territory of Morequito. The report de Vera hoped to send back to Spain included accounts of Indian talk of a city and a lake far up the river. The ship in which a copy of de Vera's report was sent to Spain, however, was captured by the privateer George Popham and the document itself eventually came into Ralegh's hands.

Written with more enthusiasm than accuracy, de Vera's account of his settling of Trinidad and his journey down the Orinoco depicted a progress that was allegedly a triumph of exploration, conquest and missionary endeavour. Tribesmen submitted and were converted. Crosses were erected to suggest the possession of these lands by Spain. Most important of all, from Ralegh's point of view, de Vera's account of his enquiries among the Indians fixed more precisely than ever the locale of Manoa and the fabulous kingdom of El Dorado. The legend now appeared to have an exact habitation. The whereabouts of the lake, the existence of a sophisticated trading people, and even of a race of men 'whose shoulders were so high that they were almost on a level with the head',[8] were all accepted as factual. Ralegh's El Dorado was thus very largely that constructed by Berrio and de Vera – the dream of other men.

Berrio himself meanwhile was alternately exultant and dismayed. The reappearance of de Vera in Trinidad, laden with golden ornaments, encouraged him to seek support from his ally Don Diego Osorio at Caracas, but after Osorio had answered 'with smooth words',[9] it became evident that he too was determined to seize the fabulous kingdom. Osorio was thus added to Berrio's known rivals. In his despair, the old man was led to confess that 'the devil himself is the patron of this enterprise'[10] and was obliged to desperate courses. His teenage son was sent to New Granada to try to raise further forces, while de Vera was despatched on his similar mission to Spain. And it was while Berrio was awaiting the result of these initiatives – an old man perched in gloomy suspicion on Trinidad – that Ralegh appeared off the island, anchored, wiped out the harbour guard at Port of Spain, surprised San Joseph, burned the little town to the ground, seized Berrio and his lieutenant, and marched them off to his ship for interrogation.

Extensive preparations had been made for this raid. Back in London, Cecil had lent his influence as well as his money. The Lord Admiral offered his ship the *Lion's Whelp*. William Sanderson, the London merchant who had contributed so generously to the Virginia enterprises was also approached, but, in this difficult period for Ralegh, there was a bitter quarrel between the two men over money. West Country relatives were also encouraged to invest, Butshead Gorges, John Grenville and John Gilbert being prepared to sail on the expedition in person.

Other practical matters were also attended to. Indians brought back by Whiddon were trained up as interpreters, and all the available information was collated. This almost certainly included de Vera's report along with a captured Spanish 'rutter' or guide to the currents in the Caribbean, knowledge that was then supplemented by interviewing those English mariners who had sailed the difficult waters of the Gulf of Paria that lay between Trinidad and the South American mainland. Finally, letters patent were granted to 'our servant Sir Walter Ralegh'[11] allowing him, in the familiar formula, to possess any lands not actually held by a Christian king. The patent also granted him permission to annoy the King of Spain in any manner that seemed appropriate. The search for the legendary Golden Man was thus allowed to pay for itself from the altogether surer prospect of privateering.

Indeed, Ralegh tried to involve a number of well-known West Indies privateering captains in the venture. George Popham, Amyas Preston and George Somers were all expected to co-operate with him off Trinidad. Others, too, were bound for the Caribbean. These included the young Sir Robert Dudley, the illegitimate son of the Earl of Leicester, who had been prevented by the queen from making the long and dangerous journey to the South Seas and was now, at the royal suggestion, sailing for the same area as Ralegh. For all that Dudley's venture was intended as little more than a youthful quest after experience – a twenty-year-old's trying out his wings – the threat Ralegh felt such expeditions exposed him to was irksome. It was a cardinal point of his policy that friendly relations must be established with the Indian chiefs, and he was fearful that these could easily be soured.

He wrote to Cecil, hoping he might use his influence to prevent rivals from sailing. He tried to argue that this was in the best interests of national policy and urged that there should be a restraint on all shipping because of the likelihood of an invasion from Spain. If uncoordinated activity was allowed in the Caribbean, then 'the Queen's purpose would be frustrated.'[12] More particularly – and a sense of venom and personal threat are patent here – Ralegh wrote that 'if Eaton's ships go, who will attempt the chiefest places of my enterprises, I shall be undone; and I know they will be beaten and do no good.'[13]

On 6 February 1595, and after considerable delays during which a number of his vessels seem to have deserted his fleet, Ralegh set sail with four ships and about three hundred men, half of whom were soldiers and adventurers. Jacob Whiddon was captain and John Douglas master of Ralegh's ship, the name of which has been lost. George Gifford captained the *Lion's Whelp* which sailed as vice-admiral. There were, in addition, a small bark and a *gallego*, probably captured from the Spaniards, which sailed under the command of a man for whom El Dorado was to become an obsession and, eventually, a personal tragedy. This was Laurence Keymis, an Oxford mathematician who, abandoning his Balliol fellowship, had joined the altogether more stimulating group of men gathered in Durham House. Harriot, although he offered technical help, did not sail on the voyage.

For the first time since 1578, when, as a young man, he had made towards the West Indies as an officer under Humphrey Gilbert, Ralegh was sailing at the head of an expedition. Then he had been in his vigorous twenties. Now, just turned forty, he would feel the strain and discomfort. At some point during their crossing of the Atlantic, Ralegh's ship and the little bark became separated from the others and made for the Canaries. Here they anchored for over a week, waiting in vain for Amyas Preston's men to join them. Their failure to appear was a first indication that the co-operation planned in London would collapse once crews became excited by the prospects of privateering. Ralegh then sailed on to Trinidad where, on 22 March, he anchored off what is now Icacos Point, the south-west extremity of the island. Neither Dudley nor Popham was there to greet him.

Dudley, who had provided himself with a hundred and forty men, an able captain and experienced navigator, was more eager for experience than avid for systematic conquest. He had reconnoitred Trinidad, questioned the Indians, prospected for gold which turned out to be sand, and erected a leaden plaque on a post which claimed the island for the queen and himself. His exploits on Trinidad were tinged with the romance as well as something of the absurdity of chivalry and, after a captured Indian had been 'threatened unto death' to reveal the whereabouts of El Dorado,[14] Dudley set off for the Orinoco. His brief expedition was a disaster that only ended when the company resolved to row back across the Gulf of Paria. Having met up with Captain Popham, Dudley resolved on a quixotic march through Trinidad. When this was concluded, Popham informed the young man of Ralegh's intentions and his insistence that the Indians be treated with respect. Hoping to avoid an embarrassing confrontation, Dudley left with Popham the next morning and, on his return to England, wrote a modest and largely inaccurate account of his exploits.

Ralegh lingered off the south-west of Trinidad for some days, occupying his time with expeditions to the island which had, he declared, 'the form of a sheephook'.[15] He noted the fertility of the soil, the exotic variety of the fruit, fish and fowl, and the 'excellent good pitch' which 'melteth not with the sun as the pitch of Norway.' He also, much to the disbelief of those back in England, observed oysters growing on the exposed roots of mangrove trees which were, he said, 'very salt and well tasted'. Meanwhile, Whiddon was sent out with a flag of truce to a landing-place guarded by Berrio's nephew.

Whiddon told the young man they were only looking for supplies since they were on their way to Florida with arms and munitions, some of which they were willing to trade. This was a blind, but when Berrio himself received the letter and ring Ralegh sent him, eight Spanish soldiers appeared. With some difficulty, they and Berrio's nephew were inveigled on board Ralegh's ship, lured perhaps by the promise of wine, which, 'poor soldiers', they had been without for many years. The Spaniards were soon drunk enough to start expatiating about the treasures of Guiana. Ralegh carefully noted what they had to say and refused to let them go.

He also noted the comments of the Indians who came aboard that evening, their laments about the cruelty of the Spaniards, the way their lands had been seized and divided up, and how those who traded with the English were sentenced to be hanged and quartered. Ralegh saw it was necessary to win these peoples' confidence, and he questioned them about Berrio's forces and the route to San Joseph. He then began laying plans while, next day, eight more men from Berrio's force appeared. Most remained on the shore, but two came to drink on the flagship. While they were carousing, a boat full of English soldiers slipped away to kill the waiting Spaniards. Berrio's nephew and his men on the English ship were then stabbed to death.

With this danger removed, Ralegh's interpreters slipped in among the Indians and roused them to arms while a captain and sixty men marched in the direction of San Joseph, Ralegh following with forty more soldiers. The little settlement was overwhelmed in a dawn raid. Some dozen Spaniards were killed, while five Cacique chiefs who had been chained, starved and tortured with burning bacon fat were freed and their people addressed through an interpreter:

> I made them understand that I was the servant of a queen, who was the great Casique of the north, and a virgin, and had more Casiqui under her than there were trees in their island: that she was an enemy to the Castellani [i.e. the Spaniards] in respect of their tyranny and oppression, and that she delivered all such nations about her, as were by them oppressed, and having freed all the coast of the northern world from their servitude had sent me to free them also, and withal to defend the country of Guiana from their invasion and conquest. I showed them her majesty's picture which they so admired and honour, as it had been easy to have brought them Idolatrous thereof.[16]

The Virgin Queen was now celebrated among the Indians as 'Ezrabeta Cassipuna Aquerewana', which is as much as 'Elizabeth, the great Princess or greatest commander'.

The destruction of San Joseph was both a revenge on the earlier murder of Whiddon's men and a strategic necessity. Ralegh was about to embark on a journey which would take him as he believed four or five hundred miles from his ships, and 'to leave a garrison in my back interested in the same enterprise, who daily expected supplies out of Spain . . . should have savoured very much of the ass.' Before he set out, however, it was necessary to extract what information he could from the captured Berrio and his lieutenant, a matter requiring both courtesy and persistence. 'This Berrio is a gentleman well descended,' Ralegh wrote, 'very valiant and liberal and a gentlemen of great assuredness and of a great heart.' Ralegh was careful to use him 'according to his estate and worth in all things I could.'

Berrio was prepared to tell Ralegh about his exploits before he came to South America. In the small panelled cabin of the Englishman's ship these events had perhaps the glow of old romance and a remoteness such as made them seem almost to belong to another man, another life. When he came to tell of his own and other Spanish expeditions along the Orinoco, however, Berrio was less forthcoming. Wary now, taciturn and resentful, he drained his accounts of colour and detail. But Ralegh was persistent. During the month that Berrio was his prisoner he focused on him the full force of his concentration. The immensely complex tale of Spain's pursuit of El Dorado began slowly to fall into shape, the detail of physical conditions and the dangers to be filled in.

When Ralegh eventually confessed that his purpose of sailing to the Caribbean was not to stop over on the way to Virginia but to engage in his own pursuit of the Golden Man, Berrio clammed up. He was 'stricken into a great melancholy and sadness', and began to use 'all the arguments he could to dissuade me'. Such a journey would be miserable, lost labour. Ralegh's boats would be grounded in the shallow rivers. The natives would refuse to talk to him and would burn their settlements rather than offer help. Manoa was a very long way off, he repeated. Besides, winter was coming and the rivers would be in flood. Tributaries of the Orinoco that Berrio had claimed were too narrow to navigate were now described as too dangerous to pass. And the natives, he added, would never trade gold with the Christians anyway.

Ralegh was not to be deflected by this. After a month of questioning Berrio, his vision of El Dorado had become fixed: fixed in terms of geography, history, political organization and customs. Above all, the empire had become fixed as a place of inexhaustible wealth, a fantasy that had objective existence:

> The Empire of Guiana is directly east from Peru towards the sea, and lieth under the Equinoctial line, and it hath more abundance of gold than any part of Peru, and as many or more great cities than ever Peru had when it flourished most: it is governed by the same laws, and the Emperor and people observe the same religion, and the same form and policies in government as was used in Peru, not differing in any part: and as I have been assured by such of the Spaniards as have seen Manoa the imperial City of Guiana, which the Spaniards call El Dorado, that for the greatness, for the riches, and for the excellent seat, it far exceedeth any of the world, at least of so much of the world as is known to the Spanish nation. . . .[17]

Now, having established the existence of this empire, the strength of the Spaniards, and a measure of co-operation with the natives, it was time to make for the fabled kingdom itself, to verify its riches and reach an understanding with its peoples. The expedition he was about to make was, Ralegh believed, merely the first stage in persuading the crown to establish an English empire in South America that would finally and fatally undermine the power of Spain. The rejected lover of the Virgin Queen, seeking to regain her favour amid the myriad intricate tributaries of the Orinoco, was blind to the fact that he was urging a policy Elizabeth herself would never finance and was pursuing a goal that did not exist. More than ever, Ralegh was the prisoner of his fantasies.

The rest of his expedition had now caught up with him, the *Lion's Whelp* and Keymis's *gallego* arriving off Trinidad the day San Joseph fell. Now, when a party under John Douglas had reconnoitred four shallow but 'goodly' entrances to the Orinoco basin, carpenters set about stripping down the smallest of the vessels. The *gallego* was remodelled as a boat of low draught that could, if necessary, be rowed up the Orinoco to the fabulous city. Accompanied by four other boats and with a crew of a hundred men provisioned for a month Ralegh's expedition set off.

They made a stormy crossing to the mainland and spent arduous days working their way through the half-submerged islands, the 'woods, prickles, bushes and thorns' of the tropical forest. Ralegh dramatized the discomfort to magnificent effect. He described the members of the expedition 'being all driven to lie down in the rain and weather in the open air, in the burning sun, and upon hard boards'. The fish they had brought began to stink, and to this was added the rank smell of 'the wet clothes of so many men thrust together'. But even here, amid 'the labyrinth of rivers' that made up the Orinoco basin, Ralegh's imagination dwelt most powerfully on his own predicament, the favour he had lost and his all-pervading sense of entrapment. 'I will undertake', he wrote – and every reader knew he was referring to himself – 'there was never any prison in England that could be found more unsavoury and loathsome, especially to myself, who had for many years before been dieted and cared for in a sort far differing.'

But now their young Indian guides were proving useless, and the sight of three natives in a dug-out canoe seemed to promise relief. One of the three – an old man – was taken prisoner and made to direct their way. The strong current was running against them, however, and the men at the oars rapidly wearied. Supplies were running low and the waters around them were unpalatable. 'We grew weaker and weaker when we had most need of strength and ability.' To keep his company from disintegrating and so dying ignominiously in the jungle, Ralegh constantly urged 'that it was but only one day's work more to attain the land where we should be relieved of all we wanted.'

The old guide, promising that bread, fish and wine would be found up a narrow tributary, tried the same expedient. The foraging party made its way upstream but, after three hours, saw no sign of human habitation. 'He told us a little further.' They rowed for three more hours. The sun was setting and Ralegh suspected a trap. 'When it grew towards night, and we were demanding where the place was, he told us but four reaches more.' Night then fell and the river narrowed ever more threateningly. Branches of overlapping trees scratched the explorers' faces, and 'we were driven with arming swords to cut a passage through'. The men had not eaten since morning, 'and our stomachs began to gnaw apace.' Ralegh felt he wanted to murder the old man.

Then, about one in the morning, still rowing the 'thick' water and with the noises of the jungle shrilling around them, 'we saw a light, and, rowing towards it we heard the dogs of the village.' They approached the settlement and were given the promised food. Then, returning by daylight along the previous night's fearful route, the beauty of the Orinoco landscape became apparent: the savannahs of short grass, the groves of trees, the flashing jungle birds, 'some carnation, some crimson, orange-tawny, purple, green'. The poet in Ralegh became one with the explorer. 'And still as we rowed, the deer came down feeding by the water's side, as if they had been used to a keeper's call.'

When the party had landed to cook their meal, fighting off some Indians in the process, Ralegh thought he discovered signs of what he had come so far to seek. There was an Indian basket hidden in the bushes. 'It was a toolkit dropped by a metal refiner containing quicksilver, saltpetre, and divers things for the trial of metals and also the dust of such ore as he had refined.' Ralegh's description of the incident kindles the reader's excitement and then deflects it with a haughty superiority that is at once characteristic and a cheat. 'I could have returned a good quantity of gold ready cast,' he wrote, 'if I had not shot at another mark than present profit.' We are encouraged to believe his mind was set on higher things. But is any man – especially one who had sailed half-way round the world – really so indifferent to the possible existence of a gold mine?

With the rivers now rising all about him, Ralegh decided to press on, and 'on the fifteenth day we discovered afar off the mountains of Guiana to our great joy.' The kingdom of El Dorado seemed to be in view and the journey appeared to become easier. Friendly natives arrived bringing fish and turtles' eggs along with fruit that was traded for some wine. Delighted by this, the chief invited the Englishmen to his village where they could sample his own brew, a spicy fermentation of herbs and fruit juices which was kept in twelve-gallon earthenware pots. The local people were, Ralegh discovered, 'the greatest carousers and drunkards of the world'. He found two visiting traders lying in hammocks, 'which we call brazil beds', getting pleasantly tipsy as they toasted each other, three cups at a time, on alcohol ladled out by two attractive women.

Ralegh himself disapproved of heavy drinking, but other aspects of village life held a strong appeal for him. For example, one of the traders had his wife with him, and 'in all my life I have never seen a better favoured woman.' She was, Ralegh noted, 'of good stature, with black eyes, fat of body, of an excellent countenance, her hair almost as long as herself, tied up again in pretty knots, and it seemed she stood not in awe of her husband, as the rest, for she spake and discoursed, and drank among the gentlemen and captains, and was very pleasant, knowing her own comeliness, and taking great pride therein.' Ralegh often found such independent-minded women attractive, and this one reminded him of 'a lady in England' save for the difference in the colour of their hair. Perhaps the reference was meant as a compliment to Bess.

Ralegh none the less insisted on the strictest sexual propriety. For the same reason, he took pains to see that the Indians' possessions were left untouched by his men. It was vital to win the natives' trust and essential also strongly to differentiate the behaviour of the English from that of the conquistadors. The Indians had told him that the Spaniards 'took from them both their wives and daughters daily, and used them for satisfying their own lusts.' Ralegh insisted that such behaviour was forbidden to his own men. 'But', he added, 'I confess it was a very impatient work to keep the meaner sort from spoil and stealing, when we came to their houses, which because in all I could not prevent, I caused my Indian interpreter at every place where we departed, to know of the loss or wrong done, and if aught were stolen or taken by violence, either the same was restored, and the party punished in their sight, or else it was paid for to their uttermost demand.'

After six days' travel, Ralegh's party passed the junction of the Orinoco and Caroni rivers and arrived at the village of Morequito, who had been executed on the orders of Berrio. The settlement was now ruled by the ageing Topiawari who, Ralegh claimed, was a hundred and ten years old. English policy towards the natives began to prove its worth, for the two men became firm friends. Topiawari himself had come to greet his visitor bearing pineapples which Ralegh declared to be 'the princess of fruits that grow under the sun', along with miniature parakeets and, most fascinating of all, an armadillo 'which seemeth to be barred all over with small plates'. The animal reminded Ralegh of a miniature rhinoceros.

Most importantly, Topiawari appeared able to give information on El Dorado. Ralegh determined to woo the old man's confidence. Having constructed a small tent in which the Indian could rest, he gently questioned him through an interpreter about Berrio's murder of Morequito and then suggested that the queen of England had sent him 'to deliver them from the tyranny of the Spaniards, dilating at large . . . Her Majesty's greatness, her justice, her charity to all oppressed nations.' Then he began sounding Topiawari out about the people who lived on the other side of the mountains:

> . . . he answered with a great sign (as a man which had inward feeling of the loss of his country and liberty, especially for that his eldest son was slain in a battle on that side of the mountains, whom he most entirely loved) that he remembered in his father's lifetime when he was very old, and himself a young man that there came down into that large valley of Guiana, a nation from so far off as the sun slept, (for such were his own words,) with so great a multitude as they could not be numbered nor resisted, and that they wore large coats, and hats of crimson colour, which colour be expressed, by showing a piece of red wood, wherewith my tent was supported, and that they were called Oreiones, and Epuremei.[18]

In a matter of a couple of paragraphs these Epuremei have been converted by wishful thinking into 'subjects to Inga, Emperor of Guiana and Manoa'.

The rivers were now rising fast and the chances were against being able to reach a silver mine up the Caroni river which Berrio's lieutenant had told them of. Instead, Ralegh hurriedly prepared three reconnaissance parties. One was sent to the Indian settlement of Capurepana which was near to the supposed frontier of the fabulous empire. Another group under Whiddon's command was sent to search for 'mineral stone', while Ralegh himself proceeded by the bank of the Caroni to where he found a succession of stupendous waterfalls, 'everyone as high over the other as a church tower, which fell with that fury that the rebound of water made it seem as if it had all been crossed over with a great shower of rain.'

But he was now beginning to tire – he was, he confessed, 'a very ill footman' – but he was urged on and was rewarded with one final vision of the borders of his promised land:

> I never saw a more beautiful country, nor more lively prospects, hills so raised here and there over the valleys, the river winding into divers branches, the plains adjoining without bush or stubble, all fair green grass, the ground of hard sand easy to march on, either for horse or foot, the deer crossing in every path, the birds towards the evening singing on every tree with a thousand several tunes, cranes and herons of white, crimson, and carnation perching on the river's side, the air fresh with a gentle easterly wind, and every stone that we stooped to take up, promised either gold or silver by his complexion.[19]

The promise was a false one however, the stones were merely *el madre del oro*, indications of deposits hidden far underground. Although convinced that 'the sun covereth not so many riches in any part of the earth' as near to where he had been, the flooding of the river and the frequent rainstorms convinced Ralegh it was now time to leave.

He returned via Topiawari's village where some of the braves urged an attack on the highland invaders with promises of 'their women for us and their gold for you'. Ralegh called the old chief a man of 'gravity and judgement', but he rejected the proposal that he leave fifty of his men there until he should himself return. Instead, as an altogether more intimate sign of trust, Topiawari gave Ralegh his son in exchange for two young Englishmen: Francis Sparrow (who was later captured and imprisoned in Spain), and Hugh Godwin, Ralegh's cabin boy who was eventually absorbed by the tribe among whom he lived, almost forgetting the use of his native tongue.

'I thought it time lost to linger any longer in that place,' and the return journey began. The weather was now so extreme, 'full of thunder and great showers', that at times Ralegh and his men were obliged to hug the banks, occasionally being carried by the current 'no less than 100 miles a day'. Just before they reached the coast, conditions became truly frightening. A mighty storm forced them as near to the shore as they dared go. 'The longer we tarried the worse it was' until, after midnight, and putting themselves 'into God's keeping', they 'thrust out into the sea'. Faint cheers kept up their spirits until, at nine the next morning, they sighted Trinidad. The South American part of the expedition was over, and 'now that it hath pleased God to send us safe to our ships, it is time to leave Guiana to the sun, whom they worship, and steer away to the north.'

This was a magnificent sentence – and a lie. Ralegh was surely aware of how little he had achieved. Trinidad had not been secured for *Ezrabeta Cassipuna Aquerewana*. In his journey up the Orinoco he had gathered a prospector's toolkit, some worthless rocks, and a deal of misinformation. Something needed to be done for the honour of the expedition and to secure a profit. Ralegh wrote haughtily that 'it became not the former fortune in which I once lived, to go journeys of picory' but 'picory' or thieving was very much what he now had in mind and, instead of steering north, he turned west.

He had first the idea of looting the pearl fisheries of Margarita, but abandoned this plan when one of his men was killed. Margarita still appeared to offer a smaller prize however, for the imprisoned Berrio had written to the governor of the island, requesting a loan of 1,400 ducats for his ransom. Alvaro Jorge was sent to secure his old master's freedom but, while disagreement erupted among the Spaniards, Ralegh veered south to Cumana on the Venezuelan coast.

He believed he was in possession of information which would allow him easily to sack the site. Two of his Indians came from the town and claimed they were familiar with its secret entrances. But the Spaniards were ready for them. They allowed Ralegh's men to land and then, after a strategic withdrawal to higher ground, fired on the invading party. The English were forced to turn and, with their backs exposed, to run through a forest of prickly pears. While four men were left dead on the shore, the agony of those wounded by the poisoned arrows of the Indians the Spaniards had recruited was appalling. Writing of the effect as if it were simply a matter of information – 'a digression not unnecessary' – Ralegh declared: 'The party shot endureth the most insufferable torment in the world, and abideth a most ugly and lamentable death, sometimes dying stark mad, sometimes their bowels breaking out of their bodies, which are presently discoloured as black as pitch, and so unsavoury, as no man can endure to cure, or to attend them.'

Ralegh himself slunk off to spend his days on two Dutch merchantmen anchored off Cumana, returning at night. Twenty-seven of his men died on their ships, and the defeat ensured that the governor of Margarita would not now pay Berrio's ransom. In the end, the old man and his lieutenant were exchanged by Ralegh for a wounded English youth. Again, the idea of sailing to Virginia that had been briefly entertained was abandoned, and the governor of Cumana, watching as Ralegh did indeed now steer for the north, informed the King of Spain that the Englishman was leaving the Caribbean not 'as pleased as he could wish'.[20]

Ralegh returned to a cold and even cynical reception. There were those who said he had not been to Guiana at all, but had spent his time skulking in some remote bay in the West Country. His samples of ore, they said, came from the Barbary coast. There was derision when an officer of the Mint declared them to be fool's gold.

Ralegh was exasperated by the petty energies of his detractors. 'This dolt and that gull must be satisfied, or else all is nothing.'[21] He bombarded Cecil with letters from 'desolate Sherborne', variously urging the place he imagined for Guiana in national policy and indulging the histrionic despair of the self-obsessed. Did Guiana 'pass for a history or a fable' among those in power? 'The like fortune was never offered to any Christian prince.' He was fearful the French and Spaniards would steal a march on his initiatives. Nor was this just a personal concern. If the Spaniards had been as 'blockish and slothful' as the English showed themselves, then 'we had not feared now their power, who by their gold from thence vex and endanger all the estates of kings.' England, Ralegh declared, could not 'maintain war' on the strength of her own revenues.[22] The country was obliged to fight and should find the money to do so through the policies he urged.

[249]

He made no effort to hide his own ambitions or his loyalty to his distant queen. 'I hope I shall be thought worthy to direct those actions that I have at mine own charges laboured in; and to govern that country which I have discovered and hope to conquer for the queen without her cost.'[23] He treasured the fantasy of being El Dorado himself, and again and again he emphasized the wealth of the legendary king. When Cecil wrote to him about some Spanish letters captured by Popham in which the writer discussed a golden idol from the region allegedly weighing 47,000 pounds, Ralegh breezily replied: 'I know that in Manoa there are store of these.'[24]

Why was nothing being done to lay hold of them? By the close of November, Ralegh was begging Cecil to 'let us know whether we shall be travellers, or tinkers; conquerors, or novices.'[25] If the winter was allowed to pass without further expeditions being sent, then 'farewell Guiana for ever'. He declared he would himself be left with the choice 'to beg or run away'. Meanwhile, he would once again take the initiative in his own hands. 'I am sending . . . a bark to the country', he told Cecil, 'to comfort and assure the people that they despair not nor yield to any composition with any other nations.'

He also sat down to write one of the supreme works of Elizabethan travel literature: *The Discovery of the Large, Rich and Beautiful Empire of Guiana*. Here, all Ralegh's powers of intellect, argument, observation, fantastication and deceit are focused on the fashioning of his role as a patriot. He plays to his audience – the literate Elizabethan public – with great versatility. But what appears as a gripping, objective account of a journey into the scarcely credible is, above all, the means by which Ralegh hoped to re-establish himself in the queen's favour. He becomes the hero of his own drama, and by the time he has finished his performance we forget how little he had accomplished and instead, like him, are beguiled by his revelation of golden opportunities;

> Guiana is a country that yet hath her maidenhead, never sacked, turned, nor wrought, the face of the earth hath not yet been torn, nor the virtue and salt of the soil spent by manurance, the graves have not been opened for gold, the mines not broken with sledges, nor the images pulled down out of their temples. It hath never been entered by any army of strength, and never conquered or possessed by any Christian prince.[26]

His public is inveigled into an act of collusion: belief in the existence of fabulous wealth and the fashioning of the hero who has, he says, discovered these riches. To achieve this, Ralegh shows himself in a variety of roles. He is the despised favourite, the pundit, the footsore and sweaty explorer, the courteous grandee, the scheming soldier and so on. Each of these roles is shrewdly presented and convincing. The pace of the narrative carries complete conviction, while the anthropological information is dense and various. We are both informed and beguiled. The story of the men whose heads grew level with their shoulders appealed even to so intelligent a reader as Shakespeare who remembered the detail when he came to write *Othello*.

Above all, Ralegh is a vivid scene painter. His portrait of himself addressing the natives of Trinidad on the virtues of Elizabeth may be variously seen as comic or repellent, but the scene strikes, perhaps for the first time, the authentic pose of the khaki imperialist on a remote frontier: the voice of England for 350 years. And throughout, the observation is remarkable – exotic but precise. Who would not be touched by the man who built a tent for old Topiawari or saw the deer by the Orinoco grazing like those in a home park?

And, as always, his performance leads Ralegh back to his queen. Here, in Guiana, was 'a better Indies for Her Majesty than the King of Spain hath'. A state initiative, he argued, was essential. But Elizabeth was no more persuaded by this than she had been by Hakluyt's similar reasoning in the *Discourse on Western Planting*. But where that work had been a private memorandum proclaiming the virtues of Virginia, Ralegh eventually published the *Discovery* in 1596. Within five years it had been translated into Dutch, twice into Latin, and four times into German. While Europe was beguiled by this Elizabethan best-seller however, Elizabeth herself merely put it to one side. Ralegh was a fallen favourite still.

If he had failed in his immediate objective Ralegh now, in concert with the intellectuals of Durham House, made a major if disturbing advance in English colonial theory. This emerges most clearly in an unpublished and anonymous document which may be the work of Thomas Harriot.

'Of the Voyage for Guiana' is a lucidly argued and novel approach to the issues surrounding the possession of colonies by the crown. It was clear that new approaches to the problem were needed. Military settlement had been tried in Virginia and failed. The trans-shipment of volunteer colonists had also failed there and was now under threat in Ireland too. Neither solution appeared practical, and both at best ignored the moral and spiritual well-being of the natives which, for the men in Durham House, were matters to which they cared to pay more than lip service. 'Of the Voyage for Guiana' attempts a solution to these difficulties through a critical appraisal of the ideas underlying Elizabeth expansion. The result was an argument of great if problematic significance.

The writer's fundamental aim was that of helping in the defeat of Catholic Spain by suggesting that the Guianan Indians be recruited to the Protestant English cause. He was seeking arguments to support this idea that appeared both pragmatic and morally respectable, in his own words: 'Just before God according to our Christian profession, and honourable among men according to the accustomed proceedings of our English nation.'[27] Convinced as he was of the duty to convert the heathen, rescue them from Spanish barbarity and elevate them to his own degree of 'civil conversation', the writer proposed a new imperialist role for England based on self-interested benevolence.

He argued that the home country would be made both rich and strong by wooing native people to her standards. Rather than crushing 'the Inga of Manoa', seizing his lands and enslaving his people (the policy pursued in Ireland), Englishmen were 'to draw the Inga to do homage' to Elizabeth and to persuade him to hold his lands from the queen as her vassal. Guiana, in other words, was to be 'united to the crown of England' as a willing tributary state, enjoying her superior laws, religion and material civilization while also contributing to her wealth. Here, in embryo, was the future British Empire.

Here too were others of its characteristic prejudices. For example, the natives of Guiana were people to be patronized rather than feared. 'The Indians for the most part are a people very faithful, humble, patient, peaceable, simple and without subtlety, malice, quarrels, strife, rancour, or desire of revengement, as meek as lambs, as harmless as children of 10 or 12 years.' In other words, they are not to be regarded as autonomous adults and, like most children, they can be won over with sweets. Among the 'allurements' the writer proposes are a series of gestures designed to portray Elizabeth herself as the benevolent queen-empress.

The Indians are to be told 'that she is a most gracious, merciful, and just princess, relieving sundry distressed nations both in her own and foreign countries.' They were then to be told about the great and wonderful material civilization which she, as queen, personified. 'She is of great magnificence and puissance, her countries populous, rich, warlike and well provided of ships as any state in the northern world.' To this material strength was then added true Protestant religion which was seen inevitably as superior to Spanish Catholicism. 'Her Majesty's religion is far differing from the Spanish, maintaining truth, justice, and faithfulness, prohibiting all murders, treasons, adulteries, thefts, and whatsoever correspondeth not with equity and reason.'

Prosperous, Protestant England is being presented as the fit arbiter of other nations' affairs. Her innate integrity and fair dealing justify her in this role. These last were matters of the utmost importance to the writer, and he envisages the presence abroad of a comparatively small but honourable force of well-disciplined missionaries, soldiers and artisans who will work with the natives and slowly raise them to their own level. They will be people 'that will not wrong the Indians in their purses, women or possessions', but who will rather labour to convert them to 'procure their loving affections, and to oblige them in assured loyalty to Her Majesty.'

Here was an image of immense future significance, and other members of the Durham House group were clearly excited by this vision of 'riches with honour, conquest without blood'.[28] In particular, Ralegh's sending Laurence Keymis on the second reconnoitring expedition he had mentioned to Cecil was the occasion for the poet George Chapman to compose his *De Guiana Carmen*. In this work the Durham House group can be seen once again fashioning images of empire of great if dubious potency.

Guiana itself for example, is personified here as a rich, exotic and ultimately submissive foreign female:

> Guiana, whose rich feet are mines of gold,
> Whose forehead knocks against the roof of stars,

Stands on her tip-toes at fair England looking,
Kissing her hand, bowing her mighty breast,
And every sign of all submission making,
To be her sister and the daughter both
Of our most sacred maid.[29]

Elizabeth is again the Imperial Virgin creating a golden world in an iron age. The 'patrician spirits' like Ralegh and Keymis who are her servants are, it is alleged, refined by the imperialist ideal beyond all merely worldly concerns. The empire, it is suggested, becomes the moral crucible of the English gentleman, testing his worth as 'a world of savages' falls tame before him. A moral rebirth will surely take place as virtuous and well-born English youths explore those ever-widening horizons where 'Britannia humbly kneels to heaven'. In the end, all the effort, imagination and initiative that went into Ralegh's pursuit of an illusory ideal in Guiana produced no more potent or dreadful a dream than this: the iconography of imperialism.

CHAPTER THIRTEEN

Ralegh and Essex

For all the vision of empire inspired by Ralegh's Guiana expedition, the threat from Spain had not diminished, and new initiatives were essential. Ralegh himself had been humiliated at Cumana while, more significantly, the expedition launched that year by Drake and Hawkins on the Spanish forts and treasure fleets of the Caribbean had been outpaced and outgunned. Its two leaders – heroes of the Armada generation – were dead, and a reinvigorated Philip was preparing a fresh invasion.

The vulnerability of England was alarmingly illustrated when four Spanish crews rowed galleys round from Brittany to Cornwall, burned Mousehole and Penzance, and then celebrated a mass of thanksgiving. Ralegh himself wrote to Cecil telling him how sixty Spanish sail were allegedly making for Ireland. 'The preparations are great, and do daily increase.' Sound intelligence was vital. 'If my lord will have a fine pinnace sent to the coast of Spain, to view what is done, I think for a matter of £40 or £50 I can get one that shall do service.'[1] A fortnight later, on 25 November 1595, Ralegh wrote a memorandum to the Privy Council urging his views on the defence of the West.

An alarmed committee resolved on an offensive. Burghley accepted that attack was the best means of defence and, conscious of his declining powers, detailed his arguments in a paper sent 'To the Queen's Majesty's only most fair hands, from a simple weak hand'. Sir Francis Vere, now England's most eminent military man, urged that an attack on Spain was essential 'to the main proceeding of this war'.[2] Admiral Lord Howard of Effingham lent his firm but crotchety support, while the Earl of Essex was thrown into intense excitement by the opportunity for glory and self-advancement offered by the proposed attack on Cadiz.

For the past two years Essex's career had been at a standstill, a position he could not abide. The motley army of his supporters was restless, while the Farm of Sweet Wines which propped up his chaotic finances had only four years to run. High military and naval endeavour would once again burnish his name and assert his undoubted glamour over hunchbacked, bureaucratic Cecil whom, in his paranoia, Essex now saw as the evil genius behind a succession of small defeats and disappointments.

Essex had recently attempted to enhance his popularity by whipping up the anti-Semitism which surrounded his accusations that one Dr Lopez had tried to assassinate the queen. Neither Elizabeth nor Cecil was entirely convinced of Lopez' guilt, but as Essex and his rival were returning by coach from an examination of the doctor, Essex broached a matter altogether nearer to his prestige. Among his followers was the brilliant young lawyer Francis Bacon, and Essex wished to secure the man's loyalty by having him appointed Attorney-General. Cecil saw objections to this. The queen disapproved of Bacon who was, besides, too young for the job. Essex indignantly pointed out that Cecil himself had achieved high office with far less experience. Cecil replied that he had been trained to this from boyhood and proved the fact by tactfully suggesting Bacon be appointed Solicitor-General. The position was altogether more appropriate and was, he suggested, 'of easier digestion to her Majesty'.[3]

Essex's response was the measure of the man. 'Digest me no digestions. For the Attorneyship for Francis is that I must have; and in that will I spend all my power, might, authority, and amity, and with tooth and nail defend and procure the same for him against whom whatsoever.'[4] This was the same histrionic fervour Essex had shown as a youth at North Hall when he had thought Ralegh was his enemy. Here was the same blazing, all or nothing fury, the same political ineptitude. Bacon himself – subtle, reptilian and vastly gifted – was to counsel Essex against such displays, but to no avail. He was also aware of the error in Essex's seeking popularity through military prestige. His patron again declined his advice.

Essex himself was convinced, perhaps correctly, that a permanent patrol of the Spanish coast from a Spanish landbase was essential to England's successful prosecution of the war. The notion was impractical, but Cadiz was to be among other things Essex's opportunity of proving his theory. The 'wretch' Ralegh was deemed a necessary component to his success for he was now one of the country's senior naval figures. The most delicate negotiations were opened to create a temporary triumvirate of Cecil, Essex and Ralegh himself.

This alliance was doomed by the very men who made it up, and contemporaries watched with circumspection as the great of the land patched up their quarrels. 'Sir Walter Ralegh', wrote one, 'hath been very often private with the Earl of Essex and is the mediator of a peace between him and Sir Robert Cecil, who likewise hath been private with him.'5 Ralegh was clearly excited by the prospects suddenly opened up and alleged 'how much good may grow of it'.6 He was at last, it seemed, back on the public stage.

He laboured with characteristic energy to help assemble the largest expeditionary force the country had ever commissioned. An army of 6,500 was to be raised, a logistical challenge made all the more difficult by the reluctance, incompetence and sheer dishonesty that attached to all Elizabethan military enterprise. Ralegh himself, who was in charge of raising troops and supplies from London and the Home Counties, spent the early months of 1596 being rowed constantly between the capital and Gravesend. His days became acutely frustrating. 'As fast as we press men one day, they come away another and say they will not serve.'7 Suspicions over what appeared as his dilatoriness were, he claimed, wholly unfounded.

He explained to Cecil what he was having to endure and tried to calm the anger of the desk men with vivid accounts of his activities: 'I cannot write to our Generals at this time, for the poursuivant found me in a country village, a mile from Gravesend, hunting after runaway mariners, and dragging in the mire from ale-house to ale-house, and could get no paper, but that the poursuivant had this.'8 Suspicions remained none the less. Anthony Bacon wrote to his brother Francis from Plymouth: 'Sir Walter Ralegh's slackness and stay by the way is not thought to be upon sloth, but upon pregnant design.'9 Essex's chronic insecurities fanned the doubts and then, with characteristic volatility, he tried to bridle his suspicions with professions of friendship.

Elizabeth made matters worse. Her inveterate hatred of war – its risk, its expense, and her own enforced position on the sidelines – caused her to blow hot and cold. She wanted her forces to sail for

Cadiz, then she did not. The men and ships, she said, were required more urgently to defend Calais. Then, since it was too late for this, she wanted to replace the commanders. When the foolishness of this was suggested, she vowed to abandon the whole enterprise. Then she changed her mind. Surely they could just send the fleet and disband the soldiers? Such prevarication was intolerable. Essex, who in the absence of adequate government funds was paying for the greater part of the men out of his own pocket, was furious. 'The queen wrangles with our action for no cause but because it is on hand.'[10] A collection of 5,000 sailors, 6,500 soldiers and £30,000 of victuals had been assembled. The Dutch had contributed men and ships with great generosity. Were the armies of England to be made fools of in front of their allies?

As soon as Ralegh himself arrived at the port there was more trouble. A quarrel broke out between the commanders over pecking-order politics. Who among these egocentric men could give orders to whom? Could Vere, as marshal of the army, issue orders to Ralegh at sea, for example? What started as a disagreement among the officers became a matter of honour to their men. Arthur Throckmorton waxed so vociferously in Ralegh's support that he was cashiered on the spot and was only reinstated when Essex solved the greater matter by deciding Ralegh should have precedence in meetings on water, Vere at those on land.

On 11 June, and with such problems at least temporarily patched up, Lord Admiral Howard ordered the signal gun to be fired from his flagship, his beloved *Ark Royal*. Over a hundred vessels, divided into five squadrons, sailed around him. Essex, as joint commander, followed in the *Due Repulse*. The Lord Admiral's brother was in the *Mere Honour*. The Dutch, under Admiral Jan van Duyvenvoord, were led by the *Neptune*. Ralegh sailed in the *Warspite*, one of two new ships provided by the queen. The fleet, its sails filled by a north-east breeze and its pennants fluttering in many-coloured gaiety, made a spectacular impression of power as it moved down the Channel from Plymouth. But the quarrels that had dogged its preparation were already seething in its cabins. When a message to the queen was placed before Essex, he signed his name so grandiloquently that there was no room for the Lord Admiral to sign his. The petulant old man took out his penknife and promptly hacked Essex's name off the document.

Then the wind dropped. Proclamations had to be issued promising death to any of those reluctant men who decided to jump overboard and swim for the shore. By 3 June, there was sufficient breeze for the fleet to sail again, and for eight days it made towards Spain, arresting on its way an Irish merchantman two days out of Cadiz. The captain informed the leaders that Cadiz itself, weakly garrisoned and ignorant of English intentions, was sheltering a convoy of fabulously laden merchant ships.

When, on Sunday 29 June, the line of English sails appeared on the horizon, the surprise and terror among the Spaniards were total. Workmen who had been repairing the defences threw down their tools as the church bells which had earlier summoned them to prayer now rang out their warning of impending disaster. Every man among the English, however, 'skipt and leapt for joy, and how nimble was every man to see all things were neat, trim and ready for the fight'.[12] Ralegh himself was assigned the task of sweeping the seas between the English fleet and the shore, so guaranteeing that none of the merchant vessels slipped from their moorings off Port Royal.

This was a tactic wholly agreeable to Essex. It meant his greatest rival was employed while he himself could argue against Howard's ludicrous idea that, instead of pressing their vastly superior forces into the harbour, the English should prepare for a landing. He was overruled. Men in armour were hurriedly ordered into boats which, as the wind freshened, turned turtle and tipped a score of helpless, screaming soldiers to their deaths.

Ralegh, making for the main body of the fleet, was rowed to the *Due Repulse* and promptly gave Essex a dressing-down before delivering a similar rebuke to the Lord Admiral. He was determined to seize the initiative after such a show of incompetence and, to jubilant cries of 'Entramos! Entramos!' – 'We're going in! We're going in!' – established the only possible strategy: the Spanish fleet was to be attacked. A suddenly exultant Essex waved his plumed hat in the air and the wind, tugging at it, cast it out over the waves. The English fleet, realizing who was really in command, hove to and readied for a dawn raid.

Ralegh dressed himself with imperious splendour for the morning's triumph. A dozen victories were within his grasp. Alone on the deck of the queen's ship, he appeared the queen's commander now. The Lord High Admiral had submitted to his advice. Essex, showing his incompetence when the landing-craft capsized, proved how easily he might be led by a man of greater powers. And now, deep in the harbour of Cadiz, the might of Spain lay at Ralegh's mercy. A lifetime's hatred focused his patriotism. Treasure beyond counting stirred his excitement. The vast mass of the *St Philip*, the flagship that had destroyed Grenville off the Azores, thrilled his resolve 'to be revenged for the *Revenge'*.[11] He ordered his ship forward, commanded loud, discordant music from his trumpets, and then, with a political adroitness that for the moment baffled all who watched, dropped anchor.

Essex at once made for the *Warspite*. When he was within distance and was himself a sitting target for the Spanish guns, Ralegh was rowed across to him. Now more than ever it was necessary to win the young man to his side, and Ralegh resolved to challenge him into complicity. For he faced a serious problem. As the commander of the queen's ship, his credit would be seriously damaged if the *Warspite* were sunk. He could not go back, but it was equally dangerous for him either to exchange broadsides with the enemy or to sail in, grapple with the Spaniards, and board their ships. Of these last alternatives the latter was the more heroic and 'I would board with the queen's ship.'[12]

He needed cover and an ally, and the volatile young favourite was the obvious choice. Essex, refusing to be outdared, fell in with the scheme enthusiastically. Having secured this tactical victory, it was now a relatively easy matter for Ralegh to sail on past the two Howards (who had used these few moments of negotiations to get ahead of him) and then to cut the rope which Vere had cunningly tied to the *Warspite* in the hope of being towed to an easy and unmerited victory.

But as the smoke thickened and the galleons cut their cables, drifting in lumbering panic, Ralegh fell – fell in sudden and excruciating pain. A cannonball had struck the deck of the *Warspite* and his calf was now a torn and bloody mess 'interlaced and deformed with splinters'.[13] The surgeon hurried forward to do what he could, while, through eyes crushed tight in agony, Ralegh watched the Spanish ships 'tumbling into the sea heaps of soldiers, so thick as if coals had been poured out of a sack'.[14] The Dutch, with memories of Spanish atrocities burned on their memories, moved gleefully in, dropping into little skiffs as the *St Philip* and the *St Thomas* exploded and shot so many burning bodies about that 'if any man had a desire to see Hell itself it was there most lively figured.'[15] Those who did not drown fell victims to the edge of the Netherlanders' swords. Victory was now in sight and, ordering the English fly-boats to sail between the agonized Spaniards and the vindictive Dutch, Ralegh, in agony himself, ordered his men to row him ashore and carry him in a litter through the streets of Cadiz. Here, plundering English soldiers ran amok. There was an orgy of looting at which Ralegh could look only with contempt. All the great riches of Cadiz were paltry compared with the wealth stowed in the merchantmen moored in Port Royal. At daybreak, he despatched John Gilbert and Arthur Throckmorton to his fellow commanders, requesting their permission to seize the ships. They all might yet be rich.

But even here Ralegh was cheated. The worried traders came to the English and offered them two million ducats' ransom. The Howards, Vere and Essex, listened and decided that this unofficial offer could probably be upped to a tremendous sum. Thinking it worth their while to wait – they hoped, perhaps, to have the ransom and seize the ships as well – they disregarded Ralegh's advice and were unmindful too of the fanaticism of the King of Spain. Commands had been issued from the Escorial on the action to be taken if Spanish ships fell prey to the English. Summoning extraordinary resolve, the Duke of Medina Sidonia – the man who had commanded the Armada of 1588 – ordered that the entire merchant fleet should be scuttled and burned. Twelve million ducats sank, a useless sacrifice to Spanish pride.

While Essex distributed knighthoods to sixty of his followers, Ralegh could do nothing. In his cabin on the *Warspite*, he lay nursing his wound, his anger and his pride:

> The town of Cadiz was very rich in merchandise, in plate and money. Many rich prisoners [were] given to the land commanders so as that sort are very rich: some had prisoners for sixteen thousand ducats, some for twenty thousand and, besides, great houses of merchandise. What the generals have gotten, I know least; they protest it is too little. For my own part, I have gotten a lame leg and a deformed. For the rest, either I spoke

too late or it was otherwise resolved. I have not wanted good words and exceeding kind and regardful usance. But I have possession of naught but poverty and pain.[17]

The bitterness and self-pity are Ralegh's authentic tone, but there was, indeed, much of which he could legitimately complain. He had barely covered his costs. A fleet of merchant ships had been sunk before his eyes, and he himself was now partly crippled. After ten days during which the other members of the expedition looted, revelled and made an inglorious attack on Faro, it was time to make for home. Even then they narrowly missed the Plate Fleet which sailed unharmed into Lisbon a mere forty-eight hours after Essex's plea that the city should be taken was rejected. The opportunity of a further twenty million ducats was lost. Much had been done, however, to damage Spanish morale, and it now remained to see if Ralegh's part in the expedition had won him back the favour of his queen.

On 1 June 1597, he was permitted to limp into Elizabeth's presence, a revenant from the glory days. He was received, it was said, 'very graciously'.[17] He was allowed once again to fill in person his place as Captain of the Guard, and that evening he 'rid abroad with the queen and had private conference with her.' Soon he was coming as 'boldly to the Privy Chamber as he was wont'.

Essex took himself off to Chatham for a few days. He had been publicly and humiliatingly rebuked for what were now seen as the lost opportunities of the Cadiz expedition, and the reinstatement of Ralegh was in part a ploy in Elizabeth's campaign to punish the earl. But the absence of Essex could not disguise the fact that the relationship between Ralegh and his queen could not be what it once was. Disgrace had sobered him and time had laid its hand on her. The mirrors in Elizabeth's palaces had long ago been covered or removed. Her hands played constantly and anxiously with the trimmings on her dress. She wore a great, reddish-coloured wig. Two locks of false hair hung either side of her ears and almost down to her shoulders. Her face was thin now, and her teeth yellow. Some of them were missing, and it was not always possible to understand her when she spoke. But she still tried to play the coquette. When entertaining a French ambassador, for example, she kept the front of her dress open, ostensibly to keep herself cool, but actually so that the man could admire her withered breasts. Ralegh could no longer extol her as Cynthia. Elizabeth was, in his truer phrase, 'a lady whom time had surprised'.[18]

The disillusion spread to her people. The second half of the 1590s were terrible years. Four summers of torrential rain rotted the harvest. People were advised to make bread from parsnips. Tapsters could no longer afford to brew beer. There were food riots, and people died of starvation. Ragged armies of the unemployed roamed the country. Those in work and those living off rents saw the value of their money tumble with alarming speed. The government could do little except arrange for food hand-outs and order prohibitions: prohibitions on the export of corn, on eating meat on Wednesdays and Fridays, prohibitions against enclosures, statutes against the decay of husbandry. Minds soured. 'The wit of the fox', complained the queen, 'is everywhere on foot, so hardly a faithful or virtuous man may be found.'[19]

There were few, certainly, in the palaces along the Strand. During the absence of his rivals at Cadiz, Cecil had been appointed Secretary. Tempers ran high again in Essex House when Ralegh successfully backed his new friend, the witty and companionable Lord Cobham, for the post of Lord Warden of the Cinque Ports. Cecil was so concerned about this – Essex had first wanted the position for a client and then nominated himself – that he decided to take Ralegh and the Earl to the theatre as part of his campaign for patching things up. *Richard II*, Ralegh declared in his thank-you letter, made Essex in particular 'wonderful merry'.[20] In Durham House itself meanwhile the old circle of friends went about their multifarious activities. Laurence Keymis was sorting through his Guiana material. Harriot had drawn a map of the region, but, with no trace of acrimony, was now turning to Northumberland for patronage. The reason for this was purely practical. There was not so much money in Durham House as there used to be.

This is apparent from the will Ralegh signed on 10 July 1597. Adequate provision was made for Bess, but the bulk of Ralegh's property was left to his son Wat, now four years old. Further bequests showed where his other affections and memories lay. Five hundred marks from the sale of the *Roebuck* – apparently the only vessel remaining from his privateering fleet – were put aside for 'my reputed daughter begotten on the body of Alice Gould now in Ireland'.[21] Harriot was also to receive £200 from the sale of the ship, a further £100 from Ralegh's patent of wines and, along with books and some furniture, 'all such black suits of apparel' as his patron had in Durham House. Laurence Keymis was left £100, while Arthur Gorges was to have Ralegh's 'best rapier and dagger', Arthur Throckmorton 'my best horse and my best saddle with the furniture'. Other small bequests were made to members of Ralegh's family and his servants.

This was all fair and reasonable, but it is clear that the great wealth Ralegh had possessed before his disgrace – the Babington lands, for example, and his privateering fleet – had gone. Ralegh was always insistent on the large sums he had spent from his own pocket on the war with Spain, whether in the Caribbean, Virginia or Guiana. His will suggests the truth of this, and provides an immediate personal motive for his wanting to launch yet another expedition against the Spanish fleet.

This need for money and personal glory was shared with Essex, and some three months before Ralegh's will was signed the earl threw a small dinner party at which Ralegh and Cecil were his guests. Conversation turned on plans they had laid for an attack on Ferrol. The English fleet was again to be a massive one, numbering upwards of a hundred ships. Seventeen of these were the queen's (Elizabeth had been persuaded to the expedition only with the greatest difficulty) and included two of the Apostles captured the previous year in Cadiz. The Dutch were again to contribute a squadron under their own officers. Essex, Thomas Howard and Ralegh were to command the three remaining squadrons. Ralegh's kinsman Sir Ferdinando Gorges was responsible for administering the fleet as a whole, while Sir Arthur Gorges was to sail as Ralegh's captain on the *Warspite*.

Six thousand troops were to be levied, including 1200 experienced soldiers of Sir Francis Vere's. Essex, who was in overall command and whose prestige has now been enhanced by being appointed Master of the Ordinance, had carefully arranged that the quarrel between Ralegh and Vere over Vere's activities at Cadiz was made up. All seemed well. The country's leading soldier was on friendly terms with the nation's leading sailors. Essex and Ralegh were in league. They would also be out of the country while Cecil pressed on in his quiet pursuit of high office.

'The Islands Voyage', as the expedition came to be known, was the last great seaborne enterprise of the Elizabethan era and its most spectacularly duplicitous and chaotic. It was ill-starred from the first. For weeks, contrary winds kept the fleet from assembling, while troops and sailors ate their way through the supplies. When they did finally set sail, a storm in the channel at once proved many of the men disastrously incompetent. Large numbers were dismissed, but those remaining faced storms of such terrible force that Ralegh's squadron was separated from the others and spent agonizing days and nights being hurled about the Bay of Biscay. Deciding that the best thing was to head for home, and dismayed that he was apparently the only leader to make for port, Ralegh wrote a letter to the Privy Council in which he described the mounting storm and its effects: 'Our men being wasted with labour and watchings and our ship being so open everywhere, all her bulkhead rent, and her very cookroom of brick shaken down into powder.'[22]

A distraught Essex then appeared, another victim of the storm. Ralegh gave him dinner on the *Warspite*, and the question arose of what had happened to Howard's squadron. The answer came some days later when a messenger reported that he had ridden out the adverse conditions and was now cruising off Corunna, trying to tempt the Spaniards to a fight while waiting for his fellow commanders to join him. It was all very humiliating. Ralegh and Essex set about readying their ships as quickly as they could, preparing a 'nimble fleet, dispestered from our worst sailors, undefensible ships and superfluous number of men'.[23] Once again, however, storms kept them in port and, on the last day of July, Howard himself appeared off the English coast, keen to know what had been happening.

It was now clear that plans would have to be changed, and that meant a meeting with the queen. Elizabeth, with her usual grip on strategy, was adamant what the objectives of the expedition should be. Her navy was first and foremost to attack the Armada harboured in Ferrol. If this had already sailed, her men were to return to defend the English and Irish coasts. Only if it were found that the Spanish threat was an insignificant one were Ralegh and Essex to sail to the Azores and there plunder the treasure fleet.

Deceit, ambition and sheer bad luck meant these priorities were now reversed. A great deal of money had been spent but nothing so far had been achieved. Supplies and morale were running low. A scheme for attacking the Armada with fireships was discussed, and five thousand of the soldiers were discharged. Elizabeth, increasingly sceptical and worried as always about how her commanders might behave once they were out of her control, insisted that Essex be made subject to the majority rulings of the council of war and that all decisions of moment be committed to writing. These were precautions in vain. Once the fleet had set sail, violent storms again arose and, when they had subsided, it was discovered that Ralegh and a score of his ships had become separated from Essex and the main body of the English forces. An attack on Ferrol was now out of the question.

A messenger was sent back to London to explain the position to the queen while, on board his ship, Essex's followers – many of them as paranoid as himself – began to whisper about Ralegh's motives. News was then received that Ralegh himself, believing the Spanish fleet had left for the Azores, was sailing after it on his own initiative. To Essex, this was intolerable insubordination. He pointed his ships in the direction of the Islands, determined that Ralegh should not rob him of his glory. King Philip of Spain meanwhile, ulcerous and close to death, resolved that now his coasts were clear he would launch a last assault on the one nation who had failed to bow before his power. Despite the warnings of his advisers that his Armada would be wrecked by storms, Philip gave orders to attack England while the greater part of the English fleet was indulging in a wild-goose chase off the Azores. Potentially, this was a moment of the utmost national peril.

The eventual meeting between Ralegh and Essex off the Islands was as cordial as the circumstances permitted, Essex 'protesting he never believed we would leave him, although divers persuaded him to the contrary.'[24] But there were practical matters to attend to as well as issues of personality. Ralegh's ships needed reprovisioning, and he requested permission to land at Flores for food and water. This was granted, but Essex, keen for action, sailed off to patrol the seas, acting 'like a high constable to arrest all in the queen's name that pass by in thirty leagues'.[25] Then, before Ralegh had completed his task, he received orders to join Essex for an attack on the island of Fayal.

Dawn revealed that Essex and his men were nowhere near the island. Whether through incompetence or deceit, Essex had failed to tell Ralegh of his change of plan. He was probably off looking for the treasure fleet, and Ralegh was left with no alternative but to drop anchor and wait for his commander while the guns of the fort were turned in his direction and the inhabitants of Fayal took measures to protect themselves. The position was both dangerous and humiliating. For Ralegh to take action on his own account meant risking the anger of the volatile Essex, while to remain where he was exposed his men to great risks.

He waited another day, another night, and then, contrary to his express orders, summoned a council of war. Those who were loyal to Essex refused to act before the return of their patron. Knowing how effectively these men could poison Essex's mind, Ralegh waited through another night. By dawn he had had enough. To remain anchored off Fayal, a target for the Spaniards, was mere foolishness. Essex's men might stay there if they chose but Ralegh had a responsibility to his own followers. He issued orders to the West Country privateers who sailed with him to weigh anchor and head off into the protection of a nearby headland.

The lush countryside tempted him to land and complete his reprovisioning. Sir Arthur Gorges described what happened:

> As we made onwards with our boats, the shot played so thick upon us as that in truth the mariners would scarce come forward, having the lesser liking to the business the nearer they came to it. And in like sort did I see some there stagger, and stand blank, that before made great shows, and would gladly be taken for valiant leaders; and some of these our Rear-Admiral did not spare to call upon openly, and rebuke aloud with disgraceful words, seeing their baseness.
>
> And withal finding a general amazement amongst the mari-

ners, and as it were a stray amongst all the boats . . . with a loud
voice [he] commanded his watermen to row in full upon the
rocks, and bade as many as were not afraid to follow him.[26]

But such encouragement was to no effect and Ralegh now ordered
his boats to head straight for the rocks, 'and bade as many as were
not afraid to follow him.'

As the bows crashed on the reefs, Ralegh jumped from his boat
and, limping and cursing in the surf as the bullets strafed about him,
ordered his men onwards. It was a superbly courageous moment,
and the abashed Spaniards 'began to shrink, and then seeing us to
come faster upon them, suddenly retiring, cast away their weapons,
turned their backs and fled.'

Now Ralegh had to make for Fayal, leading the vanguard himself. 'Our Rear Admiral', wrote Gorges, 'accompanied with divers
other gentlemen of the best sort to the number of forty, in the head
of all the troops, with his leading staff, and no other armour than
his collar (a bravery in a chief commander not to be commended)
led on the company with soft march, full in face of the fort, descend-
ing down a little hill, whilst with their great ordnance and musketry
we were very shrewdly pelted.'

The English troops fell into 'shameful disorder'[33] and Ralegh,
calling now for his armour, determined to reconnoitre the ground
himself. Neither Captain Berry nor Arthur Gorges – both of whom
put themselves forward – was at first allowed to accompany him,
but Gorges would not be restrained. 'I say truly, and so afterwards
it was much spoken of, that there was not any one more of quality
that did accompany him in that business.'

The danger indeed was great, and Ralegh

did himself go to discover the passages, and also was careful
and diligent to observe and search out the strength and ascents
of the hill. In which doing, we were shrewdly troubled with
the great artillery, which did beat upon the old walls alongst the
which we were to pass, and therewithal much endangered and
harmed us. For besides some that were hurt, two of our train
had their heads stricken clean from their shoulders; myself was
then shot through the left leg with a musket bullet, but missed

[268]

the bone being but a flesh wound, but the bullet did burn both my silk stockings and buskin, as if it has been singed with an hot iron. I was then hard by the Rear Admiral, who also was shot through the breeches and doublet sleeves in two or three places. And still they plied us so fast with small shot as that (I well remember) he wished me to put off a large red scarf which I then wore, being (as he said) a very fair mark for them. But I was not willing to do the Spanish so much honour at that time, albeit I could have wished it had not been on me, and therefore told the Rear-Admiral again that his white scarf was as eminent at my red, and therefore I now would follow his example.[27]

The town fell before such ostentatious bravado. It was a heroic victory, which the following day turned very nearly to disaster.

Essex reappeared. Whatever the purpose of his expedition, it had achieved nothing but confusion and now, in his depressed state, Ralegh's heroism seemed like a personal insult. Essex's own captains fanned his resentment as they whispered about breaches of regulations and what seemed to them Ralegh's duplicity. Essex roared for a court martial, for Ralegh's death. Messengers were sent to fetch him, but he was already on his way to Essex's ship, flushed with success and certain of his good entertainment.

As soon as he came aboard Essex's vessel 'he found all men's countenances estranged as he passed through them'. The mood in Essex's cabin was grimmer still. There was a faint welcome, and then Ralegh heard the envious young man charging him with a 'breech of order and articles'. Ralegh protested his innocence and begged to be allowed to defend himself from accusations which, if proved, would mean his death. Thinking quickly, he argued that while it was indeed an offence for a ship's captain to land 'without directions from the General' he himself was not a mere middle-ranking officer, he was 'a principal commander under your lordship'. The rule did not apply to him and he had, besides, been scrupulous in following the earl's command. What was the sacking of Fayal if not a preliminary to reprovisioning his crews? Was that not what Essex had ordered? It became obvious that such fault as there was lay with the earl. A smarting Essex brought the meeting to a close and ordered that he be rowed across to the town.

Here he at once cashiered all the officers who had taken part in the victory. An infuriated Ralegh declared that he and his men would stand and fight rather than be so humiliated. A desperate and disgraceful incident was in the making, and only the intervention of Howard saved the honour of the expedition. Essex was persuaded to accept an apology; Ralegh, with even more difficulty, to make it. 'And so', wrote Gorges, trying to play the matter down, 'all things after a little dispute came to a quiet end.' Ralegh had risked death in a military engagement and saved his life in a battle of wits. The dangerous price of both was Essex's lingering enmity. The earl did not mention the sack of Fayal in his despatches to the queen.

Yet the sacking of Fayal was the only success of the entire Islands Voyage. The expedition had failed to destroy the Armada in Ferrol and this was now lumbering towards England. Unaware of the danger, the English themselves were squabbling off the Azores. Here they might have achieved something by the capture of a treasure ship, but the rashness of Essex ensured the failure of even this, doing so in a situation where his forces had the clear advantage. By patrolling the Angra Road off Tercera they could deny the Spaniards access to their great and safe deep-water harbour. Three hours after Essex had decided to sail in the opposite direction the Spanish fleet appeared.

When Essex returned from whatever fool's errand he had gone on, he was all for attacking Tercera. His more seasoned followers managed to persuade him against an idea which would have involved exposing the greater part of the English war fleet to fire from an impregnable enemy. The only remote possibility of redeeming his reputation now lay in sailing for St Michael and there trying to ensure a blockade between the Azores and the Spanish mainland. But the same vaingloriousness reduced even this plan to failure.

When Ralegh was rowing across to reconnoitre St Michael, Essex, maddened by any action of his rival's that had a smack of honour about it, summoned him back, insisted on taking his place, and humiliated him in front of the entire fleet for Ralegh's entirely sensible precaution of wearing his armour. Then, having decided the town could not be taken by a frontal assault, Essex sailed round the island to land at Villa Franca. Ralegh was ordered to sail up and down before St Michael, his trumpets blazing, his cannon firing, and his men giving every impression they were about to land. The farce was continued for two days and a night, but still Essex did not appear to sweep down on the town. He had again changed his plans without letting Ralegh know. He had dug himself in on the other side of the island and had set to plundering Villa Franca for himself and his men.

Had he stuck to his original idea, Essex might have helped with a great prize, for an eighteen-hundred-ton East Indiaman had appeared and, since there were captured Spanish vessels in the van of Ralegh's squadron, the captain suspected no danger. Ralegh gave orders that none of his ships were to move or fire until the enemy vessel was close enough to board. But the Dutch, either through misunderstanding or greed, sailed out and holed her. The captain, true to the orders of the King of Spain, sailed for the coast, beached his craft, and burned its cargo. Had Essex attacked St Michael this loss might have been avoided. As it was, it seemed better now to take the battered and dejected fleet home, unaware that a great Armada was sailing up the Bay of Biscay through terrible storms.

It was the storms that saved the country. The Privy Council called out the county militia and erected beacons on the hills. However, as the newly landed Essex rode from Plymouth to London and Ralegh made for the West Country there to rally its forces, news came that the great fleet had already been scattered and storms had worked the defeat that Philip's commanders had predicted. In England, and in the court especially, relief was mixed with anger. Why had the Islands Voyage exposed the country to such danger? Why had the Spanish fleet been left unmolested? Why had an expedition mounted at such expense failed to achieve the capture of a single prize? The queen directed her anger at Essex. She was 'not pleased with his service at sea'. Nor was she any more impressed with 'his proceedings towards Sir Walter Ralegh in calling his actions to question before a council of war'.[28]

Despite these comments, Ralegh still did not inspire in the queen the generosity he had known in the great days of his favour when so many posts – all, that is, except a much-coveted place on the Privy Council – were his for the asking. Instead, he now sought advancement through alliances with those in the highest places in the court. In January 1598, contemporaries noted 'the too too great familiarity that is grown between the Earl of Essex, Sir Robert Cecil and Sir Walter Ralegh'.[29]

This was a triumvirate under severe strain. Elizabeth was determined to check Essex's pride, but she did so in ways that only provoked the earl's constant fear that people were plotting against him. During his absence on the Islands Voyage, for instance, the queen had given Cecil the lucrative position of Chancellor of the Duchy of Lancaster. On Essex's return, she promoted Lord Admiral Charles Howard to the Earldom of Nottingham and named him Lord Steward of the Parliament, a position that gave him precedence over Essex. Essex himself withdrew to his house at Wanstead, there to sulk under the guise of an illness. Only the gift of the title of Earl Marshal of England – a gift apparently suggested by Ralegh, perhaps in combination with Cecil – improved his spirits, for the role reestablished his seniority. Increasingly, such displays revealed the paranoid divisions in Essex's mind, and these were now visibly widening. In conjunction with his popularity, especially among the discontented, and his ever more desperate ambition for high office, such weaknesses made him a dangerous ally and, eventually, an enemy of the state.

It was necessary, however, for Ralegh to keep in with Essex and his entourage, and a little scene of court life recorded from January 1598 suggests what this entailed. Ralegh and a certain Mr Parker were up late playing primero with Essex's friend Lord Southampton. The queen had gone to bed, and Ambrose Willoughby, the Squire for the Body, 'desired them to give over'.[30] Apparently they refused to do so, and Willoughby threatened 'that if they did not leave he would call in the Guard to pull down the board'. This was enough to stop the game but Southampton was so incensed that sometime later, finding Willoughby 'between the Tennis Court wall and the Garden struck him and Willoughby pulled off some of his locks.' Ralegh, by contrast, not wishing to appear ridiculous before the men of his guard and realizing for once that discretion was the better part of valour, merely 'put up his money and went his ways'.

He was ageing, but he had lost none of his vindictive pride. Sometime in the previous year there had been a quarrel, apparently over the profits of a privateering venture, between Ralegh and his nephew, the younger Sir John Gilbert. Gilbert had clearly been whining behind Ralegh's back, claiming he had been done out of money by a tiresome uncle whom he had stuck by through difficult times. Ralegh was not the man to put up with such accusations. 'Where you say you followed the worst of my fortunes in despite of envy, I pray forget not yourself; nor do not so much mistake my fortunes, but when they were at worst they were better than the best of your own, and were able enough to stead my friends, and despise the rest.'[31] Even in its now mutilated form, the letter conveys Ralegh's venomous spirit when he felt obliged to join the sneering of a schoolboy to the wrath of a courtier.

This was the pride that flashed again in the Parliament of 1597 to which Ralegh was returned as knight of the shire for Dorset. He had been too busy to attend the opening in October, and in the following month he had been sufficiently ill for Adrian Gilbert to get a Speaker's licence to leave the House and visit him at Sherborne. By December, however, Ralegh was well enough to journey to Westminster and sit on many of the committees now framing legislation to help circumvent the effects of the dire harvests. In this capacity, Ralegh headed a delegation sent by the House to the Lords, and the old problem of precedence – the right of the peers to remain seated when conversing with members of the Lower House – infuriated him. Ralegh angrily moved a motion demanding an explanation. His illness had tired him however, and when he and Bess went to Bath to recuperate at the close of the session, the Privy Council sent him a letter expressing hopes for his recovery.

This was gratifying, but it was Cecil, now securing his leading place among the Counsellors, whom Ralegh sought as his greatest ally. His voluminous correspondence with the Secretary continued, and contained one letter of great personal interest and literary merit. In January 1597, Cecil's wife – the sister of Ralegh's friend Lord Cobham – died. 'It is true', Ralegh wrote to the genuinely grieving husband, 'that you have lost a good and virtuous wife, and myself an honourable friend and kinswoman.' He urged on Cecil the stoic reserve of which he himself was so rarely capable. 'I would but mind you of this, – that you should not over-shadow your wisdom with passion, but look aright into things as they are.'

Ralegh then wrote, decorously and with strength, of death as the common destiny of all mankind. Here was a subject later to call forth the deepest subtleties of his prose, but on this occasion Ralegh turned, as was proper, to personal consolation. 'She is now no more yours, nor of your acquaintance, but immortal, and not needing or knowing your love or sorrow.' The letter concludes with a paragraph whose power must have helped prompt the effects it counsels:

> I believe it that sorrows are dangerous companions, converting bad into evil and evil in worse, and do no other service than multiply harms. They are the treasures of weak hearts and of the foolish. The mind that entertaineth them is as the earth and dust whereon sorrows and adversities of the world do, as the beasts of the field, tread, trample, and defile. The mind of man is that part of God which is in us, which, by how much it is subject to passion, by so much it is farther from Him that gave it us. Sorrows draw not the dead to life, but the living to death. And, if I were myself to advise myself in the like, I would never forget my patience till I saw all and the worst of evils, and so grief for all at once; lest, lamenting for someone, another might not remain in the power of Destiny of greater discomfort.[33]

The letter also mentions the children of the marriage. 'She hath left behind her the fruit of her love, for whose sakes', Ralegh urged, 'you ought to care for yourself.' But Ralegh, and perhaps Bess even more, knew that little workaholic Cecil simply did not have the time to devote to fatherhood. In a gesture at once kindly and shrewd, young Will Cecil was eventually invited down to Sherborne to play with young Wat Ralegh.

Sherborne was becoming a delightful place. Ralegh had lavished money on the estate and this was, perhaps, a principal reason for the relative lack of cash suggested by his will. Sir John Harington claimed that for the cost of 'drawing the river through rocks into his garden he might very justly and without offence of the church or state have compassed a much better purchase.'[34] Having expended so much time, energy and money on the place however, Ralegh was determined to secure it for his heirs. Difficulties with the clerics lessened, and Ralegh, who was on friendly terms with the new bishop elect, managed to purchase Sherborne from him outright. By

1598, Ralegh felt able to convey the property unreserved to Wat after his death, provided the boy paid his mother £200 a year.

But still Ralegh yearned for high office. He nurtured hopes of being appointed Vice-Chamberlain. Early in 1598, Cecil was preparing for an embassy on which he intended to persuade Henri IV against negotiating a separate peace with Spain. Ralegh, it was said, 'labours mightily to have something done for him before Mr Secretary's going away, and he doth importune my Lord Essex to be a furtherer of it.'[35] The three men struck deals, Cecil hoping to cover his rear during his absence. But Essex was the greater threat and got the richer pickings – £7,000 'out of the cochineal'. When, in March, Ralegh was consulted on Irish affairs – a subject on which he had long been issuing warnings – it was rumoured he would be made Lord Deputy. Others had declined this poisoned chalice and Ralegh, it seems, was not asked to take it up. When old Burghley died in August 1598, Ralegh hoped for his place on the Privy Council. There was no hope of that. Nor was he any luckier in angling for the Vice-Chancellorship of the Duchy of Lancaster, a post which would have helped bind him in closer alliance with Cecil against Essex.

For the earl was now widening the gulf between himself and Cecil and, by so doing, was preparing his own destruction. This last was to be a complex tale of mounting paranoia and ultimately tragic ineptitude. During the Secretary's absence in France, Essex had broken his Privy Counsellor's oath of secrecy to issue an *Apology* which argued that while peace with Spain was desirable, its pursuit was unwise since the ever-duplicitous Spaniards were merely bargaining for a breathing space. This appealed to national prejudice, but Cecil, whose subtle grasp of the situation was causing him to think carefully about the possibilities of a treaty, was furious. He was made angrier still by Essex's insinuations that the Secretary and his friends had tricked Essex himself of advancement while he was fighting the enemy off the Spanish coast. But it was not Spain that became the means of Essex's fall but Ireland, and here, partly out of actual events and more decisively through imagined ones, Essex began spinning the web of intrigue that eventually was to tighten around both him and Ralegh.

The Irish situation of which Ralegh had so long been warning came to a head in the summer of 1598. A leader of genuine ability had emerged from among the petty feudal chiefs. Hugh O'Neill, setting aside his title of Earl of Tyrone to brandish the illicit rallying cry of 'The O'Neill', was a man who commanded the respect even of his enemies. 'A strong body he had,' wrote Camden, 'able to endure labour, watching and hunger; his industry was great, his mind great and able to the greatest business; much knowledge he had of military skills and a mind most profound to dissemble, insomuch as some did then foretell that he was born to the very great good or hurt of Ireland.'[36] Ralegh suggested someone be sent across to murder him. 'We have always in Ireland given head-money for the killing of rebels.'[37]

The idea was ignored, and now equally at home in the Elizabethan court and the wilds of Ulster, Tyrone had raised, equipped and trained troops that could add modern military tactics to ancient traditions of guerrilla warfare. He had also insulted the Marshal of the English Army in Ireland by abducting his sister and ill-treating her in a forced marriage. Contrary to all advice, Sir Henry Bagenal rode north with an inadequate force bent on revenge. At the Yellow Ford on the Blackwater river, he was trapped by Tyrone, humiliatingly defeated and killed. English control of Ireland was on the point of collapse. The Spaniards could now use it as a base to launch at England, while Tyrone vaunted his achievement around Europe. Elizabeth was furious 'that it must be the Queen of England's fortune (who hath held down the greatest enemy she had) to make a base Irish kerne to be accounted so famous a rebel.'[38]

Catastrophe abroad was matched by folly at home. Six weeks earlier, the volatile relationship between Elizabeth and Essex flared to violence in the Privy Chamber. Essex turned his back in contempt and the queen struck him on his face. Essex's hand reached for his sword as he screamed he would never endure to be hit by a woman and would not have accepted such an insult from Henry VIII himself. This was treason. The Earl of Nottingham hurried to interpose, and a still shouting Essex was hurried from the royal presence.

Unrepentant, Essex wrote violent letters informing Elizabeth of the wrongs she had done against the 'honour of your sex'.[39] He could only assume she was punishing herself for her gross error. By August, Elizabeth was still vowing 'to stand as much upon her

James I

Left: An alleged likeness of Lord Cobham

Below: Peace negotiations with Spain. The figures at the front right-hand side are Lord Henry Howard and, in the foreground, Robert Cecil

Count Gondomar

Robert Carr

Ralegh's lodgings in the
Tower of London

Queen Anna, wife of James I

Henry Percy, 9th Earl of Northumberland

Prince Henry, son of James I

Frontispiece to Ralegh's *History of the World*

Ralegh in later life

greatness as he hath done on stomach.'[40] None the less, she was, she confessed, 'apprehensive from the impetuosity of his temper, and his ambition, that he would precipitate himself into destruction.'[41] But now she needed a commander for her army, and Essex was perhaps the one man available who could inspire enthusiasm in the troops of famine-weary England for the near equal miseries of an Irish war.

'Unto Ireland I go. The queen hath irrevocably decreed it.'[42] She had also decided the strategy. A swift, punitive campaign in Ulster should draw Tyrone to his defeat, the English cavalry luring him to the certain disaster of an open battle. In this way Elizabeth's army, levied at great expense and in difficult times, would gain her objectives before disintegrating into yet more costly chaos. Once arrived in Dublin, Essex was to move north.

With the unanimous agreement of all present, he marched south. There were petty defeats, expensive delays, numerous casualties. Elizabeth was paying £1,000 a day, she declared, for Essex to go on a mere progress. So far it had lasted two months. Nothing had been achieved save the weakening of her exchequer and the defences of her realm. Abroad, her enemies delighted in her humiliation. Essex wrote back blaming his officers and his troops, but reserving his special venom for those of his supposed enemies who he thought were plotting behind his back, manipulating his downfall while he was out of the country and powerless to respond. 'Is it not known', he wrote, 'that from England I receive nothing but discomforts and soul's wounds?'[43] Then, after this general attack, he turned to his real and specific targets.

'Is it not lamented of Your Majesty's faithfullest subjects, both there and here, that a Cobham and a Ralegh – I will forbear others for their place's sake – should have such credit and favour with Your Majesty when they wish ill-success of Your Majesty's most important action?'[44] The veiled threat was levied at Cecil, but at this stage Essex's paranoia had not yet descended to the hopelessly uncritical state where he could openly accuse the Secretary of treason. His allegations against Ralegh, however, were as absurd as they were unfounded, for Ralegh himself was once again involved in the defence of the realm. Tyrone's successes had been welcome news in the Escorial where Philip III, hoping to surpass his predecessor by emulating his tactics, was preparing another Armada. This, like all the others, was scattered and forced to turn home, but news of its sailing sent a scare through England.

Ralegh was naturally despatched for the defence of the West, Cobham to attend to the Cinque Ports. Essex's supporters, however, claimed that they were really raising an army against the earl. The accusations were particularly absurd since Ralegh had every reason to hope that an English peace would be imposed on Ireland as quickly as possible. His own estates in the south were being threatened as Tyrone's officers began to foment disaffection there. Soon his settlers, already in a state of confusion, would be faced with abject catastrophe.

Only in the third week of August did Essex himself decide to obey the queen's orders and move north into Ulster. He knew in his heart he was now too late for success and he tried to prepare Elizabeth by sending his secretary as a messenger to Nonesuch. An embittered reply was despatched, but before it reached him Essex had embarked on the move he had already hinted at to the queen: a wholly forbidden parley with Tyrone. The two earls met and talked for half an hour. There was no witness to their conversation, but a truce was arranged and Essex believed he had persuaded his enemy to submit. There were those who thought the men had discussed other matters: the succession, for example, the mood in England, and the claims of Scottish James to a throne he might be helped to with their joint force of arms.

Whatever was in fact said, Essex presented his actions as a diplomatic triumph. Elizabeth knew they were no such thing. Tyrone was duplicitous to the core. Essex, she said, she trusted. Others were less sure of him. Why had the queen not been told 'what passed on either side'? She insisted her original policy be carried through at once. 'We absolutely command you to continue and perform that resolution'.[45] But the order was too late. In mounting panic, Essex had handed his commander's sword to his senior colleagues and now, with his less respectable friends, was heading pell-mell for Nonesuch to explain his actions. There, on 28 September, hurrying through the Presence Chamber and brushing aside Ralegh's guards in the Privy Chamber, he burst muddy and desperate into the queen's bedroom and threw himself on his knees.

She was not yet fully dressed and her hair hung about her aged, unpainted face. She let him kiss her hand, speak and calm himself slightly before recommending him to his rooms. They would talk more fully later. Then, unperturbed, resolute, Elizabeth set about discovering if she and her kingdom were safe. Had Essex come with his army or merely with an escort? Satisfied she was not at risk, Elizabeth summoned her available Privy Counsellors – Cecil, Hunsdon, North and Knollys – and ordered they hear Essex's case. Then she sent for their colleagues and prepared for her second interview with the earl. She spoke to Essex once more that afternoon, and in the evening, when Elizabeth had had a chance to read the Privy Counsellors' report, 'a commandment came from the queen to my lord of Essex, that he should keep his chamber.'[46]

The following day he was cross-examined for five hours by a full session of the Privy Council. A verdict was reached in fifteen minutes. Essex's actions had shown him in his true light: 'contemptuously disobedient', 'presumptuous', 'rash and irresponsible', 'over-bold'.[47] He was arrested, taken to York House and thence, after some months, to Essex House. Here, for a further three months, he was kept under the closest watch. He fell prey to religious melancholia, the victim of his self-destructive temperament.

Ralegh was obliged to count himself among those now suffering from Essex's catastrophic handling of the Irish situation. The scheme for plantations in Munster had for some years been going awry. By 1592, a mere fifteen of the fifty-eight undertakers were resident, and only 245 English families were permanently settled. Now in October 1598, and with Essex withdrawn and his army in confusion, Tyrone's officers succeeded in fomenting revolt. 'The Munster Rebellion', a contemporary recalled, 'broke out like lightning, for in one month's space almost all the Irish were in rebellious arms and the English were murdered or stripped and banished.'[48]

This was in large measure their own fault. The settlers had failed to establish themselves as a strong yeoman community due very largely to the dilatoriness and greed of the undertakers. 'For whereas they should have built castles and brought over colonies of English, and have admitted no Irish tenant, but only English, these and like covenants were in no part performed by them.'[49] Ralegh's notions of what could be done had simply been eroded away. He himself had already begun to grow so disillusioned with the project that in May 1598 he conveyed his Irish lands to his friend Thomas Southwell, reserving his own title but leaving the initiative to others. Now he saw his Munster colonies being depopulated and rendered valueless. In Tallow, whole families were shot, 'and in all about three score able men, ran away every one.'[50] Elsewhere, 'all the English seignory of Sir Walter Ralegh, namely John Harris, William Andrew, with others, ran away.' Spenser was forced to flee Kilcolman, and the anguish broke his heart. Only the odious Pyne survived to profit from shady deals. Ralegh's vision of an English colony that was politically strong, useful and growing prosperous from exports, faded.

But Essex's paranoia was wreaking equal if invisible damage elsewhere. Elizabeth proceeded slowly against her popular favourite. After eight months of imprisonment, Essex was brought before a court of commissioners. Two hundred of the great and the good were invited to hear the complaints against him. Francis Bacon produced incriminating letters from his old patron, and his desertion symbolized what the commissioners made certain: the Earl of Essex no longer had powerful supporters. Those who followed him were merely disaffected nobles, religious outsiders and the riff-raff of the military. All of them were broke, and most hoped to profit from Essex's lease on the Farm of Sweet Wines. At the end of October, the queen announced that this would not be renewed. By the following month Essex's mood had violently changed. 'He shifteth', wrote Harington, 'from sorrow and repentance to rage and rebellion.'[51] His sanity was openly questioned, and in this state he began to nurture conspiracy theories against Cecil, Cobham and Ralegh.

It was perfectly clear to him what these three men were trying to do. They were using their own positions and that of their kinsman to sell the country to Spain. Cecil's placemen included his brother who was President of the North; George Carew, who held a similar post in Munster; and Nottingham the Lord Admiral. To complete this encirclement of the country, Cobham was Lord Warden of the Cinque Ports, while Ralegh held undisputed sway in the West Country. What was more, Ralegh had just been appointed Governor of Jersey. How easy it would be for these men to guarantee the success of a new Armada and ensure that the Spanish Infanta succeeded to the English throne. The claims of James VI of Scotland would be completely disregarded. Messengers were at once sent from Essex House to Edinburgh assuring the king of the loyalty of the earl and his followers, and thereby poisoning his mind against Ralegh and his friends. James listened sympathetically and prepared to send an embassy south. Essex wore a secret note from the king in a little black bag tied round his throat.

Although ignorant of the damage that was now being done to his reputation with King James, Ralegh's own intentions with regard to Essex were far from innocent. He was acutely aware of the danger the earl posed, and some time between February and August 1600 he wrote a letter to Cecil which might have come from the hand of a stage machiavel: 'I am not wise enough to give you advice,' he began, 'but if you take it for a good counsel to relent towards this tyrant, you will repent it when it shall be too late.'[52] It was, Ralegh thought, vital that the edge of Cecil's malice be honed, and he appealed to the Secretary's family loyalties. 'The less you make him, the less he shall be able to harm you and yours.' Essex, in other words, was a threat to the Cecil dynasty. Once he was out of royal favour, however, 'he will again decline to a common person.' He would be at Cecil's mercy.

The murderous implication was obvious but far too dangerous to be clearly spelt out. It was better to cite some precedents for what others had safely achieved in similar circumstances. 'Somerset made no revenge on the Duke of Northumberland's heirs. Northumberland, that now is, thinks not of Hatton's issue. Kellaway lives, that murdered the brother of Horsey; and Horsey let him go by all his lifetime.'

Cecil's political intelligence was too shrewd to be drawn by this sort of backstairs insinuation. To write the letter at all was dangerous, while its advice merely showed the flaws in Ralegh's judgement. He was not, as the queen had always known, the material of which Privy Counsellors were made. He still aspired to this position however, hoping now to achieve it by being made a commissioner in the current treaty negotiations with the Dutch. 'But Her Majesty, as it is thought, begins to perceive that if he were one, he would stand to be made a counsellor ere he went, which she hath no fancy unto.'[53] Cecil, meanwhile, appeared to keep the door of opportunity open. Ralegh was asked for his advice on Irish affairs (it was not taken), while the Governorship of Jersey gave him status far from the centre of power.

Ralegh took his oath of office on 20 December 1600 and was splendidly entertained on Jersey. He declared the island to be the most beautiful he had ever seen, if poorer than he expected. He set about his duties there with characteristic energy. He established trading links with Newfoundland, Mont Orgueil castle was saved from demolition, and the old system of manning it by the compulsory call-up of local men was abolished. Ralegh also ordered the completion of the fort 'Isabella Bellisima' and, in 1602, instituted a public register of land which previous officials had been advised to do for the past forty years. He was also frequently called on to liaise between the islanders and the Privy Council while, turning to his own affairs, he now made arrangements for his daughter by Alice Gould to be married to a young local nobleman.

Children, indeed, were a frequent concern at this time. Cecil's son stayed with the Raleghs at Sherborne during March 1600. The air, Ralegh reported to the boy's father, improved young Cecil's appetite and digestion. 'He is also better kept to his book there than anywhere else.'[54] The lad clearly found Ralegh himself a glamorous alternative to his own father and, in these years of cynical letters, he sent up to Ralegh's study a little note of the utmost charm. 'Sir Walter, we must all exclaim and cry out because you will not come down. You being absent, we are like soldiers that when their Captain are [sic] absent they know not what to do: you are so busy about idle matters. Sir Walter, I will be plain with you. I pray you leave all idle matters and come down to us.'[55]

The future of his own son also craved Ralegh's attention and, with the consent of Cecil who was Master of the Court of Wards, Wat was betrothed to a ward of Cobham's worth £3,000 a year. Cobham, indeed, was now becoming a firm friend. Both men longed to be nearer the centre of power than they were, and each stimulated the other's ambition and sense of fun. There were plans for them to meet up in Bath in the spring of 1600, while in the summer of that year the two men 'stole over' to Ostend for a view of the English troops fighting there in the war between Spain and the Netherlands. In 1600, this was a largely harmless friendship, but in Essex House it was viewed with the utmost suspicion.

By the beginning of February 1601, a fight between Southampton and Lord Grey that happened to break out by Durham House convinced Essex that his enemies were seeking his death. His followers began plotting rebellion, for to lose their patron was to lose all. Sir Charles Danvers and two of Essex's Welsh followers – John Littleton and Sir John Davies – summoned Ralegh's kinsman Sir Ferdinando Gorges from Plymouth to assist them. Between them they resolved to infiltrate the palace at Whitehall and then, on a signal, seize the halberds of the royal guards and secure control of key positions. Essex himself would then arrive in state. Ralegh, as Captain of the Guard, would be arrested, along with various other enemies. Heralds would proclaim the capture of the queen to the City, and Parliament would be summoned to execute justice on Essex's rivals. The plan, as Gorges realized, was mere desperate foolishness. 'I utterly disliked that course as, besides the horror I felt at it, I saw it was impossible to be accomplished.'[56]

In the end, the conspirators decided to defer to Essex and little else was done save to persuade Shakespeare to mount a performance of *Richard II* and its then notorious deposition scene especially. The performance was given on the afternoon of 7 February. The type of people in the crowd that thronged the Globe and the dangerous nature of the play's subject alerted the queen. That evening, the Privy Council was called into session and Essex and his leading followers were required to present themselves and explain their intentions. Their refusal to obey the summons indicated their intention to revolt.

Ralegh summoned Gorges to Durham House. A hurried conference with Essex suggested it might be wiser for Gorges to meet his kinsman on neutral ground, possibly with a view to murdering him. And so, very early on 8 February, the two men were rowed separately to the middle of the Thames by Essex Stairs. Gorges had two gentlemen in his company. For Ralegh, who came alone, there were urgent matters of family honour and national security to discuss as the boats swayed and bobbed on the tide. He told Gorges there was a warrant out for his arrest and advised him that he should hasten back to Plymouth, there to resume his service as governor. Gorges refused. It was too late and he was, he said, committed to the 'two thousand gentlemen who had resolved that day to live or die free men'.[57]

Ralegh asked what such a force (greatly exaggerated in Gorges' estimate) could hope to achieve against the authority of the queen. 'My answer was, it was the abuse of that, by him and others, which made so many honest men resolve to seek a reformation thereof.' Insofar as the Essex revolt had any clear focus of grievance, this was it: the resentment of men disaffected by the inequalities of the patronage system. Ignoring the personal implication of Gorges' comment, Ralegh repeated his advice that his kinsman should show his loyalty to the queen, the better to serve his own interests.

For the moment, this was ignored, and some time during the interview Gorges issued a flamboyant warning, telling Ralegh: 'Get you back to the court, and that with speed, for my Lord of Essex hath put himself into a strong guard at Essex House, and you are like to have a bloody day of it.'[58] In fact, among the very few shots fired during the course of the revolt were the four now aimed at Ralegh himself by Sir Christopher Blount from Essex House, from where a boat containing four armed men was also seen to be moving off. It was time for the two men to part, and for Ralegh to return to the court, there to ready his guard to protect his queen.

In this atmosphere of high drama, the Privy Council resolved to move surely and by due forms. They wanted above all to avoid intensifying excitement. To fan the flames of insurrection in the narrow and disaffected streets of London would be to provoke a situation of the utmost seriousness. The deputation they had sent to Essex had already been made hostages in the earl's palace, and now Essex himself was riding out, urged by his supporters to make for the court where the queen was protected merely by her courtiers and Ralegh's guard. Characteristically, Essex refused their advice.

Half-promises and rumours suggested there were considerable forces reserved for his use in the City, and Essex now set out to summon them. This was a grave tactical error. The promised troops failed to materialize, while by the time Essex had reached the area round Fenchurch Street, the Earl of Cumberland had been sent out with troops to barricade the Lud Gate. Cry as he might 'For the queen! For the queen!' and then try to arouse the citizens by falsely claiming that Ralegh and Cobham had laid a plot for his life, Essex was cut off and his position was hopeless.

He was to remain bottled up in Fenchurch Street for three hours while Cecil's brother rode through the City proclaiming the earl's treason and pardon to his followers. The only hope remaining to the leaders of the revolt was to return to Essex House and there use their prisoners as bargaining counters. By this time however, realizing the futility of the cause, the men had been released by Sir Ferdinando Gorges. When Essex himself returned to his palace, Essex House was surrounded and the desperate earl began destroying his papers. By ten that evening he had surrendered. By three the following morning he was a prisoner in the Tower.

There followed a show trial for treason. Ralegh, as Captain of the Queen's Guard, protected the judge, Lord Treasurer Buckhurst, and listened while the treason charges were put forward by the great legal figures of the day: the Solicitor-General, Sir Edward Coke who was now Attorney-General, and a triumphantly vindictive Francis Bacon among others. Ralegh himself was summoned to give evidence – 'What booteth it to swear the fox?' Essex was heard to declare[59] – and described his interview with Gorges on the Thames. It was Bacon, however, who took up the matter of Essex's claim that Ralegh and Cobham had threatened to murder him, reducing the charge to the mere flutterings of a hysteric. When an anxious Cecil then managed to disprove Essex's allegations that he had plotted for the Spanish Infanta to assume the throne of England, Essex's entire case collapsed. He was sentenced to death.

As Captain of the Guard, it was Ralegh's duty to attend Essex's execution. The earl had already confessed himself to be 'the greatest, the most vilest and the most unthankfullest traitor that ever was born'.[60] Now, on Ash Wednesday 1601, he wanted to make his peace with the world. In his last moments he wished to clear Ralegh's and Cobham's names and declared them both 'true servants of the queen and state'.[61] But Ralegh was not there to hear. There had been murmurings that no man should stand so close to a mortal enemy at the point of death, and in deference, Ralegh had withdrawn to the armoury. This graceful action conspired to ruin his reputation among the ordinary people. His thoughts were, in truth, troubled and confused, but after Essex's death the rumour was bruited abroad that as Essex was preparing for his end Sir Walter Ralegh had sat gloating over their hero's death, smoking his pipe and joking with his friends.

This was the sort of lie disaffected people wished to believe about a man who was almost universally hated. If Essex the people's martyr could now only exist in the shrine of the people's memory, Sir Walter Ralegh could personify all their resentment, bitterness and feelings of hopeless servitude to the corrupt and self-serving court that Ralegh himself so flamboyantly embodied. The man they had loathed for over two decades became ever more clearly the 'Mischievous Machiavel', and ballad hawkers, their greasy offerings passed from hand to hand, made Raleigh the man everyone wanted to hate:

> Ralegh doth time bestride;
> He sits 'twixt wind and tide
> Yet uphill he cannot ride,
> For all his bloody pride.
>
> He seeks taxes in the tin:
> He polls the poor to the skin:
> Yet he swears 'tis no sin.
> Lord, for thy pity![62]

Suspicion and envy were darkening ever more dangerously around Ralegh's role on the public stage. He was being drawn insiduously into a drama that was not of his own contriving but from which there would be no escape but death.

CHAPTER FOURTEEN

Progress to the Tower

While the people murmured in many-headed disaffection, Ralegh himself had more immediate problems to attend to. Down at Sherborne, his agent John Meere was acting against his interests, and when Ralegh endeavoured to replace him Meere used his influence with Lord Howard of Bindon to obtain his successor's arrest. Ralegh was furious at this involvement, swearing he would 'not endure wrong at so peevish a fool's hand'.[1] There were scenes. Meere called the often difficult Adrian Gilbert a 'gorbellied rascal'. Mrs Meere hung out of her window and shouted 'undecent words concerning Lady Ralegh'. Ralegh's servants responded by singing lewd songs outside the Meeres' house at night. Eventually, Ralegh himself had his sometime bailiff placed in the stocks and walked off with the key while the locals jeered 'Where is Howard? Where is Howard?'

Amid these trying local circumstances, the Raleghs continued to entertain. The ever-busy Cecil paid a brief visit to Sherborne and was presented with a pair of gloves Bess had embroidered for him. Cobham, too, was implored to stay, Ralegh writing a delightful letter to ensure this. 'I hope your lordship will be here tomorrow or a Saturday,' he declared, 'or else my wife says her oysters will all be spoilt and her partridge stale.'[2] But even this pleasant surface was ruffled by disagreements, for a row now broke out between Bess – as ambitious in her way as her husband – and Cobham's new wife whom she accused of plotting against her return to court.

In Ireland meanwhile the objectionable Pyne was swindling Ralegh out of the returns from his plantation. These were soon found to be running at a loss of £200 a year, a figure Ralegh could not readily support. Munster was becoming another colonial adventure he would have to abandon, and it was with some relief that at the close of 1602 he succeeded in selling the entire estate to Robert Boyle, secretary to the Presidency of Munster, for £1,500. The new worlds of profit and prestige Ralegh had striven for in the days of his favour were fast contracting around him.

The comparatively small sum Ralegh accepted for his Irish plantations suggests the damage caused in Munster by unrelenting guerrilla warfare, and it was to provide money for the defence of the English interest in Ireland that Elizabeth summoned the last Parliament of her reign in 1601. The occasion gave Ralegh the opportunity to speak on a number of issues. Ever the actor, he was now to show the depth of his convictions while also revealing that impulsiveness – the almost total lack of assured guile and humbug – which made him so dangerous a political ally.

Parliament itself was in fractious mood. Money was uppermost in every member's mind: money for the war in Ireland, and the financial effects of the restraint on trade caused by the crown's granting of monopolies. Members were told that the rebellion in Ireland and the continuing struggle with Spain had accumulated a debt of £140,000. A sum over twice that amount was now called for in order to subdue the province and expel the Spaniards who had landed in Munster. A quadruple subsidy was essential. 'Neither pot nor pan, nor dish nor spoon should be spared when danger is at our elbow,' Cecil declared.[3]

Ralegh, sitting next to him, disagreed. In a debate where members had repeatedly been 'cried or coughed down', and where Ralegh had earlier been unable to make himself heard because he insisted in his right to speak while seated, he now launched a virulently patriotic attack on Cecil. 'I like not that the Spaniards, our enemies, should know of our selling pots and pans to pay subsidies,' he declared. 'Well may you call it policy, as an Honourable Person alleged, but I am sure it argues poverty in the state.'[4] This was hardly the way to secure allies.

Ralegh was equally certain that government interference in agriculture was ill-advised. Indeed, his speeches against the compulsory growing of hemp (which was made into ropes for the navy), and above all his objections to the Statute of Tillage which laid down quotas for the production of corn, show Ralegh as an early spokesman of economic liberalism, and this in a period when government control was usually thought essential to the conduct of the nation's finances. Cecil toed the traditional line when he argued: 'I do not dwell in the country, I am not acquainted with the plough, but I think whosoever doth not maintain the plough destroys the kingdom.'[5] Ralegh, who had been reared in the country and continued to pass much of his time there, saw the impracticality of the dogma.

Seeking as always to bind the weakest in loyalty to the crown, he informed the House how 'many poor men are not able to find seed to sow so much as they are bound to plough, which they must do or incur the penalty of the law.'[6] Ralegh was also aware that the European market in corn was such that corn itself could often be imported more cheaply than it could be grown at home, and he looked enviously at what had been achieved abroad by leaving entrepreneurs to their own devices. 'The Low Country man and the Hollander,' he declared, 'which never soweth corn, hath by his industry such plenty that they will serve other nations.' This was an advanced, radical insight, and Ralegh was careful to make it appeal to more conventional national sentiments. He argued that rather than the government deciding how a farmer should apportion the use of his lands, Parliament should set him 'at liberty, and leave every man free, which is the desire of a true Englishman'. Soon he was to develop these ideas of free trade into a commercial policy far ahead of its time.

But while Ralegh could advance issues of economic policy whose value would only be appreciated by a later generation, the force of his imagination and intellect – along with his enduring need to talk others down regardless of the consequences – led him into egregious errors. In earlier Parliaments, Ralegh had helped make advances in matters of procedure. Now, when a motion enforcing church attendance by giving, as Ralegh haughtily declared, 'authority to a mean churchwarden',[7] was defeated by a single vote, he revealed an arrogance that threatened to bring the House into disrepute.

It was the custom when a division was called for the Noes to sit in their places while the Ayes walked out to be counted in the lobby. It was now alleged that one member wishing to vote in favour of the motion on church attendance had been forcibly held down in his chair. Ralegh's light Devon voice rose above the hubbub. 'Why, if it please you, it is a small matter to pull one by the sleeve, for so I have done many times.'[8] The House was deeply embarrassed. Cecil muttered about slander and was widely applauded by members shocked by so tactless an interruption. Ralegh himself was summoned to be reprehended.

But it was the question of monopolies that raised the bitterest feelings, and Ralegh himself was an infamous monopolist. Francis Moore put the case for the opposition when he said: 'I cannot utter with my tongue or conceive with my heart the great grievances that the town and country which I serve suffereth by some of these monopolies; it bringeth the general profit into a private hand, and the end of all is beggary and bondage of the subject.'[9] One of the members for York recited a long list of unpopular monopolies including the manufacture of playing cards, 'whereat Sir Walter Ralegh blushed',[10] since he held the patent for these. Inside the House there were mutterings that bread itself would soon be in the hands of some monopolist, while outside in the streets, the people on whom this burden of indirect taxation fell cried: 'God prosper those that further the overthrow of these monopolies.'[11] Bacon gave his opinion that the granting of monopolies was a matter of the royal prerogative and was therefore not an issue that the House could discuss. An anxious Cecil compared the behaviour of the members to an unruly grammar school and feared the upsurge of a popular democratic movement.

The speech Ralegh himself made reveals the inconsistencies – the immaturities maybe – in his thinking on economics. Whereas, on 9 December, he had urged a vigorous argument in support of free trade, now, eleven days later, he spoke in support of the monopolists and cited his own conduct of the business of the Cornish tin mines as an example of the benefits that could be achieved under the system. Prior to his management, he declared, the tinners had been cruelly subject to the low prices offered by the London pewterers. They had been fortunate if they managed to earn two shillings a week. Ralegh claimed he had managed to double their wages, guarantee these, and increase capital for reinvestment. Then, having apparently justified the practice of monopolies, he tossed down a challenge to the opposition: he would renounce all his monopoly privileges if they would similarly forego theirs. This was hardly a political argument. It was a gesture of pure theatricality wholly typical of Ralegh and, as a contemporary reported, there was 'a great silence' after it.[12]

But this silence was far from being the end of the issue. Such was the intensity of feeling over the following days, and so resolutely did the members refuse to discuss the Subsidy Bill until the question of monopolies was settled, that by the evening of 24 November Cecil had to confess to the queen that he had lost control of the House. The ageing Elizabeth acted with characteristic resolution. She promised to revoke certain of the monopolies she had granted, while the members themselves were invited to attend her in the Council Chamber at Whitehall Palace, there to hear her 'Golden Speech'. This was the last great act of political drama in her reign.

Elizabeth was seventy now, aware of her declining powers, and still afflicted by the harrowing stress of the Essex revolt and its conclusion. Ralegh continued to serve her in any way he could. A few weeks before Parliament was called, for instance, he realized that no adequate preparations had been made to entertain Marshal Biron, envoy of Henri IV. 'I never saw so great a person neglected,' he wrote,[13] and arranged some visits and entertainments for him until the queen roused herself and royally feasted the ambassador at Lord Sandy's house. He remained in every way her loyal servant, and now, kneeling among the members of Parliament in the Council Chamber at Whitehall, he was witnessing the goddess of his devotion in her latest manifestation: old, alone, devoid of fresh ideas and yet able despite these infirmities to exercise her habitual power as the Virgin Queen.

Majesty and matriarchy were powerfully mixed in her speech. Elizabeth was addressing men who for the most part had never known another ruler and whose grievances, although genuine, touched the very nature of power and loyalty. The queen emphasized her gratitude for what she knew was their devotion. 'Though God hath raised me high, yet this I count the glory of my crown, that I have ever reigned with your loves.'[14] Her only desire was their prosperity, their well-being. She carefully hinted that she had never acted out of avarice. 'I was never any greedy, scraping grasper, nor a strait, fast-holding prince, not yet a waster.' The monopolies, she implied, had not been granted uselessly to swell her coffers or to be idly frittered away. Now, as she told the kneeling men that all she had was theirs to use to the good of the country, so she bade them rise with a gesture 'of honourable and princely demeanour'.

She knew, she continued, that monopolies were irksome, but claimed she had not realized the problem was so serious. This was at best disingenuous, but Elizabeth now held these men in the withered palms of her hands and could promise, as she had before, that the matter would be looked into. 'Yes, when I heard it, I could give no rest unto my thoughts until I had reformed it.' God would be her witness and her judge. And now her speech began to dig deeply into the myths by which she had sustained her power and held her country together for four decades. She summoned up images which, if in the day to day world were tarnished with repetition and staled with cynicism, were yet close to the hearts of all her loyal subjects. Burnished anew by her sincerity, they could still a multitude and persuade a crowd. She was, even to her last days, she declared, the humble handmaiden of the Lord, the Virgin Mother of her people. 'And though you have had and may have many princes more mighty and wise sitting in this seat, yet you never had, nor shall have, any that will be more careful and loving.'

The speech, for all its unoriginality of content, ended on these notes of emotional depth and political adroitness. When it was over, Elizabeth, with a final flourish, commanded that her Privy Counsellors should bring before her all those loyal members who wished to kiss her hand. She was Gloriana still, and her influence over Ralegh was complete. When emissaries from the King of Scotland, anxious to sound the intentions of her greatest subjects towards their probable future ruler, approached him for his views, Ralegh answered that he was so deeply in love with his queen and so profoundly in her debt that it would be treason for him to look for favour elsewhere. In so saying – and by refusing to move shrewdly with the times – Ralegh was shackling himself to an epoch now in eclipse.

Others were more calculating. Elizabeth's lifelong resolve that the succession was not a subject for open discussion was among the shrewdest of her political ploys. Not only did the decison deter the ambitious from turning to a clear rival, but it discouraged the intricate and dangerous analysis of which figures on the European stage had the most legitimate claim to her throne. The succession of

James VI of Scotland, although regarded as natural by many, was not necessarily assured. In particular, what some held to be the ambiguous nature of Elizabeth's father's will allowed the disaffected to nominate, among other claimants, the Spanish Infanta and the somewhat colourless Arabella Stuart.

These figures were minor claimants, but throughout the latter part of Elizabeth's reign, James himself made constant efforts to assure his succession. His first task, however, had been to establish his own rule in Scotland, and this he had achieved with the political ability and wisdom which went some way to justifying his boast that he was 'an experienced king needing no lessons'.[15] Ralegh was eventually to disagree with this profoundly. The loyal servant of Elizabeth was to be among the most vocal critics of her successor and of the political development that led from pragmatism to absolutism. The language of politics was undergoing a profound change, and Ralegh was to be obliged into playing the role of opposition polemicist, the man whom James was to loathe for being too 'saucy' in censoring princes.

James himself had endured a long apprenticeship. He had been separated from his mother, Mary, Queen of Scots, and crowned king at a mere thirteen months. He was then given a strenuous education in history, theology and the classics by scholars of international repute. These included the severely Protestant George Buchanan. So rigorous had Buchanan been in his insistence that 'a king ought to be the most learned clerk in his dominions'[16] that James was reputed even in his maturity to suffer from nightmare visions of his teacher. Such fears were compounded by Buchanan's insistence both in the classroom and in his printed texts that kings who disobeyed the word of God could be tumbled from their thrones by the righteous indignation of their peoples.

These ministrations had an inevitable effect. As James passed his adolescence in a Scotland riven by factional conflict (he was throughout his life to wear layers of malodorous protective clothing) his acute theoretical mind began to relish notions of absolute sovereignty. Starved of affection and finding solace in the occasional kindnesses of the handsome young men he courted with mawkish poems and lavish presents, James resolved to 'to be known as a universal king'.[17] Skilfully restraining both the nobility and the kirk, he longed

[293]

for the passing of the time when, as he declared in his *Basilicon Doron*, 'the ignorant are emboldened to cry down their betters.'[18]

The publication of such works of political theory as the *Basilicon Doron* gave James the international reputation he relished and made him of necessity a prominent figure in the constitutional debates of the early seventeenth century. He was the self-appointed spokesman of the Divine Right of Kings. In contrast both to Buchanan's belief that ungodly rulers could be violently deposed and the opinions of many English common lawyers who based their notion of a limited monarchy on legal precedent, James and the absolutists advanced ideas allegedly founded on reason and the scriptures rather than tradition. They argued that while kings themselves had an obligation to abide by the spirit of the law, they were not subject to it and could, in the interests of what they considered the public good, rule outside the law if they deemed this necessary. In the end, sovereigns were accountable to God alone.

While the royal theorist was kept waiting for his English throne, he made numerous if ineffectual efforts to obtain information and influence events. At the height of the Essex rebellion, for instance, James sent emissaries to the queen in the effort to discover her intentions on the matter of her succession. Not surprisingly, he got no more than negative answers and a promise that Parliament would not bring forward measures 'against any title he might pretend to the succession to the English crown'.[19] From his distant capital he assumed that Essex had far more influence than he in fact possessed, and James was convinced by him that Ralegh, Cobham and Cecil were in league against his favoured earl.

James was also led to believe, as a result of Essex's paranoia, that all three men were opposed to his succession to the crown. His suspicions of Ralegh seemed to him particularly well founded. Essex himself had spread rumours about Ralegh's intentions, and when James's emissary the Earl of Lennox approached him, Ralegh gave that dusty answer about unfading loyalty to his queen which James interpreted as a hostile sign. Now, however, a new and altogether more insidious enemy was poisoning James's mind against Ralegh. Lord Henry Howard had opened a secret correspondence with his future king.

Howard was an embittered polymath determined to restore his

family to what he saw as their rightful political prestige. His kin had suffered cruelly under the Tudors who had executed his father, grandfather and older brother. His nephew had died in the Tower under Elizabeth and, although he himself had assiduously cultivated royal favour from the 1570s to the 1590s, the taint on his family resulted in his being, as he lamented, as distant from the queen as America itself. His voluminous scholarly writings (Howard was the only Elizabethan aristocrat to be a Cambridge don) availed him nothing.

With James however, he shared a community of interests, above all a conviction of the necessity of the Divine Right of Kings and a delight in that wide reading which could draw illustrations and analogies from the major European languages ancient and modern, from law, history, philosophy, theology and contemporary debate. Now in his sixties and impatient for power, Howard had developed the renaissance image of the ageing courtier as the ideal adviser to his king. While Castiglione gave him his ideal however, Machiavelli offered him the means of achieving it, so making him a lethal enemy to Ralegh especially.

Howard was resolved that James should hold the Durham House group in detestation, and to ensure this he revived the old slur of atheism. Northumberland, Cobham and Ralegh were 'a diabolical triplicity, that denies the Trinity'.[20] Such views were particularly abhorrent to the royal theologian, but Howard was keen to deepen James's disgust by suggesting how their lack of belief led to crimes against the state. The three men were, Howard declared, 'wicked plotters hatching treason from cocatrice eggs that are daily and nightly sitten upon'. Having planted the suspicion that Ralegh was both an atheist and a traitor, Howard then proceeded to attack his personality. Ralegh was, he declared, a snake who had risen to influence with 'the soft voice of Jacob in courtly hypocrisy'. He then turned to Ralegh's more familiar vices, telling James that Ralegh was 'above the greatest Lucifer that hath lived in our age', a figure who 'in pride exceedeth all men alive'.

These venomous assertions were desperately dangerous, but in this period of intricate mutual deceit James was offered yet another portrait of Ralegh which, if less immediately damaging, was none the less more accurate. Northumberland, Ralegh's friend of sixteen years, also felt obliged to open up a correspondence with his future king. Unaware that his own reputation had been blackened by Howard, Northumberland hoped to ingratiate himself by offering a portrait of Ralegh that is convincing, balanced, cool. Northumberland began by assuring James that Ralegh did not dispute his right to the succession. This was followed by an appraisal of Ralegh's character in which Northumberland declared: 'Although I know him insolent, extremely heated, a man that desires to seem able to sway all men's fancies, all men's courses, and a man that out of himself when your time shall come, will never be able to do you much good nor harm, yet must I needs confess what I know, that there is excellent good parts of nature in him.'[21]

Such was the best Ralegh's friends could do, but the damage wrought by Howard meant that others had carefully to review their positions. When Cecil, concerned above all to ensure the smooth transition of power, in turn opened a correspondence with James, he immediately discovered the damage that had been done – done not just to Ralegh but also, by implication, to himself. It was now essential for the Secretary to dissociate himself from his erstwhile friend. Ralegh was a man whose reputation Cecil no longer had the power to save and he now resolved to blacken it.

Cecil's correspondence with James – secret, dangerous, and of the utmost national importance – was a masterpiece of diplomacy at its most chillingly adroit. After some lines of sinuous ingratiation, Cecil tactfully suggested his major political concern: he advised James to do nothing rash in his desire to succeed to the throne but suggested rather that he should bide his time in patience. Elizabeth was ever more determined that the matter of the succession should not be openly discussed, and Cecil hinted that 'the subject itself is so perilous to touch amongst us, as it setteth a mark upon his head for ever that hatcheth such a bird.'[22] Having advised caution, Cecil then felt able to turn to the lesser matter of Ralegh and Cobham.

'How contrary it is to their nature to resolve to be under your sovereignty,' Cecil opined. Ralegh himself, he suggested, was a man whose 'light and sudden humours' could barely be controlled. Then the Secretary proceeded to dissociate himself from anything Ralegh might say or do. 'Whatsoever he shall take upon him to say for me, upon any new humour of kindness, whereof sometimes he will be replete (upon the receipt of private benefit), you will no more believe it, be it never so much in my commendation.' Begging to excuse himself from troubling the king with these tiresome personal concerns, Cecil applied a last and dexterous turn to the screw: 'Would God I were as free from offence towards God in seeking, for private affection, to support a person whom the most religious men do hold in anathema.'

With this phrase the damage had been done. Cecil had contrived to ingratiate himself while suggesting Ralegh was dangerous, unreliable, atheistical. His future had been destroyed. All Cecil had to do now was to ensure that such friends of Ralegh's as George Carew (currently distinguishing himself in the suppression of Munster) would not prove hostile and to suggest to Ralegh and Cobham themselves that he was still their friend by joining with them in funding a privateering expedition.

Eventually, on Thursday, 24 March 1603, at three in the morning, the long-awaited climax came: 'Her Majesty departed this life, mildly like a lamb, easily like an ripe apple from the tree.'[23] As soon as her death was confirmed, a meeting of the Privy Council was summoned and Cecil drafted the proclamation announcing the succession of James to the throne. The document was first read in Whitehall and then in the City. Although there were fears of a commotion – for centuries no new dynasty had succeeded without a struggle – 'every man went about his business as readily, and as peaceably, as securely, as though there had been no change, nor any news ever heard of competitors.'[24] Three days later, King James began his progress south.

Ralegh was in the West Country when the news reached him, along with rumours that he was planning a coup. Distinguished men were quick to disown him, and despite the fact that orders had been issued commanding government officers to remain at their posts, Ralegh eventually resolved to ride out to greet his new king. By 25 April, he had reached Northamptonshire and, armed with letters he claimed were urgently in need of the royal signature, had himself announced to the monarch whose mind had been so poisoned against him.

The greeting he received was curt and ambiguous. 'When Sir Walter Ralegh's name was told, said the king, "Oh my soul, mon, I have heard rawly of thee." '[25] The chilling gracelessness of this was underlined by James's treatment of the letters. The royal secretary was told to despatch the matter as quickly as possible, and the man added in a note: 'To my seeming he hath taken no great root here.'[26] Indeed, Ralegh's place was still beside his queen – he was now the last great Elizabethan – and three days after his interview with James he was back in London leading the halberdiers of the royal guard at the tail of Elizabeth's great funeral procession. In Westminster Abbey, he watched the true symbolic end of his mistress's reign as the chief men of her household broke their wands of office across their knees and threw the shattered pieces into her grave.

A while later, the lavish household of the new monarch was entertained at Cecil's palace of Theobalds. James, disliking the crowds that thronged about him and suddenly piqued by so great an English presence, declared with characteristic tactlessness that he could have entered the country under his own strength 'should the English have kept him out'. Ralegh, his voice rising above the crowd, made an equally tactless reply: 'Would God that he had been put to the trial!' James at once asked him why he wished such a thing. 'Because', said Sir Walter, 'that then you would have known your friends from your foes.' This was a dark, ambiguous, impolitic comment, and 'was never forgotten nor forgiven'.[27] For all the subtlety of Howard and the manoeuvering of Cecil, it almost seems Ralegh himself was driven by an obscure impulse to destroy his reputation with the new king.

By May 1603, the weakness of his position under the Stuart regime was becoming evident. The king, honouring the promise made in Elizabeth's Golden Speech, called in all monopolies for scrutiny. Ralegh was at once deprived of a chief source of his income and was severely curtailed of the means to support himself at court. Two weeks later, he was quite reasonably required to surrender his captaincy of the guard to the Scottish favourite who had occupied the post in Edinburgh. He was in part compensated by being excused the annual payment of £300 asked for the Governorship of Jersey. But he realized something decisive now had to be done, a dramatic gesture made if he were to capture the king's favour.

As unaware of the depth of James's desire for a peaceful foreign policy as he was innocent of the plots that had destroyed his reputation, Ralegh offered to supply the king with a written account of his strategy for continuing the war with Spain. Nothing could have been more inimical to a monarch who hoped to prove himself a European peacemaker. With this hapless action Ralegh's old, Eliza-bethan belligerency destroyed any last hope of a rapprochement between two wholly different men. James now began simultaneously to open peace negotiations with Spain while moving against Ralegh himself.

His humiliation was to be both personal and public. On James's progress south, for instance, the Bishop of Durham had petitioned the king for the return of his London palace. At the close of May James acceded to his request. Ralegh was given peremptory orders to quit the mansion in which he had lived for twenty years and on which he had lavished, he claimed, £2,000 in improvements. The terms imposed on him were humiliating in the extreme: he was to leave within two weeks and pack up a lifetime's goods on carts and wagons before a delighted London crowd. He wrote indignantly to the Attorney-General among others: 'I am of the opinion that if the King's Majesty had recovered this house, or the like, from the mean-est gentleman and servant he had in England, that His Majesty would have given six months time for the avoidance, and I do not know but that the poorest artificer in London hath a quarter's warn-ing given him by his landlord.'[28] James's action was an insult of brutal eloquence, but worse was now to follow.

In July 1603, Ralegh was at Windsor intending to take part in one of the hunts that James so relished. He was waiting on the terrace when he was approached by Cecil who informed him that the king did not wish him to ride out but, rather, had charged the Privy Council to question him on certain matters that had come to their notice. He was ushered inside to face a committee of his enem-ies, among them Cecil himself and the newly appointed Counsellor Lord Thomas Howard. Tangled rumours of treason had come to their ears and they were determined to investigate these and impli-cate Ralegh as fully as possible, moving against him with the rigour of the law regardless of the precise details of the case.

These last were extremely difficult to determine. That there were plots and that Ralegh had knowledge of at least one of them is certain, but the degree of his involvement is questionable. To his enemies on the Privy Council, however, accuracy and justice were lesser matters than removing a man whom they had persuaded their king was an enemy of the state. Having contrived to ruin his reputation, they were now resolved on a show trial.

Ralegh was wholly innocent of the lesser of the two plots. In the month before his accession to the English throne, James, unable to judge the precise balance of religious bias in his future kingdom, had listened with apparent sympathy to overtures from both Catholics and extreme Puritans. He seemed prepared to grant a measure of latitude to both sides, but on his accession he came to realize that any significant changes would be unwise. 'Na, na,' was his reported comment, 'we'll no need Papists noo.'[29] Disappointed hopes roused the inevitable reaction. Fathers Watson and Clarke, who had previously petitioned James for a relaxation of anti-papal legislation, planned a desperate coup. Their 'Bye' or Surprise Plot aimed simply at capturing the king and holding him a prisoner until he agreed to their demands.

Among the disaffected men the priests had recruited to their side was George Brooke, the brother of Ralegh's friend Lord Cobham. But Cobham himself was engaged in other vague and treasonable activities through which he hoped to establish for himself the political prestige that had so far eluded him. Before the new king's accession, Howard had suggested to Cecil that Cobham might be lured to disaster by being encouraged to become involved with Spain's attempts to force a peace with England. Now, whether or not at Howard's instigation, Cobham was in discussion with his long-term friend the Count of Aremberg, the Ambassador from the Spanish Netherlands, over plans which involved the receipt of vast sums of money from either Brussels or Spain. This money was apparently intended to subsidize those English Catholics who wished to place on the throne a ruler apparently more sympathetic to Spanish concerns than James himself.

Ralegh certainly knew about this, and his failure to report it was technically a matter of collusion. It is extremely unlikely, however, that so virulent an anti-Spaniard was either sympathetic or personally involved in Cobham's recklessly amateur manoeuvering. Indeed, the probable truth was altogether more discreditable. Ralegh had never achieved the political influence for which he longed and, with the accession of James, was further away than ever from the centre of authority. He had failed utterly in his attempt to persuade the new king to his own ideas on foreign policy and now, as James was openly moving against him, he placed his hopes on a scheme of Machiavellian duplicity. He would lure Cobham, his closest friend, into his trust, find out all he could about his plans, and then betray them to the king. The delivery of such a notable traitor to the authorities would be a spectacular coup which would surely merit reward. Such political melodrama was typical of the workings of Ralegh's imagination, while the repellent duplicity is symptomatic of a time when even the icy-hearted Bacon could lament: 'There is little friendship in the world, and least of all between equals.'[30]

But if the ploy was despicable it was also dangerous. For Ralegh to appoint himself as an unofficial *agent provocateur* was to risk being accused of the very treason he hoped to expose. If he were caught, the result would be the loss of all his goods and, most probably, his life. In the attempt to insure his family against disaster, Ralegh set about conveying Sherborne to Wat so that the property could not be sequestered if his plans went awry. Even this device was to fail, but once the Privy Council had arrested and questioned the conspirators involved in the Bye Plot and had come to hear about what was now called the Main Plot, Ralegh fell a victim to the weaknesses of his own scheme. When he was brought before the Privy Council, he was asked what he knew about a plan to 'surprise the King's person' as well as the designs of Cobham and Aremberg. He strongly denied that he knew anything at all.

This was a blatant lie and a foolish one. Ralegh's friendship with Cobham was common knowledge, both men were regarded as highly indiscreet, while Cobham himself was passing on to Cecil such details of his discussions with Aremberg as did not implicate him in treason. Besides, his brother George had already confessed to what he knew about the Main Plot. The web of insinuation was spread finely and wide, and for Ralegh to be so adamant in his protestations of ignorance looked patently suspicious. Realizing after his first interview that this must indeed be so, he wrote a letter to the Lords of the Council. In this he was still less than frank, confessing merely that now he had thought about it he did in fact remember that on a number of occasions when Cobham had parted from him at Durham

House he had seen his friend being rowed past his own home at Blackfriars across the river to St Saviour's where one of Aremberg's supposed agents was known to live. Ralegh then wrote a second letter to Cecil suggesting the man be arrested.

Cecil decided to withhold Ralegh's first letter while his second (or, at least, a part of it) was shown to Cobham himself who was now in custody. From this Cobham at once inferred that it was Ralegh – his closest friend – who had accused him of treason. He broke down in abject terror, crying: 'I will now tell you all the truth.' Cobham then proceeded to pour out an incredible story of how he had indeed been holding suspicious conversations with Aremberg but that it was the 'traitor' Ralegh who had 'procured me to this villainy'.[31] This was mere cowardly tit for tat, and, in his continuing panic, Cobham retracted his confession, changed his mind, and then changed it again. His wretched performance was none the less sufficient to ensure Ralegh was sent to the Tower.

He was plunged into hysterical despair. On 21 July the Lieutenant of the Tower wrote to Cecil that Ralegh was still protesting his innocence, 'but with a mind the most dejected I ever saw'.[32] Two days later, he wrote again complaining that 'I am exceedingly cumbered with him; five or six times a day he sendeth for me in such passions as I see his fortitude is impotent to support his grief.'[33]

In the oppressive loneliness of the Tower, it seemed to Ralegh that he had worked his own destruction. He had listened to Cobham's treasons and had failed to report them. There was not the remotest possibility of proving his innocence. No one would believe his explanations, his probable motives, and every one in the country from the king and the Privy Council downwards relished the idea of his guilt. The verdict of a seventeenth-century treason trial was, besides, a foregone conclusion. Ralegh's execution appeared inevitable, and in utter hopelessness he asked for a knife saying, unconvincingly, that he needed it to stir his wine. The request was refused.

He revealed his desperation in a letter to Bess who was soon to join him in the Tower. His words were those of a man at the end of his tether. Hysteria, vengeance and self pity, tender affection and lucid attempts to explain his financial position, jostled with a constant preoccupation with death. These energies make the letter one of the most personally revealing documents Ralegh ever wrote. His innate sense of drama – or melodrama – is evident from the first sentence, as too is his profound and generous love of Bess whom he freed from all obligations to him, urging her to marry again after his death to protect herself and their son.

And, as always, there was Ralegh's pride, his quick, vindictive scorn of those who would slight him. 'I cannot live to think how I am derided, to think of the expectation of my enemies, the scorns I shall receive, the cruel words of lawyers, the infamous taunts and despites, to be made a wonder and a spectacle!'[34] His mind moved constantly on death and suicide. 'I know it is forbidden to destroy ourselves,' he wrote, and he produced some casuistical arguments to justify his intentions before at last abandoning himself to a statement of piercing sincerity: 'The mercy of God is immeasurable; the cogitations of man comprehend it not.'

But it is the overriding sense of personal drama that is the most telling. In his letter, Ralegh's innate theatricality recreates him before his own eyes as the protagonist of a Jacobean tragedy – which indeed he was:

> For myself, I am left of all men that have done to many. All my good turns forgotten; all my errors revived and expounded to all extremity of ill. All my services, hazards, and expenses, for my country – plantings, discoveries, fights, councils, and whatsoever else – malice hath now covered over. I am now made an enemy and traitor by the word of an unworthy man. He hath proclaimed me to be a partaker of his vain imaginations, notwithstanding the whole course of my life hath approved the contrary, as my death shall approve it. Woe, woe, woe be unto him by whose falsehood we are lost. He hath separated us asunder. He hath slain by honour; my fortune. He hath robbed thee of thy husband, thy child of his father, and me of you both. O God! thou dost know my wrongs. Know, then, thou my wife, and child; – know, then, thou my Lord and King, that I ever thought them too honest to betray, and too good to conspire against.[35]

On 27 July 1603, his despair overflowed into action. Pathetically, while a group of Privy Counsellors were interviewing other prisoners in the Tower, Ralegh picked up a table-knife and tried to stab himself. Cecil's description conveys the contempt he felt. 'Although lodged and attended as well as in his own house, yet one afternoon, while divers of us were in the Tower, examining these prisoners, Sir Walter Ralegh attempted to have murdered himself.'[36] As soon as the Counsellors heard the news they went to investigate, 'and found him in some agony, – seeming to be unable to endure his misfortunes, and protesting his innocency with carelessness of life.' Cecil was aware however that this was a party suicide, a desperate charade. Ralegh had not even aimed for his heart and 'had wounded himself under the right pap, but no way mortally; being in truth rather a cut than a stab.'

He recovered and found a new energy, a fresh resolve. Laurence Keymis was sent to Cobham to try to convince him that, far from being his betrayer, Ralegh had tried to defend him when questioned by the Privy Council. Keymis was also to provide Cobham with a morsel of legal information which, Ralegh wrongly believed, would save them both. He recalled how, in the reign of Queen Mary, his father-in-law had been acquitted at a treason trial when the prosecution could not produce the required two witnesses to testify against him. How would those trying Ralegh and Cobham be able to find two men to testify against them? Such conversations as they had had were all held in the utmost secrecy. But the idea of being saved by a legal technicality was a vain hope. Cobham, in treacherous despair, revealed the plan to the Privy Counsellors, men whose legal training was sufficient for them to know that, as a result of the Throckmorton case, the law had been changed.

A second ploy also failed. John Peyton, the son of the Lieutenant of the Tower, was persuaded by Ralegh to act as a go-between and peacemaker between himself and Cobham. But such dangerous diplomacy was not long continued for in August 1603, and by a neat irony, the Lieutenant was appointed to Ralegh's post as the Governor of Jersey. The following month, and to further Ralegh's humiliation, the High Sheriff of Cornwall was also promoted, 'the commission of lieutenancy granted to Sir Walter Ralegh being become void and determined'.[37]

A last effort was made to win Cobham over. Its comic-opera ingenuity shows the state to which Ralegh had been reduced. A letter to Cobham was wrapped round an apple and then thrown in at his window. It asked for a written declaration of Ralegh's innocence. This was forthcoming (it was carried by the son of the new Lieutenant of the Tower) but was found to be unsatisfactory, and Ralegh insisted on a revised version. This was prepared and seemed to exonerate Ralegh completely. 'I protest upon my soul,' Cobham wrote, 'and before God and his angels, I never had conference with you in any treason.'[38]

Ralegh intended to flourish this declaration at his trial as the absolute proof of his innocence. He was unaware that Cobham had had second thoughts after writing it, had confessed the contents of his letter to the Privy Council, and sworn an affidavit contradicting its contents. Ralegh, innocent of his betrayal, went to his trial with, as he believed, the proof of his innocence carefully folded up inside his doublet.

The plague was raging late and furiously in London. The court removed to a succession of palaces, and by November 1603 had established itself at Wilton House. Here the lawyers followed and resolved that Ralegh's trial should be held at the ancient episcopal palace in nearby Winchester. It fell to Sir William Waad to accompany the prisoner there.

This was a dangerous task. Despite the plague, the London mob had decided to turn out in force to jeer the traitor, the man who had betrayed their beloved Essex, and who now, for all his pride and cunning, was being led to humiliation and certain death. Waad ordered a guard of fifty light horse to surround Ralegh and his other charges. Watches were set in the streets. None the less, 'it was hob or nob whether Sir Walter Ralegh should have been brought alive through such multitudes of unruly people as did exclaim against him.' The moment marked the nadir of his public reputation.

The trial had been fixed for 17 November, and the bishop's palace had been quickly converted to house a Court of King's Bench. There were eleven Commissioners, four of them judges and seven laymen. They represented the might of royal authority, and their presence was designed to impress the jurymen – a carefully packed group of men from Middlesex – with the gravity of the matter in hand. Of the judges, Sir John Popham was Chief Justice of the King's Bench, and Sir Edmund Anderson Chief Justice of the Common Pleas. The two other judges – Gaudy and Warburton – were puisnes.

The remaining commissioners were mainly Ralegh's enemies: Lord Thomas Howard was now Lord Chamberlain of the King's Household; Lord Mountjoy had been implicated in the Essex revolt but had redeemed his reputation by defeating Tyrone in Ireland; Lord Wootton was Comptroller of the Royal Household; Sir John Stanhope was Vice Chamberlain; Ralegh's guard Sir William Waad was Clerk to the Privy Council. The two remaining commissioners were Sir Robert Cecil, now Lord Cecil of Essingden, and Henry Howard, soon to be rewarded with the Earldom of Northampton.

Ralegh had no detailed knowledge of the charges against him before they were read out on the morning of his trial. There were five indictments. He was accused of entering into a conspiracy with Lord Cobham to advance Arabella Stuart to the throne. Money from Habsburg Austria and Spain, it was alleged, had been promised for this on condition that Arabella would undertake to establish a peace with Spain, extend toleration to Catholics, and be guided by her backers as to the choice of a husband. The second charge was based on a reputed conversation between the conspirators in the Bye Plot in which it was allegedly declared: 'There will never be a good world in England till the king and his cubs are taken away.'[40] The third indictment concerned a lost manuscript book which Ralegh allegedly gave Cobham to confirm the basis of their treasonable plans. As the fourth count, Ralegh was said to have urged his fellow conspirators to entice Arabella to write to the King of Spain, an act which was itself treasonable. Lastly, Ralegh was supposed to have instigated a correspondence between Cobham and Aremberg to obtain the vast sum of 600,000 crowns of which Ralegh himself was supposedly to receive 8,000.

There was little originality of thought in this tissue of fabrications. They were no more than a version of the charges levied against Cobham and Ralegh by the Earl of Essex in the months before his death and set out in a letter that had come into Cecil's possession. For a busy man the fantasies of one traitor, lying conveniently to hand, would serve to frame Ralegh as another. Such a proceeding would appeal to the king, and justice was beside the point. Essex's ghost, it seemed, was powerful still.

Insofar as there was a fundamental point underlying the accusations it was that Ralegh had allegedly plotted with Cobham to replace King James with his cousin Arabella Stuart. The trial produced not a shred of evidence to substantiate this. None the less, as a man accused of treason, Ralegh was denied all legal representation as well as the right to give evidence on oath. Cobham, on whom so much of the prosecution case depended, was not presented for cross-examination and had demanded the right to be tried by his peers. Such proofs as the prosecution were able to produce consisted of no more than extracts from statements made to the Privy Council in Ralegh's absence. These were not necessarily made on oath and no means was allowed of establishing either that they were accurately recorded or that they were admitted to be correct by the deponents.

Ralegh naturally denied he was guilty on any of the charges and was left alone to defend himself against a tissue of hearsay. This was presented with crude forensic bullying by the prosecuting counsel, the Attorney-General Sir Edward Coke. Although Coke himself was later to become one of the great defenders of the common law, his conduct on this day – along with the supine attitudes of judges – made the trial of Sir Walter Ralegh infamous. Even Lord Chief Justice Popham was heard to declare: 'I never saw the like trial and hope I shall never see the like again.'[41]

As the trial opened, Ralegh offered no objection to the jurymen, but made one request to the court. 'Only this I desire,' he began. 'Sickness hath of late weakened me, and my memory was always bad. The points of indictment be many, and in the evidence perhaps more will be urged. I beseech you, My Lords, let me answer every point severally for I shall not carry all to the end.'[42]

The request was calm, lucid, reasonable, but to the prosecution it was anathema. Careful analysis by so articulate a man would quickly reveal the shoddy inconsistencies of their case, and Coke at once stood upon his dignity. 'The King's Evidence', he declared, 'ought not to be broken or dismembered whereby it might lose much of its grace and vigour.' This was a poor objection even in a show trial and was later to be partly overruled.

Coke then launched into his opening speech. This was an account of the Bye Plot – a matter on which Ralegh had not been charged – and was little more than a compound of irrelevance and hearsay designed to cover the weaknesses of Coke's case by impressing the jurymen with the sensation that treason and national peril were all about them. There was not a whisper of guidance from the bench about the relevance of this, not a hint of an objection or an overruling. Ralegh was obliged to intervene on his own behalf.

'You Gentlemen of the Jury,' he began, 'I pray remember, I am not charged with the Bye being the treason of the priests.'

'You are not,' Coke declared, 'but their Lordships will see that all these treasons though they consisted of several parts, closed in together like Samson's foxes, which were joined in their tails though the heads were severed.'

Coke then launched into a long, pedantic disquisition on the history of treason in England which eventually concluded with the allegation made against the conspirators in the Bye Plot that there would be 'no good world in England until the fox and his cubs were taken away'. Coke was well aware of the effect these sinister, ambiguous words would have on the jury and was determined to exploit it. 'But to whom, Sir Walter, did you bear malice? To the royal children?'

Ralegh responded with coolly contrived bewilderment: 'Master Attorney I pray you to whom, or to what end speak you all this? I protest I do not understand what a word of this means, except it be to tell me news.' Ralegh was again reminding the jury that he had not been charged with the Bye Plot, and so suave an answer unnerved the Attorney-General.

'I will then come close to you,' he replied. 'I will prove you to be the most notorious traitor that ever came to the bar. You are indeed on the "Main": but you followed them in the "Bye" in imitation. I will charge you with the words.'

Ralegh remained collected, strong. This was the one role in which he might win himself a moral victory if not a legal acquittal. He spoke out firmly. 'Your words cannot condemn me. My innocency is my defence. *Prove* against me any one thing of the many that you have broke, and I will confess all the indictment, and that I am the most horrible traitor that ever lived, and worthy to be crucified with a thousand torments.'

Coke resorted to abuse. 'Nay, I will prove all. Thou art a monster! Thou hast an English face but a Spanish heart!'

To address an erstwhile grandee by the diminutive 'thou' was an insult in a society preoccupied with rank and, having abused

Ralegh, Coke proceeded to allege how this 'monster' had seduced
Cobham to his schemes, detailing the circumstances before coming
to the proofs.

'Let me answer,' Ralegh interposed. 'It concerns my life.'

The request was denied, and Coke continued with his speech.
Cobham, he alleged, was neither a politician nor a swordsman, but
'Sir Walter Ralegh was a man fitting for both' – the apt corrupter of
a great peer. None the less, Coke's subsequent detailing of Cobham's
activities in no way proved Ralegh himself a traitor. The Attorney-
General's whole approach was merely an attempt to prove guilt by
association. Again, Ralegh rose superior to his abuse.

'No, no, Master Attorney, I am no traitor,' he affirmed. 'Whether
I live or die, I shall stand as true a subject as ever the King hath. *You*
may call me "traitor", at your pleasure; yet it becomes not a man of
quality or virtue to do so. But I take comfort in it. It is all that you
can do; for I do not hear that you charge me with any treason.'

Heedless of his victim's dignity, Coke proceeded to read out
Cobham's confessions. But Ralegh's role was now firmly that of the
innocent Englishman defending his honour and his life against
powers who had reduced themselves to vulgar insults. To those
observing the trial – men who had hurried down to Winchester in
many cases to gloat over Ralegh's destruction – such a defence
made a strong appeal. Slowly, opinions were changing, and Ralegh's
speech in his own defence was greatly to enhance this.

He addressed the court with informed common sense and a quiet
but dramatic sense of his own place in the nation's history. The
concision and reasonableness, along with the sense that in defending
himself in this bear-pit of a court he was also speaking for England,
made him wholly convincing. Everything, he argued, showed how
foolish it would be to plot the sort of treason the court seemed
determined to prove against him. Cobham, 'a man that hath neither
love nor following', was the least likely figure an intelligent plotter
would wish to be involved with. Besides, the nation had never been
stronger or more at peace with itself.

'I was not so bare of sense but I saw that, if ever this state was
strong, it was now that we have the kingdom of Scotland united,
whence we were wont to fear all our troubles; – Ireland quieted,
where our forces were wont to be divided; – Denmark assured,

whom before we were always wont to have in jealousy; – the Low Countries, our nearest neighbour. And, instead of a lady whom time had surprised, we had now an active king, who would be present at his own business. For me, at this time, to make myself a Robin Hood, a Wat Tyler, a Kett, or a Jack Cade! – I was not so mad!'

The patriot's pride in the international situation, the tributes, open and implied, to James and his wife Anna of Denmark, to Mountjoy's successes in Ireland, and to the memory of Elizabeth were all perfectly judged. So, too, was Ralegh's picture of the king of Spain's decline: 'his weakness, his poorness, his humbleness'.

The slow collapse of the national enemy and memories of the old, heroic days were finely juxtaposed. 'I know that six times we had repulsed his forces: thrice in Ireland; thrice at sea, – once upon our coast, and thrice upon his own.' These memories were still potent, and Ralegh's known share in them counted for much. 'Thrice had I served against him myself at sea, – wherein, for my country's sake, I had expended of my own property forty thousand marks.'

So eloquent a performance, so obvious a patriotism, were changing opinions. A contemporary declared that Ralegh 'behaved himself so worthily, so wisely, so temperately, that in half a day the mind of all the company was changed from the extremest hate to the greatest pity.'[43]

It was clear from the outset that Coke's charges and Ralegh's replies centred largely around Cobham's testimony, and, having explained that his 'inwardness' with Cobham 'was only in matters of private estate', Ralegh asked 'to have my accuser brought here to speak face to face'. He backed his request with what he thought was the legal ploy that might yet save his life.

'I have learned that by the law and statutes of this realm,' he began, 'in case of treason a man ought to be convicted by the testimony of two witnesses if they be living.' For Ralegh, this was the imagined climax of his trial, the moment when a legal technicality would free him from the accusations of his enemies. But Popham successfully contradicted the point (the law was on his side) and Ralegh, with quick desperation, tried now to argue that it was against equity – that it was simply unjust – to condemn a man to death without adequate testimony.

'Equity must proceed from the king,' Popham replied. 'You can only have justice from us.'

Technicalities were turning a moral victory into a legal humiliation, and Coke proceeded to read out more of Cobham's allegations. These included the fact that Ralegh's supposed friend had offered him a portion of the money promised from Spain. Ralegh was obliged to the compromising admission that this was so, and while he tried to prevaricate over details of time and place, Henry Howard brought the matter back to the main point.

'Allege me any grounds of cause why you gave ear to my Lord Cobham, as of receiving pensions, in matters you had not to deal in.'

'Could I stop my Lord Cobham's mouth?'

This was a weak reply, but when the prosecution raised the matter of the book Ralegh had allegedly given Cobham to provide him with a theoretical justification for treason, Ralegh himself managed to score a point. The book – which all present knew to be an outdated irrelevancy – had been acquired, Ralegh declared, from the library of the late Lord Burghley.

Cecil rose to his feet, desperate to prove that it was part of his father's business to have a knowledge of such dangerous works, and suggesting that Ralegh had managed to get hold of the volume largely by accident when he asked permission to search the old man's library 'for some cosmographical description of the Indies'. But it was clear that Cecil's conscience was raw, and that, for all the duplicity with which he had managed to blacken his sometime friend's reputation, there remained a trace of that affection he had once had for him.

'I ... would have trusted Sir Walter Ralegh as soon as any man – though since, for some infirmities, the bonds of my affection to him have been broken; and yet, reserving my duty to the king, my master, which I can by no means dispense with, by God I love him and have a great conflict within myself.'

This was an honest confession, even a moving one, but Ralegh spoiled whatever advantage he might have extracted from it by the rash boast that he too had a collection of such libellous works in his possession, all of them 'writ against the late queen' to whom his loyalty was unquestioned. Coke was quick to point out that only Privy Councillors had the right to such material, and he hoped Ralegh would never occupy such a position.

'He was not sworn a councillor of state,' Cecil declared, 'but he has been called to consultations.'

[311]

Ralegh tried to dismiss the whole matter. 'Here is a book supposed to be treasonable. I never read it, nor commended it, nor delivered it, nor urged it.'

Lord Henry Howard also tried to raise the matter of Ralegh's dealings with Cobham in the Tower – his attempt, in effect, to tamper with witnesses. Laurence Keymis's visit to Cobham was particularly mentioned, and Ralegh proceeded to scandalize the court by claiming that Keymis's testimony had been extracted under threat of torture. This was quickly denied by the alarmed commissioners.

'We protest, before God, there was no such matter to our knowledge.'

Ralegh turned to Waad. 'Was not the keeper of the rack sent for and he threatened with it?'

Waad tried to save the situation as best he could. 'When Mr Solicitor and myself came to examine Keymis we told him he "deserved the rack", but did not threaten him with it.'

The commissioners demurred. 'It was more than we knew.'

Ralegh then came to the main point. He had been accused concerning Arabella Stuart 'and concerning money out of Spain'. He begged once more that Cobham be produced as a witness. This was again denied, and the mere mention of the king's cousin caused concern among the commissioners. Cecil ardently professed Lady Stuart's complete innocence, and Lord Admiral Nottingham, 'being in a standing with the Lady Arabella', sprang to her defence, calling out to the court: 'The Lady doth here protest, upon her salvation, that she never dealt in any of these things.'

Yet again Ralegh begged that Cobham be produced as a witness. 'You, Gentlemen of the Jury, mark this: He said, I have been the cause of all his miseries and the destruction of his house; and that all the evil that hath happened to him by my wicked counsel. If this be truth, whom hath he cause to accuse and to be revenged on, but me?' Surely it was clear that only an innocent man would call such a witness in his defence. But the request was again denied. 'He is a party, and may not come. The law is against it.'

It was evident that Cobham would not be brought forward as a witness under any circumstances, and Coke now decided to produce the one deponent the prosecution was prepared to call. The incident is a measure of the inadequacy of their case, the depth of farce to which their theatre of cruelty was prepared to descend.

'There is one Dyer,' Coke began, 'a pilot, that being in Lisbon met with a Portugal gentleman, which asked him if the king of England were crowned yet. To whom he answered: "I think not yet, but he shall be shortly". "Nay," saith the Portugal, "that shall never be, for his throat will be cut by Don Ralegh and Don Cobham, before he be crowned." '

Dyer was produced and solemnly swore to the truth of this ridiculous incident.

Ralegh was appalled. 'What infer you from that?'

'That your treason hath wings.'

All Ralegh could do in the face of this legal abomination was to try to kindle the imaginations of the jurymen, to ask them to put themselves in his place and show mercy in their verdict. For his life's sake, he begged them to ask themselves 'if you would be content, on presumptions, to be delivered to the slaughter; to have your wives and children turned into the streets to beg their bread; – if you would be contented to be so judged, judge so of me.'

The trial was drawing to its close, but Ralegh had no right to sum up his case. One transcript of the trial, however, offers an account of what took place when the prosecution's speech was concluded.

'Mr Attorney,' Ralegh declared, 'have you done?'

'Yes, if you have no more to say.'

'If you have done, then I have somewhat more to say.'

'Nay, I will have the last word for the king.'

'Nay, I will have the last word for my life.'

It was time to produce Cobham's letter, the one final coup Ralegh hoped would save his neck.

Coke was furious. 'The king's safety and your clearing cannot agree. I protest I never knew a clearer treason.'

Cecil tried to let Ralegh be heard, but Coke sat down in such a fury that he 'would speak no more, till the commissioners urged and entreated him to go on.'

When he eventually rose to his feet, it was to inflict a cruel, surprising defeat on Ralegh's hopes. He brandished before the court Cobham's retraction of the letter Ralegh had hidden in his doublet. Betraying the whole story of how the apple had been thrown in at

Cobham's window – 'it was Adam's apple, whereby the devil did deceive him' – Coke proceeded to lambast Ralegh as a 'damnable atheist' and destroy his defence by reading out Cobham's retraction.

This was a comprehensive assault made at an hour when death seemed imminent, 'and now to dissemble with God is no time'. Ralegh's motives were transparent: 'He went about only to clear himself by betraying of me.' The repentant Cobham was 'resolved to set down the truth, and under my hand to retract what he cunningly got from me.'

It was clear to him now how foolishly he had been led and how Ralegh was the cause of all his misfortune. Then, twisting the knife of treachery, Cobham declared that Ralegh had thought of taking Aremberg's money not for the sake of procuring a peace but to betray his country's interests to Spain.

'At this confession,' a reporter observed, 'Sir Walter Ralegh was much amazed, but by and by he seemed to gather his spirits again.'

Coke, who had punctuated the reading of the letter with exclamations of his disgust – 'Is not this a Spanish heart in an English body?' – asked Ralegh what he thought of his friend's conduct now.

'I say that Cobham is a base, dishonourable, poor soul.'

Knowing that it could serve no good purpose, Ralegh now produced that letter of Cobham's he once thought would be his salvation. He bade Cecil read it to the court. The words could have no positive effect but, as the jury prepared to retire, Ralegh asked them to chose between the letters: between Cobham's retraction and a confession written 'under oath, and the deepest protestations a Christian man can make'.

The twelve men reached their verdict in fifteen minutes. Ralegh was guilty. None of the counts against him had been proved, and Popham, pronouncing sentence with brutal relish, chose to add irrelevant insult to gross injustice:

> You have been taxed by the world, Sir Walter Ralegh, with holding heathenish, blasphemous, atheistical and profane opinions, which I list not to repeat, because christian ears cannot endure to hear them. But the authors and maintainers of such opinions cannot be suffered to live in any christian commonwealth. If these opinions be not yours, you shall do well, before

[314]

you leave the world, to protest against them, and ask God forgiveness for them as you hope for another life, and let not
Harriot, nor any such doctor, persuade you there is no eternity
in heaven, lest you find an eternity of hell-torments.

The accused had been brought to trial on a charge of treason and
been condemned for being Sir Walter Ralegh. The inevitable sentence
was hanging, drawing and mutilation.

'That trial injured and degraded the justice of England', one of the
judges was later to declare.[44] Here was an early revelation of what
could be expected from Stuart absolutism, but for many at this time
it was Ralegh's own performance that caused them to think most
deeply. It had become axiomatic that he was a man to be hated.
He was a monopolist, a court parasite, a rapacious, self-seeking,
vainglorious man trapped in his own arrogance. Now they had seen
his grace and courage in the face of manifest injustice. 'Never was a
man so hated and so popular in so short a time.'[45] Even a Scottish
friend of the king's had to admit that 'whereas, when he saw Sir
Walter Ralegh first, he was so led with the common hatred that he
would have gone a hundred miles to see him hanged, he would,
'ere they parted, have gone a thousand to save his life.'[46]

But the loss of that life now seemed imminent and Ralegh wrote
with cringing desperation to anyone whom he thought could save
it: to Cecil 'if ought remain of good or love',[47] to the Privy Council
begging to have 'one year to give to God in prison',[48] to the king:
'save me, therefore, most merciful prince'.[49] He was lacerating himself on the shivered fragments of his pride and, as a month of
anguished waiting passed, his weakness came to revolt him. He
wrote, as always, his truest thoughts to Bess. 'Get those letters (if it
be possible) which I writ to the Lords, wherein I sued for my life,
but God knoweth it was for you and yours that I desired it, but it is
true that I disdain myself for begging it.'[50] The apparent truth of his
situation was dawning on him. 'I plainly conceive that my death
was determined from the first day.'

He was chastened into sincerity and hurried into genuine displays of affection. The futures of Bess and Wat preoccupied him. 'I
would not, with my last will, present you with sorrows, dear Bess.

Let them go to the grave with me, and be buried in the dust.' The lives of his wife and son – perilous and almost certainly poverty-stricken – obsessed him. Frail and potent facts, debts to be discharged or reclaimed, 'my stuff, and jewels', glimmered before the imminent black curtain of his death and seemed only to reinforce the certainty of suffering. 'For the rest, when you have travailed and wearied your thoughts on all sorts of worldly cogitations, you shall sit down by sorrow in the end.' And of himself, for once, he was modest:

> I cannot write much. God knows how hardly I stole this time, when all sleep; and it is time to separate my thoughts from the world. Beg my dead body, which living was denied you; and either lay it at Sherborne if the land continue, or in Exeter church, by my father and mother.
> I can write no more. Time and Death call me away.[51]

He paused, evidently, in the writing of the letter, thinking, perhaps, that he had said all he need. But the very act of writing carried its own imaginative momentum, and he returned to the letter: 'The everlasting, infinite, powerful and inscrutable God, that Almighty God that is goodness itself, mercy itself, the true life and light, keep you and yours, and have mercy on me, and teach me to forgive my persecutors and false accusers; and send us to meet in his glorious kingdom.' If this is conventional piety – something of which his judges would never have accused him – its patent sincerity is proved by the thoughts that followed. 'My true wife, farewell. Bless my poor boy. Pray for me. My true God hold you in both his arms.'

But now the time was coming for the sentences of death to be carried out. Of the two priests arrested for the Bye Plot, Father Clarke was pinned down screaming while he was castrated and disembowelled. George Brooke was beheaded in the yard of Winchester Castle. Here, too, Cobham and two further conspirators in the Bye Plot – Grey and Markham – were to be executed on 10 December. The special occasion of Ralegh's death was to take place three days later.

The morning of Friday, 10 December was wet and bitterly cold, but the prospect of a triple execution gave courage to the crowd. Ralegh himself, it was reported, stared down on the scene from a window. The first of the victims to face the block was Markham who bravely declined the offer of a blindfold, saying he could look on death without embarrassment. Arrived on the scaffold, Markham knelt for some moments in prayer. The waiting crowd began to stir as they became aware of someone trying to push their way through. Eventually the young James Gibb, one of the attendants of the king's bedchamber, forced his way to the scaffold and waved a warrant from his master. Markham was to be given two hours' respite – two hours more of agonized life.

The ardently Puritan Grey was then brought out. After half an hour spent in prayer, he was informed that it was the king's pleasure that Cobham should be executed first. Grey too was marched back to his cell.

It was noted that when Cobham was led to the block Ralegh was smiling at the gruesome comedy being played out below him. He watched as Cobham also spent long moments in prayer, but he was probably too far distant from him to hear his former friend swear that all the damning allegations he had made against Ralegh were true 'as I have hope of my soul's resurrection'. Then, too, Cobham's execution was stayed while his fellow victims were summoned back to the scaffold. 'Ralegh, you must think,' a contemporary wrote, 'had hammers working in his heart to beat out the meaning of this stratagem.'[52]

'Have you not been justly tried and lawfully condemned?' the sheriff asked. 'Is not each of you subject to due execution now to be performed?'

The men agreed they were.

'Then see the mercy of your prince, who of himself hath sent hither a countermand and given you your lives!'

James had resolved on a grotesque exhibition of royal clemency. Markham was to be exiled, Grey and Cobham to be imprisoned. Ralegh, in cringing wonderment, despatched another letter to his king extolling his mercy and hoping that 'although myself hath not yet been brought so very near the brink of the grave, yet I trust that so great a compassion will extend itself towards me also.'[53]

James had decided several days before that it should. The last act of this contemptible comedy was the issuing of a pardon for Ralegh. He was to be kept a prisoner in the Tower – a condemned but unexecuted traitor, a man of fifty with no hope, no apparent future, nor even any legal existence. He had been condemned to nonentity.

CHAPTER FIFTEEN

The Prisoner

Ralegh was assigned two rooms on the second floor of the Bloody Tower. Here, with the exception of occasional summonses before the Privy Council and a brief remove to another and less conspicuous gaol, he remained for nearly thirteen years.

For the man himself, there was no knowing the limits of his term, and at first he had no vision of a future beyond a solid wall. But to this familiar desolation was added a more subtle horror and one previously unknown to him. As a convicted traitor, Ralegh was a man 'civilly dead', a personality denied a public voice and shackled to a living corpse. He had no rights, no role. To struggle against this state – to assert his actual and palpable existence – was to tear himself on a legal formula, a manacle of words. A letter he wrote begging James for mercy explored his anguish with characteristic powers of self-dramatization. 'Name, blood, gentility or estate, I have none,' Ralegh declared, 'no, not so much as a being.'[1]

But James was not inclined to pardon. After the farce played out at Winchester, the new king had delighted his court with a disquisition on the trials of Ralegh and the other traitors in which the quality of mercy was considerably strained. Now James wanted pageantry to dip his hand deep into his new country's purse. He felt, he declared, 'like a poor man wandering about forty years in a wilderness and barren soil, and now arrived in a land of promise'.[2] Here was an augury of royal extravagance, a clear indication that the parsimonious ways of the Elizabethan court were a thing of the past.

In March 1604, James processed through London. While the conduits of Cheapside disgorged rivers of wine, the king himself entered the Tower under a canopy borne by members of the Privy Council. The Tower had been cleared of its more disagreeable inhabitants for the occasion. Minor prisoners had been pardoned. Those under grievous sentence, among them Ralegh, Cobham and Grey, were despatched to the squalor of the Fleet while a bull was baited for the royal pleasure. A few days later, King James opened his first parliament.

There was conflict from the outset. Shortage of money raised the vexed matter of purveyance – the right of the royal household to buy goods and services below the market rate – but, after a difficult debate, a decision was postponed. James's first parliament also touched on the painful and ultimately catastrophic struggle between the royal prerogative and the privileges of the House, doing so in a way which showed that the old Elizabethan pragmatism had died with the old queen.

The disputed election of Sir John Fortesque, for example, resulted in the members being informed that their new monarch 'desired and commanded, as an absolute king, that there might be a conference between the House and the judges'3 on the matter. There would be no more 'Golden' speeches. Here was a command implying that the liberties of the House could be determined by the judges, and considerable diplomacy was required before a compromise could be reached. For the moment, this was a position earnestly desired by the members themselves: 'For God forbid that between so gracious a sovereign and so dutiful and loving subjects any difference should arise.'4

Differences, however, continued to be only too evident, nowhere more so than over the legal problems – the issue of joint sovereignty – posed by the union of England with Scotland. The progress of this issue left all sides aggrieved: the king, the judges and parliament itself. James was particularly distressed by what he saw as the delaying tactics of certain of the members, while parliament expressed its concern in a sentence at once elegant and prophetic of the mounting crisis of the next fifty years. 'The prerogatives of princes may easily, and do daily, grow,' the members declared, 'the privileges of the subject are for the most part at an everlasting stand.'5 The lines of future conflict were becoming clear, and such problems, along with James's policies towards Spain, were all questions in which Ralegh was to involve himself as resentment at Stuart absolutism deepened and his rooms in the Tower became a focus of opposition.

But now, when Ralegh was returned to these after his brief

[319]

incarceration in the Fleet, it was to find that plague was raging all about him. Little Wat, he discovered, had 'lain this fourteen days next to a woman with a running plague sore, and but a paper-wall between.'[6] The woman's child had died, and Wat and his mother at once moved out to lodgings nearby, thereby increasing the strain on Ralegh's finances while painfully enhancing his loneliness: 'Now my wife and child, and others in whom I had comfort, have abandoned me.'[7] He wrote angrily to Cecil about the unwarranted danger in which his imprisonment placed him. 'I cannot think myself to have been either such a viper but that this great downfall of mine, this shame, loss and sorrow, may seem to your lordship's heart and soul a sufficient punishment.'[8] The complaint was wholly reasonable, but Cecil could – or would – do nothing.

Eventually, when the plague had retreated and the close conditions of Ralegh's early confinement had been relaxed, he began to construct some sort of life for himself. Two of his own people were permitted to look after him: his serving man Dean, and John Talbot who, in addition to acting as Ralegh's secretary, was also schoolmaster to Wat. Later he was allowed 'a preacher and three boys in ordinary'.[9] Ralegh's waterman brought him ale and beer, thereby saving him from the perils of the disease-infested waters of the Tower. The visits of Laurence Keymis and Thomas Harriot provided intellectual consolation, while the newly christened Indians Ralegh had brought back from Guiana came to the Tower for lessons and conversation. Shelbury, a steward of Sherborne, was allowed to discuss business affairs with his master and, above all, there were visits from Bess.

Neither her love nor her loyalty was in doubt, and she displayed both with flamboyance, driving into the Tower in her coach with her head held high. Such self-confidence had always delighted Ralegh – roused him even – and by the summer of 1604 another child had been conceived. He was born in the Tower in the February of the following year and christened with the family name Carew.

But if Bess was encumbered with a mother's cares, she was also busied about other concerns. With disgrace, the Raleghs' financial position became precarious in the extreme. Ralegh himself declared that, with the loss of his monopolies especially, his annual income had fallen from £3,000 to £300 and that he was in debt to ten times this last amount. His creditors were quick to take advantage. Even before the death of Elizabeth, Ralegh had been obliged to pawn his plate for £800 and this sum proved impossible to recover. When Bess reluctantly let him sell a diamond jewel given him by the queen, the jeweller and money-lender Peter Vanlore retained £600 against a debt which Ralegh had forgotten about – 'it was quite out of my mind as if it had never been made'[10] – and he had to be content with a mere £400.

Those more highly placed were equally rapacious. The Lord High Admiral, the Earl of Nottingham, who had received Ralegh's patent for the licensing of wine, discovered that the collection of imposts was in arrears, and Ralegh was forced to such expedients as selling his Durham House tapestries for £500. At Bess's entreaty, Cecil stepped in to save the Raleghs from the Admiral's worst depredations – he had already acted to ensure that Bess's own possessions were not subject to destraint – and now he moved to help her in the matter of Sherborne.

The position here was complex, fraught and, eventually, a catastrophe of sheer bad luck. Throughout the whole wretched proceeding Bess showed her fortitude, her tigress's instinct to protect her home. From the earliest days of her husband's disgrace, the locals at Sherborne had been quick to take advantage. 'My tenants refuse to pay my wife her rent,' Ralegh complained. 'My woods are cut down; my grounds waste; my stock – which made up my rent – sold.'[11] Such pillage was at once a heartbreaking waste and a threat, for the little under £400 the estate produced now made up the greater part of the family's income.

Ralegh wrote in desperation to Cecil lamenting that 'except some end be had, by your good favour to the king, I perish every way.'[12] Cecil roused himself again and the wilful impoverishing of the estate ceased. Ralegh expressed his heartfelt gratitude. For the moment, all seemed safe. In his relief, he could even cherish the idea that he might yet receive a pardon and be allowed to live 'confined within the hundred of Sherborne'.[13] Cecil, altogether more realistic, suggested that letters patent securing the estate in trust might be advisable.

Bess petitioned for these, hoping that they would confirm the deed drawn up for Ralegh at the time he decided to move against Cobham and which conveyed the land to Wat. But to re-examine the deed was to discover disaster. The engrossing clerk had omitted the vital phrase whereby Wat 'shall and will from henceforth stand and thereof seised' or put in possession of the property. By this wretched piece of carelessness Sherborne remained technically Ralegh's and, as such, was forfeit to the crown.

Bess, in an agony of exasperation, her hopes and efforts dashed and with her home about to be wrenched from her grasp, stormed Juno-like into the Tower. Here she berated her husband for his carelessness. Cecil was about to leave town, and Cecil was the one man who might help them. Ralegh wrote to him yet again, and something of the harassed awe Bess could stir in her husband is evident from his letter. 'She hath already,' Ralegh declared, 'brought her eldest son in one hand and her sucking child in another, crying out of her and their destruction; charging me with unnatural negligence, and that having provided for mine own life I am without sense and compassion of theirs.'[14] He was, he said, near to cursing the time that he was born. 'I beseech your Lordship, even as you must one day beg comfort from God and cry unto him for his abundant mercy, that you will be pleased to spare the time, and to finish and effect, in some sort, your heart's intent towards me.'[15]

Cecil prevaricated, and Bess approached James himself. The king was, for the moment, happy to extend his mercy to a woman in distress, and a draft warrant was made out declaring that, although the crown recognized its rights, 'all our title and interest may be passed over to his wife and children that we be no more troubled with their pitiful cries and complaints for that business.'[16] For the moment, Bess could relax. The servants down at Sherborne were ordered to clean the house and to be particularly mindful that the armour be given a good scouring.

Ralegh now had to find ways of filling his hours of enforced leisure. His old acquaintance Sir George Hervey, the Lieutenant of the Tower, was amiably disposed towards his prisoner, inviting him to dine and permitting him to exercise along the inner walls of the Tower. Eventually, he even allowed Ralegh access to his garden and to a small shed which until recently had been used as a hen-house. Ralegh proceeded to convert this into a laboratory. Here he pursued a number of experiments, many of them connected with medicine. He cured tobacco leaves as a remedy against headaches, for example, and distilled various potions such as his strawberry water and his famous 'Guiana Balsam' which was still attracting interest half a century later.

Since the garden in which these experiments took place was surrounded only by a decayed wall, it was relatively easy for all those who came by to observe Ralegh and for the prisoner himself to contrive to draw attention to his presence. The wife of the French ambassador, for instance, greeted him one day and, in the course of their conversation, asked him about his Guiana Balsam. Ralegh expatiated on its virtues, and the lady requested a sample be sent to her. Ralegh complied, sending as his messenger a certain Captain Whitelock, a member of her entourage and a client of the Earl of Northumberland. In such ways, contact could be maintained with the great in the outside world. The good effects of the Guiana Balsam soon came to the ears of James's wife Anna who in turn requested a sample. Very soon, she too was to become sympathetic to Ralegh's cause, a woman firmly convinced of his innocence.

But if the neglected queen was to become one of Ralegh's allies, her husband remained his foe. Even Ralegh's curing of tobacco leaves and his recommendation that smoking could cure headaches fell foul of a king who believed that tobacco 'makes a kitchen of the inward parts of men, soiling and infecting them with an unctuous and oily kind of soot.'[17] Since breath was God's gift of life, to stale it with tobacco smoke was a singularly wilful error, and James went on to claim in his *Counterblast Against Tobacco* (1604) that Ralegh had adopted the habit from the 'beastly Indians, slaves to the Spaniards, refuse to the world, and as yet alien from the holy covenant of God.'

The year following the royal publication saw a number of changes to life in the Tower. In August, the companionable Hervey was replaced as Lieutenant by Sir William Waad, the man who had been Ralegh's guard during his humiliating journey to his trial and subsequently one of his judges. Waad was clearly appalled by the range of comforts his most famous prisoner had managed to secure for himself, in particular the all too public laboratory 'where he doth spend his time all the day in his distillations'.[18] Waad was determined to curtail these privileges but, in November 1605, he was suddenly involved in more pressing concerns: the imprisonment and torture of Guido Fawkes for his conspiracy in the Gunpowder Plot.

While the rack was brought out for Fawkes, Ralegh, as a convicted traitor, was also looked on with suspicion. Any suggestion of his involvement with the Gunpowder Plot was absurd, but the panic which seized the authorities was such that they felt they could not ignore the slightest suspicion. Had not Lady Ralegh, after all, ordered that the armour at Sherborne was to be cleaned? Might not this indicate that a vengeful couple were preparing to take their part in the armed rising of Roman Catholics that was supposed to take place after the Houses of Parliament had been blown up?

It is a tribute to the power of Ralegh's personality – the sheer force of his presence even when in the Tower – that his wife's housework could be looked on as potentially treasonable. Besides, he had used the Earl of Northumberland's client Captain Whitelock as his messenger when sending his Guiana Balsam to the French ambassador's wife. Here was a potential conspiracy between France, Whitelock (who was clearly implicated in the Plot), and the Earl of Northumberland, that scion of a great Catholic family and an inevitable focus of suspicion. The Privy Council felt it their duty to question Ralegh and, although he acquitted himself with ease, his freedoms were curtailed.

This was doubly unfortunate since, despite his pharmacological experiments, Ralegh's health was not as resilient as it once had been. The dampness of the Tower, the limited opportunities for proper exercise, the enforced change to the pace of his life, stress, and the onset of age (he was now in his early fifties) were taking their toll. In 1605, he complained to Cecil 'that I am every second or third night in danger either of sudden death or of the loss of my limbs and sense, being two hours without feeling or motion of my hand and whole arm.' He resolved not to complain. 'I know it is vain, for there is none that hath compassion thereof.'[19]

The following year, the position was no better. His doctor reported that 'all his left side is extreme cold, out [i.e. void] of sense and motion, or numbed; his fingers on the same side begin to be contracted, and his tongue, in some part, insomuch that he speaketh weakly, and it is to be feared he may utterly lose the use of it.'[20] The physician, Dr James Turner, recommended that it might be beneficial for Ralegh if he 'were removed from the cold lodging where he lieth unto a warmer, that is to say, a little room which he hath built in the garden adjoining to his still-house.' Clearly, the doctor recognized the symptoms of a mild stroke.

The Privy Council's interrogation of Northumberland and the Gunpowder Plotters meanwhile revealed that Thomas Percy, the Earl's kinsman and steward, had set aside a large sum in support of a Catholic rising. Suspicion inevitably if unjustly fell on the Earl himself. He was arraigned before the Privy Council, fined the fantastic sum of £30,000, and sent to the Tower. Here he was often attended by Thomas Harriot who continued to live at Syon House, the Earl's London residence, rather than in the Tower itself as has sometimes been supposed. Walter Warner and the geographer Robert Hues made up the other members of a group sometimes referred to as the Earl's 'three magi'.

None of the party were men to repine at discomfort or remain in their cells growing placidly embittered with defeat. Ralegh had his laboratory and was using the Lieutenant's garden to grow the rare plants that had so delighted him at Sherborne. Northumberland lived in even greater style, paying to have his food cooked for him specially. The walkways where he took his exercise were freshly gravelled, he installed a bowling alley with a canvas roof, and managed to persuade the authorities to make new and larger windows in his cell so that he could have more light by which to conduct his experiments. These included attempts to distil spirits from stale alcohol, as well as an interest in anatomy, astronomy, geography and horology.

Sir William Waad looked on these activities – or, at least, the degree of pleasurable intellectual and physical freedom they implied – with deepening disapproval. He had been appointed the governor of a prison and was determined to assert his role. He drew up a series of 'Ordinances for the Government of the Tower'. In these he showed he was concerned to put a stop to the very public coming and going that characterized the entourages of his prisoners. He was particularly insistent that at night the Tower should be a suitable place for penitence and solitary reflection.

In a ruling at least partly aimed at Bess, Waad laid down that such prisoners' wives as were allowed access were to be 'admitted at convenient times, but shall not lodge in the Tower, and use the prisons as if they were dwelling-houses; nor shall they be permitted to come into the Tower with their coaches.'[21] The flamboyance of the Raleghs was to be curtailed and, since Waad also ruled that the cell doors should be kept locked during the day and that wives must leave at night, he was evidently denying Ralegh conjugal visits. His servants (along with the more numerous following of the Earl of Northumberland) were also to be closely regulated. They were to live in the Tower, 'dine by themselves', and were not to use their access to the kitchens as a meal-ticket for their friends.

Much of this was the detail of discipline no doubt proper in a prison, but Waad was concerned above all to limit his prisoners' contact with the outside world, to ensure that the 'civilly dead' were deprived of civil society. In his own eyes at least, Waad's aims were more prudent than vindictive. He was concerned, for instance, that there should be no chance of Ralegh's chatting with foreign dignitaries and suspected traitors over the garden fence. He desired 'not to remove him' from his laboratory, but 'if a brick wall were built, it would be more safe and convenient.'[22] The wall was duly built, a high, broad wall on which Ralegh, to the dismay of his gaoler, chose to walk for his exercise. He realized the advantages of displaying himself 'to the view of the people, who gaze upon him and he stares at them, which he does in his cunning humour that it might be thought that his being before the Lords was rather to clear than to charge him.'[23]

With his shrewdly imperious gesture, Ralegh turned his prison into a stage and began fashioning for himself a principal role in the drama of political opposition. Amid deepening resentment at James's rule, Ralegh became a symbol of past glory. The crowd that had once hated him for his pride and jeered as he rode in humiliation to Winchester, came now to see the last great Elizabethan limping on his stick as, high above them, he patrolled the confines of his cage. The injustice of his state was manifest. He was deliberately fashioning himself as an object lesson in Stuart absolutism – a national totem in an increasingly disillusioned state.

This role – so dangerous to authority because so potent and yet so imprecise – was unwittingly enhanced by Waad. In his wish to constrain his charges, the Lieutenant ruled that once the afternoon bell had been rung and the gates of the Tower were closed, then 'all the prisoners, with their servants, are to withdraw themselves into their chambers, and not to go forth again for that night.'²⁴ To the scholar, such enforced inactivity was a golden opportunity and, as his long evenings passed in voracious reading, Ralegh could say with Cicero that he was never less alone than when alone. Gradually, a stream of prose works issued from the Bloody Tower that was profoundly to influence opposition to Stuart rule. As Bishop Hall was to declare: 'The court had his youthful and freer times, the Tower his later age: the Tower reformed the court in him, and produced those worthy monuments of art and industry, which we should have in vain expected from his freedom and jollity.'²⁵

Ralegh's Jacobean writings began with his *War with Spain*. This was almost certainly the tract he had mentioned to James during the opening weeks of his reign and which, Ralegh declared at his trial, 'I had intended to present unto the king.' Its belligerent tone ran wholly counter to James's policies, however, and, as such, was a first indication of the opposition stance Ralegh was later consciously to adopt. The tenor of its argument, in the early months of Stuart rule, was more certainly a sign of Ralegh's inability to read both the mind of his new sovereign and the current mood of the country.

The expense of the long Elizabethan war with Spain (a burden augmented by the increasingly successful campaign to subdue Ireland) cost the crown and country dear. Elizabeth had accumulated over £200,000 of debt, and her people were wearied of war with an increasingly exhausted empire. Despite pressure from the Dutch and French, James concluded that peace was an altogether more attractive policy and, in negotiating the Treaty of London, Cecil and Howard especially achieved a satisfactory conclusion amid general rejoicing. Trade with Holland and the Mediterranean was encouraged, and the difficult problem of the Caribbean was shelved while England observed the continuing struggle between Spain and the Netherlands from the comfortable vantage of unfamiliar peace.

Ralegh, however, feared that the Dutch fleet might yet fall into the hands of Spain and so revivify an old enemy's declining navy. English shipping in the seas around her own coast would be put under threat, he argued, while, as a veteran of the Armada, Ralegh also feared that Spain might once again find the power to launch an attack on England herself. Ralegh advanced his argument with what he doubtless considered an apt combination of logical order and abject flattery. None the less, he was unmindful not only of James's desire to appear before Europe as *rex pacificus* but also of the sheer cost of continuing the war and the resolute independence of the Dutch themselves who would fight for the Protestant cause regardless of the wavering of their erstwhile allies.

In maintaining his hostility towards Spain, Ralegh was in tune with the country's deeper prejudices and the loathing of an old enemy that surfaced again once the initial delight in peace had worn off. This deeply entrenched hatred was a factor James himself constantly disregarded. While memories of what had been achieved by the sailors of the Elizabethan age hardened to myth in the minds of his subjects, the king, asserting his prerogative in matters of foreign policy, rarely explained his policies to parliament.

Guided by his prejudices, James schemed constantly for a strong diplomatic link with Spain and, as his financial crisis deepened, so hopes of a marriage between the Infanta and his eldest son were quickened by prospects of a vast dowry. So careless a disregard for national prejudice, along with fears that Spain might yet seek for 'universal monarchy' in the ten-year truce secured with the Dutch, increasingly alienated him from the people. As this dislike deepened, so the thoughts of many turned to the old prisoner in the Tower.

Before his term of imprisonment there had begun – indeed, probably while he was awaiting death in Winchester – Ralegh composed a work that was to bring him considerable posthumous renown: his *Instructions to his Son*. Here, believing he was about 'to depart this world',[26] Ralegh gave Wat the benefit of his thoughts on topics such as the right choice of friends and a wife, flattery, conversation, deportment and the management of estates and servants. His mood was one of the utmost seriousness: 'I have had my part in this world, and now must give place to fresh gamesters. Farewell. All is vanity and weariness, yet such a weariness and vanity that we shall ever complain of it and love it for all that.'[27] Small personal touches, individual inflections of the voice, and a poet's command of the resources of prose save the work from the platitudes of a Polonius.

But Wat was no Laertes. The little boy seen so touchingly imitating the pose of his father in a portrait from 1602 inherited the temperament of both his parents. During the early years of his father's imprisonment, Ralegh's secretary John Talbot educated him in preparation for Oxford, but whatever the boy's taste for scholarship may have been, it is the records of his high spirits and recklessness that survive to give us the picture by which we know him.

When, for example, Wat was sent to Paris to complete his education with no less a tutor than the poet and classical pundit Ben Jonson, Wat got the older man so drunk that he was laid on a cart and carried spread-eagled through the streets with the boy crying out that here was the best crucifix in Paris. On another occasion he shocked the Parisians by pinning the gifts given to him by various girlfriends on to his codpiece. In April 1615, he had to flee England after wounding an opponent in a duel. Bess had on one occasion to remind her husband that he himself had been quite as wild in his youth; there is no question that Ralegh's love for the lad ran deep in his nature. Wat was the 'dear boy' and 'pretty knave' of Ralegh's wittily gruesome lyric 'Three things there be'.

The early years of Ralegh's imprisonment were also the likely occasion for one of his most concise yet serious lyrics, a poem whose imagery, if conventional, lies at the heart of his concern with role-playing, morality and death. 'What is our life?' was a widely popular poem and exists in some forty contemporary transcriptions. Many of these vary widely in the form they take, and while the text printed by Orlando Gibbons in his *First Set of Madrigals* of 1612 is the best known, modern scholarship has reconstructed a version which is almost certainly closer to Ralegh's original intentions:

> What is our life? It is a play of passion.
> What is our mirth? The music of division.
> Our mothers, they the tiring houses be,
> Where we are dressed for time's short tragedy.
> Earth is the stage, heaven the spectator is
> Who doth behold whoe'er doth act amiss.
> The graves that hide us from the parching sun
> Are but drawn curtains till the play be done[28]

The man who throughout his career had seen the world as a stage on which to act out his own complex and ambitious role here reduces the idea to eight lines packed with vivid particularization and stern, absolute morality.

Meanwhile, a new scene in the hapless drama of Sherborne was unfolding. In 1607, the king's attention had been caught by the lissom form of Robert Carr, an impoverished Scottish follower, and as interest turned to infatuation so presents were heaped on the youth. James's munificence towards his Scottish followers was a source of mounting resentment against a king who, contrary to Elizabeth, regarded lavish display by the crown as a duty despite the fact that it was 'a horror to me to think upon the height of my place, the greatness of my debts, and the smallness of my means'.[29] Indeed, by 1607, James had been obliged to entail the crown lands, and the promise of a gift of £20,000 to Carr so appalled Cecil that he persuaded the king to a less obvious course.

Whether through deviousness or pressure of work, Cecil had not complied with James's ruling that Sherborne should be secured for Bess and Wat. Ralegh's own unfortunate conveyance was still the operative document, and Cecil now suggested the king wriggle through its loophole to provide his favourite with an estate. Sherborne was to become the means by which James could indulge his favourite without breaking the entail on crown lands. While the Court of Exchequer requested Ralegh to procure evidence of proper title, James sent a carefully worded note of gratitude to Cecil: 'The more I think of your remembrance of Robert Carr for yon manor of Sherborne, the more cause I have to conclude that your mind ever watcheth to seek out all advantage for my honour and contentment.'[30]

Bess, caught in a position at once repellent and cruel, resolved on the only course open to her. A request for an audience with James had already been ignored, and so she now stationed herself in a strategic position at Hampton Court where, as the king waddled by, she threw herself down before his spindle-shanked legs and begged for mercy – a house for herself and her child. The king merely mumbled in colloquial embarrassment: 'I mun have the land, I mun have it for Carr.'[31] He was later to offer reasonable compensation – £8,000 and an annuity of £400 – but in January 1609, the conveyance of 1602 was pronounced void.

There was no concept of equity competent to deal with the

engrossing clerk's trivial but tragic slip, and blame for the Raleghs' ruin – the collapse of all their worldly hope – had to be placed elsewhere. Writing of the 'flaw in the conveyance', a contemporary noted that 'the error or oversight is said to be so gross, that men do merely ascribe it to God's own hand, that blinded him and his counsel.'[32] Ralegh, stripped as naked as he came into the world, was soon being seen as a Jacobean Job.

He wrote pathetically to Carr, swallowing his pride to beg for what was 'lost in law for want of words'. He stressed Carr's youth and promise, and contrasted to these his own age and humiliation. 'I beseech you not to begin your first buildings upon the ruins of the innocent; and that their griefs and sorrows do not attend your first plantation.'[33] The appeal went unheard amid the bibulous laughter and machiavellian whispering of the king's court.

Ralegh turned elsewhere. In the first years of the reign he had sent Queen Anna a sample of his Guiana Balsam, and perhaps as early as 1603 had begun to think of her as a possible ally. A sad lady, neglected by her husband, Anna was none the less England's queen, and an early draft of a poem addressed to her (a poem that Ralegh may not have completed or sent to her at this time) makes much of her role. Adapting passages from 'The Ocean to Cynthia', the new queen becomes the virtuous successor to the old. She alone, Ralegh suggests, has the greatness of mind to see that his desolation is the result of a world where malice had long been busy about discrediting him. Now he finds the hearts of the world and his former friends to be as stony as the walls of his cell:

> To whom then shall I cry, to whom shall wrong
> Cast down her tears, or hold up folded hands?[34]

The only appeal can be to his new queen. The erstwhile lover of the virgin moon, reshaping an old lament to a new occasion, created thereby a new image of feminine power. Great, good and graceful, nutritive and succouring, Anna is the queen who can bring to her country 'equal, if not greater bliss' than Elizabeth herself. She is above all things a mother:

> Who hath brought glory, and posterity
> Unto a widow land and people hopeless.[35]

*

While it appears that Anna herself made no appeal to the king at the time of Ralegh's trial, she was afterwards convinced of his innocence and always spoke in his favour. When, in 1606, her brother the king of Denmark paid a visit to England, it may well have been at her prompting that, after a series of entertainments in which Christian IV taught even the Jacobean court to drink deep, he asked for Ralegh to be released so he might be made Admiral of the Danish fleet. The request was turned down.

But if the queen's brother could not help, there remained her eldest son. Ralegh's reference in his poem to Anna's 'posterity' reflects the nation's delight, that, for the first time in many decades, there were royal children to ensure the succession. Hopes gathered particularly about Henry, Prince of Wales, who, as he grew to young manhood, became the focus of a cult whose martial spirit and muscular Protestantism defined itself in opposition to the tenor of his father's court. Where Whitehall could too often be seen as licentious, drunken and profligate, bent on appeasement abroad and self-indulgence at home, Henry's court – founded when he was a mere fifteen – took its character from the prince himself.

A contemporary described him as 'tall and of an high stature, his body strong and well proportioned, his shoulders were broad, his eyes quick and pleasant, his forehead broad, his nose big, his chin broad and cloven.'[36] Shrewder contemporaries such as Sir Francis Bacon, however, noted that the young man's gravity was the expression of a temperament essentially cold and guarded. Henry had the interest in high morals and good conduct of the born martinet. The swear-boxes to be found in his apartments were not an ornamental warning.

Unlike his father, who had failed to convert him to his own relish for pedantry, Prince Henry was not over-bookish, although he was far from disparaging scholarship. His mind, more dogged than brilliant, was concerned principally with the task of fashioning himself as a young Protestant worthy, a youth born to high office, a latter-day Sidney. He was a considerable patron with advanced interests in the arts, as well as in those forms of architecture and gardening that might one day enhance his status as a great European prince.

Henry was also – and for the same reasons – deeply interested in war, in strategy and the martial arts. He was an expert horseman, a good shot, a youth fascinated by new inventions, 'also delighting to confer, both with his own, and other strangers, and great captains, of all manner of wars, battle, furniture, arms by sea and land, disciplines, orders, marches, alarms, watches, stratagems'.[37] The contrast to his cowardly and pacific father could hardly have been more marked, and this was a contrast underlined by the prince's zealous and even aggressive Protestantism.

James belonged to that humanist literary tradition which was appalled by the bloody divisions of religious war and, for sound ideological and financial reasons, he hoped for a rapprochement with the Catholic powers. His role as a peacemaker flattered his self-regard and, like every contemporary monarch, he considered his children as pawns in his policy. Marriages arranged with other Catholic powers would, he presumed, cement his efforts at European conciliation. He was also aware of the benefits such alliances might bring to his dwindling coffers.

Henry, by contrast, was an extreme anti-Catholic. It was said of his household that 'there was not one known or suspected papist' to be found there, with the result that 'his magnetic virtue drew all the eyes, and hearts, of the protestant world.'[38] Among these last were inevitably the survivors of the old Elizabethan war party, including Sir Arthur Gorges. In 1607, Gorges presented Henry with his account of the Azores expedition. Few narratives could have been more attractive to a thirteen-year-old boy or more surely have directed his attention to Ralegh in the Tower. 'None but my father', the prince allegedly declared, 'would keep such a bird in a cage.'[39]

The phrase exactly defines the position. There is no evidence to suggest that the youth and the old man ever met (Gorges was probably their intermediary) but in raising Henry's interest in him, Ralegh caught the attention of a figure who seemed of the utmost future importance. He thereby found for himself a new role. Unofficially, he took on the venerable task of tutor to a future king and, in so doing, became an *éminence grise* of the opposition party. A stream of prose works followed. These were theoretical, scholarly and practical, concerned with politics, history and Henry's passion for maritime affairs especially.

Henry's interest in the navy had been awoken when in 1604, aged just ten, he had been presented by the Lord High Admiral with an exquisitely detailed model of a ship. Twenty-eight feet in length, the model was large enough to sail with passengers on the Thames. Three years later, the master shipwright Phineas Pett presented another model and, in 1608, laid the keel for the huge, three-decker *Prince Royal*. This last was a project in which Ralegh was deeply interested and capable of giving expert advice. Indeed, his critical awareness of the problems involved was in some areas sharper than Pett's.

Ralegh had first composed his *Observations and Notes Concerning the Royal Navy and Sea Service* for Elizabeth soon after his return from Cadiz. He had then outlined, in a manner that clearly revealed his practical experience, a considerable number of general and specific problems which he believed tended to the weakening of English power at sea. Now, when he revised the work in about 1608, the position had deteriorated. James's interest in his navy was small and ineffective.

In view of the danger Ralegh believed was posed by the Spanish peace, this decline was an alarming prospect. While he was not so impolitic as to name Spain as England's chief enemy, Ralegh argued forcibly that the possibility of peace had 'proceeded out of the former trial of our forces in times of war'.[40] The Spaniards had negotiated with a nation whose power they feared. The conclusion was clear. A continuing royal concern with the navy such as Henry showed was essential to national security. Danger had not gone away, and if the Spaniards believed the country to be weak then, 'these proud mastering spirits, finding us at such advantage, would be more ready and willing to shake us by the ears as enemies, than to take us by the hand as friends.'[41]

The detailed criticisms of English naval practice Ralegh offered in his treatise helped Henry towards a precise knowledge of the state of things. The situation was indeed disgraceful. Ralegh's comments on ill-qualified officers, bad provisioning, the dishonest use of press-gangs and the varieties of peculation indulged by suppliers painted a grim picture of incompetence. Even Pett, the prince's shipwright, was not above this. Indeed, Pett made himself a considerable profit from dishonest dealing with the *Prince Royal*, a fact to which Henry's admiration blinded him.

Nor was this vast and ambitious vessel an example of the most competent and up-to-date engineering. The ship rose too high above the water-line and was far from being the stout, swift vessel Ralegh espoused. He was particularly concerned to emphasize – it was a constant theme in his writings – that more guns led not to greater power but to diminished manoeuvrability. The original eighty cannon on the *Prince Royal* were eventually reduced to fifty, perhaps because of this advice. None the less, the occasion of her launch was a heartbreaking embarrassment for the prince. It was found that the dockhead was too narrow to let the ship through. Most of the royal party went home, and it was only at 2 a.m. the following morning that the young man was able to launch his vessel to the sound of trumpets blowing in the dark.

Ralegh clearly intended to present Henry with a comprehensive view of his naval policy in what remain as the notes and fragments of a projected *Art of War by Sea*. This was to be a work in fifteen chapters beginning with a history of ships and naval combat. Only much later was Ralegh to expand his notes for this section into his again unrevised *Discourse on the Invention of Ships*. Here he dealt knowledgeably with the general history of naval technology up to the present day, while in a second part he urged themes of central importance to his strategic thinking. He voiced his strong disapproval, for instance, of the export of English cannon. He made clear his conviction that 'trade by force' in areas where states or competitors were hostile was of great importance to training a strong navy. He reiterated his belief that a firm alliance with the Dutch was essential and suggested that Spain's colonies could easily be wrested from her grasp.

Lethal to him as this last idea was to prove, it was a part of a coherent strategy which, in the *Art of War by Sea*, he attributed to the ancient Greek Themistocles: 'He that commands the sea, commands the trade, he that is lord of the trade of the world is lord of the wealth of the world.'[42] This was a vision of empire two and a half centuries ahead of its time, and Ralegh commended it to Henry by a shrewd appeal to his self-esteem. 'There is nothing that so much discovers the judgement of a prince', he wrote, 'as his enterprises.'[43]

Significant among these 'enterprises' was the belief Prince Henry shared with Ralegh in the importance of American colonization. Despite disappointments, Ralegh himself had not easily abandoned Roanoke or wholly given up his hopes of settlement in the region of Chesapeake Bay. Hakluyt continued to urge the advantages of Virginia over Ireland and Guiana, while at some unspecified point Ralegh despatched two expeditions captained by Samuel Mace to see what had happened to his colonists there. These expeditions returned with no information of value. The sea war with Spain ensured that few if any other ships were despatched to the region in the decade from 1591, and it was only with the diminution of hostilities from 1602 that active interest in the region revived.

In that year, Ralegh had sent Mace and two vessels to trade and reconnoitre the coast south of Cape Hatteras. Instructions were also issued to search again for the colonists from John White's last expedition, but the crew did not follow these, 'pretending that the extremity of weather and loss of some principal ground tackling forced and feared them' from the endeavour. A cargo of sufficient value was brought back to pay for the expedition, but the opportunities afforded by the relative peace with Spain encouraged competitors to trade with what is now North Virginia.

The valuable quantity of sassafras brought back by an expedition led by Bartholomew Gosnold, Bartholomew Gilbert and John Brereton in particular threatened the profits from Ralegh's own voyage. He at once took steps to see that their cargo was confiscated. None the less, because his rivals' primary interest was to the north rather than to the south of the region, Ralegh was eventually prepared to concede retrospective permission for the voyage, a generous move encouraged by the enthusiastic advertising for Virginia afforded by the publication of Brereton's *Brief and True Relation* of his voyage. 'I shall yet live to see it an English nation,' Ralegh had written of Virginia to Cecil.[45] Bristol merchants now sailed to the area while, in 1603, Ralegh despatched Bartholomew Gilbert on an ill-starred expedition to the Chesapeake. When this returned to report that its leader had been killed by the Indians, Ralegh himself was a prisoner in the Tower, his rights in America forfeited to the crown.

Ralegh was thereby denied a leading role in the colonization of America at the very moment when the tide of events seemed at last to be turning in favour of his schemes. Although James himself strongly disapproved of privateering and was concerned to arrange a Spanish marriage for his eldest son, he was equally determined to defend the rights to North America that reverted to him with Ralegh's fall, and he supported Cecil and Nottingham in their resolve not to abandon these during the peace negotiations that led to the Treaty of London. By 1605, the king seemed prepared to act – or at least to assert his sovereignty over Virginia – and it was probably the influence of Cecil that resulted in the setting up of the Virginia Council and the granting of its charter in 1606.

The gentlemen of the West lent their eager support. Sir Ferdinando Gorges encouraged the old argument that the unemployed should be urged 'to spend themselves in seeking a new world'. Gilbert's sons and the recorder of Plymouth lent their voices, as did many others. By a cruel irony, however, it was Sir John Popham, Lord Chief Justice of the King's Bench and presiding judge at Ralegh's trial, who became the most active promoter of colonization in the West Country.

Along with Cecil and others, Popham joined the expertise of his compatriots to the financial resources of the City, thereby creating two companies in one, the London company in particular having rights in the region around Chesapeake Bay. However, much to the annoyance of the merchants and shareholders who hoped to profit from what was essentially a joint-stock venture, the King's Council of Virginia and two sub-committees were given overall authority. Such a set-up proved unwieldy and unfair, and when it was found that these disadvantages were combined with insufficient capitalization, the scheme fell through.

From the Tower, Ralegh tried to use his influence with the queen to gain some say in the enterprise. No man had more experience of its aims, and 'I long since presumed to offer your majesty my service in Virginia,' he wrote later, 'with short repetition of the commodity, honour and safety which the king's majesty might reap by that plantation.'[46] He was not asked to participate however, and the great hardships suffered by Christopher Newport's men at what later came to be known as Jamestown showed that an altogether more substantial community was required for successful colonization.

To enhance interest in the project, the government embarked on what Ralegh had long considered a necessity: an advertising campaign of widespread and blatant nationalism. Deep reserves of anti-Spanish feeling were tapped and, much to the concern of the Spanish ambassador, his nation's ancient enemy in the Tower again offered his advice, whether asked or no. The ambassador managed to get hold of a copy of Ralegh's document (which is now lost) along with the company's map of the region. He then wrote anxiously to his king to inform him that the members of the Council of Virginia were following Ralegh's written instructions which ought to be translated at once and compared with the map to determine precisely what plans were afoot.

This effort was Ralegh's last known contribution to the ideal of an empire in North America: a dream he had nurtured for thirty years and on which he had lavished both his intellect and his fortune. No Elizabethan had contributed more to a movement which, stumbling and insecure though it appeared, was yet to have the utmost importance for the future of world history. Ralegh was still a prisoner, and now, while a newly incorporated Virginia Company pursued the agonizing and often brutal path of colonization, Ralegh himself was obliged to turn to more immediate problems at home.

Ralegh's fragmentary *On the Seat of Government* elaborates a theme of the greatest importance to his thought: his belief that reason should be the guide that taught monarchs to win the love of their people, and that these two forces – reason and love – were essential to the proper relation of the monarch to those he ruled. In the London that pulsed outside the Tower and in the nation at large, however, it was becoming all too evident that reason and love were threatening to turn into their opposites and pull disastrously apart.

The marriages James proposed for the royal children appeared to increase this tension, and two responses to these which cannot be attributed to Ralegh with complete confidence suggest the depth of concern felt by many. The tract on the proposed match of Henry's sister Princess Elizabeth to the Duke of Savoy discussed the purposes of dynastic marriage in general, illustrating its dangers with an unwieldy collection of historical precedents. Much of this material was repeated in a more satisfactory form in the 'Discourse Touching a Marriage between Prince Henry . . . and a Daughter of Savoy'. The disadvantages of a weak ally are clearly exposed here, as are the moral and strategic dangers of an alliance with a crown so closely associated with Spain.

Ralegh's loathing of what he saw as the malicious ambitions

of Catholic Europe and the Jesuits especially found its strongest expression in his 'Dialogue between a Jesuit and a Recusant'. Ralegh himself had been attacked as a Puritan in the Jesuit-inspired *Apologia pro Henrico Garneto*, and his anger at this, combined with his mounting exasperation over James's policies, resulted in a new departure for his prose: satiric attack.

By a shrewd manipulation of the dialogue form, Ralegh has his recusant confess to the range of the Jesuits' international terrorism and then, as the irony deepens, compares the Jesuits unfavourably to the Apostles. 'They humbled themselves, ye exult your selves.'[47] The moral and political anarchy Ralegh had associated with the Jesuits in his 'Revenge' pamphlet is again made to appear as an all-encompassing threat, but his strongest attack is reserved for the king himself.

The cowardly and pacific James, Ralegh declares, 'wants all that should make a king fearful to his enemies.'[48] Poor and hated at home, he is the dupe of international conspiracy abroad. To advance such arguments was desperately dangerous, even if the 'Dialogue' itself was intended only for the inner circle of Henry's court. What the work reveals most clearly, however, is how powerfully the last great Elizabethan could be a focus for opposition under the new Jacobean regime. Imprisoned, shamed and 'civilly dead', Ralegh was as never before a spokesman at one with his disillusioned countrymen.

So dangerously subversive was the 'Dialogue between a Jesuit and a Recusant' that only one contemporary manuscript of it survives, compared to the sixteen transcripts of *War with Spain* and the more than two dozen copies of the tract on Prince Henry's marriage. None of these works could be printed, but clearly they earned the prince's gratitude and he did what he could to help the old man's cause. In particular, Henry persuaded his father to grant Sherborne to him rather than to Carr, hoping thereby to hold it for Ralegh against the day of his release. This generous move was in large part a recognition of Ralegh's literary labours, in particular the vast masterpiece on which his reputation as a writer principally rests: *The History of the World*.

The stately frontispiece of the first edition of this work offers a visual interpretation of Ralegh's concept of history. The figure of history herself is seen trampling on the corpses of death and oblivion, and is flanked by representations of experience and truth. On the columns beside her are engraved Latin phrases, borrowed from Cicero, which praise her as the witness of time, the messenger of ancient days, the light of truth, and the light of memory. History – strong, bright and vital – is thus a force of wisdom, the embodiment of human effort and, as the fifth of Cicero's phrases emblazoned on her gown declares, the guide to existence. History is thus presented as the mortal world's defence against ignorance and oblivion.

But for Ralegh – the atheist taunts of his enemies notwithstanding – the conduct of life was not a merely human affair. History holds the globe above her head, thereby 'raising the world', in Jonson's explanatory poem, both 'to good and evil fame' and to the region of divine judgement. Thus suspended between the mortal and the immortal, the globe places England at its centre. To the east, Europe, Asia and Africa suggest the history of the Old World – the Fall, Noah's ark and so on – while, from the western coasts of these ancient civilizations, a fleet sails in discovery of the New World.

The opposing figures of good and evil reputation balance this sphere of human endeavour, while above them beams the all-seeing eye of Providence – the will of God in human affairs and the ultimate arbiter of all. Throughout *The History of the World*, heaven is the judicious sharp spectator as the will of an omniscient God works itself out through the desires – and, all too often, the wickedness – of men. In the human tragedy, God has 'appointed all the parts we are to play', but the fact that His inscrutable will has foreknowledge of how men will act does not absolve them from moral responsibility.[49] History – Ralegh's *History* – may help, however, since it is one of the principal duties of the historian 'to teach by examples of times past such wisdom as may guide our actions'.[50]

Ralegh's own passage in praise of history makes these ideas explicit, doing so in a prose that, while magniloquent and swelling, is always attuned to the rhythms and vocabulary of intelligent, natural discourse. These aspects of a style capable of grandeur where necessary, but also of detailed factual analysis, narrative and anecdote are ideally suited to sustaining his vast enterprise through close on a million words. Writing of the nature of history, Ralegh declared:

True it is than among many other benefits for which it hath been honoured, in this one it triumpheth over all human knowledge, that it hath given us life in our understanding, since the world itself had life and beginning, even to this day: yea, it hath triumphed over time, which beside it nothing but eternity hath triumphed over: for it hath carried our knowledge over the vast and devouring space of so many thousands of years, and given so fair and piercing eyes to our mind, that we plainly behold living now, as if we had lived then, that great world, *Magni Dei sapiens opus*, 'the wise work', saith Hermes, 'of a great God', as it was then, when but new to itself. By it, I say that it is that we live in the very time when it was created; we behold how it was governed; how it was covered with waters; and again repeopled; how kings and kingdoms have flourished and fallen; and for what virtue and piety God made prosperous, and for what vice and deformity he made wretched, both the one and the other. And it is not the least debt which we owe unto history that it hath made us acquainted with our dead ancestors; and out of the depth and darkness of the earth, delivered us their memory and fame. In a word, we may gather out of history a policy no less wise than eternal; by the comparison and application of other men's forepassed miseries with our own like errors and ill deservings.[51]

For Ralegh, history offered a sense of human plenitude which, albeit often oppressive, was yet a moral pageant which revealed the workings of a just God and so encouraged readers in a period of increasing autocracy to believe in some intuition of justice beyond man's evident pursuit of worldly power. Its study became a means of criticizing the present on the basis both of accumulated experience and in the light of eternity.

As such, the writing of history was no harmless antiquarianism, a prisoner's way of filling his hours. For Ralegh, the composition of *The History of the World* was a way of evaluating an existence in which the tyranny of a Stuart king denied him any other role. To write history was thus a potentially radical and dangerous activity, and the result was a subversive masterpiece which a monarch, convinced that divine right placed him beyond criticism, tried actively but ineffectually to suppress for being 'too saucy in censuring princes'.[52]

But the rulers of the earth were necessarily Ralegh's principal interest since they were the most conspicuous objects of God's judgements, whether these were recorded in Scripture (which Ralegh regarded as a sacred text largely beyond criticism) or in the works of secular writers. God's judgements 'upon the greater and the greatest have been left to posterity,' he declared, 'first by those happy hands which the Holy Ghost hath guided; and secondly by their virtue who hath gathered the acts and ends of men, mighty and remarkable in the world.'[53] It was such people who, in the end, most clearly and forcefully allowed Ralegh his purpose of justifying the ways of God to man.

The scale of the *History* was encyclopaedic in its ambition to trace man's existence from the time of the creation (in fact the work terminates with the rise of Rome and focuses on biblical and classical narrative) and this involved Ralegh in complex issues of chronology, in the evaluation of contradictory evidence, and a justification of the use of conjecture. The reading he had pursued throughout his life was supplemented and supported by a library of over 500 volumes, some of which were his own while others were borrowed from eminent scholarly contemporaries.

Some of Ralegh's surviving notes – the maps he drew and his attempts to marshal information under alphabetical headings – reveal the methodical way in which he assembled the vast mass of information he required. This suggests, as the tone of the work as a whole tends to confirm, that his was the shaping mind behind the enterprise, the controlling intellect. Ben Jonson was probably exaggerating when he claimed that he himself had drafted the section on the Punic Wars which Ralegh then 'altered and set in his book'.[54] Assistants were used, however, in fields where Ralegh recognized the limitations of his scholarship. Robert Burnhill, his chaplain, for example, offered help with Greek and Hebrew.

The encyclopaedic nature of the *History* also reflected the fact that the book was intended as a work of instruction for Prince Henry who took a keen interest in its progress. This in part accounts for Ralegh's many digressions into such areas as military and naval tactics, geography, historical curiosities such as the existence of the Amazons, duelling, the law and, above all, the nature of kingship and tyranny. These last were all-pervasive themes.

In the *History*, Ralegh showed that the ways of tyranny are the ways of death: death in its spiritual, moral and physical senses. For tyrants themselves: 'Death which hateth and destroyeth man, is believed; God which hath made him and loves him, is always deferred.'[55] Only the imminence of his end brings man a full awareness of the human condition, a liberation from the prison of human vanity. 'It is therefore death alone that can make a man know himself.'[56] Only death can show him the vanity of his efforts – even, as events were now to prove, the efforts of the historian himself.

In the autumn of 1612, Prince Henry was struck down with a fever after swimming in the filthy Thames. As he lay dying it seemed that England's hope – the one young man who might have heeded the lessons of Ralegh's book, stemmed the flood of Stuart tyranny, and returned the country to its martial pride – was to be lost to the nation. When the doctors had exhibited the uselessness of such knowledge as they possessed, the queen begged that a phial of Guiana Balsam be administered to her son.

The Privy Council were reluctant to agree. It was unheard of folly that the heir to the throne should be fed potions from a convicted traitor. Only when it was too late did they finally consent. A measure of the balsam was brought from the Tower accompanied by ominous warnings that it would only work if the prince had not been poisoned. For a moment on 6 November, as the elixir was fed to him, the prince opened his eyes. He sat up – spoke even – and then sank back in death.

Henry's demise was the silencing of his historian. 'It hath pleased God to take that glorious prince out of the world,' he lamented. All indeed had proved to be vanity, even the hope of political reform, even the hope of one day regaining Sherborne which was now given to Carr. Life was a thoroughfare of woe, and the epitaph that closed over the grave was also apt to close *The History of the World*:

> O eloquent, just and mighty death! Whom none could advise, thou hast persuaded; what none hath dared, thou hast done; and whom all the world hath flattered, thou only hast cast out of the world and despised: thou hast drawn together all the far stretched greatness, all the pride, cruelty, and ambition of man, and covered it all over with these two narrow words, *Hic iacet*.[57]

*

If death concluded the *History*, royal absolutism tried to silence it. The influence of Prince Henry had ensured that the work was entered on the Stationers' Register – the list of approved books – in April 1611. The great labour of typesetting began almost at once and continued for almost three years as Ralegh's manuscript advanced towards Book Five. By March 1614, finished copies were ready and the *History* appeared on the bookstalls around St Paul's. Nine months later, agents of the Archbishop of Canterbury began seizing copies. The *History* had come to the attention of the king, and James had been appalled by Ralegh's attitude of criticism towards monarchs. For two years the book lay under the heavy hand of the censor, a move which only served to increase interest and boost sales once the work was freely available again two years later.

The year of the royal embargo on Ralegh's *History*, 1614, showed how strongly opinion had turned against James. Desperate for money, he had reluctantly summoned parliament, but the members proved themselves so hostile that the 'Addled Parliament' as it came to be called passed no legislation whatsoever. This was in large part a result of the wrecking measures instigated by the rising Howard faction at court after the death of Cecil in 1612.

As they gained in confidence and prestige, the Howards began to enrich themselves with spectacular aplomb and to urge on the king a pro-Spanish policy and a relaxation of penal laws against Catholics. The Protestant faction that opposed them included Sir Ralph Winwood who eventually succeeded to the Secretaryship and, more alarmingly for the Howards, Robert Carr and his mentor Sir Thomas Overbury. James handled this rivalry with some skill, then, suddenly, the royal favourite became smitten by Lady Frances Howard, the wife of the third Earl of Essex. Overbury, unaware of how serious the affair would become, played his part in the matter of the lady's seduction.

While this secret crisis was maturing, the king – much to the Howards' intense concern – summoned parliament in the hope they would settle his £680,000 of debt. The Howard faction, knowing how antipathetic the members were to their views, entered on a whispering campaign about corrupt electioneering. A time-wasting committee was set up to investigate the matter but found virtually no evidence of malpractice. In spite of this, the mood of the members became ugly, and when Secretary Winwood suggested the House vote a supply to the king they insisted on discussing impositions, the unpopular taxes levied by the crown on imports.

This was a matter on which the king would not compromise since it affected the basis of his prerogative. Bishop Neile accused the Lower House of sedition and their attention was at once turned on him as the chaotic session hurried ever more furiously towards a threatened dissolution. Finally, when his favourites were viciously attacked, parliament was indeed dissolved. Better, the king decided, to live on gifts, loans and the selling of titles. The dowry from a Spanish marriage would also prove extremely useful. Parliament, he told Count Gondomar, the Spanish ambassador, was a body without a head and it was beyond his comprehension why his predecessors had ever allowed it to come into existence.

Ralegh was appalled by this violent upset to the traditional balance of power. Throughout the later Elizabethan parliaments he had laboured to enhance the queen's influence by striving for harmony between the commons and the crown. The serenity of a nation united was an ideal at the heart of his political thinking. It was also a subject on whose history he was well informed. In a work entitled 'The Prerogative of Parliaments' which he now composed, Ralegh ironically undertook to play the part of the king's good adviser and explain to him how the crown and parliament had, at their best, striven for the common good since the time of the Norman conquest. The Justice of the Peace in the dialogue speaks for Ralegh's anti-absolutist position and sets out to prove 'that the kings of England have never received loss by parliament'.[58] While much of what he has to say is a dry rehearsal of historical precedent, this is occasionally enlivened in the manner of the *History* by the telling parallels drawn between past and present.

Parliament itself, however, was not recalled, and to the problems of royal debt were now added those of royal scandal. Delighted that the beauties of Lady Frances had won Carr to their side, the Howards resolved to make assurance double sure by arranging for Carr's now furious mentor to be sent on a mission abroad. Overbury refused the post and was sent to the Tower. One obstacle was thus removed, but the Howards found more formidable opposition in the figure of Lady Frances's husband, the Earl of Essex.

Resolved that Carr should marry Lady Frances, they sought an annulment of her marriage on the grounds of non-consummation. Two investigations pronounced her *virgo intacta*, a state the lady herself believed she had maintained through the use of drugs administered to her husband, a small wax effigy of whom she had persuaded a witch to make and then pierce through the testicles with a pin. With these preparations for her marriage thus advancing, Lady Frances arranged with her uncle, Ralegh's enemy Lord Henry Howard, that poisoned tarts and jellies should be smuggled into the Tower and there, with the connivance of the new Lieutenant, be offered to the imprisoned Overbury. His corpse, it was said, 'stank intolerably' and, after a year, the smell of scandal reached out beyond the walls of his cell.

Coke was summoned to investigate. While the revelations about Carr, Lady Frances, her uncle and other members of the pro-Spanish faction seriously impaired the reputation of the crown, the anti-Spanish faction began to ingratiate themselves with the king, using for bait the charms of George Villiers, said by some to be the most beautiful young man in England.

The position of the crown became delicate in the extreme and James was obliged to play a double game. While revelations from the Howard scandal pushed him towards the arms of Villiers and Winwood's Protestant faction, the mounting crisis of the royal debt led him to consider once again the possibilities of a marriage between his son Charles and the Infanta. The urbane brilliance of Gondomar, 'the Spanish Machiavelli', encouraged his hopes. James delighted in his company, his intelligence and his master's wealth. To the disgust of the nation, 'the two Diegos' were seen sharing wine from the same bottle and complimenting each other on their elegant Latin. In 1615, the English ambassador in Madrid sent James the terms on which the Spaniards would sell their princess.

These were wholly unacceptable. Any children of the marriage were to be baptized and educated as Catholics but were not thereby to forfeit their right to the throne. The penal laws were to be repealed and Catholics allowed freedom of worship in such places as the

Infanta's public chapel. Aware that these conditions could not be seriously entertained and ever more desperate about his financial position, James began to lend a sympathetic ear to Secretary Winwood's mention of Ralegh's plan that all might yet be put to rights by the fool's gold glittering on the banks of the Orinoco.

CHAPTER SIXTEEN

Last Acts

To revive the idea of Guiana was to revive Ralegh's vision of empire. This he had never abandoned, and the variety of his attempts to gain a foothold in South America shows the versatility of his intelligence and the persistence of his illusion.

The year after his first expedition returned, Laurence Keymis was despatched with orders to find a new route to Manoa and more certain evidence of gold mines. Keymis sailed the coast between the mouths of the Amazon and the Orinoco and, on the advice of the natives, navigated the Essequibo to where he found a lake he could identify with that supposedly belonging to El Dorado. Having satisfied himself this part of his mission was accomplished, Keymis moved on to the confluence of the Orinoco and Caroni rivers, there to assure the natives of Ralegh's continuing interest and to search for gold.

On the most slender evidence, both Keymis and Ralegh himself believed this gold was to be found near the junction of the two rivers as well as around Mount Inconuri which, the Indians had promised, was auriferous. However, what Keymis now actually discovered was a cause for discouragement and – ultimately – for tragedy. Old Topiawari had died, while Berrio, the better to secure his passage to El Dorado, had built the small fort of San Thomé at the mouth of the Caroni. With the enemy thus barring Keymis's way, the precise location of the mines became ever more treacherously a matter of memory. 'We all', he wrote, 'were not without grief to see ourselves thus defeated.'[1]

Such setbacks did not end the venture. Keymis concluded his report with a rousing statement of his faith in the ease with which England could, he believed, establish for herself a South American empire. 'All my thoughts live only in that action.' Fired by such enthusiasm, Leonard Berry was despatched in the *Wat* to explore

[348]

three of the rivers that flow from the Guiana highlands to the Atlantic. Berry, too, believed he could reach the great lake, and he continued to assure the natives of Ralegh's kindly intentions.

Royal support was not forthcoming, however, and Ralegh felt obliged to look for other means. In 1598, he was reported to be assembling thirteen ships for what appears to have been an attempt to transport a body of settlers. These were to be accompanied by a similar number of support vessels supplied by the future king of Sweden. Such involvement suggests that, for Ralegh, the Guiana project remained a firmly Protestant ideal, the lynchpin of his strategy to undermine the Spanish empire in the Americas. The Spaniards themselves were certainly aware of this and, despite the collapse of the 1598 venture, realized the risk it implied. 'Against the present measure', the Council of the Indies declared, 'all possible measures of defence have been resolved upon and put into execution.'[2] Walter Ralegh was ever more clearly identified as a threat to Spanish imperialism.

Spanish control over the Guiana region was uncertain none the less. The Wild Coast between the Orinoco and the Amazon had become the unprofitable fag end of empire. While the Council of the Indies looked to the riches of Mexico and Peru, traders and privateers sailed in unobserved. The Spanish colonists were willing to risk illicit trade with these *rescates*, and where the French and Dutch led, the English followed. Ralegh's *Discovery* in particular had raised expectations about the region and, soon after James had confined him to the Tower, attempts at founding trading colonies were launched by Charles Leigh and (with the encouragement of Prince Henry) by Robert Harcourt. Having taken formal possession for the crown, Harcourt found Ralegh's name still current and respected by the local Indian chiefs.

One of the principal trading interests of these men was tobacco, a commodity with a ready market at home and a keen supplier in the figure of Fernando de Berrio, the son of the old conquistador. Between 1607 and 1612 the region under his command enjoyed a tobacco boom. Almost from the moment of his succession, however, James made clear that Englishmen trading in this area did so at their own risk and, in accordance with the king's foreign policy, the majority of the London tobacco merchants complied with James's wishes when, in 1612, the Spaniards moved to suppress the *rescates* trading around the Orinoco basin.

Others, meanwhile, were looking for gold. These included Ralegh himself. In 1607, he wrote a letter to Cecil from the Tower in which he described how an assayer, 'a man very skilful but poor', had found gold in some previously unregarded rocks brought back from the first Guiana expedition. He then told Cecil how he had 'reserved a little quantity of each to make a second trial'. Ralegh's description of this experiment offers a vivid picture of what went on in his laboratory by the Lieutenant's lodgings:

> I tried the ore of Guiana in this sort. I took of the ore beaten small 12 grains, of filed lead half an ounce, of sandiver a quarter of an ounce. I beat the sandiver small and then mixed all together and put it into a cruset, covering it with another cruset that had a little hole in the top and luted both together. Then I covered all with good coal, and with two pairs of ordinary bellows we blew to it till the lead was consumed, and had of the 12 grains a quarter of a grain of gold.[3]

Careful experiment led to boundless fantasy. In Guiana there was such gold, he told Cecil, of 'an abundance sufficient to please every appetite'. Moreover, it was easy to transport it by river to the coast. In the damp monotony of the Bloody Tower, when scholarship palled, a fettered imagination was spinning fantasies of boundless wealth and personal and national salvation.

The letter continues with a pathetic appeal to be allowed to go and exploit the gold. Hoping to move pity, Ralegh lamented his age and poverty. Hoping to prove his trustworthiness, he declared that 'I am content to both go and come as a private man; that both the charge of the ship be given to another . . . and he have order that if I do but persuade a contrary course to cast me into the sea.' He even offered to raise the finance for the journey himself. The Privy Council showed some interest, but insisted Keymis be sent to reconnoitre. Ralegh demurred. What if Keymis – the only man sure about the whereabouts of the mine mentioned by the Indians – died? Besides, the Spaniards were certain to exploit the treasure if the English did not set up a strongly guarded camp and start extraction at once.

The negotiations fell through, but when, three years later, the great Jacobean traveller and diplomat Sir Thomas Roe took up the project Ralegh contributed £600 to his costs. The expedition also had the active backing of Cecil who, as a master in the labyrinthine twists of foreign policy, was currently negotiating an alliance with France against Spanish interference with Caribbean shipping. Ralegh's Guiana dreams and strategies might be useful in this, and Roe was despatched to discover a route to El Dorado and to report on Spanish defences in the area.

In his absence, Ralegh wrote again to the Lords of the Council. He was now prepared to submit to their earlier conditions and send Keymis on a preliminary reconnoitring expedition if they wished. He was fully aware of the problems. 'And though it be a difficult matter – of exceeding difficulty – for any man to find the same acre of ground again in a country desolate and overgrown, which he hath seen but once, and that sixteen years since (which were hard enough to do upon Salisbury Plain), yet that your Lordships may be satisfied of the truth I am contented to venture all I have, but my reputation, upon Keymis's memory.'⁴ The Council turned the application down.

Roe eventually returned with an extensive knowledge of the Guiana region and the largely settled conviction that El Dorado was a myth. He none the less provided vivid pictures of the vengeance wrought by the Spanish authorities on those *rescates* who were trading with their colonists. Most dangerously of all, he believed San Thomé could be easily captured and held, and that the usefulness of so doing was enhanced by the presence in the region of a renegade Spaniard who could be persuaded to offer his knowledge of gold mines to the English. The Secretary gave this information cautious consideration but, by the end of May 1612, he was dead. A king now deeply in debt began negotiating the *entente* with Spain that might assure him the Infanta's dowry. For Ralegh, there would be no sailing to Guiana now.

Hope seemed momentarily to shine from another quarter. If the king of England was content to parley with Catholic Spain, the Huguenots remained loyal to the Protestant cause. The Prince de Rohan approached James and asked if he might employ Ralegh as an admiral. The king was too wily not to see through this device – the French wanted Ralegh to command a handful of their ships in an attack on the Plate Fleet – and he refused. The interest of the

Huguenots was significant none the less, for Ralegh himself was soon to see them as an important ally.

Meanwhile, with the death of Lord Henry Howard and the waning influence of Carr, the anti-Spanish faction in the court and Privy Council was enjoying a brief ascendancy. Archbishop Abbot of Canterbury urged his influence as spokesman of the nation's Church. The vehemently anti-Spanish Sir Ralph Winwood succeeded to the Secretaryship, and the queen, her loathing of Carr now finding means of expression, allied herself with Villiers and urged Ralegh's case. Villiers himself was personally approached and, on his half-brother and one of his clients receiving a bribe of £750 each, proceeded to urge Ralegh's Guiana plans on the king. Winwood, too, lent his voice, and James listened as both his favourite and his chief minister recommended a plan which might yet save the royal finances and (just as importantly for their purposes) wreck the chances of a Spanish marriage by provoking hostilities along the Orinoco.

On 19 March 1616, the Lieutenant of the Tower received a warrant authorizing Ralegh's release so that, accompanied by a keeper, he might prepare for his voyage. After thirteen years he was free and, as a contemporary noted, 'goes up and down seeing sights and places built or bettered since his imprisonment.'[5] But Ralegh was an old man now, frailer than he cared to admit, and, as he limped past Durham House, so he was moving towards his final role in a Jacobean tragedy of vengeance, political duplicity and greed.

Preparations for the voyage took over a year and, during that time, Ralegh may have lived in a house in Broad Street owned by Bess. He was constantly occupied. A matter of days after his release he gave £500 on account to Phineas Pett for a vessel of 450 tons. In all, the expedition was to cost some £30,000 (over three times the detailed estimate Ralegh had made in 1614) and the raising of such a sum proved difficult.

Privateering was no longer officially countenanced. The City preferred to invest in more substantial initiatives such as the explorations of the Muscovy and East India Companies. The Virginia settlers had had to raise funds by means of a lottery. Ralegh himself, having sold everything he owned, was thrown back on his family and friends. Bess plied her relatives – the Earls of Huntingdon, Pembroke and Arundel – for sureties, and managed thereby to raise £15,000. The £8,000 paid in compensation for Sherborne was called in and Bess sold her own estate in Mitcham for a further £2,500. Such efforts were proof, if it were needed, of her generous, unquestioning love for her husband. Ralegh's efforts proved his devotion to his cause. 'What madness could have made me undertake this journey,' he later wrote, 'but the assurance of the mine; thereby to have done his majesty service, to have bettered my country by the trade, and to have restored my wife and children their states they had lost.'[6]

Wat was to play an important part at his father's side. Aged twenty-two, he was still the reckless, energetic young man who had pinned his girlfriends' presents to his codpiece. Now returned from his period of self-banishment after his duel, he was beside Ralegh whether down in the Deptford dockyards, recruiting men, or dining with the great. His presence could prove a liability to even the most loving of fathers however, and Aubrey (with what degree of accuracy it is impossible to say) tells the story of how, before some great dinner, Ralegh declared: 'Thou art such a quarrelsome, affronting creature that I am ashamed to have such a bear in my company.' Wat promised to behave himself 'and was very demure at least half the dinner time.' Then he opened his mouth:

> 'I this morning, not having the fear of God before my eyes, but by the instigation of the devil, went to a whore. I was very eager of her, kissed and embraced her, and went to enjoy her, but she thrust me from her and vowed I should not: "For your father lay with me but an hour ago." '
>
> Sir Walter, being so strangely surprised and put out of his countenance at so great a table, gives his son a damned blow over the face. His son, as rude as he was, would not strike his father, but strikes over the face the gentleman that sat next to him, and said:
>
> 'Box about. 'Twill come to my father anon.'[7]

Preparations for a fleet of vessels, some of them heavily armed, meanwhile proceeded. Then, suddenly, in the winter of 1616, it

[353]

seemed they might be required for a wholly different purpose from the expedition to Guiana. Count Scarnafissi arrived in England seeking help for Savoy in its war against Spain. James, whose ability to see all sides of a problem frequently led his policies into a labyrinth of indecision and crossed purpose, had already provided money for this cause. Now, considering the possibilities of a leading part in a Protestant alliance, he hinted that more cash might be forthcoming.

The anti-Spanish faction leapt at the chance. The opportunity of an officially sanctioned attack on the Spaniards at Genoa was greatly to be preferred over the hazards of a conflict in Guiana. Ralegh himself, despite his earlier reservations about an alliance with Savoy, was keenly aware of the personal and strategic advantages in the new situation. The Count reported that he was eager 'to attack the Spaniards wherever he could'.[8] Here was the old Elizabethan enthusiasm in the new Jacobean world. This sorted ill with the true temper of the king, however, who, on the receipt of encouraging news from Madrid, broke off negotiations with Savoy as suddenly as he had entered them. Ralegh, he declared, could not be diverted from Guiana and, in the closing days of 1616, the keeper appointed to watch over him was relieved of his duties.

This swing of royal policy in the direction of Spain was a cause for the deepest anxiety. As Count Gondomar had reasonably enquired, how could James with one hand offer friendship to Spain while, with the other, commanding Ralegh and his ships to sail within the confines of the Spanish empire? Guiana, the ambassador boldly asserted, was wholly subject to that empire, and a ruthless policy against foreigners was in force there. If Ralegh's sole purpose was to seek a gold mine, why was he arming so great a number of ships? His aim, surely, was to turn pirate and seize the Plate Fleet or sack the towns along the Spanish Main.

The ambiguity of Ralegh's position was cruelly heightened when, on 26 August, he received his commission. This was not issued to a man 'trusty and well-beloved' – that conventional phrase was scratched out – but to one who was 'under the peril of the law'.[9] Despite the arguments of some lawyers which suggested that the commission was a *de facto* pardon, Ralegh was a condemned traitor still, a man 'civilly dead'.

Under the circumstances, a promise was given that Ralegh would be required to stand surety against injuries inflicted on Spanish subjects and that if this condition were contravened then his life would be forfeit. The burden of responsibility for the Guiana voyage was thus shifted from the crown (who hoped for a percentage of the profits) to a subject who could barely expect to preserve his life. As Ralegh was fully aware, to pass through enemy territory, seize a mine close to the enemy's fort, and then work it and transport its treasures without a fight was an all but impossible task.

In desperation, Ralegh looked for other means to free himself from this net of contradictions. Delicate hints to the French ambassador as to the advantages to his country that might accrue from an offer of help proved largely inconclusive, but Ralegh was also negotiating with the Huguenots, believing that these Protestant allies might be persuaded to his side. He hoped that, in return for a share of the profits from the mine, they would agree 'to displant the Spanish at San Thomé, that the English might after pass up to the mine without offence'.[10] In other words, the Huguenots were to wreak the damage which, if inflicted by Ralegh himself, would cost him his life. Furthermore, the Huguenots were also to provide him on his return with a safe harbour where he could wait while James resolved the delicate issue of whether to side still with Gondomar or fill his empty treasury with the ingots stacked in the holds of Ralegh's fleet.

Even while this last was sailing down the Channel, Ralegh was continuing to negotiate with the Huguenots. A certain Captain Faige returned from a meeting with Montmorency, the Admiral of France, in which he had pressed for ships and the use of a port. The nature of the Admiral's reply is unknown, but Faige was immediately sent back to France and returned with a letter from Montmorency promising he would do his utmost to persuade the boy king Louis's advisers to his side. When, a little later, the chief Catholic power at the French court was murdered, Faige was despatched once again to collect ships and men now fitting out at Dieppe and Le Havre.

Accompanied by Anthony Belle, another of Ralegh's confidants, Faige crossed the Channel a third time, only to ignore his instructions. Instead of reconnoitring with the Huguenots, the two men joined a Mediterranean trading expedition which was subsequently captured by pirates. While Faige himself languished in a Genoese debtors' prison, Belle made his way to Rome. Here he confessed his acquaintance with the infamous Protestant Ralegh and, at his own request, was sent to Madrid. Here he told the whole story of his dealing between the English and the French, producing as evidence of his involvement one of Ralegh's letters along with a copy of his map of Guiana, a copy of his original instructions to Faige, and Montmorency's promise of assistance.

And now, to betrayal by his subordinates was added the treachery of his king. Gondomar had throughout relentlessly opposed an expedition launched into so strategically important a region of his master's empire. James responded that the force of public opinion meant he could do little to stop it. The Privy Council were on Ralegh's side and all the king could do was repeat his earlier assurances – that and hand over to Gondomar an inventory of Ralegh's ships, his armaments, his ports of call and probable dates of arrival.

These details were hurriedly despatched to Madrid and eventually forwarded to Guiana. The *junta*, supine and short of cash, could do little more however. In the end, Ralegh's expedition was compromised less by Spain than by his fellow-countrymen. His only hope now lay in the riches of the supposed mine, and it was essential that his belief in this was not seen to waver. He was, he boasted, 'as confident of finding the Guiana gold as . . . of not missing his way from his dining-room to his bedchamber'.[11] In this mood, Ralegh named the ship that would transport him to his triumph his *Destiny*. It was to be captained by Wat.

But this confidence was all on the surface. The crews Ralegh assembled were, he declared, 'scum' – a thousand wild-eyed men sufficiently desperate to follow him on his fool's errand half-way round the world.[12] There was trouble at Gravesend where a fight broke out and the townspeople drove Ralegh's men ignominiously into the mud of the river. Seven vessels had sailed down the Thames and were joined by three pinnaces at Plymouth. Here, the mayor and corporation, mindful of the old Elizabethan days and Ralegh's popularity in the West, organized a banquet and paid for a drummer to beat a tattoo as the ageing hero walked up the gang-plank to his *Destiny*.

None the less, after leaving port, there were 'continual quarrels and fighting amongst our own company with many dangerous

[356]

hurts'.[13] Ralegh's Orders for the voyage laid down detailed instructions about the discipline and training that were to be enforced on his ships and, mindful of the all-seeing eye of Providence, he took measures to enforce what godliness he could. Blasphemy was to be checked and, 'because no action nor enterprise can prosper (be it by sea or land) without the favour and assistance of Almighty God, the Lord and strength of hosts and armies, you shall not fail to cause divers services to be read in your ship morning and evening.' Before the mounting of the evening watch especially, the crew were to join in 'praising God every night with singing of a psalm'.[14]

But if rigorous Protestant discipline was to give a shape to the long days and nights of the voyage, accidents and ill-management during the delays in getting to the ocean caused continuous frustration. Captain Pennington, putting into the Isle of Wight for provisions, had to send to London to beg Bess for money with which to pay for them. Ralegh had to sell the remains of his own plate to bail out Captains Whitney and Bailey. Then, when the flotilla was preparing to leave Plymouth, a storm drove them back into the port.

A second storm forced them into Falmouth. A third was the cause of one of the pinnaces being lost off the Scillies and of another being obliged to shelter in Bristol while the rest harboured off Kinsale. By now, Ralegh's senior officers knew they could expect no help from the foreign powers their leader had approached. 'We hear of none, neither French nor Dutch, that mean to accompany us.'[15] Meanwhile, for over three weeks, contrary winds kept them anchored off Cork.

Here Ralegh was entertained by Lord Boyle who took the old man round the Lismore estate he had purchased from him in 1602 for a mere £1500. Of this, Ralegh only ever received a third, the down payment. When the rest was due he was a prisoner in the Tower. Boyle himself only managed to secure the estate from the hands of the king by agreeing to pay James the £1000 outstanding. During his occupancy, however, Boyle had made the estate flourish and he could well afford to advance Ralegh money and provide his fleet with generous supplies of beef, beer and a thirty-two-gallon cask of whiskey. By 19 August, the weather had cleared sufficiently for the flotilla to set sail once again.

Ralegh had issued orders against the harassment of enemy

shipping which his officers intended to ignore. A few days out, Captain Bailey approached four French vessels and, claiming their cargoes had been stolen, declared the ships to be prizes. Ralegh, as convinced as Bailey himself that the French captains were privateers, none the less stuck to his resolve, paying sixty-one crowns for one of their pinnaces and for a quantity of oil. Scrupulous conduct was essential, and 'I did not suffer my company to take from them any pennyworth of their goods.'[16]

Such behaviour was 'greatly to the discontentment of my company',[17] and when three of the crew were killed by Spaniards as they were trying to get supplies at Lancerota, Bailey, in angry contempt at Ralegh's refusal to respond, turned his ill-provisioned ship for England. Arrived there, he began a whispering campaign which led 'those that malice him boldly'[18] to affirm that Ralegh had turned pirate. The pro-Spanish faction were jubilant. 'His Majesty is very disposed and determined against Ralegh, and will join the king of Spain in ruining him.'[19] This plan was to be kept secret for the moment, but when a certain Captain Reeks, who had witnessed Ralegh's restraint under the difficult conditions at Lancerota, returned to London to tell the true state of affairs, the Privy Council had Bailey arrested.

Ralegh found a better reception on the island of Gomera. Here, the half-English wife of the Spanish governor sent the crew (many of whom were now ailing) much-needed supplies of fruit. When Ralegh returned this kindness with some suitable luxuries and 'a very excellent picture of Mary Magdalene',[20] more fruit, bread, chicken and fresh water were forthcoming. Finally, the governor himself 'sent his friar aboard my ship', Ralegh recorded in his journal, 'with a letter to D. Diego Sarmiento [i.e. Count Gondomar], ambassador in England, witnessing how noble we had behaved ourselves, and how justly we had dealt with the inhabitants of the island.'[21]

But now the sickness on board the ships swelled rapidly to epidemic proportions. Three days after leaving Gomera, fifty of the crew on the *Destiny* were out of action, and Ralegh decided to make for the Cape Verde Islands, there to recuperate and search for supplies of fresh meat and fruit. As they entered the Brava roads, however, a hurricane fell on them. One of the pinnaces had no watch and careered under the bowsprit of the *Destiny* and sank. 'But the men were saved though better worthy to have been hanged than saved.'

Then, after the hurricane passed, they lay becalmed. The death toll began to mount. Previously, Ralegh's record of the losses among his men had been confined to the margins of his journal. Now, idle and desperate, they were virtually all he had to report. It was a grim litany. 'Friday one of my trumpeters and one other of the cookroom died.' Four days later, 'died Mr John Haward, ensign to Cap. North, and Lieutenant Payton and Mr Hwes fell sick. There also died to our great grief our principal refiner Mr Fowler.' Hwes – 'a very honest and a civil gentleman' – died six days later.

And throughout, the weather remained hostile. 'From Sunday noon to Monday noon we made not above twelve leagues. Observe we could not for the dark weather, a lamentable twenty-four hours it was' – a period made all the worse by the death of 'my honest friend Mr John Talbot, one that had lived with me eleven years in the Tower, an excellent general scholar and a faithful true man as lived. We also lost Mr Gardner and Mr Mordant two very fair conditioned gentlemen, and mine own cook Francis.' Looking out over this alien, infernal waste, and with men lured by the force of his ambition now dropping around him, Ralegh 'observed this day, and so I did before, that the morning rainbow doth not give a fair day as in England.'

Then he fell sick himself – too ill even to write his journal. There is a blank for a fortnight. For twenty dreadful days and nights, sweating so profusely that he often had to change his shirt six times in twenty-four hours, he lay in his cabin, able to eat nothing except 'now and then a stewed prune'. These and will-power enabled him to survive while, with the smell of 'so many sick men' rising about him, the desperate voyage continued. 'From the Cape de Verde Islands,' Keymis recorded, 'before we could seize the coast of America we spent about forty days; which course formerly I have performed in twelve.'[22]

At last, on 14 November, they dropped anchor, and Ralegh sent a barge ashore 'to inquire for my servant, Harry the Indian' who had been with him in the Tower. Harry's brother and two other Indians came to attend him and 'stayed with me that night, offering their services and all they had'. Ralegh then had himself carried ashore and, on 17 November, Harry himself appeared, 'who had almost forgotten his English'. The supplies he brought were welcome none the less: 'A great store of very good cassava bread, with which I fed my company some seven or eight days, and put up a hogshead full for store.' There were other treats as well:

> He brought great plenty of roasted mullets which were very good meat, great store of plantains and pines with divers other sorts of fruit and pistachios, but as yet I durst not adventure to eat of the pine which tempted me exceedingly. But after a day or two being carried ashore and sitting under a tent, I began to eat of the pine, which greatly refreshed me. And after that I fed on the pork of the country, and of the armadillos and began to gather a little strength.[23]

It was time for writing letters home, relaxation, and a moment of pride to share with Bess: 'To tell you I might be here king of the Indians were a vanity; but my name hath lived among them.'[24] Peter Alley, too ill for further service, was entrusted to bear the letter back to London in the ship of one Janssen of Flushing who was found to be anchored nearby. Alley was also entrusted with a report entitled 'News of Sir Walter Ralegh from the River of Calina'. Alley's own poor state of health and his first-hand account of storms and deaths made quite as vivid an impression however – tales of suffering and misfortune from the mouth of the Orinoco.

Ralegh was too weak to lead his expedition up the river itself and, besides, his captains refused to embark on the mission at all unless he remained behind in person to guarantee their retreat. They feared that the sight of Spanish ships would cause anyone else to flee. Ralegh gave his word. 'You shall find me at Punto Gallo, dead or alive. And if you do not find my ships there, you shall find their ashes. For I will fire with the galleons, if it come to extremity: run will I never.'[25]

The explicit instructions Ralegh gave for the conduct of the expedition were clear. Keymis was to lead his men twenty miles downstream from San Thomé and there establish a screen of armed soldiers between the fort and the site of the supposed mine. Only if the Spaniards attacked first was George Ralegh to order his troops to fight. The business of the expedition was to locate the mine and then work it. If Keymis found the mine to be rich, he was to stay there and exploit it. If it were poor or dangerously positioned, he was to take just 'a basket or two' of gold to prove the existence of the mine and save Ralegh's reputation.

In the circumstances, this was all he could do. The leadership of this last and most desperate of ventures would have to be handed to others. These men – a scholarly enthusiast, a relative, and a barely bearded youth – would be responsible for the success of the mission and for Ralegh's own fate. His life and reputation had been given into the hands of others. Ralegh himself meanwhile would await news of the pursuit of the illusory mine off the shores of nearby Trinidad. Omens in the sky greeted his arrival there. A sequence of fifteen rainbows scintillated above him, 'and one of the rainbows brought both ends together at the stern of the ship making a perfect circle which I never saw before nor any man in my ship had seen the like.'[26]

For a fortnight Ralegh lingered off the south west of the island, then, the strain of waiting beginning to tell, he made for Port of Spain to observe the great bitumen lake. He was revisiting old sites, but he was no longer the man who had taken possession of the island for *Ezrabeta Cassipuna Aquerewana*. He was taciturn now and, when he spoke, bitter.

Slowly, the simple, perilous facts began to scratch at the golden fantasy he had nurtured in the Tower. If he spoke about the mine at all, 'it was with far less confidence than formerly'.[27] More than ever the soldiers he had ordered to find the mine were 'scum'. They too were part of the soiling process – a principal part perhaps – and they could be made to bear the burden of his self-doubt, his self-hate. 'They were good for nothing but to eat victuals and were sent to sea on purpose that their friends might be rid of them.'[28]

He span fantasies and thought of tobacco trading. This last idea was abandoned when the Spaniards fired on his boat and it had to turn back. A similar incident drove him from the bitumen lake, but when Ralegh returned to his first anchorage, he captured a canoe with some Spaniards on board that was being rowed by Indians.

The Spaniards escaped, and the captured Indians claimed they spoke no European language.

This was a lie. While three of the men were kept on Ralegh's ship, the rest were sent back to their village under a guard, there to be forced to trade. While they were under escort, however, a member of the guard, thinking he recognized one of the Indians, remembered also that his captive spoke Spanish. The Indian eventually confessed to this and admitted that one of his companions of Ralegh's ship also spoke Spanish. This news was relayed back, and Ralegh questioned his captive. The man had heard, he said – it was only a rumour – that the English had sacked San Thomé, killed the governor and others, and lost two of their own leaders. If this were true, it was the end of everything. Another Indian, confessing a similar story, was brought to the ship and interrogated hour after hour. The details of their stories twisted and changed, and days passed. Then one of the launches from Ralegh's expedition appeared bringing news.

The men told of incompetence and tragedy. Instead of following Ralegh's written instructions and making for the supposed mine, Keymis had led his expedition to within five miles of San Thomé, dropped anchor, and then had his larger boats rowed out to besiege the fort.

There had been answering Spanish gunfire, but at first the English refused to return it. They marched forward with Captain Cosmor in the van. Behind him came the bulk of the musketeers, and behind them the pikes led by Wat. A Spanish advance guard watched them form up and, as the English moved on, so they fired again. An experienced leader might have chosen this moment to retreat, but a young voice, ardent and clear, now rose above the night sounds of the Orinoco jungle: 'Come on my hearts. Here is the mine you must expect; they that look for any other mine are fools.'[29]

Young Wat Ralegh, determined to save his father's honour and ensure the expedition at least one success, rushed forward as he spoke. A bullet killed him instantly. The rest of the company, their blood up now, stormed the walls of the fort, possessed the settlement and razed it to the ground. When, weeks later, the news reached Gondomar, it was said he burst in on the king shouting 'Piratas, piratas, piratas!'[30] Walter Ralegh's death was assured by a pathetic skirmish in a tiny jungle fort. It was a skirmish in which he had played no part and which his orders had tried to prevent.

Keymis was numbed by the stupidity of what he had allowed to happen. For years the mine had been his obsession. He had willed it into existence even as his memories of the Orinoco became ever more imprecise. Now however, as day after day he had been rowed into the dark heart of the forest, so his illusion had been laid bare and the whole elaborate fantasy on which he had reared his hopes collapsed. He could only stare in blank fatuity. For a week he could not even bring himself to write to Ralegh about the death of his son. The pathos and the folly of it all were destroying him.

The morale of his men collapsed with his own. One of them later wrote that Keymis 'trifled up and down some twenty days, keeping us in hope ... but at last we found all his delays mere illusions.'[31] They called him a Machiavel and implied that he had deliberately led them into this dreadful situation for his own purposes. This was unfair and untrue. Keymis was no skilled manipulator of men, that was his trouble. He was an innocent fool trapped in his own ambition, and now the responsibility of it all oppressed him utterly. 'It is ... on your judgement that I rely, whom I hope God will direct for the best', Ralegh had written.[32] But Keymis had killed Ralegh as surely as if he had stuck a knife in his back.

He sent out parties to reconnoitre and they were fired on. More men were killed. Inert hopelessness turned to spite. Keymis took a priest and an Indian woman from out of his prisoners and threatened them with torture. There was a mine, he was sure there was a mine. Why were the Spaniards here if there was no mine? He would make them scream until they confessed where the mine was. He bound a Portuguese lad with ropes and thrashed him until he cried out. Would the town be so poor, the boy whimpered, if it were near to gold?

George Ralegh, roused by family honour, resolved an equally desperate measure. Had not old Topiwari said the border people up-river traded the gold of El Dorado along the length of the Orinoco? He would find them. Taking a handful of men, he made a journey of three hundred miles and discovered nothing. On his return, the sullen company would believe no more stories. All they had got for their efforts were two gold ingots stolen from the Spaniards along with three Negroes, a couple of Indians and several tons of tobacco.

These would have to suffice. When, on their passage back down the river, they passed the point on the bank that lay parallel with Mount Inconuri and Keymis told them of the wealth he believed lay thereabouts, the men merely shrugged their shoulders and rowed on.

The party finally met up again at the mouth of the Orinoco, and Ralegh turned on it the full vengeance of his despair. They should have 'pinched' the governor's servant until he confessed to the existence of the mine. Ralegh took the servant aside and bullied him and shook him until he knew 'the precise way to five or six of the richest mines which the Spaniards have'.[33] Keymis trembled and lied before the onset of such fury. The water was too shallow for them to land, he said. Their party was too weak. A handful of men could not work the mines around Mount Inconuri. To work them and leave them would be merely to show their whereabouts to the Spaniards. But such stammerings melted in the fire of Ralegh's wrath, and Keymis retreated to his cabin. Some moments later, a single shot ran out. A cabin boy was sent to investigate. Keymis said he had been cleaning his pistol, lying again to cover his botched suicide. When the boy had gone, he stuck his dagger through his heart.

Ralegh patched up some excuses to Secretary Winwood who, unknown to him, had died. He too lied to cover his abject failure. His son was dead, his closest friend was dead – both of them victims of the illusion he himself had so desperately followed. Now there remained only Bess, and to her he would not lie:

> I was loth to write because I do not know how to comfort you; and, God knows, I never knew what sorrow meant till now. All that I can say to you is, that you must obey the will of Providence . . . Comfort your heart (dearest Bess), I shall sorrow for us both. I shall sorrow the less because I have not long to sorrow, because not long to live.[34]

He folded the letter and sealed it. Then, wanting to write more, opened it again and wrote a long post-script in his old authentic manner, a passage many sheets long that swung between wounded pride, hatred of the men who had let him down, truths and half-truths he hoped would limit the wrecking of his reputation.

Ralegh's letter was that of a man trying to still the whirlwind, to master the chaos sheering about him. But by now he was barely in control of himself. To those who had followed him, he was a wild, lying old man whose words were nothing and whose promises were lies. He would capture Trinidad, he said. He would lead them back up the Orinoco himself. They would capture the Plate Fleet, he suggested, in words he would later regret. He would go to Virginia. But he could do nothing. Captains Whitney and Wallaston cut their losses and deserted. The fly-boat was sent home 'and in her a rabble of idle rascals, which I know will not spare to wound me; but I care not.'[35]

He decided to sail to Newfoundland with his remaining men. Then he discovered they intended to turn pirate and slip out of the harbour while his own ship was beached for cleaning. He confronted them with their treachery and they, having possession of the weapons, replied that they would under no circumstances return to England. He persuaded them with promises of pardons to cross the Atlantic and make for the pirate base of Killibeg in Ireland. Although, he later boasted, he could have made £100,000 by turning pirate himself, the temptation had no real meaning for him. He had a little tobacco to sell for his and Bess's support, and the still centre in this hurricane of chaos lay in his honour. He had vowed to return, and he would.

Ruined, broken and confused, believing wildly that his only worldly salvation lay in justifying his cause, Ralegh ordered his *Destiny* to make for Plymouth. Here, ten days before his arrival, the king who had betrayed his plans issued a proclamation condemning Ralegh's 'hostile invasion of the town of San Thomé'.[36] He also ordered his arrest at the hands of Sir Lewis Stukely, the vice-admiral and a distant relative of Ralegh's.

Bess was at Plymouth to meet him. 'My brains are broken'[37] he had written in his last, desperate letter, and the truth of this was now apparent to her. For all his resolve on leaving Ireland, the old clarity of purpose had gone. He vacillated, shifting with every wind.

For over a month, he was left unmolested by the government. Fearing public anger if they proceeded too obviously against him, they hoped perhaps he might slip away. Instead, he did nothing. He would not yet consider saving his skin by destroying his name, and by the second week of July Ralegh had finally determined to face his enemies. He set out for London, there to confront his king.

He had ridden barely twenty miles when he encountered Stukely who had orders to escort him back to Plymouth, sell the tobacco in the hold of the *Destiny*, and wait for further instructions. No doubt the government still hoped Ralegh would flee. Stukely did nothing to hinder his movements. Bess, in the anguish of her grief, arranged for a West Country acquaintance – one Captain King – to negotiate with the Huguenots for both her and her husband to be taken to France. Her pleading was enough to persuade Ralegh for a while, but, even as he was being rowed to freedom, he changed his mind and ordered the men to return him to the shore. He would indeed face his king and justify his name.

But he was riding into a trap. Under pressure from Gondomar, James had declared that 'Ralegh's friends and all England shall not save him from the gallows.'[38] The ambassador, whose tour of duty was soon to end, was determined to return to Madrid with a diplomatic triumph. James had rashly promised that Ralegh might be executed by the King of Spain himself if Philip so wished. Gondomar was resolved this promise should be kept. As if Britain were a tributary state, he demanded a meeting of the Privy Council. James, in the face of opposition, declared he would consider all those who crossed him to be traitors. While Stukely was ordered to bring Ralegh to London, James confided in writing that Philip would indeed be welcome to dispose of the English traitor how he liked.

The King of Spain was too wise to accept, but the government in England were determined to assemble such evidence against Ralegh as they could. 'All this was mine and it was taken from me unjustly,' Ralegh supposedly lamented as he rode for a last time by Sherborne.[39] The comment was duly passed on. He was still enfeebled from his voyage, prone to make such careless remarks, and prone as well to take the most unsuitable men into his confidence. These now included the French doctor Manourie whom Stukely had brought with him to attend his charge.

As the party were approaching Salisbury where, they knew, the king was in residence, Ralegh asked Manourie to provide him with an emetic, foolishly exposing to him the fact that he wanted this not for health reasons but so that he could feign sickness and buy time to set his affairs in order, rally his friends and write an appeal to the king. This last would justify his conduct of the voyage to Guiana. He believed, as always, that the force of his prose might change the mind of his monarch. Just in case he should fail, he also agreed that Bess and King should ride to London and there arrange for his transshipment to France.

On arrival in Salisbury, Ralegh feigned sickness with hysterical panache, going so far as to hit his head against a pillar in his imagined delirium. When he knew that Bess and Captain King were safely on the way to London, he threw himself down on the floor, foamed at the mouth, and acted all the parts of lunacy with such conviction that Manourie was called to administer his medicines. Three doctors of Salisbury confirmed the seriousness of Ralegh's condition and, while Manourie's other drugs caused Ralegh's skin to break out in hideous but harmless blisters, the patient sat down to enjoy 'a leg of mutton and three loaves'.[40] that had been smuggled into him by Manourie himself. Then he composed his 'Apology for his Voyage to Guiana'.

The manner of Ralegh's defence was the measure of the man. Using his journal to refute some of the detailed charges levelled against him, he also broadened his defence to place his expedition in the context of similar ventures launched by such great Elizabethans as Sir Francis Drake. He suggested that when 'chance had left them to the trial of their own virtues'[41] they too had failed. Ralegh was also meanly particular in laying special blame on his men. He once again described his crew as 'the very scum of the world, drunkards, blasphemers, and such others as their fathers, brothers, and friends thought it an exceeding good gain to be discharged of.'

The final part of the 'Apology' addressed the king himself. Ralegh tried to refute the charge that the mine was merely his own invention designed to free him from the Tower. No man, he suggested, would sell his all and risk his life for what he knew to be a fool's errand. As for the charge of robbing Spanish territory, Ralegh insisted – as he was now to continue to do – that England had a claim to the country and that James's encouragement of his expedition seemed to prove this. If the region did indeed belong to Spain, then exploiting the goldmine would have been just as illegal as sacking the town. 'Either the country is the king's or is not the king's.' It was for James to show his hand.

He would do no such thing. Instead, he ordered Stukely to take

Ralegh to London at once. The royal mood was clear, and royal vengeance would only be a matter of time. Ralegh, in desperation, tried to bribe Stukely and Manourie to help him escape. He also made overtures to the new French ambassador and, most foolishly of all, allowed Bess and Captain King to continue their negotiations for his flight with two of his former servants who betrayed his plans even as they were being laid. When Stukely came to hear of these, the authorities agreed that, rather than arresting him there and then, Ralegh should be given enough rope to hang himself. His plans for liberty condemned him to a certain death.

They also showed how desperate a man he had become and how, under this intense strain, cunning and even natural caution had left him. Almost as if he wished to destroy himself, Ralegh unnecessarily revealed the details of his plans to Stukely who listened with interest and even volunteered to accompany him. During the night of 9 August, the two men made their way down the river to where Captain King and a couple of wherries were waiting for Ralegh, now ludicrously disguised in a false beard. Seeking to confirm his treacherous appearance of friendship, Stukely asked 'whether thus far he had not distinguished himself as an honest man.' King muttered that he hoped 'he would continue so'.[42] He was aware that they were being trailed by a larger vessel.

Ralegh, becoming suspicious and fearful himself, asked the crew of his boat if they would continue rowing even if they were asked to stop in the king's name. They gave an ambiguous answer and, by the time they had started rowing again, the tide had begun to turn. Since it was now impossible to reach Gravesend, they would go back to Greenwich. As the boat turned, a voice from the vessel that had been trailing them ordered them to stop in the name of the king. Ralegh hurriedly passed some valuables to Stukely and received his treacherous embrace. Only after his arrest at Greenwich did he realize how completely his kinsman had betrayed him. And in this moment of defeat he stood on his dignity as a gentleman. He made no protest, showed no anger. He merely turned and said: 'Sir Lewis, these actions will not turn out to your credit.'[43] That at least was a shrewd observation. Some short while later, having been accused of clipping coin, Sir 'Judas' Stukely was to die a lonely lunatic on Lundy Island, a man hated by the entire nation for his betrayal of Ralegh.

Meanwhile, early on the morning of 10 August, Ralegh himself was once again a prisoner in the Tower.

They took from him the few treasures he had hoped to smuggle abroad. There was £50 in coin, two ingots of gold and a quantity of jewellery – an easily portable form of wealth – that suggested the magnificence Ralegh had once been used to: a gold chain and gold buttons set with diamond chips, another jewel mounted with a ruby, a diamond ring. Other items were more personal. Ralegh had taken with him his silver seal with its proud roebuck crest. Another seal, cut with a figure of Neptune, was surmounted with a sample of Guiana ore. Charts and descriptions of Guiana itself suggested he still hoped to encourage others to investigate the area, while a diamond ring, given to him by Elizabeth, was the only memento of the days of his true greatness.

For the authorities, there remained the problem of how to secure Ralegh's death by something that would appear like a due process of law. Bess was imprisoned in the Tower in the effort to coerce her, but she proved resolute. Ralegh's gaoler tried ineffectively to insinuate himself into his prisoner's confidence. The king set up a commission to advise him on the best means of proceeding. This deliberated for many weeks, but when, on 15 October, a letter from the King of Spain was received sparing Ralegh from execution in Madrid but urging, in the light of the delicate negotiations for a marriage, that his death in London would be gratifying to his Most Catholic Majesty, matters were speeded up.

Three days after the receipt of the letter, Coke gave his opinion that since Ralegh was still technically a man 'civilly dead', he could not be tried for events that had occurred in Guiana. The king should therefore publish a narrative of his 'late crimes and offences'[44] to persuade public opinion, while, at the same time, issuing a warrant for his execution on the old charges of high treason. The body of the commission recommended there should be a hearing before the Privy Council and a packed selection of judges and others great and good.

James rejected this last proposal. He knew only too well the danger of having Ralegh appear as a witness in his own defence 'as was found by experiment at the arraignment at Winchester where, by his wit, he turned the hatred of men into compassion for him.'[45]

Such a turn of events must be avoided this time at all costs. Many in the nation from the queen down were loud in Ralegh's support, and besides, a letter Ralegh had written from the Tower showed how profoundly and with what skill he could defend himself. To allow him to speak now would be to put hopes of the Infanta's dowry in jeopardy. A safer means of destroying him must be found.

In the end, the king suggested the plan that was adopted. There would be a final hearing before a small group of those commissioners who had already questioned him. This would be followed by an immediate execution. To reassure himself of success, James signed Ralegh's death-warrant in advance of the hearing while, at the same time, arranging for a *Declaration* of his offences to be drawn up – a document which, James hoped, would silence public opinion. Then, on 22 October, Ralegh was brought, hugger-mugger, before his accusers to be arraigned for crimes committed before, during and after his last voyage.

He was charged by the Attorney-General with four 'impostures': that the mine was a deliberate fabrication, that 'he proposed to set war' between England and Spain, that he had 'abandoned and put in danger all his company', and that his behaviour towards the king had been 'unfaithful'.[46] To these charges the Solicitor-General added that Ralegh intended to flee from justice and that his behaviour at Salisbury had been a fraud intended to deceive the king and state.

The fragmentary record of the hearing suggests that Ralegh, despite his recent illness, answered his accusers with elegance and courage. The king, he declared, had never believed him guilty of treason and he cited Justice Gaudy's death-bed comment that in the trial of 1603 'the justice of England was never so degraded and injured'.[47] Ralegh affirmed that his belief in the mine was genuine by citing the elaborate preparations he had made to exploit it. He had patently not abandoned his men, for they had deserted him. The accusation of trying to foment war and of 'unfaithful carriage' to the king he merely denied. As to his feigning madness, Ralegh excused himself on the grounds that the Biblical David had acted in a similar manner to save his skin. He had not sought to escape, he declared, 'till his arrest by Sir Lewis Stukely'. Finally, in the matter of his behaviour towards James, 'he said that his confidence in the king deceived, but denieth that he used any other ill speeches.'[48]

[370]

When the hearing was over, it was considered necessary that Ralegh be brought before a sessions of the King's Bench in order that his death sentence should have a greater appearance of validity. On 28 October, he was driven from the Tower to Westminster Hall, a bedraggled and apparently broken man. A servant was shocked by the sight of his uncombed hair. 'Let them kem it that are to have it,' he replied and, in this mood of gallows humour, added: 'Dost thou know, Peter, of any plaster that will set a man's head on again, when it is off?'[49]

But while Ralegh stood by irony, his judges were determined to assert the majesty of the law. They were not without an awareness of the tragedy to be inflicted on their dishevelled prisoner, and Mr Attorney-General Yelverton's words were a painful combination of the judicially impartial and the humanly apt:

> My Lords, Sir Walter Ralegh, the prisoner at the bar, was fifteen years since convicted of high treason, by him committed against the person of his Majesty and the state of this kingdom, and then received the judgement of death, to be hanged, drawn, and quartered. His Majesty, of his abundant grace hath been pleased to show mercy on him till now that justice calls for execution. Sir Walter Ralegh hath been a statesman, and a man who in regard of his parts and quality is to be pitied. He hath been a star at which the world gazed; but stars may fall, nay they must fall when they trouble the sphere wherein they abide. It is therefore his Majesty's pleasure now to call for the execution of the former judgement, and now I require order for the same.[50]

The record of the 1603 conviction and judgement was then read out, and Ralegh was asked what he could say in his own defence.

'My Lords, my voice is grown weak by reason of my late sickness, and an ague which I now have, for I was now brought hither out of it.'

'Sir Walter,' the Lord Chief Justice responded, 'your voice is audible enough.'

Ralegh tried to argue the point that may have been made to him by Francis Bacon prior to his sailing to Guiana, namely that the granting of a commission such as his was a *de facto* pardon. But this was not an argument the bench would accept. The Lord Chief Justice interrupted to explain that in the case of treason a defendant could not be implicitly pardoned. It was necessary that 'words of a special nature' make the pardon explicit. These words had not been used.

Ralegh had employed the only substantial legal argument he had, and had lost. He could now only throw himself on the mercy of the king. He expressed the vain hope that 'he will be pleased to take commiseration on me', and began to suggest that grounds for this lay in the obvious faults of the trial in 1603.

The Lord Chief Justice again declared his opinion. 'Sir Walter Ralegh, you must remember yourself; you had an honourable trial, and so were justly convicted.'

The might of the law veiled its own injustice, and Walter Ralegh was a condemned man.

The judge went on to extol the mercy of a king who had refused to execute his prisoner 'fifteen years since', and to deliver his opinion that 'new offences have stirred up his Majesty's justice'. Yet, even while these mendacious technicalities were stifling hope, the judge recognized the worth of the man standing before him. His reputation and his *History*, mute and powerless witnesses in this terrible court, were achievements to honour all the same. The lawyers who had examined the proceedings of 1603 had recommended something be said to mitigate the spiritual insults hurled at Ralegh from the bench, and the judge felt it behoved him to show what justice he could.

'I know you have been valiant and wise,' he began, 'and I doubt not but you retain both these virtues, for now you have occasion to use them. Your faith hath heretofore been questioned, but I am resolved you are a good Christian, for your book which is an admirable work, doth testify as much.'

Having said this, the Lord Chief Justice passed sentence in the normal, impersonal way:

'Execution is granted.'

The court rose.

The execution was to take place the following morning in Old Palace Yard, Westminster. To avoid drawing attention to the prisoner, he was not returned to the Tower but housed overnight in the Abbey gatehouse. Here he would have to make his peace with the world and prepare for his life's last scene.

Bess came to hold her living husband for a final time. The Lords, she told him, had granted her the disposing of his body.

'It is well, Bess, that thou mayst dispose of it dead, that hadst not always the disposing of it when it was alive.'[51]

After midnight she left, and in the chilly silence, as her warmth and perfume faded from his clothes, he thought of her as he had when he was a younger man:

> Her eyes he would should be of light,
> A violet breath and lips of jelly,
> Her hair not black, nor over bright,
> And of the softest down her belly.[52]

Some means had to be found of joining that exultation to what he was experiencing now. The poem had, in the deepest sense, remained unfinished for half a lifetime. Its last stanza lacked a final couplet. He read it over again and added what was necessary:

> Even such is Time which takes in trust
> Our youth, our joys and all we have,
> And pays us but with age and dust,
> Who in the dark and silent grave
> When we have wandered all our ways
> Shuts up the story of our days.
> > And from which earth and grave and dust
> > The Lord shall raise me up I trust.[53]

That trust was absolute, as certain as his death. It gave him a clarity of purpose far beyond that of those people who, drawn by love and duty, now came to visit him. His nearness to God restored his humanity, and men of less strong conviction were concerned by his seeming lightness. Charles Thynne, a friend from the Sherborne days, counselled him directly:

'Sir, take heed you go not too much upon the brave hand, for your enemies will take exception to that.'[54]

'Good Charles,' he replied, 'give me leave to be merry, for this is the last merriment that ever I shall have in this world. But when I come to the sad part, thou shalt see, I will look on it like a man.'

Fussy and ambitious Dean Tounson, sent to Ralegh for his

spiritual comfort, was disturbed by this Christian cheerfulness. He sensed spiritual peril, and warned Ralegh 'that the dear servants of God, in better causes than his, had shrunk back and trembled a little.'[55] Ralegh, thanking God, replied that he did not fear death itself and preferred, indeed, to die by the axe than of some fever. Tounson admonished him and said that pagans could die as bravely. He was impressed by Ralegh's reply. 'He answered that he was persuaded that no man that knew God and feared him could die with cheerfulness and courage except he were assured of the love and favour of God unto him; that other men might make shows outwardly, but they felt no joy within.'

Communion was celebrated, and Ralegh cheerfully declared he 'hoped to persuade the world that he died an innocent man.' Tounson was again shocked. This looked like 'an oblique taxing of the justice of the realm'. Ralegh's reply suggested how he viewed man's justice now – the justice meted out the day before in Westminster Hall. 'He confessed justice had been done,' Tounson wrote, 'and by course of law he must die; but yet, I should give him leave, he said, to stand upon his innocency in the fact.' Ralegh then 'ate his breakfast heartily, and took tobacco, and made no more of his death than if he had been to take a journey.'

He dressed himself magnificently for his last appearance before the world. He wore a hair-coloured satin doublet with a black embroidered waistcoat beneath it and a pair of black breeches in cut taffeta. His silk stockings were ash coloured. He wore a hat over his embroidered nightcap and wrapped himself in a black velvet cloak. Imperious to the last, he was also convivial as never before. He was brought a cup of sack and, being asked how he liked it, replied that 'it was a good drink if a man might tarry by it.'[56] By such pleasantries he would be remembered. In the last hour of his life he was scrupulous about his image, careful to act his part.

Then the time came for the last scene. Old Palace Yard was crowded. King James had hoped the pageantry of the Lord Mayor's show being held that morning would keep people away, but the drama and importance of Ralegh's execution were such that few could be diverted by bread and circuses. The people knew – and their presence there assured – that this stately murder of an innocent man was a moment which focused all their lives, all their criticism of the house of Stuart. The death of this man would change opinions, change lives. In so doing, it would also help change history.

There in the crowd, three unregarded young men in particular watched the grim pageant: John Eliot, John Hampden, John Pym. Serious, intelligent and idealistic, they were youths whose passion for justice would not pale in comfortable middle age. They were watching the death of the last Elizabethan and they sensed what it symbolized for those who believed in parliament and the law. John Eliot especially, who was himself to die for this cause, drew strength from Ralegh's courage. 'All preparations that are terrible were presented to his eye,' he recalled. 'Guards and officers were about him, the scaffold and the executioner, the axe and the more cruel expectation of his enemies. And what did all this work on the resolution of our Ralegh? Made it an impression of weak fear to distract his reason?' Of course not. 'Nothing so little did that great soul suffer.'[57] He was 'our Ralegh' now.

Tounson and two sheriffs led him up to the scaffold and comedy undercut high drama. They met Sir Hugh Beeston who had gone to some pains to get himself a letter guaranteeing him a good place near the block. When he handed the letter to one of the sheriffs, however, the man found he had left his glasses at home. He put the letter in his pocket and Sir Hugh was elbowed aside.

'I know not what shift you make,' Ralegh declared, 'but I am sure of a place.'[58]

He had been made breathless by the buffeting of the crowd and it took him a little time to recapture his spirits on the scaffold and to greet the company of lords gathered there. Other peers were crowded in a window nearby. There was a call for silence. Ralegh doffed his hat. He asked his audience to bear with him. He was still weak with ague. None the less, 'I thank God of his infinite goodness that he hath vouche-safed to me to die in the light, in the sight of so honourable an assembly, and not in darkness.'[59]

The Lords in the window called out that they could not hear.

'I will strain my voice, for I would willingly have your honours hear me.'

The Lords Arundel, Notttingham and Doncaster thought they had better come up on to the scaffold. They were not going to miss this, and there was a round of hearty handshaking. Ralegh began again:

'As I said, I thank God heartily that he hath brought me into the light to die, and hath not suffered me to die in the dark prison of the Tower, where I have suffered so much adversity and a long sickness. And I thank God that my fever hath not taken me at this time, as I prayed God it might not.'

The same God would witness to the truth of what he was now to say. A number of charges had been made against him and he was concerned in these last minutes to rebuff them in great detail. He denied that he had entertained any idea of colluding with France in the matter of Guiana. He refuted the notion that he had spoken 'dishonourably and disloyally' of the king. He admitted he had tried to escape Stukely's custody since 'I desired to save my life'. None the less, he refused vehemently to admit any of the charges Stukely himself had laid on him.

Then he looked down at his notes and, realizing perhaps that the crowd was getting restless, begged them for a little more time. There were the various accusations that had been levied against his expedition to Guiana to clear, and he called Lord Arundel to witness that he had vowed before parting to return. Then he craved a little time 'to speak of one thing more'. The rumour of his callous behaviour at the death of Essex when, it was said, he had sat puffing his pipe and relishing the destruction of an enemy, was something he was particularly concerned to rebuff. When that was done and he was satisfied he had cleared his name before men, Ralegh came to his conclusion:

And now I entreat you to join with me in prayer, that the great God in Heaven, whom I have grievously offended, being a great sinner of a long time and in many kinds, my whole course a course of vanity, a seafaring man, a soldier, and a courtier – the temptations of the least of these were able to overthrow a good mind and a good man; that God, I say, will forgive me, and that he will receive me into everlasting life. So I take my leave of you all, making my peace with God.[60]

The scaffold was cleared for the high solemnity of his death. Ralegh put aside his hat and his nightcap. He gave money to the attendants and bade leave of the peers. Then he took off his gown and his doublet and asked the headsman to show him the axe. The man delayed.

'I prithee, let me see it. Dost thou think I am afraid of it?'

He ran his finger along the edge.

'This is a sharp medicine,' he said, turning to the sheriff, 'but it is a physician that will cure all my diseases.'

He begged the few remaining functionaries on the scaffold to pray for him. The executioner asked his forgiveness. He gave it and laid his head down on the block. There was a murmuring of disapproval. He was facing west. A good Christian should die facing east, the direction from which his saviour would return.

Ralegh got up, declaring, 'So the heart be right, it is no great matter which way the head lieth.'

He would please them, though, and he knelt down on the other side of the block and began to pray. He had refused a blindfold, and he had arranged that he would be ready for the axe when he stretched out his hands. He did so once, twice. The headsman delayed.

'Strike, man, strike!'

The axe fell.

And fell again.

Ralegh's severed head was shown on each side of the scaffold.

The people were heard to mutter. 'We have not such another head to be cut off!'[61]

That evening, Bess took the head home in a red leather bag. Later, she had it embalmed and kept it in a cupboard to show her husband's admirers. 'This was the news a week since,' wrote Dean Tounson, 'but it is now blown over, and he is almost forgotten.'[62]

Ralegh's *History of the World* and Alexander the Great

While the scale of the *History* forbids comprehensive analysis, Ralegh's chapter 'Of Alexander the Great' in the fourth book shows many of the techniques he employed and the purposes he was aiming at, the deftly critical manipulation of parallels between the ancient world and Stuart England especially.

Alexander is first presented as the ideal young king: strong, virile and just. He is a ruler as fair with his subjects as he is competent with his army. Having secured his throne and won the love of his people 'by freeing them from all exactions, and bodily slavery, other than their service in his wars', he stirs the martial pride of his subjects by leading them against the enemy Persians.

Contemporary readers may have felt the implied contrast to the cowardly James and his appeasement with Spain (by Book Four this technique of implicit comparison has been well established) but they would also have noted how the portrait of Alexander is woven into a wider moral pattern. The weaknesses of the great hero are evident, early on. Before moving against Persia, Alexander has slaughtered or humiliated those he considers dangerous, 'thinking by unjust cruelty to assure all things, both in the present and future'.

This, Ralegh suggests, is the ultimately self-defeating behaviour of a tyrant, an over-weaning pride inevitably subject to divine punishment. 'The end of all fell out contrary to the policy which his ambition had commended unto him, though agreeing very well with the justice of God; for all that he had planted, was soon after withered, and rooted up; those, whom he most trusted, were the most traitorous; his mother, friends, and children, fell by such another merciless sword as his own, and all manner of confusion followed his dead body to the grave, and left him there.'

Alexander's victory over the effeminate Persians is that of a virile nation over the self-indulgent. The followers of Darius, like the followers of the Stuart court, are 'men that took more care how to embroider with gold and silver their upper garments, as if they attended the invasion but of the sunbeams, than they did to arm themselves with iron and steel against the sharp pike, swords, and darts of the hardy Macedonians.'

Alexander's victory however, carefully described by Ralegh the military historian, is no greatly glorious matter. The personal, pragmatic tone of his comments suggests at once accuracy of research and a refusal to be blinded by worldly spectacle. 'It seems to me', he wrote, 'that the victory thus gotten was exceeding easy, and that the twenty thousand Persian footmen, said to be slain, were rather killed in the back, in running away, than hurt in the bosoms by resisting.' Such military observation (like Ralegh's many allusions to contemporary European history a matter of much interest to Prince Henry) is followed by 'a digression concerning the defence of hard passages'. This is an argument to prove that no general should rely simply on the lie of the land for his defence, and its insertion is a well-argued passage typical of the *History*'s techniques and purposes.

So too is a famous passage in which Ralegh apostrophizes the empire-building Alexander as the hero whose energies are the expression of God's providential plan for the world. This paragraph is often quoted as an example of Ralegh's praise of great men, but this is to deny the *History*'s continuous exposure of human vanity:

> For so much hath the spirit of some one man excelled, as it hath undertaken and effected the alteration of the greatest states and commonwealths, the erection of monarchies, the conquest of kingdoms and empires, guided handfuls of men against multitudes of equal bodily strength, contrived victories beyond all hope and discourse of reason, converted the fearful passions of his own followers into magnanimity, and the valour of his enemies into cowardice; such spirits have been stirred up in sundry

[379]

ages of the world, and in divers parts thereof, to erect and cast down again, to establish and to destroy, and to bring all things, persons and states; to the same certain ends, which the infinite spirit of the Universal, piercing, moving, and governing all things hath ordained. Certainly the things that this king did were marvellous, and would hardly have been undertaken by any man else: and though his father determined to have invaded the lesser Asia it is like enough that he would have contented himself with some part thereof, and not have discovered the river of Indus, as this man did. The swift course of victory, wherewith he ran over so large a portion of the world, in so short a space, may justly be imputed unto this: that he was never encountered by an equal spirit, concurring with equal power against him. Hereby it came to pass that his actions being limited by no greater opposition, than desert places, and the mere length of tedious journeys could make, were like the Colossus of Rhodes, not so much to be admired for workmanship, though therein also praiseworthy, as for the huge bulk.[1]

The full effect of the passage certainly shows how 'great men' work out in their destinies the will of God, yet Ralegh is careful to show that in Alexander's case this is no cause for pride. His mighty successes have been won against supine enemies. The moral judgement is ironic and exact. The military historian is at one with the theologian.

Darius, meanwhile, 'who had been accustomed to nothing so much as to his own praises, and to nothing so little as to hear truth', reveals himself as the archetypal tyrant condemning men to arbitrary death, refusing advice and so proving that, 'the infinite wisdom of God does not work always in one and the same way, but very often in the alteration of kingdoms and estates, by taking understanding from the governors, so they can neither give nor discern counsels.' The parallels with James are evident, but it is Alexander himself who now begins to show this pattern of tyrannical behaviour at its most terrible. He reveals first his cruelty and then his delusions of grandeur. The High Priest of Jerusalem, issuing 'out of the city covered with his pontifical robes', convinces him that he is the mighty conqueror mentioned in the prophecies of Daniel. The sovereign authority of Scripture clearly indicates that he is thus an embodiment of evil.

Such folly is compounded when Alexander reaches the temple of Jupiter Amon and insists on being recognized as a deity. Ralegh makes his allusions to the vain and homosexual court of James I clear and biting. 'When Alexander came near the place, he sent some of his parasites before him to practise the priests attending the oracle, that their answer might be given in all things, agreeable to his mad ambition, who affected to the title of Jupiter's son.'

Disillusioned contemporary readers – that freemasonry of the sub-text trained to see parallels between the ancient world and their own – would have recalled such disturbing moments as James's address to his parliament of 1610 when, delighting in a pedantic display of absolutism, he told the members: 'Kings are justly called gods for that they exercise a manner of resemblance of divine power upon earth, for if you will consider the attributes to God you shall see how they agree in the person of a king. God hath power to create or destroy, make or unmake, at his pleasure; to give life or send death, to judge all and to be judged not accountable to none; to raise low things and to make high things low at his pleasure; and to God are both soul and body due. And the like power hath kings.'[2] With analogies such as these established, the working out of God's justice on Alexander could be seen as a foretaste of the Almighty's view of the Stuarts.

These satiric analogies are drawn tighter when Alexander enters on the rich lands of Babylon, Susa and Persepolis. The once temperate and prudent prince declines to become 'a lover of wine, of his own flattery, and of extreme cruelty'. Revelling in voluptuous pleasure like the bibulous James, he becomes the perfect image of a tyrant.

> Now as Alexander had begun to change his conditions after the taking of Persepolis: so at this time his prosperity had so much over-wrought his virtue, as he accounted clemency to be but baseness, and the temperance which he had used all this lifetime, but a poor and dejected humour, rather becoming the instructors of his youth, than the condition and state of so mighty a king,

as the world could not equal. For he persuaded himself that he now represented the greatness of the gods; he was pleased that those that come before him, should fall to the ground and adore him; he ware the robes and garments of the Persians, and commanded that his nobility should do the like; he entertained his court, and his camp, the same shameless rabble of courtesans, and sodomitical eunuchs, that Darius had done, and imitated in all things the proud, voluptuous, and detested manners of the Persians, whom he had vanquished.[3]

A Jacobean reader would inevitably recall the debauchery of Whitehall, a degree of self-indulgence 'unpractised', as a contemporary wrote, 'by the most luxurious tyrants'.[4] The same writer went on to describe what he called 'the vanity of ante-suppers', an innovation of James Hay's, 'the manner of which was, to have the board covered, at the first entrance of the guests, with dishes, as high as a tall man could well reach, filled with the choicest and dearest viands sea or land could afford: and all this once seen, and having feasted the eyes of the invited, was in a manner thrown away, and fresh set on to the same height, having only this advantage of the other, that it was hot.'

The writer then adds an extraordinary detail to this Trimalchian debauch. 'I cannot forget one of the attendants of the king, that at a feast, made by this monster in excess, eat to his single share a whole pie, reckoned to my lord at ten pounds, being composed of ambergris, magisterial of pearl, musk, etc.' It was amid scenes like this that his opponents could imagine James, the drunken advocate of divine right, condemning men like Ralegh to unjust imprisonment, revelling in the prostrate adoration of his flatterers, and dandling with the codpieces of his ' sodomitical eunuchs'.

The culmination of this grotesque corruption is Alexander's murder of Calisthenes who had declared that a man might only be deified after his death. ' Alexander', Ralegh wrote, 'stood behind a partition and heard all that was spoken, waiting but an opportunity to be revenged on Calisthenes, who being a man of free speech, honest, learned, and a lover of the king's honour, was yet soon after tormented to death, not for that he had betrayed the king to others, but because he never would condescend to betray the king to himself, as all his detestable flatterers did.'

In passages such as these, righteous indignation over events in the past becomes a means of exciting opposition in the present. Irony becomes political awareness, and the oppressed subjects of an absolute state must take such comfort as they can when the 'cruel and ungrateful traitor Antipater' probably (Ralegh is deliberately ambiguous on this dangerous issue) arranges for the poisoning of the king's wine. Another generation – the generation of Cromwell, Milton and Pym who revered Ralegh's *History* for its lessons – were eventually to see regicide as the only solution to the tyranny of the Stuarts. However, Ralegh's picture of Antipater's actions clearly reveals that his own thoughts could not willingly extend so far.

Notes and References

PREFACE

1. Ralegh, *History of the World*, Book I, ch. ii, in *Works*, ed. Oldys and Birch, vol. I, p. 53; hereafter cited as *Works*.

THE GENTLEMEN OF THE WEST

1. *Best's Farming Book*, p. 6, quoted in Mildred Campbell, *The English Yeoman*, pp. 199–200.
2. v. A.H. Slee, 'Braunton and its Manors', *Transactions of the Devon Association*, 1941, p. 195–6; quoted in A.L. Rowse, *The Elizabethan Renaissance*, p. 172.
3. John Hooker, *Description of the City of Exeter*, quoted in Anthony Fletcher, *Tudor Rebellions*, p. 45.
4. Ibid., pp. 46–7.
5. PRO HCA. Libels, etc., file 18, no. 208. This and the ensuing quotations are taken in modernized form from the transcriptions in Michael J.G. Stanford, 'The Raleghs Take to the Sea', *Mariner's Mirror*, 48, no. 1 (Feb. 1962), 18–35.
6. PRO *SP Dom, Mary*, vol. III, no. 10, f. 34, quoted in Stanford, loc. cit., p. 32.
7. Quotation from Hooker's account in Fox's *Acts and Monuments* (ed. 1583), 2050–52.
8. Cited from R.G. Marsden, *Select Pleas in the Court of Admiralty* (1897), vol. II, pp. 31–4, in Stanford, loc. cit., p. 26.
9. PRO *SP Dom, Mary*, vol XII, no. 67, 18 April 1558, quoted in Stanford, 'A History of the Ralegh Family of Fardel and Budleigh in the Early Tudor Period', p. 229.
10. v. Neville Williams, *The Sea Dogs*, p. 63.
11. Richard Hakluyt, *Principal Navigations*, vol. II, p. 204.
12. Cited in Kenneth R. Andrews, *Trade, Plunder and Settlement*, p. 68.
13. Humphrey Gilbert, 'Petition from Humphrey Gilbert to the Queen', quoted in *The Voyages and Colonising Enterprises of Sir Humphrey Gilbert*, ed. D.B. Quinn, vol. I, p. 105; hereafter cited as Gilbert, *Voyages*, vols I and II.
14. Gilbert, 'A Discourse of a Discovery for a new Passage to Cataia', ibid., vol. I, p. 134.
15. Ibid., p. 160.
16. John Camden, *History of the Reign of Elizabeth* (ed. and trans. 1675), p. 82.
17. Ibid., quoted in Rowse, *Sir Richard Grenville of the 'Revenge'*, p. 63.

18. v. Robert Lacey, *Sir Walter Ralegh*, p. 22.
19. v. Adamson and Folland, *The Shepherd of the Ocean*, p. 36; hereafter cited as Adamson and Folland.
20. Theodore Agrippa D'Aubigne, *Histoire Universelle*, III, 130, quoted in J.W. Thompson, *The Wars of Religion in France*, p. 224.
21. These and the following passages on the state of France are cited from B.M. Titus, B. ii, 468, in Thompson, op. cit., pp. 227–8.
22. v. Adamson and Folland, p. 43.
23. Ibid.
24. Ibid., p. 41.
25. Ibid., p. 43.
26. Ralegh, *Works*, vol. II, p. 53.

EDUCATION

1. Anthony à Wood, *Athenae Oxoniensis*, ed. P. Bliss (1815), vol. II, col. 235.
2. Ralegh, *Works*, vol. II, p. xlv.
3. v. Adamson and Folland, p. 26.
4. John Aubrey, *Brief Lives*, ed. Andrew Clark, vol. II, p. 7; hereafter cited as Aubrey.
5. Francis Bacon, *Apothogems New and Old* (1625), no. 269, quoted in Norman Lloyd Williams, *Sir Walter Ralegh*, p. 9; hereafter cited as Lloyd Williams.
6. Middlesex County Records, 19 December 1577, quoted in Lloyd Williams, p. 16.
7. Aubrey, pp. 183–4.
8. 'Walter Ralegh of the Middle Temple, in Commendation of "The Steel Glass" ', ll. 11–12.
9. Gilbert, 'Queen Elizabeth's Academy'; quotations are taken in modernized form from the text established by F.J. Furnivall in *E.E.T.S.*, extra series no. 8, 1869, pp. 1–12.
10. John Camden, *Annals* (1635), p. 394.
11. v., for example, D. Wilson, *Sweet Robin: A Biography of Robert, Earl of Leicester*, p. 95, for comments by Spanish and Italian observers.
12. Hakluyt, *Principal Navigations*, vol. X, p. 8.
13. The phrase is Hakluyt's, v. Andrews, op. cit., p. 121.
14. PRO, *SP* 12/44, no. 13, quoted in Andrews, ibid., p. 126.
15. v. Neville Williams, op. cit. p. 57.
16. Hakluyt, *Principal Navigations*, vol. X, p. 74.
17. v. Andrews, op. cit. p. 141.
18. v. Gilbert, *Voyages*, op. cit., pp. 170–80.
19. Gilbert, 'A Discourse how Her Majesty may Annoy the King of Spain', ibid., p. 173.
20. Ibid., p. 175.
21. Letters Patent to Sir Humphrey Gilbert, ibid., p. 193.

22. Ibid.
23. Raphael Holinshed, *Chronicles*, 1587, III, 1369, in ibid., p. 237.
24. Ibid.
25. John Hooker, in ibid., quoted ibid., p. 236.
26. Privy Council to Sir John Gilbert, *Acts of the Privy Council, 1578–80*, pp. 142–3, quoted in ibid., p. 221.

THE FRINGES OF POWER

1. v. *Acts of the Privy Council*, 7 February 1580, quoted in Lloyd Williams, p. 21.
2. The surgeon George Baker, quoted in Steven May, 'The Poems of Edward de Vere . . .', *Studies in Philology*, 77 (1980), p. 8.
3. Mendoza in a despatch of 1581, cited in J.A. Bossy, 'English Catholics and the French Marriage', *Recusant History*, v (1959), p. 6.
4. John Camden, quoted in Paul Johnson, *Elizabeth I*, p. 255.
5. v. Christopher Hibbert, *The Virgin Queen*, p. 189.
6. Ibid., p. 191.
7. John Stubbs, *The Discovery of a gaping gulf whereunto England is like to be swallowed by another French marriage if the Lord forbid not the banns by letting Her Majesty see the sin and punishment thereof*, v. ibid., p. 192.
8. Ibid.
9. John Stow, op. cit., quoted in ibid., p. 193.
10. PRO, *Calendar of State Papers, Spanish, 1580–1596*, 29, 36, 49, cited in D.C. Peck, 'Ralegh, Sidney, Oxford and the Catholics', *Notes and Queries*, n.s. 25 (1978), p. 430.
11. *SP* 12/151, 45. The deposition is cited in Rowse, *Elizabethan Renaissance*, p. 160.
12. *SP* 12/1511, 45, cited in D.C. Peck, loc. cit.
13. v. Rowse, op. cit. pp. 96–100.
14. Edmund Spenser, *A View of the Present State of Ireland*, ed. W.L. Renwick, p. 223.
15. Fynes Morrison, quoted in Quinn, *The Elizabethans and the Irish*, p. 78.
16. Father William Good, v. Quinn, ibid., p. 47.
17. Sidney, *Letters and Memorials* ed. Collins, vol. I, p. 24, quoted in Rowse, *Grenville*, p. 65.
18. v. Gilbert, *Voyages*, vol. I, p. 17.
19. Ibid.
20. Holinshed, *Chronicles*, ed. Hooker, 1587, III, 1369.
21. v. Lacey, op. cit., p. 37.
22. Spenser, op. cit., *Prose Works*, ed. R. Gottfried, p. 161.
23. v. Steven May, *Sir Walter Ralegh*, p. 4.
24. Ralegh to Sir Francis Walsingham, in Edwards, *The Life of Sir Walter Ralegh*, vol. II, p. 11; hereafter cited as Edwards, vols I and II.
25. Ralegh to Lord Grey of Wilton, ibid., p. 16.
26. Spenser, op. cit, p. 158.

27. v. Adamson and Folland, p. 56.
28. Ralegh to Sir Francis Walsingham, Edwards, op. cit., p. 10.
29. Ralegh to the Earl of Leicester, ibid., p. 17.
30. Ibid.
31. Ralegh to Sir Francis Walsingham, ibid., p. 13.
32. Sir Robert Naunton, *Fragmenta Regalia*, in Lacey, op. cit., p. 43.
33. Ibid.
34. Naunton, op. cit. p. 60.

THE WORSHIP OF THE VIRGIN QUEEN

1. The word is used by Aubrey, p. 182.
2. Thomas Fuller, *The History of the Worthies of England*, 1663, p. 262.
3. Ibid.
4. Aubrey, p. 182.
5. v. Adamson and Folland, p. 175.
6. Ralegh to Lord Burghley, Edwards, op. cit., p. 21.
7. Aubrey, p. 182.
8. v. Lacey, op. cit., p. 47.
9. Ralegh to Sir Robert Cecil, Edwards, op. cit., p. 51.
10. For the canon of Oxford's poetry v. May 'Poems of Edward de Vere, Seventeenth Earl of Oxford', loc. cit., pp. 25–42.
11. George Puttenham, *The Art of English Poetry*, ed. Willcock and Walker, p. 63.
12. The text is a modernized version of that given in A.G. Latham, ed., *The Poems of Sir Walter Ralegh*, p. 111, ll. 1–4.
13. Ibid., ll. 17–18.
14. Ibid., ll. 9–16.
15. Giordano Bruno, *Degli Eroici Furori*, trans. Paul Eugene Memmo Jr., p. 217.
16. v. Lacey, op. cit., p. 40; Clark suppresses the anecdote.
17. John Norden, *Speculum Britanniae: Pars Middlesex*, 1593, quoted in E. Beresford-Chancellor, *The Annals of the Strand*, p. 276.
18. Aubrey, p. 183.
19. For Browne's letter v. *The New Found Land of Stephen Parmenius* ed. and trans. D.B. Quinn and Neil M. Cheshire, Appendix I, letter 9, 25 April to 3 May, 1583, pp. 203–8.
20. Middlesex County Records, 5 October, 1584, quoted in T.N. Brushfield, *Transactions of the Devon Association*, xxxv (1903), p. 546.
21. v. Jane Ashelford, *Dress in the Age of Elizabeth I*, p. 74.
22. Ben Jonson, *Every Man Out of His Humour*, II, iv, 42–8.
23. John Stubbs, *Anatomy of Abuses*, quoted Ashelford, op. cit., p. 46.
24. Quinn and Cheshire, op. cit., p. 205.
25. Sir John Harington, Epigram 315, 'Of Paulus, A Flatterer', ll. 1–6.

26. Ralegh to the Vice-Chancellor and others, the Senate of the University of Cambridge, Edwards, op. cit., p. 28.
27. Cited in Lloyd Williams, p. 65.
28. v. Andrews, *Elizabethan Privateering*, p. 25.
29. For von Wedel's account v. von Klarwill, *Queen Elizabeth and Some Foreigners*, p. 336.
30. v. Johnson, op. cit., p. 214.
31. von Wedel, in Klarwill, op. cit.

VIRGINIA

1. Gilbert to Sir Francis Walsingham, cited in Gilbert, *Voyages*, vol. II, p. 241.
2. Ibid., p. 339.
3. Ralegh to Sir Humphrey Gilbert, ibid., p. 348.
4. Ibid.
5. Examination of John Carter, ibid., p. 378.
6. Gilbert to Sir George Peckham, ibid., p. 383.
7. This and the ensuing accounts of Gilbert's last voyage are taken from Edward Hayes' narrative, ibid., pp. 385–423.
8. The terms of Ralegh's patent are given in *The Roanoke Voyages, 1584–1590*, ed. D.B. Quinn, vol. I pp. 82–9; hereafter cited as *Roanoke Voyages*, vols I and II.
9. Cited in Lloyd Williams, p. 52.
10. Hakluyt, Dedicatory Epistle to Sir Walter Ralegh from his edition of Peter Martyr, *The Decades of the New World*; for the original Latin version v. *The Original Writings and Correspondence of the Two Richard Hakluyts*, vol. II, pp. 256–62; hereafter cited as *Hakluyts*.
11. For Arthur Barlowe's 'Discourse' of the first voyage from which this and the ensuing quotations are taken, v. *Roanoke Voyages*, vol. I, pp. 91–115.
12. v. Quinn, *Fair Set for Roanoke*, p. 43.
13. Hakluyt, 'Inducements to the Liking of the Voyage Intended Towards Virginia', in *Hakluyts*, p. 334.
14. Hakluyt, 'Discourse of Western Planting', ibid., p. 216. The full text, from which the ensuing quotations derive, is reprinted in *Hakluyts*, pp. 211–326.
15. v. *Roanoke Voyages*, op. cit., p. 116.
16. v. ibid., p. 233.

THE ROYAL SERVANT

1. v. Lacey, op. cit., p. 54.
2. Cecil to Sir Robert Heneage, v. PRO *SP Dom*, ccxliii, p. 17.
3. 'A. B.' to Lord Burghley, v. PRO *SP Dom*, xxix, p. 126.
4. Richard Carew, *The Survey of Cornwall*, quoted in Lloyd Williams p. 69.

5. Ralegh to the Devon Justices, quoted in A.H.A. Hamilton, 'The Jurisdiction of the Lord Warden of the Stannaries in the Time of Sir Walter Ralegh', *Transactions of the Devon Association*, viii (1876) p. 381.
6. For arms and equipment, v. Cruickshank, *Elizabeth's Army*, pp. 102–29.
7. Thomas Digges, quoted in ibid.
8. v. Rowse, *Expansion*, p. 370.
9. Ralegh to Richard Duke, in Edwards, op. cit., p. 26.
10. PRO *Calendar of State Papers, Spanish, 1587–1603*, p. 23.
11. Quoted in E. Thompson, op. cit., p. 49.
12. Ralegh, *The Discovery of Guiana*, ed. V.T. Harlow, p. 4.; hereafter cited as *Discovery*.
13. The following translations from de Oviedo are taken from John Flemming, *The Search for El Dorado*, pp. 97–9.
14. v. Andrews, op. cit., p. 22.
15. Evesham's account of his privateering voyage is taken from Hakluyt, *Principal Navigations*, vol. VI, pp. 434–7.
16. *Botler's Dialogues* ed. Perry, pp. 39–40, quoted in Andrews, op. cit., ibid., p. 41.
17. Cited in Johnson, op. cit., p. 268.
18. For Ralegh's letter to Leicester v. Edwards.
19. T. Lant, *Funeral of Sir Philip Sidney*, quoted in Lacey, *Elizabethan Icarus*, p. 38.
20. Ralegh, 'An Epitaph upon the Right Honourable Sir Philip Sidney Knight: Lord Governor of Flushing', ll. 1–12.
21. Sidney's will, cited in Lacey, op. cit., p. 38.

RALPH LANE'S COLONY

1. Holinshed, *Chronicles*, vol. III, p. 1401, quoted in *Roanoke Voyages*, op. cit., p. 174.
2. For the anonymous *Tiger* journal of the 1585 voyage v. ibid., pp. 178–93.
3. Ibid.
4. Ibid., p. 186.
5. Jan Huygen van Linschoten, *Discourse of Voyages into the East and West Indies* (trans. 1598), quoted in Peter Earle, *The Last Fight of the 'Revenge'*, p. 35.
6. For the supply problem, v. Quinn, *Ralegh and the British Empire*, pp. 82–3.
7. Ralph Lane to Sir Francis Walsingham, in *Roanoke Voyages*, op. cit., p. 211.
8. Ibid., p. 212.
9. Ibid., p. 424.
10. Ibid., p. 419.
11. Thomas Harriot, *A Brief and True Report*, ibid., p. 370.
12. Ibid., p. 422.
13. Ibid., p. 344.
14. v. E. Thompson, op. cit., p. 46.
15. *Roanoke Voyages*, op. cit., pp. 422–3.
16. Ibid., p. 425.

17. Ibid., p. 427.
18. Ibid., p. 422.
19. Grenville to Sir Francis Walsingham, ibid., p. 219.
20. v. Rowse, *Grenville*, p. 217.
21. Harriot, op. cit., *Roanoke Voyages*, op. cit., p. 323.
22. v. Quinn, op. cit., p. 84.
23. Harriot, op. cit. in *Roanoke Voyages* op. cit., p. 384.
24. Lane's 'Discourse' on the first colony, *Roanoke Voyages*, op. cit., p. 257.
25. This and the following quotations are taken from Harriot, op. cit., ibid., pp. 317–87.
26. *Roanoke Voyages*, op. cit., p. 431.
27. Lane, op. cit., ibid., p. 258.
28. This and the following quotations are from ibid., pp. 255–94.

'THE BEST HATED MAN IN THE WORLD'

1. v. Lacey, *Ralegh*, p. 71.
2. PRO *SP Dom*, xxix, p. 126, quoted Lloyd Williams, pp. 69–70.
3. Thomas Fuller, *Worthies* (1840), vol. I, p. 420.
4. Aubrey, p. 186.
5. Edward Bohun, *The Character of Queen Elizabeth*, 1693, quoted Lloyd Williams, p. 73.
6. Warrant Book, B.M. Add Mss., V, p. 750, quoted Lacey, op. cit., p. 102.
7. Aubrey, p. 180.
8. v. Adamson and Folland, p. 115.
9. Ibid., p. 116.
10. Thomas Wright, *Queen Elizabeth and her Times*, 1838, vol. II, p. 320, quoted in Johnson, op. cit., p. 288.
11. J.E. Neale, *Elizabeth I and her Parliaments*, vol. II, p. 116.
12. Letter of Anthony Bagot, quoted in Lacey, *Elizabethan Icarus*, p. 43.
13. 'A Sonnet', ll. 1–4, v. May, *Sir Walter Ralegh*, p. 32.
14. Details of the quarrel at North Hall from Ms Tanner, 76, fol. 84b–85a, quoted Lloyd Williams, pp. 81–2.
15. v. Johnson, op. cit., p. 305.
16. Ralegh, *History of the World*, quoted ibid., p. 304.
17. PRO *SP Dom.*, *Elizabeth*, 206, no. 40, quoted in Rowse, *Grenville*, p. 254.
18. Howard to Lord Burghley, *SP Dom*, ccvii, 87, quoted in Lloyd Williams, p. 84.
19. Ralegh, quoted in Johnson, op. cit., p. 308.
20. Ibid., p. 314.
21. J.H. Laughton, ed., *State Papers Relating to the Defeat of the Spanish Armada*, 1894, vol. I, p. 357.
22. Ralegh, *A Report of the Truth of the Fight about the Isles of Azores, this last summer, betwixt the 'Revenge', one of Her Majesty's Ships, and an Amada of the King of*

Spain, v. Hammond, *Sir Walter Ralegh: Selected Writings*, pp. 65–6; hereafter cited as *Report*.

23. Edwards, vol. I, p. 245.
24. Francis Allen to Anthony Bacon, Thomas Birch, *Memoirs of the Reign of Elizabeth I*, vol. I, p. 56.
25. Ralegh to Sir George Carew, Edwards, vol. II, p. 41.
26. v. Lloyd Williams, p. 91.
27. v. Quinn, op. cit., p. 152.
28. Ralegh to Sir George Carew, Edwards, op. cit., p. 41.
29. Ibid.
30. Ralegh, 'Farewell to the Court', ll. 1–4.
31. Ralegh, *The Eleventh and Last Book of the Ocean to Cynthia*, ll. 344–50.
32. Spenser, *Colin Clout's Come Home Again*, ll. 56–79.
33. Ibid., l. 183.
34. Ibid., ll. 198–9.
35. Ibid., l. 66.
36. Ibid., l. 253.
37. Spenser, 'To the Right Honourable and Valorous Knight, Sir Walter Ralegh', in A.C. Hamilton, ed., *The Faerie Queene*, p. 743.
38. Ralegh, 'A Vision upon the Conceit of *The Faerie Queene*', ibid., p. 739.
39. Spenser, 'A Letter of the Author's . . . to . . . Sir Walter Ralegh', ibid., p. 737.
40. Spenser, *The Faerie Queene*, III, v, st. 16, l. 2.
41. I, John, 2. 16.
42. Spenser, *The Faerie Queene*, III, v, st. 15, l. 6.
43. Ibid., st. 25.
44. Ibid., st. 27, l. 9.
45. Ibid., st. 32, l. 6.
46. Ibid., st. 52, l. 9.
47. Robert Ashley. *Of Honour*, ed. Virgil B. Heltzel, San Marino, Cal, 1937, p. 50, quoted in Thomas P. Roche, *The Kindly Flame*, p. 144.

THE LOST COLONY

1. Hakluyt to Ralegh, in *Hakluyts*, p. 355.
2. John White's narrative of the voyage, *Roanoke Voyages*, vol. II, p. 517. White's is the only narrative source for his colonizing efforts and the ensuing quotations are taken from it. The text appears in full in *Roanoke Voyages*, vol. II, op. cit., pp. 515–38.
3. Ibid., p. 563.
4. Ibid., p. 567.
5. Ibid., p. 568.
6. Ibid., p. 569.

7. Agreement between Ralegh, Thomas Smythe, etc., for the continuance of the City of Ralegh venture, ibid., p. 573.
8. White's narrative of the 1590 voyage, ibid., p. 612. The full text, from which the following quotations derive, appears in full in *Roanoke Voyages*, ibid., pp. 598–622.
9. Jonson, *Eastward Ho!*, III, iii, ll. 17–20.
10. Ralegh, quoted Johnson, op. cit., p. 338.

THE FAVOURITE'S FALL

1. Ralegh, 'Now we have present made', ll. 5–8. The most readily available text is in Hammond, op. cit., p. 50.
2. Arthur Throckmorton, *Diary*, quoted in Rowse, *Ralegh and the Throckmortons*, p. 104; hereafter cited as *Diary*.
3. Ralegh, 'Nature, that washed her hands in milk', ll. 7–10.
4. Ibid., l. 31.
5. Sir Roger Williams, v. Earle, op. cit., p. 62.
6. Ibid., p. 66.
7. Ibid., p. 77.
8. Ibid., p. 35.
9. Ralegh, *Report*, Hammond, op. cit., pp. 66–7.
10. Ibid., pp. 69–70.
11. Ibid., p. 75.
12. Robert Parsons, *An Advertisement Written to a Secretary of My L. Treasurer's Of England* (abridged contemp. trans. of *Responsio*), quoted in Ernest Strathman, *Sir Walter Ralegh: A Study in Elizabethan Scepticism*, p. 31; hereafter cited as Strathman.
13. Dove, *Confutation of Atheism* (1605), quoted Strathman, p. 86.
14. Ibid., p. 5.
15. Ralegh, *Works*, vol. III, p. 100.
16. George Peele, *The Honour of the Garter*, quoted in Charles Nicholl, *The Reckoning*, p. 211; hereafter cited as Nicholl.
17. Giordano Bruno, *Cenna della Ceneri*, quoted in Nicholl, p. 206.
18. George Abbot, *The Reasons of Dr Hill for the Upholding of Papistry*, (1604), pp. 88–9, quoted in Nicholl, p. 206.
19. Alnwick Household Accounts, quoted in John W. Shirley, *Thomas Harriot, Renaissance Scientist*, p. 23; hereafter cited as Shirley.
20. v. Nicholl, p. 194.
21. v. Shirley, pp. 29–30.
22. Thomas Digges, quoted in Nicholl, p. 207.
23. v. Shirley, pp. 5–6.
24. Ibid.

25. Robert Greene, *Greene's Groatsworth of Wit Bought with a Million of Repentence*, (1592), quoted in Nicholl, p. 44.
26. Gabriel Hervey, *Four Letters*, quoted in ibid., p. 54.
27. Richard Cholmeley, 'Remembrances', quoted in ibid., p. 293.
28. Christopher Marlowe, 'The Passionate Shepherd to his Love', in Latham, op. cit., p. 39, ll. 5–8.
29. Ralegh, 'The Nymph's Reply to the Shepherd', ll. 21–4.
30. For the Martin Marprelate controversy v. J. Black, *The Reign of Elizabeth I*, pp. 201–2.
31. v. Edwards, vol. I, p. 132.
32. Ibid., p. 133.
33. Report of Father Henry Garnet, quoted in Nicholl, p. 111.
34. For this incident, v. Ms Stonyhurst, Anglia vi, 117, quoted in Philip Caraman, *The Other Face*, pp. 258–60.
35. Sir John Harington, *Nugae Antiquae* (ed. 1779), vol. I, pp. 105–6.
36. Ibid.
37. *Diary*, quoted Lloyd Williams, p. 109.
38. Ibid., quoted Rowse, op. cit., p. 160.
39. v. Edwards, op. cit., p. 147.
40. Ibid., p. 148.
41. Ibid., p. 46.
42. *Diary*, quoted in Rowse, op. cit., p. 160.
43. Ibid., p. 161.
44. Edwards, vol. II, pp. 50–51.
45. v. H.E. Sandison, 'Arthur Gorges, Spenser's Alcyon and Ralegh's Friend' *P.M.L.A.* 43 (1928), pp. 645–74.
46. Sir Edward Stafford to Sir Anthony Bacon, quoted in E. Thompson, op. cit., p. 83.
47. *Diary*, quoted in Rowse, op. cit., p. 162.

THE YEARS OF DISGRACE

1. Edwards, op. cit., p. 51.
2. H.M.C. *Finch Mss*, I, 333–4, quoted Rowse, op. cit., p. 164.
3. Ralegh, *The Ocean to Cynthia*, ll. 21–3.
4. Ibid., ll. 61–8.
5. Ibid., ll. 120–24.
6. Ibid., ll. 209–12.
7. Ibid., ll. 497–508.
8. Ibid., ll. 517–22.
9. Edwards, op. cit., p. 53.
10. Ibid., p. 62.
11. Deposition of Vincent de Fontesco, quoted ibid., p. 64.

12. Letters of Cecil to Lord Burghley, quoted in Edwards, vol. I, pp. 153–4.
13. Hawkins to Lord Burghley, ibid., p. 151.
14. *SP. Dom.* ccxliii, 17, quoted Lloyd Williams, p. 115.
15. v. Rowse, op. cit., p. 167.
16. Ralegh to Lord Burghley, quoted in Edwards, vol. II, pp. 70–71.
17. *SP. Dom.* ccxliii, 17, quoted Lloyd Williams, p. 114.
18. Edwards, op. cit., p. 72.
19. Ralegh to Lord Burghley, ibid., pp. 67–8.
20. Sir John Fortesque to Lord Burghley, Edwards, vol. I, p. 156.
21. *Diary,* quoted in Rowse, op. cit., p. 169.
22. Salisbury Mss, IV, 507–8, quoted ibid., p. 180.
23. Ralegh to Cecil, quoted ibid., p. 181.
24. John Hooker, quoted J.E. Neale, *The Elizabethan House of Commons,* pp. 364–5.
25. Ibid.
26. Ralegh, untitled tract of the succession, v. Pierre Lefranc (ed.) 'Un Inédit de Ralegh Sur La Succession', *Etudes Anglaises* 13 (1960), p. 43.
27. For Ralegh's speech to the House of Commons v. Lloyd Williams, p. 116.
28. Ibid.
29. H. Townshend in *Historical Collections, or . . . the Four Last Parliaments of Queen Elizabeth,* quoted in ibid., p. 117.
30. Ibid.
31. v. Nicholl, p. 39.
32. D'Ewes, quoted in Lloyd Williams, pp. 117–18.
33. v. Lacey, op. cit., p. 190.
34. v. Nicholl, p. 39.
35. Ibid., p. 40.
36. Ibid.
37. Ibid., p. 42.
38. For Kyd's confession, v. ibid., p. 45.
39. Ibid., p. 46.
40. Ibid., p. 17.
41. Ibid., p. 19.
42. Ralegh to Cecil, Edwards, op. cit., pp. 50 and 79.
43. Ralegh to Cecil, ibid., p. 51.
44. Ibid., pp. 49–50.
45. For a printed version of Ironside's note (Ms Harleian 6849, fol. 183–190) v. *Willobie his Avisa* ed. G.B. Harrison, Appendix III.
46. Ralegh, 'The Lie', ll. 43–8.
47. Ibid., ll. 7–18.
48. Ibid., ll. 73–8.
49. v. *Willobie his Avisa,* op. cit.
50. Ralegh to Cecil, Edwards, op. cit., p. 91.
51. Records of the English Province of the Society of Jesus, 1878, vol. III, p. 462.

Notes and References

THE PURSUIT OF EL DORADO

1. Dedication to *Discovery*, p. 3.
2. Hakluyt, 'Discourse of Western Planting', in *Hakluyts*, p. 255.
3. *Discovery*, p. 9.
4. Ibid., p. 10.
5. Edwards, op. cit., p. 397.
6. Letter from Berrio to the king of Spain, in *Discovery*, Appendix, A, ii, p. 92.
7. v. *Discovery*, p. lxxv.
8. Ibid., p. lxxii, the original passage is in ibid., p. 82, fn. 1.
9. Ibid., p. lxxxiv.
10. Ibid.
11. This is a significant variation from the usual form of 'our trusty and well-beloved servant'.
12. v. Quinn, op. cit., pp. 180–81.
13. Ibid.
14. v. V.S. Naipaul, *The Loss of El Dorado*, p. 52; hereafter cited as Naipaul.
15. *Discovery*, p. 12.
16. Ibid., p. 15.
17. Ibid., p. 17.
18. Ibid., p. 51.
19. Ibid., pp. 54–5.
20. Francisco de Vides, Governor of Cumana, to Simon Bolivar, trans. in ibid., Appendix B, v, p. 131.
21. Quinn, op. cit., p. 197.
22. Ibid., pp. 196–7.
23. Ibid., p. 197.
24. Ibid.
25. Ibid., p. 198.
26. *Discovery*, p. 23.
27. 'Of the Voyage for Guiana', in ibid., Appendix C, p. 41.
28. George Chapman, *De Guiana Carmen*, l. 15.
29. Ibid., ll. 18–24.

RALEGH AND ESSEX

1. Edwards, op. cit., p. 108.
2. v. Lacey, *Elizabethan Icarus*, p. 139.
3. Birch, op. cit. vol. I, p. 152.
4. Roland Whyte to Sir Robert Sidney, in Arthur Collins ed., *Letters and Memorials of State*, 1746, vol. II, p. 24.

5. Ibid.
6. Ibid.
7. Edwards, op. cit., p. 129.
8. Ralegh to Cecil, ibid., p. 129.
9. Anthony Bacon to Francis Bacon, quoted in Birch, op. cit., vol. I, p. 486.
10. v. Lacey, *Ralegh*, pp. 226–7.
11. v. Lloyd Williams, p. 142.
12. Edwards, op. cit., p. 151.
13. Ibid., p. 154.
14. Lloyd Williams, p. 143.
15. Ibid.
16. Edwards, op. cit., p. 137.
17. For Ralegh's return to court v. Roland Whyte to Sir Robert Sidney, in Collins, op. cit., vol. II, p. 54.
18. Ralegh at his trial, in Lloyd Williams, p. 180.
19. For economic conditions in these years v. Black, op. cit., pp. 408–10.
20. Edwards, op. cit., p. 169.
21. For Ralegh's will, v. Lacey, *Ralegh*, p. 247, and Agnes Latham, 'Sir Walter Ralegh's Will' *Review of English Studies*, xxii (1971), 129–31.
22. Edwards, op. cit., p. 172.
23. v. Lacey, op. cit., p. 242.
24. Ibid., p. 249.
25. v. Lacey, *Elizabethan Icarus*, p. 188.
26. This and the following quotations from Gorges are taken from his 'Relation of the . . . Islands Voyage' in *Purchas His Pilgrims* vol. XX, pp. 34–129, p. 81.
27. Ibid., p. 88.
28. v. Lacey, op. cit., p. 257.
29. Collins, op. cit., vol. II, pp. 79 and 83.
30. For the primero incident, v. Whyte to Sidney in Collins, op. cit., vol. II, p. 83.
31. Edwards, op. cit., p. 197.
32. Ralegh to Cecil in Edwards, ibid., 161–3.
33. Ibid., p. 163.
34. Harington, *Nugae Antiquae*, (1779), vol. I, pp. 104–5.
35. Collins, op. cit., vol. II, pp. 82, 86, 90.
36. v. Rowse, *Expansion*, p. 147.
37. Edwards, op. cit., p. 198.
38. v. Johnson, op. cit., pp. 385–6.
39. v. Lacey, *Elizabethan Icarus*, p. 214.
40. John Chamberlain, quoted in Johnson, op. cit., p. 391.
41. Report of the French Ambassador, ibid.
42. H.M. C. *Sidney Mss* IX, 6, quoted ibid., p. 392.
43. Essex to Elizabeth, quoted ibid., p. 393.
44. Ibid.
45. Elizabeth to Leicester, v. *Letters of Queen Elizabeth I*, ed. G.B. Harrison, pp. 264–8.

46. Roland Whyte, quoted in Johnson, op. cit., p. 401.
47. For the charges in full, v. Lacey, op. cit., p. 245.
48. v. Rowse, op. cit., p. 144.
49. Ibid.
50. For this and the ensuing quotation v. Quinn, op. cit., pp. 158–9.
51. v. Black, op. cit., p. 438.
52. Ralegh to Cecil, Edwards, op. cit., p. 198.
53. Collins, op. cit., vol. II, p. 178.
54. Edwards, op. cit., p. 202.
55. Lloyd Williams, p. 154.
56. v. Lacey, op. cit., p. 282.
57. v. Lacey, *Ralegh*, p. 266.
58. Ibid., p. 265.
59. v. Lacey, *Elizabethan Icarus*, p. 304.
60. Ibid., p. 313.
61. v. Lacey, *Ralegh*, p. 267.
62. Lloyd Williams, p. 156.

PROGRESS TO THE TOWER

1. v. Lloyd Williams, p. 157.
2. Edwards, op. cit., p. 227.
3. Lloyd Williams, p. 158.
4. Ibid.
5. Ibid., p. 159.
6. Ibid.
7. v. Rowse, op. cit., p. 224.
8. Ibid.
9. Black, op. cit., p. 230.
10. v. Rowse, op. cit., p. 225.
11. Ibid., p. 232.
12. Ibid., p. 225.
13. Edwards, op. cit., p. 233.
14. For the text of Elizabeth's 'Golden Speech' v. J.E. Neale, *Elizabeth I and her Parliaments, 1584–1601*, pp. 388–93.
15. v. S.J. Houston, *James I*, p. 8.
16. Ibid., p. 5.
17. For James and the divine right of kings, v. ibid., pp. 37–9.
18. Ibid., p. 8.
19. Black, op. cit., p. 442.
20. *Secret Correspondence*, v. Lacey, op. cit., p. 274.
21. Lloyd Williams, p. 164.
22. For Cecil's correspondence with James v. Edwards, vol. I, pp. 312–15.

23. Dr John Manningham, *Diary*, quoted Lloyd Williams, p. 165.
24. Ibid., quoted in Johnson, op. cit., p. 439.
25. Aubrey, p. 186.
26. Thomas Lake to Cecil, quoted in Lloyd Williams, p. 186.
27. Aubrey, p. 187.
28. Ralegh to the Royal Commissioners, Edwards, op. cit., p. 270.
29. v. Lacey, op. cit., p. 289.
30. Bacon, *Essays*, 'Of Followers and Friends'.
31. v. Lacey, op. cit., p. 289.
32. Ibid., p. 290.
33. v. Lloyd Williams, p. 171.
34. Ralegh to Lady Ralegh, Edwards, op. cit., pp. 383–87.
35. Ibid., p. 384.
36. For Cecil's account of Ralegh's attempted suicide v. Edwards, vol. I. p. 375.
37. v. Lacey, op. cit., p. 293.
38. Edwards, vol. II., p. 485.
39. Edwards, vol. I, p. 386.
40. Lacey, op. cit., p. 296.
41. The outstanding modern legal exposition of the trial is J. Bruce Williamson, *The Trial of Sir Walter Ralegh*.
42. This account of Ralegh's trial is based on *Criminal Trials*, vol. I, pp. 384–452 (in turn derived from Herleian Mss, vol. XXXIX, and a transcript made by Thomas Overbury), *Complete State Trials*, and material in Edwards, op. cit., pp. 383–439.
43. *Criminal Trials* vol. I, p. 451.
44. Justice Gaudy, Edwards, op. cit., p. 388.
45. Dudley Carleton, quoted in C. Williams, *Court and Times of James I*, vol. I, p. 20.
46. v. Lacey, op. cit., p. 300.
47. Edwards, vol. II, p. 279.
48. Ibid., p. 277.
49. Ibid., p. 280.
50. Ibid., p. 284.
51. Ibid., p. 287.
52. Williams, op. cit., vol. I, p. 31.
53. Edwards, op. cit., p. 282.

THE PRISONER

1. Ralegh to James I, Edwards, op. cit., p. 296.
2. D.H. Wilson, *King James VI and I* p. 17, quoted in Roger Lockyer, *The Early Stuarts: A Political History of England, 1603–1642*, p. 159.
3. *Commons Journals*, quoted ibid.
4. J.R. Tanner (ed.), *Constitutional Documents of the Reign of James I*, quoted ibid., p. 159.

5. Ibid., quoted, ibid., p. 164.
6. Edwards, op. cit., p. 315.
7. Ibid.
8. Ibid., p. 314.
9. Rowse, op. cit., p. 249.
10. Ibid., p. 247.
11. Ralegh to Cecil, Edwards, op. cit., p. 293.
12. Ibid.
13. Ralegh to Cecil, Edwards, op. cit., p. 304.
14. Ibid., p. 318.
15. Ibid.
16. v. Rowse, op. cit., p. 250.
17. Quoted in Lacey, op. cit., p. 315.
18. Ibid., p. 318.
19. Edwards, op. cit., pp. 317–18.
20. For Turner's diagnosis, v. Edwards, vol. I., p. 491.
21. Ibid., pp. 490–91.
22. Ibid., p. 489.
23. v. Rowse, op. cit., p. 252.
24. Edwards, op. cit., pp. 490–91.
25. v. E. Thompson, op. cit., p. 243.
26. Ralegh, 'Instructions to his Son', v. May, op. cit., p. 68.
27. Ibid.
28. Text established by Michael Rudick in 'The Text of Ralegh's Lyric "What is our life?" ', *Studies in Philology* 83 (1986), 76–87.
29. *Letters of King James VI and I*, ed. G.P.V. Akrigg, p. 261, quoted in Lockyer, op. cit., p. 74.
30. S.R. Gardiner, *History of England from the Accession of James I to the Outbreak of the Civil War, 1603–1642*, vol. II, pp. 42–9, quoted in Lockyer, op. cit., p. 73.
31. v. Lacey, op. cit., p. 321.
32. *Letters of John Chamberlain*, in Rowse, op. cit., p. 256.
33. Ralegh to Robert Carr, Edwards, vol. II, p. 327.
34. Ralegh, 'Petition', ll. 49–50.
35. Ibid., ll. 59–60.
36. W.H. *The True Picture and Relation of Prince Henry* (Leiden 1634), p. 31, quoted in R. Strong, *Henry, Prince of Wales*, p. 12.
37. Sir Charles Cornwallis, *An Account of the Baptism, Life, Death and Funeral . . . of Henry, Prince of Wales*, (1751), p. 26, quoted ibid., p. 68.
38. Daniel Price, *Prince Henry His First Anniversary*, p. 6, quoted, ibid., p. 54.
39. Roger Coke, *Detection of the Court and State of England* (1694), quoted, ibid., p. 51.
40. Ralegh, 'Observations', *Works* vol. VIII, p. 349.
41. Ibid.
42. Lefranc, *Sir Walter Ralegh*, p. 600.
43. Ibid., p. 598.

44. v. Quinn, op. cit., p. 213.
45. Edwards, op. cit., p. 252.
46. Ralegh to Queen Anna, Edwards, op. cit., p. 333.
47. v. May, op. cit., p. 82.
48. Ibid., p. 83.
49. Ralegh, *Works*, vol. II, p. xlii.
50. v. Lloyd Williams, p. 222.
51. Ralegh, op. cit., pp. v–vi.
52. John Chamberlain to Dudley Carleton, quoted Lloyd Williams, p. 231.
53. Ralegh, op. cit., pp. vi–viii.
54. Ralegh, *History of the World* ed. C. Patrides, p. 23, fn. 3.
55. Ralegh, *Works*, vol. VII, p. 900.
56. Ibid.
57. Ibid., pp. 900–901.
58. Ralegh, *Works*, vol. VIII, p. 163.

LAST ACTS

1. v. V.T. Harlow, *Ralegh's Last Voyage*, p. 3; hereafter cited as *Last Voyage*.
2. The Council of the Indies to the King of Spain, quoted in Harlow, *Discovery*, p. 115.
3. Ms Sloane 359, fol. 52b, quoted Lloyd Williams, p. 217.
4. Edwards, op. cit., p. 338.
5. John Chamberlain to Sir Dudley Carleton, quoted Lloyd Williams, p. 233.
6. *Last Voyage*, pp. 331–2.
7. Lacey, op. cit., p. 343.
8. *Last Voyage*, p. 28.
9. v. Lacey, op. cit., p. 344.
10. v. *Last Voyage*, p. 29.
11. v. Lloyd Williams, p. 236.
12. v. *Last Voyage*, p. 52.
13. Ibid.
14. Ralegh, 'Orders to be Observed by the Commanders of the Fleet', *Last Voyage*, p. 121.
15. James Hancock to Nathaniel Rich, quoted in *Last Voyage*, p. 143.
16. *Last Voyage*, p. 53.
17. Ibid.
18. Ibid.
19. Ibid., p. 55.
20. Lacey, op. cit., p. 349.
21. For Ralegh's journal of the voyage, from which this and the following extracts are taken, v. Ralegh, *The Discovery of Guiana*, ed. R.H. Schomburgk, 1848.
22. Lawrence Keymis to Silvanus Scorie, *Last Voyage*, p. 161.

23. v. Schomburgk, op. cit., p. 197.
24. Ralegh to Lady Ralegh, Edwards, op. cit., p. 347.
25. v. *Last Voyage*, p. 57.
26. v. Naipaul, op. cit., p. 96.
27. Ibid., p. 97.
28. Ibid.
29. *Last Voyage*, p. 344.
30. James Howell, *Epistolae Ho-Elianae* (1645), quoted Lloyd Williams, p. 241.
31. Charles Parker to Captain Alley, *Last Voyage*, p. 231.
32. v. Edwards, vol. I, p. 617.
33. v. Adamson and Folland, p. 427.
34. Edwards, vol. II, p. 359.
35. Ibid., p. 363.
36. 'A Proclamation Declaring His Majesty's Pleasure Concerning Sir Walter Ralegh', *Last Voyage*, p. 246.
37. Edwards, op. cit., p. 362.
38. v. Lacey, op. cit., p. 363.
39. v. Adamson and Folland, p. 431.
40. v. Lacey, op. cit., p. 365.
41. For Ralegh's 'Apology', v. *Last Voyage*, pp. 316–34.
42. v. Lacey, op. cit., p. 367.
43. Ibid.
44. Ibid., p. 372.
45. James's reply to a letter from his commissioners, *Last Voyage*, p. 296.
46. For the charges against Ralegh, v. *Last Voyage*, pp. 297–300.
47. Ibid., p. 300.
48. Ibid.
49. v. Lacey, op. cit., p. 373.
50. *Complete State Trials*, vol. II., col. 33.
51. John Chamberlain to Sir Dudley Carleton, quoted in Lloyd Williams, p. 255.
52. Ralegh, 'Nature that washed her hands in milk', ll. 7–10.
53. Ralegh, 'The Author's Epitaph'.
54. John Pory to Sir Dudley Carleton, quoted Lloyd Williams, p. 256.
55. Robert Tounson to Sir John Isham, quoted Lloyd Williams, p. 254.
56. John Chamberlain to Sir Dudley Carleton, quoted Lloyd Williams, p. 256.
57. v. Lacey, op. cit., p. 380.
58. For accounts of Ralegh's execution v. Lloyd Williams, pp. 257–64.
59. Ibid., p. 257.
60. Ibid., p. 263.
61. Ibid., p. 264.
62. Robert Tounson to Sir John Isham, quoted in Lloyd Williams, p. 265.

APPENDIX

1. Ralegh, *Works* vol. V, pp. 310–11.
2. Speech of James to Parliament 1610, quoted Houston, op. cit., p. 116.
3. Ralegh, *Works*, vol. V, p. 353.
4. Francis Osbourne, *Traditional Memories on* (sic) *the Reign of King James the First,* quoted in Houston, op. cit., p. 115.

Select Bibliography

Unless otherwise stated, the place of publication is London

Adamson, J. H. and Folland, H. F., *The Shepherd of the Ocean: An Account of Sir Walter Ralegh and his Times*, 1969

Andrews, K. R., *Elizabethan Privateering: English Privateering during the Spanish War, 1585–1603*, Cambridge, 1964

——— 'The Elizabethan Seaman', *Mariner's Mirror*, 68 (1982), 245–62

——— *Trade, Plunder and Settlement: Maritime Enterprise and the Genesis of the British Empire*, Cambridge, 1984

Andrews, K. R., Canny, N. P. and Hair, P. E. H., *The Westward Enterprise: English Activities in Ireland, the Atlantic and America, 1480–1650*, Liverpool, 1979

Andrews, K. R. (ed.), *English Privateering Voyages to the West Indies, 1585–95*, Hakluyt Society, second series, cxi, Cambridge, 1956

Anonymous, 'Ralegh and the Middle Temple', *Law Times*, 180 (1935), 271–2

Armitage, Christopher, *Sir Walter Ralegh: An Annotated Bibliography*, 1987

Ashelford, Jane, *A Visual History of Costume: The Sixteenth Century*, 1983

——— *Dress in the Age of Elizabeth I*, 1988

Ashton, Robert, *Reformation and Revolution*, The Paladin History of England, 1985

Bagwell, Richard, *Ireland under the Tudors, With a Succinct Account of the Earlier History*, 1885–90; reptd. 1963

Barker, Felix and Jackson, Peter, *The History of London in Maps*, 1990

Bednarz, James P., 'Ralegh in Spenser's Historical Allegory', *Spenser Studies*, 4 (1984), 49–70

Bedwell, C. E. A., *A Brief History of the Middle Temple*, 1909

Bell, Douglas, *Elizabethan Seamen*, 1936

Bennett, Josephine Waters, 'Oxford and *Endimion*', *P.M.L.A.* lvii (1942), 354–69

Bishop, Carolyn J., 'Ralegh Satirised by Harrington and Davies' *R.E.S.* n.s. 23 (1972), 52–56

Black, J. B., *The Reign of Elizabeth, 1558–1603*, The Oxford History of England, 2nd ed., Oxford, 1959

Bossy, John, 'English Catholics and the French Marriage, 1577–1581', *Recusant History* v, (1959), 2–16

Bowen, Catherine Drinker, *Francis Bacon: The Temper of a Man*, 1963

——— *The Lion and the Throne: The Life and Times of Sir Edward Coke*, 1956

Boynton, Lindsay, *The Elizabethan Militia, 1588–1638*, 1967

Bremer, Francis, 'Thomas Harriot: American Adventurer and Renaissance Scientist', *History Today*, 29 (1979), 639–47

Bruno, Giordano (trans. Paul Eugene Memmo Jr), *Giordano Bruno's 'The Heroic Frenzies': A Translation with Introduction and Notes*, University of North Carolina Studies in the Romance Languages and Literatures, no. 50, Chapel Hill, 1964

Buisseret, David, *Huguenots and Papists*, 1972

Campbell, Mildred, *The English Yeoman under Elizabeth and the Early Stuarts*, rev. ed., 1959

Canny, Nicholas P., *The Elizabethan Conquest of Ireland: A Pattern Established, 1565–76*, Hassocks, 1976

Clanton, Stacy M., 'The "Number" of Sir Walter Ralegh's *Booke of the Ocean to Scinthia*, *Studies in Philology* 82, (1985) 200–11

Clulee, Nicholas H., *John Dee's Natural Philosophy: Between Science and Religion*, 1988

Connell-Smith, Gordon, *Forerunners of Drake, a Study of English Trade with Spain in the Early Tudor Period*, 1954

Cunnington, C. W. and P., *Handbook of English Costume in the Sixteenth Century*, 1962

Dee, John, *General and Rare Memorials Pertaining to the Perfect Art of Navigation*, 1577

Dudley, Edwards, R., *Ireland in the Age of the Tudors: The Destruction of Hiberno-Norman Civilisation*, 1977

Duncan-Jones, Katherine, *Sir Philip Sidney: Courtier Poet*, Oxford, 1991

Durant, David N., *Ralegh's Lost Colony*, 1981

Earle, Peter, *The Last Fight of the 'Revenge'*, 1992

Edwards, Edward, *The Life of Sir Walter Ralegh*, 2 vols, 1868

Elliott, J. H., *The Old World and the New, 1492–1650*, Cambridge, 1970; reptd, 1992

Ellis, Steven G., *Tudor Ireland, Crown, Community and the Conflict of Cultures, 1470–1603*, 1985

Emden, Cecil Stuart, 'Sir Walter Ralegh: His Friends at Oriel', *Oriel Papers*, Oxford, 1948, 9–21

Falls, Cyril, *Elizabeth's Irish Wars*, 1950

Ferguson, Arthur B., *Clio Unbound: Perception of the Social and Cultural Past in Renaissance England*, Durham, North Carolina, 1979

Fletcher, Anthony, *Tudor Rebellions*, Seminar Studies in History, 3rd ed., 1983

French, Peter, *John Dee: The World of an Elizabethan Magus*, 1972

Fussner, F. Smith, *The Historical Revolution, English Historical Writing and Thought, 1580–1640*, Columbia, 1962

Gilbert, Sir Humphrey (ed. F. J. Furnivall), 'Queen Elizabeth's Academy', E.E.T.S. extra series no. 8, 1869

Glanville, Philippa, *London in Maps*, 1972

Graham, Winston, *The Spanish Armadas*, 1972

Greenblatt, Stephen J., *Sir Walter Ralegh: The Renaissance Man and his Roles*, Yale, 1973

von Hagen, Victor W., *The Golden Man: A Quest for El Dorado*, Westmead, Farnborough, 1974

Haigh, Christopher, *Elizabeth I*, Profiles in Power, 1988

Haigh, Christopher (ed.), *The Reign of Elizabeth I*, Problems in Focus, 1984
_____ *The English Reformation Revised*, Cambridge, 1987

Harlow, V. T., *Ralegh's Last Voyage*, 1932

Hakluyt, Richard (ed. James MacLehose), *The Principal Navigations, Voyages, Trafficks and Discoveries of the English Nation*, 12 vols, Glasgow, 1904

Harington, Sir John (ed. Norman Eybert Mclure), *The Epigrams of Sir John Harington*, Philadelphia, 1926

Hemming, John, *The Search for El Dorado*, 1978

Hibbert, Christopher, *The Virgin Queen: The Personal History of Elizabeth I*, 1990

Hill, Christopher, *Intellectual Origins of the English Revolution*, Oxford, 1965

Hopkins, Lisa, *Queen Elizabeth and her Court*, 1990

Houston, *James I*, Seminar Studies in History, 1973; rev. ed., 1988

Hughes, G. B., 'Ralegh and the Farm of Wines', *Country Life* 147, (1970), 194–5

Hulton, Paul and Quinn, D. B. (eds), *The American Drawings of John White* 2 vols, 1964

Johnson, Paul, *Elizabeth I: a Study in Power and Intellect*, 1974

Johnson, Ronald C., *George Gascoigne*, Twayne's English Authors Series, 135, New York, 1972

Knecht, R. J., *The French Wars of Religion, 1559–1598*, Seminar Studies in History, 1989

Lacey, Robert, *Robert, Earl of Essex: An Elizabethan Icarus*, 1971
_____ *Sir Walter Ralegh*, 1973

Latham, Agnes M. C., 'Sir Walter Ralegh's Will', *R.E.S.* 22 n.s. (1971), 129–36

Lefranc, Pierre, *Sir Walter Ralegh Ecrivain: l'oeuvre et les Idées*, Paris, 1968

Levy, F. J., *Tudor Historical Thought*, San Marino, Cal., 1967

Lewis, George R., *The Stannaries: A Study of the Medieval Tin Miners of Cornwall and Devon*, Truro, 1908

Linthicum, M. C., *Costume in the Drama of Shakespeare and his Contemporaries*, Oxford, 1936

Lloyd-Williams, Norman, *Sir Walter Ralegh*, Cassell Biographies, 1962

Lockyer, Roger, *The Early Stuarts: A Political History of England*, 1989

MacCurtain, Margaret, *Tudor and Stuart Ireland*, The Gill History of Ireland, Dublin, 1972

Marsden, R. G., 'The Vice Admirals of the Coast', *E.H.R.* xxii (1907), 468–77 and xxiii (1908), 736–57

Mattingly, Garrett, *The Defeat of the Spanish Armada*, 1959

May, Steven, 'The Poems of Edward De Vere, Seventeenth Earl of Oxford and of Robert Devereux, Second Earl of Essex: an edition and commentary', *Studies in Philosophy 77*, (1980), 25–42

____ *Sir Walter Ralegh*, Twayne's English Authors Series, 469, Boston, 1989

____ *The Elizabethan Courtier Poets: The Poems and their Contexts*, 1991

'Mc', 'Sir Walter Ralegh, East Londoner, *N&Q* 12th ser. 4 (1918), 296–7 and 5 (1919), 15

McGowan, A., *Tiller and Whipstaff: the Development of the Sailing Ship, 1400–1700*, 1981

McGurk, J. J. N., 'The Fall of the Noble House of Desmond, 1579–1583', *History Today 29*, (1979), 578–85, 670–75

Naipaul, V. S., *The Loss of El Dorado: A History*, 1969, rev. ed., 1973

Neale, J. E., *Queen Elizabeth I*, 1934

Nicholl, Charles, *The Reckoning: The Murder of Christopher Marlowe*, 1992

Notestein, Wallace, *The English People on the Eve of Colonisation*, 1954

Oakeshott, Walter, *The Queen and the Poet*, 1960

____ 'Sir Walter Ralegh's Library', *Library* 5th ser. 23 (1968), 285–327

Openhein, M. M., *A History of the Administration of the Royal Navy, 1509–1660*, 1896

Page, John T., 'Sir Walter Ralegh, East Londoner', *N&Q* 12th ser. 5 (1919), 51

Palliser, D. M., *The Age of Elizabeth: England under the Later Tudors*, Longman Social and Economic History of England, 1983

Parks, G. B. (ed. J. A. Williamson), *Richard Hakluyt and the English Voyages*, American Geographical Society, Special Publication no. 10, New York, 1928

Peck, D. C., 'Ralegh, Sidney, Oxford and the Catholics,' 1579 *N&Q*, n.s. 25 (1978), 427–31

Peck, Linda Levy (ed.), *The Mental World of the Jacobean Court*, Cambridge, 1991

Pegge, Samuel, *Curialia*, I, 1791

Prouty, C. T., *George Gascoigne*, New York, 1942

Quinn, David B., *Ralegh and the British Empire*, Teach Yourself History Library, 1947; rev. ed., 1962

——— 'Sir Thomas Smith, 1513–1577, and the Beginnings of English Colonial Theory', *Proceedings of the American Philosophical Society* 89, (1945), 543–60

——— *The Elizabethans and the Irish*, Ithaca, 1966

——— 'The Munster Plantation: Problems and Opportunities', *Journal of the Cork Historical and Archaeological Society* 71, (1966), 19–40

——— *Set Fair for Roanoke: Voyages and Colonies, 1584–1606*, 1985

Quinn, David B. (ed.), *The Voyages and Colonising Enterprises of Sir Humphrey Gilbert*, Hakluyt Society, 2nd ser., vols 83–4, 1940

——— *The Roanoke Voyages, 1584–1590*, 2 vols, Hakluyt Society, Cambridge, 1955

——— *The Hakluyt Handbook*, 2 vols., Hakluyt Society, Cambridge, 1974

Quinn, David B., and Cheshire N. M. (eds), *The New Found Land of Stephen Parmenius*, Toronto, 1972

Quinn, David B., and Quinn, Alison M. (eds), *Virginia Voyages from Hakluyt*, Oxford, 1973

——— *New American World: A Documentary History of North America to 1612*, 5 vols, New York, 1979

Racin, John, *Sir Walter Ralegh as Historian: An analysis of the History of the World*, Salzburg, 1974

Ralegh, Sir Walter (eds William Oldys and Thomas Birch), *The Works of Sir Walter Ralegh*, 8 vols, Oxford, 1829

Ralegh, Sir Walter (ed. V. T. Harlow), *The Discoverie of Guiana*, 1928

Ralegh, Sir Walter (ed. Agnes M. C. Latham), *The Poems of Sir Walter Ralegh*, 1929

Ralegh, Sir Walter (ed. Pierre Lefranc), 'Un inédit de Ralegh sur la conduite de la Guerre (1596–97)', *Etudes Anglaises* 8 (1955), 204–11

——— 'Un inédit de Ralegh sur la Succession', *Etudes Anglaises* 13 (1960), 42–46

——— 'Une Nouvelle Version de la "Petition to Queen Anne" de Sir Walter Ralegh', *Annales de la Faculté des Lettres et Sciences Humaines de Nice* 34, (1978), 65–6

Ralegh, Sir Walter (ed. Louis B. Wright), 'Instructions to his Son' in *Advice* to a Son, Precepts of Lord Burleigh, Sir Walter Ralegh, and Francis Osborne, Ithaca, 1962

Ralegh, Sir Walter (ed. Michael Rudick), 'The Poems of Sir Walter Ralegh', unpublished doctoral dissertation, University of Chicago, 1970

Ralegh, Sir Walter (ed. C. A. Patrides), *The History of the World*, 1971

Ralegh, Sir Walter (ed. Gerald Hammond), *Sir Walter Ralegh: Selected Writings*, Manchester, 1984

Read, Conyers, 'Walsingham and Burleigh In Queen Elizabeth's Privy Council', *E.H.R.* xxviii (1913), 34–58

Ridley, Jasper, *Elizabeth I*, 1987

Roberts, J. C., 'The Parliamentary Representation of Devon and Dorset, 1559–1601', unpublished M.A. dissertation, University of London, 1958

Roberts, J., 'The Second Marriage of Walter Ralegh', *Devon and Cornwall Notes and Queries* xxxiv (1978), 11–13

Roche, Thomas, *The Kindly Flame: A Study of the Third and Fourth Books of Spenser's 'Faerie Queene'*, Princeton, N.J., 1964

Rosenberg, Eleanor, *Leicester, Patron of Letters*, New York, 1955

Routh, C. R. N. (rev. by Peter Holmes), *Who's Who in Tudor England*, Who's Who in British History, vol. 4, 1990

Rowse, A. L., *Sir Richard Grenville of the 'Revenge'*, 1937

_____ *Tudor Cornwall: Portrait of a Society*, 1941

_____ *The Expansion of Elizabethan England*, 1955

_____ *The Elizabethans and America*, 1959

_____ *Ralegh and the Throckmortons*, 1962

_____ *The Elizabethan Renaissance: the Life of the Society*, 1971

Rudick, Michael, 'The "Ralegh Group" in *The Phoenix Nest*', Studs in Bib 24, (1971), 131–7

_____ 'The Text of Ralegh's Lyric "What is Our Life?" ', *Studies in Philology* 83, (1986), 76–87

Ryan, Michael, T., 'Assimilating New Worlds in the Sixteenth and Seventeenth Centuries', *Comparative Studies in Society and History* 23, (1981), 519–38

Salaman, Redcliffe N., *The History and Social Influences of the Potato*, Cambridge, 1949

Salmon, J. H. M., *Society in Crisis: France in the Sixteenth Century*, 1975

Sandison, H. E., 'Arthur Gorges, Spenser's Alcyon and Ralegh's Friend', *P.M.L.A.* 43, (1928), 645–74

Scott-Thomson, G., *Lords Lieutenant in the Sixteenth Century*, 1923

Shirley, John. W., 'The Scientific Experiments of Sir Walter Ralegh, the

Wizard Earl and the Three Magi in the Tower, 1603–17' *Ambix*, Dec. 1947, 52–66

_____ *Thomas Harriot: A Biography*, Oxford, 1983

Shirley, John W. (ed.), *Thomas Harriot: Renaissance Scientist*, Oxford, 1974

St Clare Byrne, M., *Elizabethan Life in Town and Country*, rev. ed., 1961

Spenser, Edmund, *The Faerie Queen* (ed. A. C. Hamilton), Longman Annotated English Poets, 1977

Stanford, Michael J. G., 'A History of the Ralegh Family of Fardel and Budleigh in the Early Tudor Period', unpublished M.A. dissertation, University of London, 1955

_____ 'The Raleghs take to the Sea', *Mariner's Mirror* 48, no 1 (Feb. 1962), 18–35

Starkey, David (ed.), *Rivals in Power: Lives and Letters of the Great Tudor Dynasties*, 1990

Starnes, De Witt T. and Talbot, Ernest William, *Classical Myth and Legend in Renaissance Dictionaries: A Study of Renaissance Dictionaries in their Relation to the Classical Learning of Contemporary English Writers*, Chapel Hill, 1955

Strathmann, Ernest A., *Sir Walter Ralegh: A Study in Elizabethan Scepticism*, New York, 1951

Strong, Sir Roy, *The Cult of Elizabeth: Elizabethan Portraiture and Pageantry*, 1977

_____ *Henry, Prince of Wales and England's Lost Renaissance*, 1986

_____ *Gloriana: The Portraits of Queen Elizabeth I*, 1987

Strong, Sir Roy and Oman, J. T., *Elizabeth R*, 1971

Taylor, E. G. R., *Tudor Geography, 1485–1583*, 1930

_____ *Late Tudor and Early Stuart Geography, 1583–1650*, 1934

Taylor, E. G. R. (ed.), *The Original Writings and Correspondence of the Two Richard Hakluyts*, Hakluyt Society, 2nd ser., vols 76–7, 1935

Thomas, Keith, *Religion and the Decline of Magic: Studies in Popular Beliefs in Sixteenth- and Seventeenth-Century England*, 1971

Thompson, Edward, *Sir Walter Ralegh: the Last of the Elizabethans*, 1935

Thompson, J. W., *The Wars of Religion in France*, 1957

Trattner, Walter I., 'God and Expansion in Elizabethan England: John Dee, 1527–1583', *Journal of the History of Ideas*, 25 (1964)

Tugwood, R. M. S., 'Piracy and Privateering from Dartmouth and Kingswear, 1540–58', unpublished M.A. dissertation, University of London, 1953

Vines, Alice Gilmore, *Neither Fire nor Steel: Sir Christopher Hatton*, Chicago, 1974

Waddington, Raymond B., *The Mind's Empire: Myth and Form in George Chapman's Narrative Poems*, 1974

Wallace, W. M., *Sir Walter Ralegh*, 1959

Ward, B. M., *The Seventeenth Earl of Oxford, 1550–1604*, 1928

Williams, Neville, *All the Queen's Men: Elizabeth I and her Courtiers*, 1972

_____ *The Sea Dogs: Privateers, Plunder and Piracy in the Elizabethan Age*, 1975

Williams, Penry, *The Tudor Regime*, 1979

Williamson, Bruce J., *Sir Walter Ralegh and his Trial*, 1936

Williamson, James, A., *The Age of Drake*, The Pioneer Histories, 1946

Wrightson, Keith, *English Society, 1580–1680*, Hutchinson Social History of England, 1982

Yates, Frances A., *Giordano Bruno and the Hermetic Tradition*, 1964

_____ *Astrea: The Imperial Theme in the Sixteenth Century*, 1975

_____ *The Occult Philosophy in the Elizabethan Age*, 1979

Youings, Joyce, 'The South-Western Rebellion of 1549', *Southern History* 1 (1979)

_____ *Sixteenth-Century England*, The Pelican History of England, 1984

_____ *Ralegh's Country: The South West of England in the Reign of Elizabeth I*, North Carolina, 1986

Youings, Joyce (ed.), *Ralegh in Exeter 1985: Privateering and Colonisation in the Reign of Elizabeth I*, Exeter Studies in History, no. 10, Exeter, 1985

Index

Index

Counter-Reformation 48, 181 *see also* Catholicism; Catholics; Jesuits
Courteny, Sir William 93
courtier, concept of 22, 23, 156
Crediton 5
criminals 91
Croatoan 88, 163, 165, 171–2
Cuba 30
Cumana 236, 248–9, 255
Cumberland, George Clifford, 3rd Earl of 196, 208, 210, 211, 284

Danvers, Sir Charles 283
Dare, Ananias 162
Dare, Virginia 166, 167
Darius of Persia 379, 380
Dasemunkepuec 165
Davies, Sir John 283
Davis, John 228
Davison, William 139
de Bry, Theodore 121
de Fever, George 7–8
de Passe, Crispin 147, 148
de Vera Ybarguen, Domingo 236, 237
Dee, John 24–5, 26, 66, 81
Democritus 189
Denmark 309–10
Desmond family 52, 183, 184
Desmond, Gerald Fitzgerald, 15th Earl of 44, 46, 48, 52, 100, 101, 157, 158
Devereux, Dorothy 140
Devereux, Robert, *see* Essex, Robert Devereux, 2nd Earl of
Digges, Thomas 98
Divine Right of Kings 294, 295, 381
Dominica 116, 163
Douglas, John 238, 243
Drake, Bernard 118, 134
Drake, Sir Francis 28, 93, 103, 134–5, 142, 144, 145, 148, 167, 178, 232, 255
  circumnavigation of globe 29, 107
Drake, Gilbert 7
Drake, Joan 1–2, 3
Drake, John 1, 2
Dublin, the Pale 43, 45
Dudley, Robert *see* Leicester
Dudley, Sir Robert (son of Leicester) 237–8, 239
Duke, Richard 99
Dumaresq, David, Seigneur de Saumarez 53
Durham, Bishop of 299
Durham House 67–8, 70, 195, 198–9, 200, 202, 299
Durham House circle 81–3, 88, 187, 189, 192, 220–1, 227, 251, 252, 253–4, 263, 295

East Budleigh, Devon 2
East India Company 169, 352
Eastern trading empire 12, 13, 14
Eastward Ho! 172

economic liberalism 288–9, 290
Eden, Richard 9, 12
Edward VI, reign of 8
Effingham, Lord Howard of *see* Howard, Lord Charles
El Dorado, SWR and 105–6, 231–54, 348–65, 367, 370 *see also* gold
Eliot, John 375
Elizabeth I
  dancing 74
  death and funeral 297, 298
  dress and appearance 66–7, 262–3
  and Duc of Alençon 17, 39–42, 57–8
  and forbidden marriages 140, 176
  'Golden Speech' 291–2, 298
  and parliament 212–19, 288–92
  plots against 101–2, 187–8
  portraits 61–2, 147
  as Princess 3, 11
  and religion 48, 192, 193, 217
  and succession 214–15, 292–3
  as Virgin Queen 24–5, 39, 60, 61–2, 65, 147, 148, 155–9, 174, 175, 254, 291
  as Weroanza 132
  see also under Essex; Leicester; SWR
Elizabeth, Princess (daughter of James I) 338
Epuremei 246
Eskimos 83
Essequibo River 348
Essex, Lettice, Countess of (née Knollys) 40, 71, 141, 149, 176
Essex rebellion 283–6, 294, 305, 306
Essex, Robert Devereux, 2nd Earl of 148, 192–3, 213, 255–7, 294, 306, 376
  and Bacon 256, 280, 285
  and Cadiz 258, 259–60, 261, 262
  and Cecil 256, 257, 263, 275, 277, 280, 285
  and Elizabeth 71, 113, 139–42, 149–50, 176, 199, 206, 258, 262, 271, 272, 276–7, 278–9, 283
  and Ireland 275, 277
  and Islands Voyage 264–71
  SWR 113, 140–2, 149–50, 153, 192, 206, 219–22, 256, 257, 259, 260, 264–5, 266–7, 269–71, 272, 277, 280, 281, 284, 285–6, 294, 305, 306
Essex, Robert Devereux, 3rd Earl of 345, 346
Evesham, John 107, 108–10
Exeter, religious revolts in 5, 6, 8

Faige, Captain 355–6
Falcon, description of 33–5
Fawkes, Guido 323–4
Fayal, Azores 267–70
Fenny Bridges 5
Fernandez, Simon 31, 34, 76, 84, 115, 117, 162–4, 166
Ferrol 178, 179, 264, 265, 266, 270
Fitzgerald, Sir James 47

[413]

Index

Index

Marlowe, Christopher 190–1, 219, 220–2
Marprelate tracts 192
Martens, Veronio 152
Mary, Queen of Scots 28, 101–2, 110, 138–9, 293
Mary Tudor 8–9
mathematics 24
Maule, Richard 150
May, James, Viscount Doncaster 375
Medina Sidonia, Duke of 142, 261
Meere, John 212, 287
Menatonon 130–1, 132
Mendoza, Bernardino de (Spanish Ambassador) 31, 105
'merchant adventurers of England' 7
  see also privateering
Mexico (New Spain) 27–8, 179, 349
military training 98–9
missionaries (Protestant and Catholic) 88, 89, 90, 128, 129, 184, 232, 252, 253, 349
Mitcham, Surrey 175, 353
Mogeely Castle 152
Mohun, Sir William 93
Moncado, Hugo de 146
Moncontour, Battle of 15
monopolies 71, 72–3, 137, 203, 288, 290–1, 292, 298, 321
Mont-de-Marsan 17
Montgomerie, Comte de 15, 16, 17
Montluc, Blaise de 17
Montmorency, Admiral, of France 355, 356
Moore, Francis 290
Moratuc tribe 130
Morequito 235
Morgan, Thomas 102
Mountjoy, Charles Blount, Lord 306, 310
Moyle, Henry 51
Munster, Ireland 44, 46, 48, 50, 100, 150–1, 152, 223–4, 279–80, 287, 288, 297
Muscovy Company 12–13, 77, 352

Navarrens 17
navigation 24, 82–3
Neile, Bishop 345
Netherlands 17, 349
  trade with 217–19, 327
  war with Spain at home 26, 28, 142, 143, 148, 327
    English help 110–11, 282
    French help 39, 58, 110
  war with Spain at sea 260–1, 264, 271
New Spain (Mexico) 27–8, 179, 349
Newfoundland 30, 78, 79, 134, 282
Newport, Christopher 337
Nombre de Dios 29, 179
Nonesuch Palace 65
Norden, John (map of Westminster) 67
Norris, Sir John 'Black John' 143, 149, 179
North America 30–6, 75, 76–94, 114, 115–36, 143, 159, 160–73, 217, 251, 252, 335–6, 337, 338 see also under Gilbert; Grenville; SWR

North Carolina 81, 84
North Hall 140, 256
North, Lord 32, 279
North West and North East Passages 12
Northumberland, Henry Percy, 'Wizard Earl', 9th Earl of 38, 188–9, 263, 281, 295–6, 323, 324, 325, 326
Northumberland, John Dudley, Duke of 281
Norumbega 31
Nottingham, Earl of see Howard, Lord Charles
Nugent, Edward 133

O'Neill, Hugh, 3rd Earl of Tyrone 223, 276, 277, 278, 306
O'Neill, Shane, 2nd Earl of Tyrone 'Prince of Ulster' 43, 45, 46
Oreiones 246
Orinoco River 235, 236, 239, 241, 242, 243–5, 248, 251, 347, 348, 350, 352, 360, 365
Ormonde, Earl of 44, 48, 50, 51, 54, 55, 149
Orphic Hymns 189
Ortelius, Abraham 13
Osorio, Don Diego 236
Overbury, Sir Thomas 344, 345, 346
Oviedo, Fernandez de 106
Oxford, Edward de Vere, 17th Earl of 37–9, 40, 41–2, 58–9, 62, 65, 74
Oxford University 19–20, 67

Pamlico River 118, 122
Panama 29, 196, 198, 211
papacy
  and American colonies 26
  and Ireland 45, 48–9
parliament 212–19, 288–92, 319, 344–5
Parma, Duke of 142, 145
Parsons, Robert 185–6, 190, 191, 219
Patagonia 103
Paunsford, Richard 21
Peele, George 187
Pennington, Captain 357
Percy, Henry see Northumberland
Percy, Thomas 325
Perrot, Sir Thomas 37, 140
Persians, ancient 378, 379, 381–2
Peru 103, 105–6, 349
Peter Martyr 9, 12
Petrarch 61
Pett, Phineas 334, 352
Peyton, John 304
Philip II, of Spain
  and double agents 104–5
  and Mary Queen of Scots 101
  and Mary Tudor 8
  see also Netherlands, war with Spain; Spain
Philip III, of Spain 277

Index

Index

Index